Web Developer's Reference Guide

A one-stop guide to the essentials of web development including popular frameworks such as jQuery, Bootstrap, AngularJS, and Node.js

Joshua Johanan

Talha Khan

Ricardo Zea

BIRMINGHAM - MUMBAI

Web Developer's Reference Guide

First published: March 2016

Production reference: 1180316

Published by Packt Publishing Ltd.
Livery Place
35 Livery Street
Birmingham B3 2PB, UK.

ISBN 978-1-78355-213-9

www.packtpub.com

Credits

Authors
Joshua Johanan

Talha Khan

Ricardo Zea

Reviewers
Chetankumar Akarte

Gergo Bogdan

Rahul Devaskar

David Ellenwood

Philippe Reneiver Gonin

Robert Mion

Natalie Olivo

Mateus Ortiz

Commissioning Editor
Edward Gordon

Acquisition Editor
Meeta Rajani

Content Development Editor
Samantha Gonsalves

Technical Editor
Abhishek R. Kotian

Copy Editor
Pranjali Chury

Project Coordinator
Kinjal Bari

Proofreader
Safis Editing

Indexer
Monica Ajmera Mehta

Graphics
Disha Haria

Production Coordinator
Conidon Miranda

Cover Work
Conidon Miranda

About the Authors

Joshua Johanan is a web developer who currently lives in South Bend, Indiana. He has been a web developer for five years. He has built sites using many different languages, including PHP, Python, JavaScript, and C#; although if asked, he would prefer using Python and JavaScript. These languages have led him to use different MVC frameworks, such as Zend Framework, Django, and .Net's MVC.

As you can see from this book, Joshua has also used JavaScript on both the backend with Node.js and frontend using many different libraries. These include Backbone, React, jQuery, and plain old JavaScript.

He currently works for a healthcare organization, writing websites in C#. This does not allow him to utilize the latest flashy browser technologies, but it does enforce good development skills, such as maintainability and scalability.

This is his first book, but he does post somewhat regularly on his blog at `http://ejosh.co/de/`.

I would like to thank my wife, Liz, for her support through the writing of this book. I would also like to thank Dexter and Gizmo, who hung out by my feet as I wrote most of this book.

Talha Khan is a passionate web developer, JavaScript enthusiast, software consultant, and coffee freak from Pakistan who is currently residing in UAE. He has more than five years of experience in this field. Despite graduating in mathematics and statistics, his love for web technologies pushed him toward the field of web technologies. He is experienced in developing interactive websites and web applications using PHP, MYSQL, and Dot Net Suite along with HTML, CSS, and JavaScript libraries. He has been teaching web development as well and is an active contributor on programming forums such as StackOverflow. Occasionally, he tweets at `@alphaprofile`.

Talha has worked and consulted on various projects for several major brands and companies. `Tossdown.com`, a leading restaurants and food search engine of Pakistan, is among one of his major achievements. He is also running his own start-up while educating newbies on technology. He is currently working as a software architect for UAE's biggest swimming academy, Hamilton Aquatics.

I want to thank my parents for keeping me motivated and my friends who supported me in writing, as I could count on them anytime if I had to use their laptop. I am also grateful to Tahir Ali Khan, who helped me at every step throughout my career and was like a guiding light.

I would like to take this opportunity to thank all the teachers and mentors who helped me shape my career and helped me whenever I needed it. These people were my source of inspiration. A special thanks to Omair Bangash, who took the risk of employing someone from a non-IT background and taught me to a level where I am now teaching others. His confidence in me was enough to push me to reach to my goals. I worked under many projects of various scales and technologies under his supervision. He helped me at every step to hone my skills. I don't think I would be have been able to write this book had it not been for his constant support and motivation. Without learning from these teachers, there is not a chance I could be doing what I do today, and it is because of them and others who I may not have listed here that I feel compelled to pass my knowledge on to those willing to learn.

Ricardo Zea hails originally from Medellín, Colombia. He is a passionate and seasoned full-stack designer who is now located in Dayton, Ohio, USA. He is always looking for ways to level up his skills and those around him. Constantly wondering how things are made on the Web, how they work, and why, have made Ricardo a very technical designer, allowing him to explain to others the intricacies of design and the technicalities of the Web in ways that are very easy to understand and assimilate.

Ricardo has a master's degree in publicity and advertising and has deep passion for understanding human behavior. He also has a fiercely competitive PC gaming hunger. Together, all this has allowed him to switch from the creative side of the brain to the rational side very easily, allowing him to visualize and create technically sound web and mobile designs that are responsive, perform well, and convey the proper message through design.

Ricardo is the author of *Mastering Responsive Web Design*, *Packt Publishing*. He's also the organizer of the CodePen Dayton meetup group. He's a member of the Dayton web developers and UX Dayton meetup groups. He's also one of the first members of SitePoint's Ambassadors program. He's also the author of the monthly web design and development newletter Level Up!. He was also a technical reviewer for *Sass and Compass, Designers Cookbook*, and *Sass Essentials*, all by Packt Publishing. For several years, he was also a Flash and CorelDRAW professor at different universities in his home country, Colombia.

Ricardo has 15 years of experience in web design and 20 years of experience in visual and graphic design.

A huge and infinite thanks to my wife, Heather, and my beautiful son, Ricardo. They are my inspiration to be a better professional, a better person, a better husband, and a better dad.

To my mom, Socorro, who showed me the values that made me the man I am today. To my dad, Ricardo "Pinta" Zea, for teaching me to be determined to not only be good at what I do but to be the best I can be.

To God, for allowing me to share with everyone my knowledge of CSS.

And to you, the readers, for giving me the chance to help you be better web professionals.

About the Reviewers

Chetankumar Akarte is the CEO of Renuka Technologies Private Limited, Nagpur, located in central India. He is an engineer (electronics) from Nagpur University with more than 10 years of experience in the design, development, and deployment of web-based, Windows-based, and mobile-based applications with expertise in PHP, .NET, JavaScript, Java, Android, and more.

Chetankumar likes to contribute to newsgroups and forums. He has written articles for Electronics For You, DeveloperIQ, and Flash and Flex Developer's Magazine. In his spare time, he likes to maintain his technical blog (`http://www.tipsntracks.com`) to get in touch with the developer community. He has been the technical reviewer for four books published by Packt Publishing. He has released more than 96 applications on the Android market! One of his applications, an English to Hindi Dictionary, is like a pocket dictionary for students, which has more than a hundred thousand downloads. You can find it at `https://play.google.com/store/apps/details?id=com.sachi.hindi.dictionary`.

Chetankumar lives in Nagpur with wife, Shraddha, and his two children, Kaiwalya and Hrutvij. You can visit his websites, `http://www.sahityachintan.com` and `http://www.tipsntracks.com`, or get in touch with him at `chetan.akarte@gmail.com`.

I'd like to thank my wife, Shraddha, and my parents for their consistent support and encouragement. I'd also like to thank my lovely children, Kaiwalya and Hrutvij, who allowed me to dedicate all of their playtime with me to this book. I'd also like to thank Packt Publishing for this opportunity to do something useful, especially the project coordinator, Kinjal Bari, for all the valuable support.

Gergo Bogdan is a software engineer with over eight years of experience in the IT industry. During this time, he worked at small companies as well as multinational organizations. He has vast expertise in multiple technologies, starting from .NET and Python to JavaScript and Java. He loves to create technical articles and tutorials for fellow developers, and he is a passionate blogger (`http://grelution.com`). He is the author of the *Web API Development with Flask* video course, *Packt Publishing*.

Rahul Devaskar is a software engineer with experience of building real-time event-driven applications, context-aware applications, and web applications. His expertise includes web apps development, mobile apps development, API server development, and real-time analytics. He has built apps using AngularJS, Node.js, MongoDB, and Ionic.

> I'd like to thank my wife, Niyati, for her constant support and encouragement.

David Ellenwood is a frontend developer and WordPress expert with more than 15 years of experience on the Web. As the owner and solo developer at DPE Websmithing and Design, LLC, he enjoys providing consulting services to midsize customers looking to update or extend their existing websites beyond traditional brochureware. He lives with his beautiful wife and two amazing boys at the westernmost tip of Lake Superior in Superior, Wisconsin.

Philippe Renevier Gonin has been an assistant professor at the University Nice Sophia Antipolis (UNS), France, since 2005. He teaches web technologies, software engineering (architecture and development), and HCI (Human Computer Interaction). On the research front, Philippe works on connections between user-centered design (for example, user and tasks models) and software engineering (for example, component architecture and UI development).

Robert Mion takes every effort to design experiences that continually delight, empower, and inspire people, often by repeatedly triggering that magical moment when your brain makes your mouth go A ha! or Of course!. This passion was ignited when watching Pixar's Toy Story at the age of eight. The fire has only grown since then.

Robert continues to use his amassed knowledge of storytelling, color, typography, layout, design, human psychology, and web technologies as an excuse to have fun every day by crafting experiences designed to go beyond solving problems — to emotionally connect with users and to help them become more awesome.

Robert and his wife, Laura, currently live in Fort Mill, SC — minutes south of the Queen City — with their two pugs (one, a pug-boxer mix).

Natalie Olivo has worked with web-based technologies for almost a decade and began her career in coding when the majority of HTML pages were tabular and inflexible. She remembers the excitement and satisfaction in the creative process of building her first prototype for a messaging application while she was employed at one of the first popular social networks in the age before Facebook. Natalie's wide ranging experience include key development roles in companies such as Godiva, Barnes and Noble, and The Daily Beast. She has spent the last year building out the mobile web experience at The Daily Beast, and enjoys the challenges of building applications that are performant for mobile web. She is currently a senior frontend engineer at Business Insider.

Mateus Ortiz is the creator of some cool open source projects such as Web Components Weekly (webcomponentsweekly.me), the first weekly World of Web Components, and web components the right way, and other projects. He is only 17 years old and spends his days helping and creating new open source projects. Mateus lives in Brazil where he makes several talks on the frontend. You can find him on Twitter at twitter.com/mteusortiz.

First of all, I'd like to thank God. I'd like to thank my mother, who always supports me and helps me in everything, my father, and all my family and friends. I'd also like to thank Packt Publishing for the opportunity to assist in the review of this book.

www.PacktPub.com

eBooks, discount offers, and more

Did you know that Packt offers eBook versions of every book published, with PDF and ePub files available? You can upgrade to the eBook version at www.PacktPub.com and as a print book customer, you are entitled to a discount on the eBook copy. Get in touch with us at customercare@packtpub.com for more details.

At www.PacktPub.com, you can also read a collection of free technical articles, sign up for a range of free newsletters and receive exclusive discounts and offers on Packt books and eBooks.

https://www2.packtpub.com/books/subscription/packtlib

Do you need instant solutions to your IT questions? PacktLib is Packt's online digital book library. Here, you can search, access, and read Packt's entire library of books.

Why subscribe?

- Fully searchable across every book published by Packt
- Copy and paste, print, and bookmark content
- On demand and accessible via a web browser

Table of Contents

Preface

This book covers many concepts that any web developer may need to know. These concepts may be new or known, but forgotten. The first two chapters in this book will cover the basic elements and attributes of HTML. The next four chapters will cover the concepts and syntax of CSS. JavaScript will be the focus of the next five chapters. Finally, we will cover external libraries. These include Bootstrap, jQuery, and Angular. Because this is a reference guide, it is not set up as a read-through tutorial. Each section and concept is written to stand on its own so that you can find the piece of information that you need quickly.

What this book covers

Chapter 1, HTML Elements, covers all the elements that you will need when building a web page. This is focused on HTML5.

Chapter 2, HTML Attributes, focuses on any the attributes that can be used with HTML elements.

Chapter 3, CSS Concepts and Applications, focuses on selectors. Selectors are core to determining which elements the CSS attributes apply to.

Chapter 4, CSS Properties – Part I, covers properties for animation, background, the box model, CSS units, columns, and the mighty Flexbox.

Chapter 5, CSS Properties – Part II, covers properties for fonts, transforms, transitions, positions, text, tables, words and paragraphs, and paging.

Chapter 6, CSS Properties – Part III, covers properties for the page box, lists, counters, drop shadows, display and visibility, clipping and masking, user interface, and 3D.

Chapter 7, CSS Functions, covers functions for filters, transforms, colors, gradients, and values. It covers a few extra concepts like at-rules, global keyword values, and miscellaneous.

Chapter 8, JavaScript Implementations, Syntax Basics, and Variable Types, talks about JavaScript implementations and language basics, including syntax and variables and their types. This chapter will enable us to understand and get started with basic scripting.

Chapter 9, JavaScript Expressions, Operators, Statements, and Arrays, enables us to advance with our basic JavaScript language understanding and introduces JavaScript expressions, basic operators, statements, loops, conditions, and arrays. This also covers examples for better understanding.

Chapter 10, JavaScript Object-Orientated Programming, explains the basic concepts of object-oriented programming, that is, inheritance, polymorphism, abstraction, and encapsulation. You will also learn the usage of objects, classes, and related methods. We will cover examples for better understanding.

Chapter 11, Extending JavaScript and ECMA Script 6, covers all the newly introduced features of ECMAScript 6, which was released in 2015, such as new objects, patterns, syntax changes, and new methods on existing objects. This chapter covers all these features in detail.

Chapter 12, Server-side JavaScript – NodeJS, continues to focus on JavaScript. The difference is that we will now write JavaScript on the server side instead of the client side. We can use the concepts covered in the other JavaScript chapters in addition to learning specific NodeJS objects and paradigms.

Chapter 13, Bootstrap – The Stylish CSS Frontend Framework, talks about Bootstrap, which is an intuitive framework for creating responsive websites. It uses JavaScript, HTML, and CSS. This chapter will give you a detailed look at the Bootstrap framework and will enable you to create responsive layouts and web pages. Each topic in this chapter has a relevant example.

Chapter 14, jQuery – The Popular JavaScript Library, focuses on jQuery, which is a JavaScript library that simplifies dealing with various aspects of an HTML document. In this chapter, you will learn to traverse elements of an HTML document, methods, event handling, animations, and AJAX for rapid development.

Chapter 15, AngularJS – Google's In-Demand Framework, is where we conclude this book by finishing the external library section. Angular has been one of the most popular frameworks since it was introduced by Google. We will look at all the main concepts that you will need to begin writing applications with Angular.

What you need for this book

Most likely, for this book, you will need nothing that you are not already using! You will need a computer, a browser, and a text editor. Each chapter will cover different concepts and languages, so there may be differences between each chapter.

Here is a summary of the various things you will need throughout the chapters:

- For Chapters 1-5, you will only need a text editor and a browser.

- For Chapters 6-11, you will need the same text editor and browser, but with JavaScript being a programming language, I would recommend an integrated development environment (IDE). JetBrains makes a great IDE called WebStorm for web development. However, this is not necessarily needed for these chapters.

- For Chapters 12-14, you will again need a text editor and browser. An IDE would also be very helpful for this section. Anytime you are dealing with complex frameworks, an IDE will make your life easier.

Although you can just use a notepad and a browser to do any sort of development, an IDE is always preferred and suggested for development in any specific language. I would suggest using Adobe Dreamweaver for beginners. The intellisense of IDE makes it a lot easier to code as it auto-suggests various methods, names, and variables, so you don't have to remember everything. As we will be dealing with the elements and document nodes in the JQuery section, you should have extensions enabled in your browser. ECMA Script 6 is very recent and not fully supported by all browsers. In some examples, you might have to load ES6 compilers to enable that feature in your browser. However, I would highly recommend that you use the latest version of Google Chrome as a client, as it covers most of the sections in ES6.

Who this book is for

This book is intended for beginners as well as advanced web developers. This book will be a valuable resource for anyone who is a web developer. You can look up any concept that deals with HTML, CSS, JavaScript, NodeJS, Bootstrap, jQuery, or Angular in this book.

Conventions

In this book, you will find a number of text styles that distinguish between different kinds of information. Here are some examples of these styles and an explanation of their meaning.

Code words in text, database table names, folder names, filenames, file extensions, pathnames, dummy URLs, user input, and Twitter handles are shown as follows: "HTML5 has a simple document type declaration, `<!DOCTYPE html>`."

A block of code is set as follows:

```
<div class="example">
  This is an example HTML element
</div>
```

When we wish to draw your attention to a particular part of a code block, the relevant lines or items are set in bold:

```
try{
  JSON.parse(jsonObject);
} catch (ex) {
  //do something with this error
}
```

Any command-line input or output is written as follows:

```
# cp /usr/src/asterisk-addons/configs/cdr_mysql.conf.sample
  /etc/asterisk/cdr_mysql.conf
```

New terms and **important words** are shown in bold. Words that you see on the screen, for example, in menus or dialog boxes, appear in the text like this: "Clicking the **Next** button moves you to the next screen."

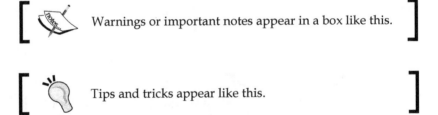

> Warnings or important notes appear in a box like this.

> Tips and tricks appear like this.

Reader feedback

Feedback from our readers is always welcome. Let us know what you think about this book — what you liked or disliked. Reader feedback is important for us as it helps us develop titles that you will really get the most out of.

To send us general feedback, simply e-mail feedback@packtpub.com, and mention the book's title in the subject of your message.

If there is a topic that you have expertise in and you are interested in either writing or contributing to a book, see our author guide at www.packtpub.com/authors.

Customer support

Now that you are the proud owner of a Packt book, we have a number of things to help you to get the most from your purchase.

Downloading the example code

You can download the example code files for this book from your account at http://www.packtpub.com. If you purchased this book elsewhere, you can visit http://www.packtpub.com/support and register to have the files e-mailed directly to you.

You can download the code files by following these steps:

1. Log in or register to our website using your e-mail address and password.
2. Hover the mouse pointer on the **SUPPORT** tab at the top.
3. Click on **Code Downloads & Errata**.
4. Enter the name of the book in the **Search** box.
5. Select the book for which you're looking to download the code files.
6. Choose from the drop-down menu where you purchased this book from.
7. Click on **Code Download**.

Once the file is downloaded, please make sure that you unzip or extract the folder using the latest version of:

* WinRAR / 7-Zip for Windows
* Zipeg / iZip / UnRarX for Mac
* 7-Zip / PeaZip for Linux

Errata

Although we have taken every care to ensure the accuracy of our content, mistakes do happen. If you find a mistake in one of our books—maybe a mistake in the text or the code—we would be grateful if you could report this to us. By doing so, you can save other readers from frustration and help us improve subsequent versions of this book. If you find any errata, please report them by visiting `http://www.packtpub.com/submit-errata`, selecting your book, clicking on the **Errata Submission Form** link, and entering the details of your errata. Once your errata are verified, your submission will be accepted and the errata will be uploaded to our website or added to any list of existing errata under the Errata section of that title.

To view the previously submitted errata, go to `https://www.packtpub.com/books/content/support` and enter the name of the book in the search field. The required information will appear under the **Errata** section.

Piracy

Piracy of copyrighted material on the Internet is an ongoing problem across all media. At Packt, we take the protection of our copyright and licenses very seriously. If you come across any illegal copies of our works in any form on the Internet, please provide us with the location address or website name immediately so that we can pursue a remedy.

Please contact us at `copyright@packtpub.com` with a link to the suspected pirated material.

We appreciate your help in protecting our authors and our ability to bring you valuable content.

Questions

If you have a problem with any aspect of this book, you can contact us at `questions@packtpub.com`, and we will do our best to address the problem.

1
HTML Elements

HyperText Markup Language (HTML) is a language that annotates text. Annotation of text is done using elements. Using the following p element, as an example, we will see how to use HTML:

```
<p>This is an example</p>
```

HTML elements also have attributes that will modify how they are rendered or interpreted. Attributes are added inside of the starting tag. Here is the class attribute in a div element:

```
<div class="example">This is an example</div>
```

There have been multiple specifications of HTML so far, but we will just look at the most commonly used and important elements of HTML5. HTML5 is the latest official specification, so we will be as future-proof as possible at the time of writing this book. You will want to follow the specifications of HTML as closely as possible. Most browsers are very forgiving and will render your HTML, but when you go beyond the specifications, you can and will run into strange rendering issues.

 All HTML elements will have global attributes. The attributes listed for each element in the sections that follow are the attributes beyond the global attributes.

DOCTYPE

The DOCTYPE element defines the document type of the file, as follows:

```
<!DOCTYPE documentType>
```

Attributes

The documentType attribute that you can see in the preceding code lets the browser know the type of document you will use.

Description

HTML5 has a simple document type declaration, <!DOCTYPE html>. This lets the browser know that the document is HTML5. The previous versions of HTML needed a formal definition of the version being used, but HTML5 has removed this for simplicity.

Most browsers will enforce strict adherence to the document type declared and try and figure out what it is based on looking at the document. This can lead to rendering issues, so it is recommended that you do follow the standards.

Here is an HTML5 declaration:

```
<!DOCTYPE html>
```

html

The html element is the root element of the HTML document:

```
<html manifest></html>
```

Attributes

The manifest attribute links to a resource manifest that lists which files should be cached.

Description

The html element must directly follow the DOCTYPE element. This is the root element that all other elements must be descendants of.

The html element must have one head element and one body element as its children. All other elements will be inside these tags.

Here is what a simple HTML page looks like:

```
<!DOCTYPE html>
<html manifest="offline.appcache"><head>
</head>
<body>
    Hey
</body>
</html>
```

Document metadata

The next elements will give metadata about the document. In addition to this, you can also include links to resources, such as CSS and JavaScript.

head

The head element is the metadata parent element. All other metadata elements will be children of this element:

```
<head></head>
```

Description

The head element usually must have a title element inside it. The elements that can go in head are title, link, meta, style, script, noscript, and base. These elements are explained next.

Here is an example of the head element that defines a title and stylesheet element:

```
<head>
    <title>Title that appears as the tab name</title>
    <link href="style.css" rel="stylesheet"
      type="text/css" media="all" />
</head>
```

title

The title element displays the title of the document. This is what is displayed in the browser's tab or the browser window:

```
<title></title>
```

Description

The `title` element is an aptly named element. This is a required element in `head`, and there should only be one `title` element for a document. Here is a simple example of `title` element:

```
<head>
    <title>Example</title>
</head>
```

link

The `link` element links a resource to the current document:

```
<link crossorigin href media rel sizes type></link>
```

Attributes

The attributes that are used in the `link` element are as follows:

- `crossorigin`: This tells the browser whether to make the **Cross-Origin Resource Sharing (CORS)** request or not
- `href`: This indicates the URL of the resource
- `media`: This selects the media that this resource applies to
- `rel`: This indicates the relationship of this resource to the document
- `sizes`: This is used with `rel` when it is set to `icons`
- `type`: This indicates the type of content of the resource

Description

The `link` element has a lot of attributes, but most of the time, it is used for loading the CSS resources. This means that you will want to use the attributes `href`, `rel`, `type`, and `media` at least.

You can have multiple `link` elements in a `head` element. Here is a simple example of how to load CSS:

```
<link href="style.css" rel="stylesheet"
  type="text/css" media="all" />
<link href="style.css" media="screen"
  rel="styleshhet" sizes type="text/css"></link>
```

See also

You can also refer to the `crossorigin`, `href`, `media`, `rel`, `sizes`, and `type` attributes to find out more details about the `title` element.

meta

The meta element contains metadata about the document. The syntax is as follows:

```
<meta content http-equiv name></meta>
```

Attributes

The attributes that are used in the meta element are as follows:

- content: This states the value of either the name or http-equiv attribute.

- http-equiv: This attribute, in the case of HTML5, can be set to default-style, which sets the default style. Alternatively, it can be set to refresh, which can specify the number of seconds taken to refresh the page and a different URL for the new page if needed, for example, http-equiv="1;url=http://www.google.com".

- name: This states the name of the metadata.

Description

The meta tag has many nonstandard applications. The standardized applications can be viewed in *Chapter 2, HTML Attributes*.

Apple has many meta tags that will pass information to an iOS device. You can set a reference to an App Store application, set an icon, or display the page in the full screen mode, as just a few examples. All of these tags are nonstandard, but useful when targeting iOS devices. This is true for many other sites and companies.

You can use multiple meta tags in a head element. Here are two examples. The first example will refresh the page every 5 seconds and the other will define the author metadata:

```
<meta http-equiv="refresh" content="5" />
<meta name="author" content="Joshua" />
```

See also

You can also refer to the name attribute to find out more details about the meta element.

style

The `style` element contains the style information.

CSS:

```
<style media scoped type></style>
```

Attributes

The attributes that are used in the `style` element are as follows:

- `media`: This is a media query
- `scoped`: The styles contained in this element only apply to the parent element
- `type`: This sets the type of document; the default value is `text/css`

Description

The `style` element is usually in the `head` element. This allows you to define CSS styles for the current document.

The preferred method of using CSS is to create a separate resource and use the `link` element. This allows styles to be defined once and used everywhere on a website instead of defining them on every page. This is a best practice as it allows us to define the styles in one spot. We can then easily find and change styles.

Here is a simple inline stylesheet that sets the font color to blue:

```
<style media="screen" scoped type="text/css">
    body{
        color: #0000FF;
    }
</style>
```

See also

You can also refer to the global attributes and Chapters 3-7 to know more details about the style element.

base

The `base` element is the base URL for the document. The syntax is as follows:

```
<base href target>
```

Attributes

The attributes that are used in the base element are as follows:

- href: This indicates the URL to be used as the base URL
- target: This indicates the default target to be used with the URL

Description

The base URL is used whenever a relative path or URL is used on a page. If this is not set, the browser will use the current URL as the base URL.

Here is an example of how to set the base URL:

```
<base href="http://www.packtpub.com/">
```

See also

You can also refer to the target attribute to find out more details about the base element.

script

The script element allows you to reference or create a script for the document:

```
<script async crossorigin defer src type><script>
```

Attributes

The attributes that are used in the script element are as follows:

- async: This is a Boolean attribute that tells the browser to process this script asynchronously. This only applies to the referenced scripts.
- crossorigin: This tells the browser whether to make a CORS request or not.
- defer: This is a Boolean attribute that tells the browser to execute the script after the document has been parsed.
- src: This distinguishes the URL of the script.
- type: This defines the type of the script that defaults to JavaScript if the attribute is omitted.

Description

The `script` element is the way to get JavaScript into your document and add enhanced interactivity. This can be done using a bare `script` tag and adding JavaScript into the element. Also, you can use the `src` attribute to reference an external script. It is considered a best practice to reference a script file as it can be reused here.

This element can be a child of `head` or can be placed anywhere in the body of the document. Depending on where the `script` element is located, you may or may not have access to the DOM.

Here are two examples of using a `script` element. The first example will reference an external script, the second will be an inline `script` element, and the last will show how to use the `crossorigin` attribute:

```
<script src="example.js" type="text/javascript"></script>
<script>
    var a = 123;
</script>
<script async crossorigin="anonymous" defer
  src="application.js" type="text/javascript"><script>
```

noscript

The `noscript` element will be parsed if scripting is turned off in the browser. The syntax is as follows:

```
<noscript></noscript>
```

Description

If scripting is enabled, the content inside of this element will not appear on the page and the code inside it will run. If scripting is disabled, it will be parsed.

This element is mainly used to let the user know that the site may not work with JavaScript. Almost every website today not only uses JavaScript, but requires it.

Here is an example of the `noscript` element:

```
<noscript>
    Please enable JavaScript.
</noscript>
```

Semantic content sections

The next elements are the main elements to use when adding content to the document. For example, using the `article` element instead of an arbitrary `div` element allows the browser to infer that this is the main content of the page. These elements should be used to give structure to a document and not be used for styling purposes. Semantic elements make our HTML document more accessible using an ever-increasing amount of different devices.

body

The `body` element is the main content section of the document. There must be only one main element, its syntax is as follows:

```
<body></body>
```

Attributes

The attributes of the `body` element include the `inline` event attributes.

Description

The `body` element is the main content section of most documents. It must be the second child element of `html`, and there should only be one `body` element in a document.

Here is an example of the `body` element:

```
<body>
    <span>Example Body</span>
</body>
```

section

The `section` element describes the content section of a document. For example, this can be a chapter of a book:

```
<section></section>
```

Description

The `section` element is a new element that was introduced in HTML5. A `section` element should group the content together. While not a requirement, using a `heading` element as the first element in the code is a best practice. The section should be viewed as another part of the outline of the document. It groups related items into an easily targeted area. You can use this element multiple times in a document.

Here is an example of the `section` element:

```
<section>
    <h2>Section Heading</h2>
    <p>Section content.</p>
</section>
```

nav

The `nav` element is the navigation element:

```
<nav></nav>
```

Description

The `nav` element is another semantic element introduced with HTML5. This lets the browser know that the content of this element is the parent and is for navigation. The `nav` element enhances accessibility by giving screen readers a landmark for navigation. This element should wrap any site navigation or other links that are grouped together for ease of navigation. You can use this multiple times.

Here is an example of using the `nav` element:

```
<nav>
    <ul>
        <li><a href="#">Home</a></li>
    </ul>
</nav>
```

article

The `article` element is designed to wrap content that can stand on its own:

```
<article></article>
```

Description

The `article` element is a new element introduced in HTML5. The `article` element is similar to the `section` element; in that, it denotes that the content in the element is the core part of the page. The `article` element should be a complete composition that can stand on its own. For example, in a blog, the actual blog post should be wrapped with an `article` element.

Content can then be further broken down using either an `article` element or a `section` element. There is no standard rule for when to use either. However, both should be related to the content in the outer `article` element.

Here is an example of the `article` element being used:

```
<article>
    <header>
        <h1>Blog Post</h1>
    </header>
    <p>This post covers how to use an article element...</p>
    <footer>
        <address>
            Contact the author, Joshua
        </address>
    <footer>
</article>
```

Headings

The `heading` elements are the elements that specify different levels of headings according to their importance:

```
<h1></h1>
<h2></h2>
<h3></h3>
<h4></h4>
<h5></h5>
<h6></h6>
```

Description

These should be used to give relative importance to different headings. For example, `h1` should be used for the title of the document. The importance of a heading goes down as the heading value goes up, that is, `h6` is the least important level of heading in the example that follows.

Here is an example using all the headings:

```
<h1>Heading Importance 1</h1>
<h2>Heading Importance 2</h2>
<h3>Heading Importance 3</h3>
<h4>Heading Importance 4</h4>
<h5>Heading Importance 5</h5>
<h6>Heading Importance 6</h6>
```

See also

You can also refer to the global attributes to learn the heading element in more detail.

header

The header element groups the content that is considered to be the header for a particular group of content, its syntax is as follows:

```
<header></header>
```

Description

The header element is usually one of the first content elements on the page. It will most likely contain navigation options, a logo, and/or a search box. The header is usually repeated on multiple pages of a website. Each section or article can also contain a header. This is a new element introduced in HTML5.

Here is an example of the header element:

```
<header>
    <img src="logo.png" />
</header>
```

See also

You can also refer to the global attributes to find out about the header element in more detail.

footer

The `footer` element provides a footer of a particular group of content, its syntax is as follows:

```
<footer></footer>
```

Description

The `footer` element wraps all the content that is considered to be the footer of the document. Usually, this will include copyright, author, and/or social media links. Of course, what you decide to put into a footer is arbitrary. Each section or article can also contain a footer.

Here is an example of the `footer` element:

```
<footer>
    Written by: Joshua Johanan
</footer>
```

address

The `address` element is used for the contact address of the author or organization, its syntax is as follows:

```
<address></address>
```

Description

Use the `address` element when you have the contact information of the user. The `address` element will add semantic value to the content, contrary to a regular `div` element.

Usually, this will be placed in the footer, but it can be used in an article or body section. It will apply to the nearest `article` element or to the entire document. Do not use any of the content section elements in an `address` element.

Here is the `address` element in use:

```
<footer>
    <address>
        Please contact me at my <a href="#">website</a>
    </address>
</footer>
```

aside

The `aside` element is for supplemental content:

```
<aside></aside>
```

Description

Use the `aside` element to highlight the content that is tied to the main article. Some examples in the context of the blog would be the author's profile, other posts by this author, or even related advertisements.

Here is an example of `aside`:

```
<aside>
    Peyton Manning is a 5-time MVP (2003, 2004, 2008, 2009, 2013)

</aside>
```

p

The `p` element is known as the paragraph element. This is a block element, its syntax is as follows:

```
<p></p>
```

Description

The `p` element should be used to distinguish between separate paragraphs in a document. This element is associated with the `text` and `inline` elements. You will not want to use a `div` element, for example. If you find yourself wanting to do this, you may want to build your document differently.

Here are a couple of paragraphs:

```
<p>This is an intro paragraph.</p>
<p>This paragraph will build upon the opening.</p>
```

Content sections

The `content` sections are quite similar to the semantic content sections. The main difference is that the use of all the given elements are not driven by the outline or purpose of the document like the semantic sections are.

hr

The `hr` element is the horizontal rule element, its syntax is as follows:

```
<hr>
```

Description

By default, the `hr` element will draw a horizontal line in the content. You can change the look of this element through CSS.

This element should never have any content inside of it:

```
<p>This is a paragraph.</p>
<hr/>
<p>This paragraph goes in another direction.</p>
```

pre

The `pre` element is the preformatted text:

```
<pre></pre>
```

Description

The text in an HTML document is usually not shown in the browser with the same whitespace or line breaks as it is in a text document. The `pre` element allows you to display text in the same way as it is in the document. Whitespace and line breaks will be preserved.

Here is an example of using line breaks:

```
<pre>This text
has some
line breaks.</pre>
```

blockquote

The syntax of a `blockquote` element is as follows:

```
<blockquote cite></blockquote>
```

Attributes

The `cite` attribute is used in the `blockquote` element to point to the URL of the cited document.

Description

The blockquote element is used when pulling a quotation out of a document or text.

Here is an example:

```
<blockquote cite="https://www.packtpub.com/">
    <p>Contact Us</p>
</blockquote>
```

ol

The ol element is the ordered list element, which has the following syntax:

```
<ol reversed start type></ol>
```

Attributes

The attributes that are used in the ol element are as follows:

- reversed: This is a Boolean value. It denotes that the list is in a reverse order.
- start: This accepts a value as a number to start with.
- type: This will change the type of the numbered elements. By default, we can have a numbered list (1), but we can change to other types, such as lowercase letters (a), uppercase letters (A), lowercase Roman numerals (i), and uppercase Roman numerals (I).

Description

The ol element can be used in the same situations as a ul element, except that an ol element is numbered instead of bulleted. For example, you would use a ul element for a grocery list and an ol element for a numbered set of instructions. You can have multiple ul or ol elements nested within each other.

The items in the list will be the li elements.

Here is an example of a list that uses Roman numerals and starts at 10.

```
<ol start="10" type="i">
    <li>Roman numeral 10</li>
    <li>Roman numeral 11</li>
</ol>
```

See also

You can also refer to the `ul` and `li` elements to find out more about the `ol` element.

ul

The `ul` element is an unordered list element:

```
<ul></ul>
```

Description

The `ul` element can be used in the same situations as an `ol` element, but a `ul` element will be bulleted and an `ol` element will be numbered.

When you style this list, you should use CSS and not the older HTML 4 attributes.

You can nest the `ul` and `ol` elements multiple times.

Here is an example of the `ul` element:

```
<ul>
    <li>Items in</li>
    <li>no particular</li>
    <li>order</li>
</ul>
```

See also

You can also refer to the `ol` and `li` elements to learn more about the `ul` element.

li

The `li` element is the list item element:

```
<li value></li>
```

Attributes

The `value` attribute is used in the `li` element with the `ol` element and it is the value of the item in the ordered list.

Description

You will use the li element for each item in a list.

Here is an example:

```
<ul>
    <li>Item 1</li>
    <li>Item 2</li>
    <li>Item 3</li>
</ul>
```

See also

You can also refer to the ol and ul elements to know more details about the li element.

dl

The dl element is the definition list element:

```
<dl></dl>
```

Description

The dl element is a list where the items have a term and definition; however, the dl element can be used for more than just terms and definitions.

You must use the dt element followed by the dd element when building the list for the dl element. Each dt element can have multiple dd elements after it.

Here is an example:

```
<dl>
    <dt>PactPub</dt>
    <dd>Packt Publishing</dd>
</dl>
```

See also

You can also refer to the dt and dd elements to find out more about the dl element.

dt

The dt element is the definition term element:

```
<dt></dt>
```

Description

The dt element is the first item in a definition list, the dd element being the other item.

Here is an example:

```
<dl>
    <dt>PactPub</dt>
    <dd>Packt Publishing</dd>
</dl>
```

See also

You can also refer to the dl and dd elements to find out more about the dt element.

dd

The dd element is the definition description element:

```
<dd></dd>
```

Description

The dd element is the second item in a definition list, the other one being the dt element.

Here is an example:

```
<dl>
    <dt>PactPub</dt>
    <dd>Packt Publishing</dd>
</dl>
```

See also

You can also refer to the dl and dd elements to find out more about the dd element.

figure

The syntax of the `figure` element is as follows:

```
<figure></figure>
```

Description

The `figure` element is a new element introduced with HTML5. In much the same way as an article adds some meaning where there was none, a figure adds meaning too. A figure is an image or any other item of information that is related to the document. This has more meaning than just using an `img` element.

Here is an example:

```
<figure>
     <img src="figure1.jpg" title="Figure 1" />
     <figcaption>Figure One</figcaption>
</figure>
```

See also

You can also refer to the `figcaption` element to find out more about the `figure` element.

figcaption

The `figcaption` element is the figure caption element:

```
<figcaption></figcaption>
```

Description

The `figcaption` element was introduced in HTML5 along with the figure. This element provides the caption for a figure. This element must be inside a `figure` element and it must be either the first or last child of the `figure` element.

Here is a simple example of the `figcaption` element:

```
<figure>
     <img src="figure1.jpg" title="Figure 1" />
     <figcaption>Figure One</figcaption>
</figure>
```

See also

You can also refer to the `figure` element to find out more about the `figcaption` element.

div

The `div` element is the division element:

```
<div></div>
```

Description

The `div` element is one of the most used elements in HTML today. It is the element used to split up your document into arbitrary divisions. The `div` element has no default styling. These divisions could be for placement, styling, or any other reason. A `div` element does not affect the semantic meaning of the document. It should only be used when no other element suits your requirements.

Here is an example:

```
<div>
    You can put whatever you want in here!
    <div>
        More elements.
    </div>
</div>
```

main

The syntax of the `main` element is as follows:

```
<main></main>
```

Description

The `main` element should have the main content of the document inside it. You cannot have this element as a descendant of the `article`, `aside`, `footer`, `header`, or `nav` elements. This differs from an article, in that, an article should be a self-contained element.

Here is an example of the `main` element in use:

```
<main>
    This is the main content of the document.
    <article>
        Here is the article of the document.
    </article>
</main>
```

Inline elements

The following elements can all wrap text- and block-level elements to give them functionality, style, and meaning.

a

The a element is the anchor element. This is where HTML gets the **HyperText (HT)**, the syntax is as follows:

```
<a download href media ping rel target type></a>
```

Attributes

Here are the attributes that are used in the a element:

- `download`: This attribute lets the browser know that the item should be downloaded. The dialog will default to the filename in this attribute.
- `href`: This is the link target.
- `media`: This states the media that the stylesheet should apply to based on a media query.
- `ping`: This makes a URL to ping and notify if the link is followed.
- `rel`: This states the relationship of the document being linked to.
- `target`: This states where the target link is to be displayed.
- `type`: This states the MIME type of the linked resource.

Description

The a element is one of the most important and useful elements. It allows you to link documents together and you can easily jump between elements. We can say that the Web would not be as popular as it is now without this very easy-to-use element.

The link can be that of an `anchor` tag in the document, a relative URL, or any external resource. When linking to an `anchor` tag in the current document, use the `a` tag and the `id` attribute.

The content you put inside the `a` element will become part of what the user can click on to follow the link. This includes the `text`, `img`, and `div` elements, to name a few.

Here is an example of an `img` element with an image:

```
<a href="http://www.packtpub.com">
    <img src="packt_logo.png" />
</a>
```

Here is an example of a PDF document that will be downloaded; this will track each click:

```
<a download="report.pdf" href="assests/report.pdf"
  media="min-width: 1024px" ping="track/click" rel="alternate"
  target="_blank" type=" application/pdf"></a>
```

abbr

The `abbr` element is the abbreviation element:

```
<abbr></abbr>
```

Description

The `abbr` element is used to show what an abbreviation stands for. You should put the full word in the `title` attribute. Most browsers will display this as a tooltip when you hover over this element.

Here is an example:

```
<abbr title="abbreviation">abbr</abbr>
```

bdo

The `bdo` element is the bi-direction override element:

```
<bdo dir></bdo>
```

Attributes

The `dir` attribute is used in the `bdo` element, which gives the direction of the text. Its values can be `ltr`, `rtl`, and `auto`.

Description

The `bdo` element will override the current direction of the text for the direction defined in the element.

Here is an example:

```
<bdo dir="rtl">Right to Left.</bdo>
```

br

The `br` element is the line break element:

```
<br>
```

Description

The `br` element adds a line break. This is needed as line breaks in text are ignored when rendered in the browser. This should not be used to help place elements, as that is the job of CSS.

Here is an example:

```
First Name<br>
LastName
```

cite

The `cite` element is the citation element:

```
<cite></cite>
```

Description

The `cite` element is used to cite another source. Most browsers will render this in italics.

Here is an example:

```
This quote is from <cite>Web Developer's Reference</cite>
```

code

The syntax of the code element is as follows:

```
<code></code>
```

Description

The code element is used to display the programming code in a document. The browser will use a monospace font for it.

Here is an example:

```
Here is some JavaScript: <code>var a = 'test'</code>
```

dfn

The dfn element is the defining instance element:

```
<dfn></dfn>
```

Description

The dfn element is used to create a defining instance or the first time a specific word is introduced and explained.

Here is an example of the dfn element:

```
<dfn>HTML</dfn>, or HyperText Markup Language.
```

em

The em element is the emphasis element:

```
<em></em>
```

Description

The em element is used to add more emphasis to a specific word or phrase. By default, browsers will render this in italic font, but it should not just be used for italics.

kbd

The kbd element is the keyboard input element:

```
<kbd></kbd>
```

Description

The kbd element is used for text that the user should input. This does not mean that the user inputs data into the element, rather they will enter it into a window, console, or some application on their computer.

Here is an example:

```
Press <kbd>Win + R</kbd> to open the Run dialog.
```

mark

The syntax of the mark element is as follows:

```
<mark></mark>
```

Description

The mark element is used to highlight text.

Here is an example:

```
<mark>This</mark> will be highlighted
```

q

The q element is the quote element:

```
<q cite></q>
```

Attributes

The cite attribute used in the q element states the URL of the source of the quote.

Description

The q element is used for short quotes. For longer quotes, use `blockquote`.

Here is an example:

```
<q cite="http://en.wikiquote.org/">Don't quote me on this.</q>
```

See also

You can also refer to the `blockquote` attribute to learn more about the q element.

s

The s element is the strikethrough element:

```
<s></s>
```

Description

The s element should be used when a piece of information in the document is no longer accurate. This is different than a revision made to the document.

Here is an example:

```
Today is the <s>twenty-fifth<s> twenty-sixth.
```

samp

The samp element is the sample output element:

```
<samp></samp>
```

Description

The samp element is used to show the sample output from a command or program.

Here is an example:

```
The command should output <samp>Done!</samp>
```

small

The syntax of the small element is as follows:

```
<small></small>
```

Description

The small element is used to make the text smaller. This is usually done with text such as the copyright or legal text.

Here is an example:

```
<small>Copyright 2014</small>
```

span

The syntax of the span element is as follows:

```
<span></span>
```

Description

The span element is much like the div element; in that, it is just an arbitrary container. The div element is a block-level element, and the span element is an inline element. The element does not add any semantic meaning to the text or document. Often, it is used to add a CSS style to the text:

```
<span>This text is in the span element.</span>
```

strong

The syntax of the strong element is as follows:

```
<strong></strong>
```

Description

The strong element should be used when certain text needs more importance. This carries some semantic meaning. The strong element's default style in most browsers is bold. This should not then be interchangeable with the b element, as that does not carry any semantic meaning.

Here is an example:

```
<strong>Warning!</strong> JavaScript must be enabled.
```

sub

The sub element is the subscript element:

```
<sub></sub>
```

Description

The sub element will render the text as a subscript.

Here is an example:

```
H<sub>2</sub>O
```

sup

The sup element is the superscript element:

```
<sup></sup>
```

Description

The sup element will render the text as a superscript.

Here is an example:

```
x<sup>2</sup> is what x squared should look like
```

time

The syntax of the time element is as follows:

```
<time datetime></time>
```

Attributes

The datetime attribute used in the time element gives a string that is the date and time value.

Description

The datetime element allows browsers to easily parse dates out of a document. You can wrap a date or the description of a date (tomorrow or July 4, for example) and still have an exact date for the browser to read.

Here is an example:

```
The party is on <time datetime="2014-11-27 14:00">
   Thanksgiving @ 2PM</time>
```

var

The var element is the variable element:

```
<var></var>
```

Description

The var element is used for variables in a mathematical expression or for programming.

Here is an example:

```
The variable <var>x</var> is equal to the string test
   in this example.
```

wbr

The wbr element is the word break opportunity element:

```
<wbr>
```

Description

The wbr element is a new element that was introduced with HTML5. We use this element to let the browser know of a good spot to break between words. This does not force a break, but if a break is needed, then the browser will respect the element.

It is an empty tag, meaning that it should not have an ending tag.

Here is an example:

```
If you have a really short width <wbr>then you <wbr>
   could have breaks.
```

Embedded content

The following elements are used to embed media or other objects into the document.

img

The img element is the image element:

```
<img alt crossorigin height ismap sizes src srcset width />
```

Attributes

The attributes that are used in the img element are as follows:

- alt: This is the alternate text for the image. Use this to describe the image. This is used to enhance accessibility.

- crossorigin: This lets the browser know whether this image should be fetched with a CORS request. If the image will be modified in a canvas element and not from the same domain name, then a CORS request must be used.

- height: This is an attribute to set the height of the image.

- ismap: This lets the browser know whether the image is used in a server-side map.

- sizes: This is a list of media conditions that will map to a size. This is used to help the browser determine which image to use. By default, this will be 100 VW, which is 100% of the view width.

- src: This is the most important attribute, it is the image URL.

- srcset: This is a list of multiple images that can be used for display on our web page. This is used to target different screen sizes or pixel densities.

- width: This is an attribute to set the width of the image.

Description

The img element is used if you want an image in the document. This element has many attributes, but the src and alt attributes are the only required attributes. The alt attribute should be used to describe the image in almost 100% of the cases. The main exception is when the image is only used as a decorative image, for example, when an image is used instead of a horizontal rule. The width and height can be used if the image is of a different size than what is needed on the page; otherwise, it defaults to the size of the image.

The crossorigin element can be confusing. It is used to ensure that you have ownership of an image before you modify the image in a canvas element. The image needs to either be from the same fully qualified domain name or the server's response must let the browser know whether the current domain can use the image.

Finally, srcset is used to give the browser a list of images that it can use. This is done with a comma-separated list of URLs and a descriptor. A descriptor can either be a width descriptor, which would be a number followed by w, or a pixel descriptor, which is a number followed by x. The width descriptor tells the browser the width of the image. The pixel descriptor tells the browser the pixel density it should use for the image.

The width descriptor can also be used by the browser when the pixel density changes. For example, if you have an image that is double the resolution and the pixel density doubles as well, the browser will choose the larger resolution.

The `sizes` element is used along with `srcset` to help the browser identify a break point. This is done using a media condition, for example, `"(min-width: 1600px) 25vw, 100vw"`. This states that if the width of the page is at least `1600` pixels, the images will be 25% of the view width, otherwise the view width is 100%. This helps the browser know where you want a break point and how large you want the image to be.

 The best way to think about `srcset` is that you are letting the browser know about all the images that can be used in a specific `img` element. You include the information that the browser is most concerned about—width and pixel density—and let the browser choose.

Here are a few examples. The first example is a simple `img` tag and the next one uses `crossorigin`:

```
<img src="example.png" alt="This is an example image"/>
<img src="example.png" crossorigin="anonymous"
  alt="This is an example image"/>
```

Here is a `srcset` example that lets the browser choose the image based on pixel density:

```
<img src="normal.jpg" srcset="normal.jpg 1x,
  retina.jpg 2x" alt="Image of Person in article" />
```

The following is an example using `srcset` and widths:

```
<img src="regular.jpg" srcset="double_size.jpg 1000w,
  regular.jpg 500w" sizes="100vw" alt="A bird"/>
```

iframe

The `iframe` element is the inline frame element:

```
<iframe height name seamless src width></iframe>
```

Attributes

The attributes that are used in the `iframe` element are as follows:

- `height`: This is the attribute to set the height.
- `name`: This states a name that can be used in the target attribute.
- `seamless`: This makes `iframe` appear as part of the content of the document. This will apply the outer context CSS and enables us to open links in the outer context.
- `src`: This is the URL of the embedded document.
- `width`: This is the attribute to set the width.

Description

The `iframe` element is used to embed another full HTML document inside the current document.

Here is an example that loads the Google homepage and another that loads Packt Publishing's page:

```
<iframe src="http://www.google.com"></iframe>
<iframe height="100px" name="remote-document"
   seamless src="https://www.packtpub.com/" width="100px"></iframe>
```

embed

The syntax of the `embed` element is as follows:

```
<embed height src type width/>
```

Attributes

The attributes that are used in the `embed` element are as follows:

- `height`: This is the attribute to set the height
- `src`: This is the URL of the object to be embedded
- `type`: This is the MIME type of the object
- `width`: This is an attribute to set the width

Description

The embed element is used to embed other objects in the document. There are other elements for embedding objects as well, depending on their type. For example, you can embed a video using the video element, as follows:

```
<embed src="example.mp4" type="video/mp4"/>
```

See also

You can also refer to the audio, video, and object elements to learn more about the embed element.

object

The syntax of the object element is as follows:

```
<object data height type width></object>
```

Attributes

Here are the attributes that are used in the object element:

- data: This is the URL of the object to be embedded
- height: This is the attribute to set the height
- type: This is the MIME type of the object
- width: This is the attribute to set the width

Description

The object element can be used very much like the embed element. This has historically been used for the Flash objects.

Here is an example:

```
<object data="example.swf" type="application/x-shockwave-flash">
  </object>
```

See also

You can also refer to the audio, video, embed, and param attributes to find out more about the object element.

param

The `param` element is the parameter element:

```
<param name="movie" value="video.swf"/>
```

Attributes

The attributes that are used in the `param` element are as follows:

- `name`: This is the name of the parameter
- `value`: This is the value of the parameter

Description

The `param` element defines a parameter for the object element. The parent of this element should be an `object` element.

Here is an example. This example is useful when using objects on older browsers:

```
<object data="example.swf" type="application/x-shockwave-flash">
    <param name="movie" value="example.swf" />
</object>
```

video

The syntax of the `video` element is as follows:

```
<video autoplay buffered controls crossorigin
  height loop muted played poster src width></video>
```

Attributes

The attributes that are used in the `video` element are as follows:

- `autoplay`: This is a Boolean attribute that tells the browser to start playing the video as soon as it can play after the loading has stopped
- `buffered`: This is a `read` object that tells how much of the video has buffered
- `controls`: This is a Boolean attribute to decide whether to display the controls
- `crossorigin`: This attribute is used make a CORS request if you plan on modifying the video in a canvas and the video is not hosted at the same fully qualified domain name

- `height`: This is the attribute to set the height
- `loop`: This states whether or not to loop the video
- `muted`: This states whether or not to mute the audio
- `played`: This is a `read` object, which reads how much of the video has been played
- `poster`: This is a URL of an image that will be displayed until the video can played
- `src`: This is the URL of the video
- `width`: This is the attribute to set the width

Description

The `video` element is a new element introduced in HTML5. You can use this to play a video directly in the browser. This is very useful as the user does not need a plugin or special player to view the video. In addition to this, you can use the `video` element as a source for the `canvas` element.

You can also use the `source` element to include multiple sources in case the browser can only play a certain type of file. If the browser does not support the `video` element or the file type, you can put the fallback content into the element.

Here is an example using the `video` element and another that demonstrates possible values for all of the attributes:

```
<video src="example.mp4" autoplay poster=
  "example-poster.png"></video>
<video autoplay buffered controls crossorigin="anonymous"
  height="100px" loop muted played poster="cover.jpg"
  src="video.ogg" width="100px"></video>
```

See also

You can also refer to the `source` and `track` attributes to find out more about the `video` element.

audio

The syntax of the `audio` element is as follows:

```
<audio autoplay buffered controls loop muted played
  src volume></audio>
```

Attributes

The attributes that are used in the `audio` element are as follows:

- `autoplay`: This is the attribute in which the browser will start playing the audio as soon as it can without loading
- `buffered`: This is the attribute that has the buffered time ranges
- `controls`: This is the attribute that has the browser display controls
- `loop`: This is the attribute that decides whether or not to loop the audio
- `muted`: This is the attribute that decides whether or not to mute the audio
- `played`: This is the attribute that has the time ranges of the audio played
- `src`: This is the attribute that gives the URL of the audio
- `volume`: This is the attribute that ranges the volume from 0.0 to 1.0

Description

The `audio` element was introduced in HTML5. You can add an audio to your page and make the browser play it.

You can also use the `source` element to include multiple sources in case the browser can play a certain type of file. If the browser does not support the audio element or the file type, you can put fallback content into the element.

Here is an example using the `audio` element:

```
<audio src="test.mp3" autoplay loop>
    Your browsers does not support the audio element.
</audio>
```

See also

You can also refer to the `source` and `track` attributes to find out more about the `audio` element.

source

The syntax of the `source` element is as follows:

```
<source src type />
```

Attributes

The attributes that are used in the source element are as follows:

- src: This is the URL of the resource
- type: This is the MIME type of the resource

Description

The source element is used to add multiple sources to the audio, picture, and video elements. It must be a child of one of these elements. You can use this to specify multiple formats of the same resource. For example, you can have two different video encodings for a video. If the browser cannot play the first, it will fall back to the other.

Here is an example with an audio element:

```
<audio autoplay controls>
    <source src="test.ogg" type="audio/ogg" />
    <source src="test.mp3" type="audio/mpeg">
</audio>
```

See also

You can also refer to the audio and video attributes to find out more about the audio element.

track

The syntax of the track element is as follows:

```
<track default kind label src />
```

Attributes

Here are the attributes that are used in the track element:

- default: This states whether the chosen track is the default track or not.
- kind: This states the different kinds of tracks that can be loaded. Here are the values: subtitles, captions, descriptions, chapters, or metadata.
- label: This is the title of the track.
- src: This is the URL of the resource.

Description

You will mainly use the `track` element to add captions or subtitles to videos.

Here is an example video with captions:

```
<video src="test.mp4">
    <track label="English" kind="captions" src="en.vtt" default>
    <track label="Spanish" kind="captions" src="sp.vtt">
</video>
```

Tables

Tables are useful for showing data. They make defining rows and columns very easy. In the past, tables were used to create layouts, but today, that is done with CSS. They should be used to only display the tabular data.

table

The syntax of the `table` element is as follows:

```
<table></table>
```

Description

The `table` element is the root element for creating a table. All the other elements in this section must be children of this element.

Here is a simple example of the `table` element:

```
<table>
    <tr>
        <td>Column in Row 1</td>
    </tr>
</table>
```

caption

The syntax of the `caption` element is as follows:

```
<caption></caption>
```

Description

The `caption` element will be the title of the table. This element must be the first child of the `table` element.

Here is a simple example:

```
<table>
    <caption>Caption for the table</caption>
    <tr>
        <td>Column in Row 1</td>
    </tr>
</table>
```

colgroup

The `colgroup` element is the column group element:

```
<colgroup span></colgroup>
```

Attributes

The `span` attribute states the number of columns the group spans.

Description

The `colgroup` element is used to define styles that are common to all columns or groups of columns. This element is not as useful as it once was as the new CSS selectors can target all the columns and even some specific columns.

tbody

The `tbody` attribute is the table body element:

```
<tbody></tbody>
```

Description

The `tbody` attribute is the main part of a table. All of the data rows and columns should go in this element. This element should have one or more `tr` elements as its children.

Here is an example:

```
<table>
    <tbody>
        <tr>
            <td>Column in Row 1</td>
        </tr>
    </tbody>
</table>
```

thead

The thead element is the table head element:

```
<thead></thead>
```

Description

The thead element is the row that has all of the column headings. It must appear before the tbody or tfoot elements.

Here is an example:

```
<table>
    <thead>
        <tr>
            <th>Heading 1</th>
        </tr>
    </thead>
    <tbody>
        <tr>
            <td>Column in Row 1</td>
        </tr>
    </tbody>
</table>
```

tfoot

The tfoot element is the table footer element:

```
<tfoot></tfoot>
```

Description

The tfoot element is the footer for the table. It must be used after any thead elements, but can be either before or after tbody. The placement of the tfoot element does not affect where it is rendered, which is always at the bottom.

Here is an example:

```
<table>
    <tbody>
        <tr>
            <td>Column in Row 1</td>
        </tr>
    </tbody>
    <tfoot>
        <tr>
            <td>Footer 1</td>
        </tr>
    </tfoot>
</table>
```

tr

The tr element is the table row element:

```
<tr></tr>
```

Description

The tr element is the row element. Every time you need another row in a table, use this element. This element can be the child of a table, tbody, thead, or tfoot element. You must use either a td or th as its child.

Here is an example:

```
<table>
    <tbody>
        <tr>
            <td>Column in Row 1</td>
        </tr>
    </tbody>
</table>
```

td

The `td` element is the table cell element:

```
<td colspan headers rowspan></td>
```

Attributes

The attributes that are used in the `td` element are as follows:

- `colspan`: This tells how many columns it will span as an integer
- `rowspan`: This tells how many rows the `rowspan` attribute will span as an integer
- `headers`: This is a space-separated list of strings that match the ID of any `th` element

Description

The `td` element is the basic table column element. The `colspan` and `rowspan` attributes allow you to make the column wider and taller, respectively.

Here is an example:

```
<table>
    <tbody>
        <tr>
            <td>Column in Row 1</td>
        </tr>
    </tbody>
</table>
```

th

The `th` element is the table header cell element:

```
<th colspan rowspan></th>
```

Attributes

The attributes that are used in the `th` element are as follows:

- `colspan`: This states the number of columns the `colspan` attribute will span as an integer
- `rowspan`: This states the number of rows the `rowspan` attribute will span as an integer

Description

The th element is used when we add a column to the thead element.

Here is an example:

```
<table>
    <thead>
        <tr>
            <th>Header</th>
        </tr>
    </thead>
</table>
```

Forms

Forms are great for getting information from the user. They usually have multiple elements inside them that accept input from the user. The data acquired from the input of the user is then sent to the server to process.

Form

The syntax of the form element is as follows:

```
<form accept-charset action autocomplete enctype
    method name novalidate target></form>
```

Attributes

The attributes that are used in the form element are as follows:

- accept-charset: This is a list of character encodings that the server accepts. This can be a space- or comma-delimited list.

- action: This is the URL that will process the form.

- autocomplete: This lets the browser know whether it can autocomplete this form with previous values.

- enctype: This sets the MIME type for the content being sent to the server.

- method: This is the HTTP method that will be used to submit the form. It can be Post or Get.

- name: This is the name of the form.

- novalidate: This tells the browser not to validate the form.

- target: This states where the response will be displayed. This can be: _self, _blank, _parent, or _top.

Description

The form element is the root element of a form in a document. When submitted, the form will contain all the data that is entered into the different elements inside of the form.

Here is a simple form of the syntax:

```
<form action="processForm" method="post">
    <input type="text" name="text-input"/>
    <button type="submit">Submit!</button>
</form>
```

fieldset

The syntax of the fieldset element is as follows:

```
<fieldset disabled form name></fieldset>
```

Attributes

The attributes that are used in the fieldset element are as follows:

- disabled: This disables all the elements in the fieldset
- form: This is the ID of the form the form attribute belongs to
- name: This is the name of fieldset

Description

The fieldset element allows us to group related inputs together. The default style of most browsers is to put a border around the fieldset.

If the first element is a legend element, then the fieldset will use that as its label.

Here is an example of using the fieldset element:

```
<form action="processForm" method="post">
    <fieldset>
        <legend>This is a fieldset</legend>
        <input type="text" name="text-input" />
    </fieldset>
</form>
```

See also

You can also refer to the `legend` attribute to find out more about the `fieldset` element.

legend

The syntax of the `legend` element is as follows:

```
<legend></legend>
```

Description

The `legend` element will become the label of the `fieldset` element that it is a child of.

See also

You can also refer to the `fieldset` element to find out more about the `legend` element.

label

The syntax of the `label` element is as follows:

```
<label accesskey for form></label>
```

Attributes

The attributes that are used in the `label` element are as follows:

- `accesskey`: This is a shortcut for the `accesskey` element
- `for`: This is the ID of a form element that this is the label for
- `form`: This is the ID of the form the `form` attribute is associated with

Description

The `label` element is for labeling inputs. You can either put the element in the label or use the `for` attribute. When the label is correctly linked to an input, you can click the label and the cursor will be in the input.

Here is an example that covers each different way of labeling an element:

```
<form action="processForm" method="post">
    <label>First name: <input type="text"
      name="firstName" /></label>
    <label for="lastNameInput">Last name:
      </label><input id="lastNameInput" type="text"
      name="lastName" />
</form>
```

input

The syntax of the `input` element is as shown:

```
<input accept autocomplete autofocus checked disabled form
   formaction formenctype formmethod formnovalidate
   formtarget height inputmode max maxlength min minlength
   multiple name placeholder readonly required size spellcheck
   src step tabindex type value width></input>
```

Attributes

The attributes that are used in the `input` element are as follows:

- `accept`: This is used to specify which file types are accepted for the web page.
- `autocomplete`: This says whether the browser can autocomplete this input based on previous values.
- `autofocus`: This lets the browser automatically focus on the element. This should only be used on one element.
- `checked`: This is used with the radio or checkbox. This will select the value on page load.
- `disabled`: This says whether or not to disable the element.
- `form`: This states the ID of the form.
- `formaction`, `formenctype`, `formmethod`, `formnovalidate`, and `formtarget`: These will override the form's value if these attributes are associated with a button or image.
- `height`: This is used to set the height of the image.
- `inputmode`: This gives a hint to the browser of what keyboard to display. For example, you can use numeric to specify only the keypad.
- `max`: This is the maximum number or date-time of the system.

- maxlength: This is the maximum number of characters that can be accepted in the web page.
- min: This is the minimum number or date-time of the system.
- minlength: This is the minimum number of characters.
- multiple: This says whether there can be multiple values or not. This is used with email or file.
- placeholder: This is the text that is displayed in the element when there is no value assigned to this attribute.
- readonly: This makes the element of the read-only format.
- required: This is the element that is required to be assigned a value and cannot be blank.
- size: This is the size of the element.
- src: This will be the URL of the image if it is of the img type.
- step: This is used with the min and max attributes to determine the incremental steps.
- tabindex: This is the order of the elements when using tab.
- type: Refer to the next section for the description.
- value: This is the initial value of the element.
- width: This is the attribute to set the width.

Description

The input element is the main way to get data from the user. This element can vary quite a bit based on the type that is used. HTML5 has added a few inputs that also give you validation. For example, the email type will also validate that the e-mail is a valid email. In addition to this, the type can give hints to the browser about what keyboard to display. This is important for mobiles, which have many different virtual keyboards. For example, the tel type will show a number pad instead of the regular keyboard. Here is a rundown of the different types of keyboards and their description:

- button: This is a button.
- checkbox: This is a checkbox.
- color: For most browsers, this will create a color picker; however, it is not required by HTML5.
- date: This creates a date picker.

- datetime: This creates a date and time picker using a time zone.
- datetime-local: This creates a date and time picker without a time zone.
- email: This is a text input for e-mail addresses. This type validates e-mails.
- file: This selects a file.
- hidden: This attribute will not be displayed, but the value will still be part of the form.
- image: This essentially creates an image button.
- month: This can enter the month and year.
- number: This is used for a floating point number.
- password: This is a text input where the text is not shown.
- radio: This is a control to group multiple elements using the same name attribute. Only one from the provided list can be selected.
- range: This a way to select a range of numbers.
- reset: This resets the form.
- search: This is a text input.
- submit: This is a button that will submit the form.
- tel: This is an input to enter a phone number.
- text: This is your basic text input.
- time: This is the time without a time zone.
- url: This an input to enter a URL. This will do validation as well.
- week: This is to enter the week number.

Here is an example of the text, e-mail, and tel inputs:

```
<input type="text" name="name" placeholder="enter email"/>
<input type="email" />
<input type="tel" />
```

button

The syntax of the button element is as follows:

```
<button autofocus disabled form formaction formenctype
    formmethod formnovalidate formtarget name type value></button>
```

Attributes

The attributes that are used in the button element are as follows:

- autofocus: This lets the browser automatically focus on the element that this is an attribute of. This should only be used on one element.
- disabled: This states whether or not to disable the element.
- form: This is the ID of the form.
- formaction, formenctype, formmethod, formnovalidate, and formtarget: These will override the form's value if this is a button or image.
- name: This is the name of the button for the form.
- type: This changes what the button does. The values are submit — which submits the form, reset — which resets the form, button — which is the default that does nothing.
- value: This is the initial value of the element.

Description

The button element creates a button that can be clicked on. Changing the type attribute will change its behavior.

Here is an example of the reset and submit buttons:

```
<button type="reset">Reset</button>
<button type="submit">Submit</button>
```

select

The syntax of the select element is as follows:

```
<select autofocus disabled form multiple name required
  size ></select>
```

Attributes

The attributes that are used in the button element are as follows:

- autofocus: This lets the browser automatically focus on this element. This should only be used on one element.
- disabled: This states whether or not to disable the element.
- form: This is the ID of the form.

- `multiple`: This states whether or not multiple items can be selected.
- `name`: This is the name of the element.
- `required`: This checks whether the option needs a value.
- `size`: This determines the number of rows for the element.

Description

The `button` element is used with the `option` element. Multiple `option` elements can be added to the list to select or choose from. The value of the selected option is used when the form is submitted.

Here is an example:

```
<select name="select">
    <option value="1">One</option>
    <option value="2">Two</option>
</select>
```

See also

You can also refer to the `optgroup` and `option` attributes to find out more about the `button` element.

optgroup

The `optgroup` element is the option group element:

```
<optgroup disabled label></optgroup>
```

Attributes

The attributes that are used in the `optgroup` element are as follows:

- `disabled`: This disables the group
- `label`: This is the heading in the drop-down menu

Description

The `optgroup` element allows you to group options together. The children of this element need to be the `option` elements. They are not selectable and do not have a value.

Here is an example of the `outgroup` element with car makes and models:

```
<select name="cars">
   <optgroup label="Ford">
       <option value="Fiesta">Fiesta</option>
       <option value="Taurus">Taurus</option>
   </optgroup>
    <optgroup label="Honda">
        <option value="Accord">Accord</option>
        <option value="Fit">Fit</option>
    </optgroup>
</select>
```

See also

You can also refer to the `option` and `select` elements to learn more about the `optgroup` element.

option

The syntax of the `option` element is as shown:

```
<option disabled selected value></option>
```

Attributes

The attributes that are used in the `option` element are as follows:

- `disabled`: This states whether or not the element is disabled.
- `selected`: This states whether or not the option is selected. We can set only one option per selected element.
- `value`: This states the value of the `option`.

Description

The `option` elements are the actual items in the `select` element. They can either be the child of a `select` or `optgroup` element.

Here is an example:

```
<select name="select">
    <option value="1">One</option>
    <option value="2">Two</option>
</select>
```

See also

You can also refer to the `select` and `optgroup` elements to find out more about the `option` element.

textarea

The syntax of the `textarea` element is as follows:

```
<textarea autocomplete autofocus cols disabled form
    maxlength minlength name placeholder readonly required
    rows spellcheck wrap></textarea>
```

Attributes

The attributes that are used in the `textarea` element are as follows:

- `autocomplete`: This states whether the browser can autocomplete this input based on previous values or not.

- `autofocus`: This lets the browser automatically focus on this element. This should only be used on one element.

- `cols`: This states the width of the `textarea` element in characters.

- `disabled`: This states whether or not to disable the element.

- `form`: This is the ID of the form.

- `maxlength`: This is the maximum number of characters.

- `minlength`: This is the minimum number of characters.

- `name`: This is the name of the element.

- `placeholder`: This is the text that is displayed in the element when there is no value.

- `readonly`: This makes the element read-only.

- `required`: This states that the element is required and cannot be blank.

- `rows`: This states the number of rows for `textarea`.

- `spellcheck`: This states whether or not the element should have the spelling checked.

- `wrap`: This states how the lines are wrapped.

Description

You will use this when you need more text than just a single line.

Here is an example:

```
<textarea cols="20" rows="10"
  placeholder="Input text here"></textarea>
```

Drawing elements

In previous versions of HTML, if you wanted a graphic or image, you had to create it in another application and use the img element to pull it into your document. HTML5 has brought some new elements and features to replace the old elements that allow you to draw your own images in the browser.

canvas

The syntax of the canvas element is as follows:

```
<canvas height width></canvas>
```

Attributes

The attributes that are used in the canvas element are as follows:

* height: This is an attribute to set the height
* width: This is an attribute to set the width

Description

The canvas element is used for drawing. You can use JavaScript to draw lines, shapes, and images; pull frames from videos; and use WebGL, to name just a few features. The HTML element is just the canvas (aptly named!) that you use to make a drawing. All of the interaction happens in JavaScript.

Here is an example of a small canvas element:

```
<canvas height="400" width="400">
    Your browser does not support the canvas element.
</canvas>
```

svg

The svg element is the **Scalable Vector Graphics (SVG)** element:

```
<svg height viewbox width ></svg>
```

Attributes

The attributes that are used in the svg element are as follows:

- height: This is the attribute that sets the height.
- viewbox: This sets the bounds for the element. It takes four numbers that map to min-x, min-y, width, and height.
- width: This is the attribute that sets the width.

Description

SVG is not a true HTML element. It is its own specification with many elements and attributes. There are books written entirely about SVG. This element is here because you can now create inline SVG in an HTML document. This gives you a lot of flexibility with two-dimensional drawings that images do not give you.

Here is an example that demonstrates the difference between height, width, and viewport. The viewport takes up the bounds of the element, and height and width give the element its size:

```
<svg xmlns="http://www.w3.org/2000/svg"
  preserveAspectRatio=""
    width="200" height="100" viewBox="0 0 400 200">
    <rect x="0" y="0" width="400" height="200"
      fill="yellow" stroke="black" stroke-width="3" />
</svg>
```

2
HTML Attributes

HTML is built using elements. Each of these elements will have attributes. The attributes can change how the browser renders the element, configures it, and the behavior involving the element.

The focus of the chapter will be entirely on attributes. If you are unsure about which attributes apply to which elements, the previous chapter goes over almost all the elements and the attributes that apply to them.

Global attributes

These are attributes that are available for every HTML element. However, you should note that just because the attribute is available, it does not mean that it will actually do anything.

accesskey

The `accesskey` attribute creates a keyboard shortcut to activate or focus on the element:

```
<element accesskey></element>
```

Description

The `accesskey` attribute allows you to create a keyboard shortcut. This can be a space-delimited list of characters. Most browsers on Windows will use *Alt* + accesskey and most browsers on Mac use *Ctrl* + *Option* + accesskey.

Here is an example using a textbox that can be focused on with the character q:

```
<input type="search" name="q" accesskey="q"/>
```

class

The class attribute is often used to help group similar elements for CSS selectors:

```
<element class></element>
```

Description

The class attribute is one of the most used attributes. The class attribute allows CSS to target multiple elements and apply a style to them. In addition to this, many people also use the class attribute to help target elements in JavaScript.

Class takes a space-delimited list of class names.

Here is an example that applies the search-box class to an element:

```
<input type="search" name="q" class="search-box"/>
```

contenteditable

The contenteditable attribute sets the element's content as editable:

```
<element contenteditable></element>
```

Description

The contenteditable attribute tells the browser that the user can edit the content in the element. The contenteditable attribute should have a value of true or false, where true means that the element is editable.

Here is an example with a div element:

```
<div contenteditable="true">
   Click here and edit this sentence!</div>
```

data-*

The data-* attribute is the custom attribute for elements:

```
<element data-*></-></element>
```

Description

You can name the data attribute whatever you want as long as the name does not start with XML, does not use any semicolons, and does not have any uppercase letters. The value can be anything.

Here is a list of items with the `data-id` attributes. Note that the attribute name `data-id` is arbitrary. You can use any valid name here:

```
<li data-id="1">First Row</li>
<li data-id="2">Second Row</li>
<li data-id="3">Third Row</li>
```

dir

The `dir` attribute defines the text direction:

```
<element dir></element>
```

Description

The `dir` attribute is the direction attribute. It specifies the text direction. The following are its possible values:

- `auto`: This lets the browser choose the direction automatically
- `ltr`: This lets the browser choose the left to right direction
- `rtl`: The browser chooses the right to left direction

Here is an example for the `ltr` and `rtl` attributes.

```
<div dir="ltr">Left to Right</div>
<div dir="rtl">Right to Left</div>
```

draggable

The `draggable` attribute defines whether the element is draggable:

```
<element draggable-></element>
```

Description

The `draggable` attribute allows the element to be dragged around. Note that most elements require JavaScript as well for this to work fully:

Here is an example:

```
<div draggable="true">You can drag me.</div>
```

hidden

The `hidden` attribute prevents the rendering of the element:

```
<element hidden></element>
```

Description

The `hidden` attribute is used to hide elements. However, a hidden element can be overridden and displayed through CSS or JavaScript. This is a Boolean attribute so including this attribute sets the value to `true` and excluding it sets the value to `false`.

Here is an example:

```
<div hidden>This should not show</div>
```

id

The `id` attribute is a unique identifier of the element:

```
<element id></element>
```

Description

The `id` attribute is a unique identifier of the element. This is used for fragment linking and easily accessing the element in JavaScript and CSS.

Here is an example using a `div` element:

```
<div id="the-first-div">This is the first div.</div>
```

lang

The `lang` attribute defines the language used in the element:

```
<element lang></element>
```

Description

The `lang` attribute sets the language for the element. The acceptable value should be a BCP47 language. There are too many to list here, but you can read the standard at `http://www.ietf.org/rfc/bcp/bcp47.txt`. The language is important for things such as screen readers to use correct pronunciation.

Here is a simple example using English:

```
<div lang="en">The language of this element is English.</div>
```

spellcheck

The `spellcheck` attribute specifies whether spell check can be used:

```
<element spellcheck></element>
```

Description

The `spellcheck` attribute was introduced in HTML5. It will tell the browser whether to spellcheck this element or not. The value should either be `true` or `false`.

Here is an example using textarea:

```
<textarea spellcheck="false">
  Moste fo teh worsd r mispeld.</textarea>
```

style

The `style` attribute is used to set the inline style:

```
<element style></element>
```

Description

You can add CSS styles directly to an element with the `style` attribute. Any style rule that you can use in CSS, you can use here. Remember that this will take precedence over any other styles defined in CSS.

Here is an example that sets the background to red and text to white:

```
<div style="background: #ff0000; color: #ffffff">
  This has inline styles.</div>
```

tabindex

The `tabindex` attribute sets the tab order:

```
<element tabindex></element>
```

Description

The `tabindex` attribute element defines the order in which elements will focus when the *Tab* key is used. There are three different types of values you can use. The first is a negative number. This defines that it is not in the list of elements for tab order. A `zero` value means that the browser should determine the order of this element. This is usually the order in which the elements occur in the document. This is a positive number and it will set the tab order.

The following example demonstrates that you can set `tabindex` in a different order to where the elements are in the document:

```
<input type="text" tabindex="1" />
<input type="text" tabindex="3" />
<input type="text" tabindex="2" />
```

title

The `title` attribute is the text for a tooltip:

```
<element title></element>
```

Description

The `title` attribute gives extra information about the element. Usually, the title is shown as a tooltip for the element. For example, when using an image, this could be the name of the image or a photo credit:

```
<p title="Some extra information.">
  This is a paragraph of text.</p>
```

Miscellaneous

The miscellaneous grouping of attributes will have no hierarchy as they can be used on many different elements.

accept

The `accept` attribute gives the list of types for the server:

```
<element accept></element>
```

Elements

The elements used in the `accept` attribute are `form` and `input`.

Description

The `accept` attribute allows you to suggest the file type that this form or input should accept. You can use `audio/*`, `video/*`, `image/*`, a MIME type, or the extension.

Here is an example looking for PNG files:

```
<input type="file" accept=".png, image/png"/>
```

accept-charset

The `accept-charset` attribute gives the list of support charsets:

```
<element accept-charset></element>
```

Elements

The `form` element is used in the `accept-charset` attribute.

Description

The `accept-charset` attribute sets the charset that the form will accept. UTF-8 is most commonly used as it accepts many characters from many languages.

Here is an example of using the `charset` attribute:

```
<form accept-charset="UTF-8"></form>
```

action

The `action` attribute is where the form is processed, the syntax is as follows:

```
<element action ></element>
```

Elements

The `form` element is used in the `action` element.

Description

The `action` attribute consists of the URL that will process the form's data.

Here is an example:

```
<form action="form-process.php"></form>
```

alt

The `alt` attribute is an alternative text for the element:

```
<element alt ></element>
```

Elements

The elements that are used in the `alt` attribute are `applet`, `area`, `img`, and `input`.

Description

The `alt` attribute is an alternate text in case the element cannot render the code. The text should pass the same information to the user that the image would have.

Some browsers (Chrome being the most commonly used) will not display the text, and you may need to use the `title` attribute. This is not the standardized behavior.

Here is an example using an image:

```
<img alt="Login button." src="non-loading-image.png"/>
```

async

The `async` attribute is used for the asynchronous execution of the script:

```
<element async ></element>
```

Elements

The `script` element is used in the `async` attribute.

Description

The `async` attribute tells the browser to load and execute the script asynchronously. By default, the browser will load scripts synchronously. An asynchronous load will immediately download and parse the script without blocking the rendering of the page.

Here is an example:

```
<script src="application.js" async></script>
```

autocomplete

The `autocomplete` attribute defines whether the element can be autocompleted:

```
<element autocomplete ></element>
```

Elements

The `form` and `input` elements are used in the `autocomplete` attribute.

Description

The `autocomplete` attribute lets the browser know whether or not it can autocomplete the form or input from the previous values. This can have `on` and `off` as the values.

Here is an example:

```
<input type="text" autocomplete="off"
  placeholder="Will not autocomplete"/>
```

autofocus

The `autofocus` attribute defines whether the element would be focused automatically on the elements:

```
<element autofocus ></element>
```

Elements

The `button`, `input`, `select`, and `textarea` elements are used in the `autofocus` attribute.

Description

The `autofocus` attribute will set the focus to the element. This should only be used on one element.

Here is an example of the `autofocus` attribute with a text input:

```
<input type="text" autofocus/>
```

autoplay

The `autoplay` attribute defines whether the audio or video track should play as soon as possible:

```
<element autoplay ></element>
```

Elements

The `audio` and `video` elements are used in the `autoplay` attribute.

Description

The `autoplay` attribute will make the element play as soon as it can, without having to stop to load.

Here is an example with an audio file:

```
<audio autoplay src="audio.mps"></audio>
```

autosave

The `autosave` attribute defines whether the previous values should be saved:

```
<element autosave ></element>
```

Elements

The `input` element is used in the `autosave` attribute.

Description

The `autosave` attribute tells the browser to save values entered into this input. This means that on the next page load, the values will be persisted. It should have a unique name that the browser can associate the saved values to. This attribute may or may not work in some browsers as it is not fully standardized.

Here is an example:

```
<input type="text" autosave="textautosave" />
```

cite

The `cite` attribute has the source of the quote:

```
<element cite ></element>
```

Elements

The `blockquote`, `del`, `ins`, and `q` elements are used in the `cite` attribute.

Description

The `cite` attribute points to the source of a quote by providing a URL.

Here is an example:

```
<blockquote cite=
  "http://en.wikiquote.org/wiki/The_Good,_the_Bad_and_the_Ugly">
    After a meal there's nothing like a good cigar.
</blockquote>
```

cols

The `cols` attribute gives the number of columns:

```
<element cols ></element>
```

Elements

The `textarea` element is used with the `cols` attribute.

Description

The `cols` attribute gives the number of columns in a `textarea` element.

Here is an example of it in use:

```
<textarea cols="30"></textarea>
```

colspan

The `colspan` attribute gives the number of columns a cell should span:

```
<element colspan ></element>
```

Elements

The `td` and `th` elements are used in the `colspan` attribute.

Description

The `colspan` attribute gives the number of columns a table cell should span.

Here is an example using a table element:

```
<table>
    <tr><td colspan="2">1 and 2</td></tr>
    <tr><td>1</td><td>2</td></tr>
</table>
```

datetime

The `datetime` attribute gives the date and time associated with this element:

```
<element datetime ></element>
```

Elements

The `del`, `ins`, and `time` elements are used with the `datetime` attribute.

Description

The `datetime` attribute should be the time that the action implied by the element was taken. This attribute is mainly used with the `del` and `ins` elements to show when the deletion or insertion occurred.

Here is an example using `del`:

```
My name is <del datetime="2014-12-16T23:59:60Z">John</del>Josh.
```

disabled

The `disabled` attribute defines whether the element can be used or not:

```
<element disabled ></element>
```

Elements

The `button`, `fieldset`, `input`, `optgroup`, `option`, `select`, and `textarea` elements are used in the `disabled` attribute.

Description

The `disabled` attribute makes the element unusable. If the element is disabled, it cannot be used. This means that buttons cannot be clicked, text areas and text inputs cannot have text entered, dropdowns cannot be changed, and so on.

Here is an example with a `button` element:

```
<button disabled>This is a disabled button</button>
```

download

The `download` attribute sets a link to download a resource:

```
<element download ></element>
```

Elements

The `a` element is used in the `download` attribute.

Description

The `download` attribute tells the browser to download the resource when clicked on. This means that when the `a` element is clicked, a save dialog will appear with the value of the attribute as the default name.

Here is an example:

```
<a href="example.pdf" download="example.pdf">Save the PDF</a>
```

content

The `content` attribute gives a value to go with the name attribute:

```
<element content ></element>
```

Elements

The `meta` element is used in the content attribute.

Description

The `content` attribute is an attribute for the `meta` tag. It is used as the value of the `name` attribute.

Here is an example:

```
<meta name="example" content="value for example" />
```

controls

The `controls` attribute defines whether the controls should be displayed:

```
<element controls ></element>
```

Elements

The `audio` and `video` elements are used in the `controls` attribute.

Description

The `controls` attribute tells the browser to display controls for a media file. This is a Boolean attribute.

Here is an audio example:

```
<audio controls src="example.mp3"></audio>
```

for

The `for` attribute sets the element this attribute is associated with:

```
<element for ></element>
```

Elements

The `label` element is used with the `for` attribute.

Description

The `for` attribute specifies which form input the label is associated with. This is specified using the ID of the input element. The label will also allow the user to click on it and focus on the input.

Here is an example with a text input:

```
<label for="username">Username</label>
<input type="text" id="username" name="username" />
```

form

The `form` attribute sets the form with which this input is associated:

```
<element form ></element>
```

Elements

The `button`, `fieldset`, `input`, `labellable`, `object`, `output`, `select`, and `textarea` elements are used in the `form` attribute.

Description

The `form` attribute references the form that these controls are in:

```
<form method="get" id="example-form">

</form>
<input type="text" form="example-form" />
```

formaction

The `formaction` attribute sets the form action for the element:

```
<element formaction ></element>
```

Elements

The `button` and `input` elements are used in the `formaction` attribute.

Description

The `formaction` attribute will override the action of the form for this element. This should be a URL. If used on the form element itself, this attribute specifies the target for the form data. If used on an element within the form (for example, button), this overrides the declared value on the form itself.

Here is an example with a button:

```
<form method="get" action="formaction.php">
    <button formaction="buttonaction.php">Press me</button>
</form>
```

height

The `height` attribute sets the height of an element:

```
<element height ></element>
```

Elements

The `canvas`, `embed`, `iframe`, `img`, `input`, `object`, and `video` elements are used in the `height` attribute.

Description

The `height` attribute sets the height of the element. Only the elements listed in the previous section should use this attribute and all other elements should use CSS to set their height.

 You may see many HTML documents that use `height` on many elements. This is not valid anymore and CSS should be used to set the height on any other elements.

Here is an example with a canvas:

```
<canvas height="400" width="400"></canvas>
```

href

The `href` attribute gives the URL of the resource:

```
<element href ></element>
```

Elements

The `a`, `base`, and `link` elements are used in the `href` attribute.

Description

The URL for the element is given by the `href` attribute.

Here is an example with an anchor element:

```
<a href="http://www.google.com">Google</a>
```

hreflang

The `hreflang` attribute states the language of the resource:

```
<element hreflang ></element>
```

Elements

The `a` and `link` elements are used in the `hreflang` attribute.

Description

The `hreflang` attribute is the language of the linked document. The acceptable values should be in the BCP47 language. There are too many to list here, but you can read the standard at `http://www.ietf.org/rfc/bcp/bcp47.txt`.

Here is an example:

```
<a href="http://www.google.com" hreflang="en">Google</a>
```

label

The `label` attribute states the title of the track:

```
<element label ></element>
```

Elements

The `track` element is used in the `label` attribute.

Description

The `label` attribute is used with the `track` element to give a title to the track.

Here is an example with subtitles for a video:

```
<video src="sample.mp4">
    <track kind="subtitles" label="English Subtitles"
       src="en.vtt" />
</video>
```

list

The `list` attribute gives the list of options:

```
<element list ></element>
```

Elements

The `input` element is used in the `list` attribute.

Description

The `list` attribute ties to a `datalist` attribute with a list of options for `input`.

This example has a list of fruits for a text input:

```
<input type="text" list="fruit" />
<datalist id="fruit">
    <option>Apple</option>
    <option>Banana</option>
</datalist>
```

loop

The `loop` attribute defines whether the element should loop the media:

```
<element loop ></element>
```

Elements

The `audio` and `video` elements are used in the `loop` attribute.

Description

The `loop` attribute is a Boolean attribute which will play the media on a loop.

Here is an example with an `audio` element:

```
<audio src="example.mp3" loop></audio>
```

max

The `max` attribute defines the maximum value:

```
<element max ></element>
```

Elements

The `input` and `progress` elements are used in the `max` attribute.

Description

The `max` attribute sets the maximum numeric or date-time value allowed.

Here is an example with an input:

```
<input type="number" min="0" max="5" >
```

maxlength

The `maxlength` attribute defines the maximum number of characters:

```
<element maxlength ></element>
```

Elements

The `input` and `textarea` elements are used in the `maxlength` attributes.

Description

The `maxlength` attribute sets the maximum number of characters.

Here is an example with an input:

```
<input type="text" maxlength="5">
```

media

The media attribute sets the media for the linked resource:

```
<element media ></element>
```

Elements

The a, area, link, source, and style elements are used in the media attribute.

Description

The media attribute specifies which media this resource is for. Usually, this attribute is used with link and the CSS. The standardized values are screen, print, and all. The screen value is for displaying on a monitor, the print value is when printing, and the all value is both. Different browsers do have a few other values, but nothing that works across all.

Here is an example with CSS to create a print stylesheet:

```
<link rel="stylesheet" href="print.css" media="print"/>
```

method

The method attribute defines the HTTP method of form:

```
<element method ></element>
```

Elements

The form element is used in the method attribute.

Description

The method attribute sets the HTTP method of the form. The two values are GET, which is the default, and POST.

Here is an example of a form that submits using the POST HTTP method:

```
<form method="post" action="formaction.php"></form>
```

min

The min attribute defines the minimum value:

```
<element min ></element>
```

Elements

The `input` element is used in the `min` attribute.

Description

The `min` attribute is the opposite of `max`. It sets the minimum value for an input.

Here is an example:

```
<input type="number" min="2">
```

multiple

The `multiple` attribute defines whether multiple values can be selected:

```
<element multiple ></element>
```

Elements

The `select` element is used in the `multiple` attribute.

Description

The `multiple` attribute allows you to select multiple values. This is a Boolean attribute.

Here is an example:

```
<select multiple>
    <option>First</option>
    <option>Second</option>
</select>
```

name

The `name` attribute is the name of the element:

```
<element name ></element>
```

Elements

The `button`, `form`, `fieldset`, `iframe`, `input`, `object`, `select`, `textarea`, and `meta` elements are used in the `name` attribute.

Description

The name attribute names an element. This allows you to get the value of the element in a submitted form.

Here is an example with an input:

```
<input type="text" id="username" name="username" />
```

novalidate

The novalidate attribute defines whether the validation should be skipped:

```
<element novalidate ></element>
```

Elements

The form element is used in the novalidate attribute.

Description

The novalidate attribute sets the form to not validate when submitted. The browser will validate the input without adding any client-side code. This is a Boolean attribute.

Here is an example:

```
<form method="post" action="formaction.php" novalidate></form>
```

pattern

The pattern attribute defines a regular expression:

```
<element pattern ></element>
```

Elements

The input element is used in the pattern attribute.

Description

You can use a regular expression in this attribute to validate the input.

Here is an example that will only be valid with numbers:

```
<input pattern="[0-9].+" type="text" />
```

placeholder

The `placeholder` attribute gives a hint for the user in the element:

```
<element placeholder ></element>
```

Elements

The `input` and `textarea` elements are used in the `placeholder` attribute.

Description

When the element has not been interacted with (no value and is not in focus), it will display the text in this attribute. The value will disappear once the element is interacted with.

Here is an example with `input`:

```
<input type="text" name="username"
  placeholder="Please enter username"/>
```

poster

The `poster` attribute gives an image for a video:

```
<element poster ></element>
```

Elements

The `video` element is used in the `poster` attribute.

Description

The `poster` attribute should point to an image that will be the poster (or placeholder) for a video element until the video is loaded.

Here is an example:

```
<video src="video-about-dogs.mp4"
  poster="images/image-of-dog.png"></video>
```

readonly

The `readonly` attribute defines whether the element is editable:

```
<element readonly ></element>
```

Elements

The `input` and `textarea` elements are used in the `readonly` attribute.

Description

The `readonly` attribute makes the element readonly or not editable. This is a Boolean attribute.

Here is an example with a text input:

```
<input type="text" readonly />
```

rel

The `rel` attribute defines the relationship of the element:

```
<element rel ></element>
```

Elements

The `a` and `link` elements are used in the `rel` attribute.

Description

The `rel` attribute is the relationship between the linked resource and the document. Usually, you will see this used with the `link` element and CSS or with the `a` element and the value of `nofollow`.

Here is a CSS example:

```
<link rel="stylesheet" href="style.css"
  type="text/css" media="screen" />
```

required

The `required` attribute defines whether the element is required when submitting a form:

```
<element required ></element>
```

Elements

The `input`, `select`, and `textarea` elements are used in the `required` attribute.

Description

The `required` attribute makes the element required in the form. The form will not get submitted until the element is filled out. This is a Boolean attribute.

Here is an example with a text input:

```
<input required type="text" />
```

reversed

The `reversed` attribute changes the list order display:

```
<element reversed ></element>
```

Elements

The `ol` element is used in the `reversed` attribute.

Description

The `reversed` attribute is only an attribute of an ordered list, and it will render the list in the reverse order. The items are not in reverse, but rather the numbered list indicators are. This is a Boolean attribute.

Here is an example:

```
<ol reversed>
    <li>1</li>
    <li>2</li>
    <li>3</li>
</ol>
```

rows

The `rows` attribute sets rows in a text area:

```
<element rows ></element>
```

Elements

The `textarea` element is used in the `rows` attribute.

Description

The `rows` attribute sets the number of rows in `textarea`.

Here is an example:

```
<textarea rows="30"></textarea>
```

rowspan

The `rowspan` attribute sets the number of rows that a cell will span:

```
<element rowspan ></element>
```

Elements

The `td` and `th` elements are used in the `rowspan` attribute.

Description

The `rowspan` attribute is used on the table cell elements. It will make the cell span the number of rows in the value.

Here is an example:

```
<table>
    <tr><td rowspan="2">Pets</td><td>Dogs</td></tr>
    <tr><td>Cats</td></tr>
</table>
```

scope

The `scope` attribute defines the cell with which the element is associated:

```
<element scope ></element>
```

Elements

The `td` and `th` elements are used in the `scope` attribute.

Description

The `scope` attribute indicates what the cell is associated with. For example, this could be `row` or `col`. This is a great benefit for accessibility. It helps to convey the relationship of the rows and columns in the table when a screen reader is used.

Here is an example with a table cell:

```
<table>
    <tr><th>Name</th><th>Age</th></tr>
    <tr><td scope="row">Gizmo</td><td>4</td></tr>
</table>
```

selected

The `selected` attribute sets the default selection:

```
<element selected ></element>
```

Elements

The `option` element is used in the `selected` attribute.

Description

The `selected` attribute will set the option to be selected when the page loads. This should only be set on one `option` element per `select` element. This is a Boolean attribute.

Here is an example:

```
<select>
    <option>Cats</option>
    <option selected>Dogs</option>
</select>
```

size

The `size` attribute sets the width of element:

```
<element size ></element>
```

Elements

The `input` and `select` elements are used in the `size` attribute.

Description

The `size` attribute determines the width of the element unless the element is an input and text or password. It will then determine the number of characters the element can display. This is specified as the number of characters in the integer form. The default for this is `20`.

Here is an example with a text input:

```
<input type="text" size="100" />
```

src

The `src` attribute gives the URL for the element:

```
<element src ></element>
```

Elements

The `audio`, `embed`, `iframe`, `img`, `input`, `script`, `source`, `track`, and `video` elements are used in the `src` attribute.

Description

The `src` attribute gives the URL of the resource for the element.

Here is an example with an `image` element:

```
<img src="dogs.png" />
```

start

The `start` attribute sets the starting number:

```
<element start ></element>
```

Elements

The `ol` element is used in the `start` attribute.

Description

The start attribute will change the starting number for an ordered list.

Here is an example:

```
<ol start="10">
    <li>1</li>
    <li>2</li>
</ol>
```

step

The step attribute determines the jump between each number:

```
<element step ></element>
```

Elements

The input element is used in the step attribute.

Description

The step attribute is used with an input element and the type attribute of number or date-time. It determines how far to step for each increment.

Here is an example with a number input. You will only be able to increment by 5 four times before reaching the max:

```
<input type="number" min="0" max="20" step="5" />
```

type

The type attribute defines the type of the element:

```
<element type ></element>
```

Elements

The `button`, `input`, `embed`, `object`, `script`, `source`, and `style` elements are used in the `type` attribute.

Description

The `type` attribute is one of the most complex attributes. It can completely change the look and behavior of an element. For example, `input`.

Here is a list for each element:

- `button`: Following are the values of the `button` attribute:
  - `button`: This is the default value
  - `reset`: This resets the form
  - `submit`: This submits the form
- `input`: Please view the input element section from the previous chapter.
- `embed`: This will be the MIME type of the embedded resource.
- `object`: This will be the MIME type of the object.
- `script`: This will be the MIME type. Usually `text/javascript` are used.
- `source`: This will be the MIME type.
- `style`: This will be MIME type. Usually `text/css` are used.

Here is an example with an input:

```
<input type="password" />
```

value

The `value` attribute sets the value of the element:

```
<element value ></element>
```

Elements

The `button`, `input`, `li`, `option`, `progress`, and `param` elements are used in the `value` attribute.

Description

The `value` attribute will set the value of the element at page load.

Here is an example with a text input:

```
<input type="text" value="Hey!"/>
```

width

The `width` attribute sets the width of the element:

```
<element width ></element>
```

Elements

The `canvas`, `embed`, `iframe`, `img`, `input`, `object`, and `video` elements are used in the `width` attribute.

Description

The `width` attribute sets the width of the element.

 You may see many HTML documents that use width on many elements. This is not valid any more; CSS should be used to set the width on any other elements.

Here is an example with a `canvas` element:

```
<canvas width="200" height="200"></canvas>
```

wrap

The `wrap` attribute sets how the text is wrapped:

```
<element wrap ></element>
```

Elements

The `textarea` element is used in the `wrap` attribute.

Description

The wrap attribute decides whether or not text can be wrapped in textarea. The values can be hard or soft. A hard value will insert line breaks into the text. It must also be used with the cols attribute, so it knows where the end of the line is. A soft value will not insert any line breaks.

Here is an example:

```
<textarea cols="10" wrap="hard"></textarea>
```

3
CSS Concepts and Applications

Cascading Style Sheet (**CSS**) is the preferred way to style HTML. HTML has a style element and a global style attribute. These make it very easy to write unmaintainable HTML. For example, let's imagine that we have 10 elements on an HTML page for which we want the font color to be red. We create a span element to wrap the text that has the font color red, as follows:

```
<span style="color: #ff0000;"></span>
```

Later, if we decide to change the color to blue, we will have to change 10 instances of that element and then multiply this by the number of pages we have used the span element on. This is completely unmaintainable.

This is where CSS comes in. We can target specific elements/groups of elements to which we wish to apply a specific style. CSS allows us to define these styles, easily update them, and change them from one place to another.

This book will focus on the most used CSS selectors, units, rules, functions, and properties from CSS1, CSS2.1, and CSS3. For the most part, these should all work in any browser, but there are exceptions. A great rule of thumb is that newer browsers will have fewer issues.

We will get started with a quick overview of the different types of basic selectors.

Basic selectors

A selector represents a structure. This representation is then used in a CSS rule to determine what elements are selected to be styled by this rule. CSS style rules apply in the form of a waterfall effect. Each rule that is matched is also passed on to each of its children, matched and applied based on the weight of the selector. This section will only focus on the most basic of selectors.

The basic selectors are either type selectors, universal selectors, attribute selectors, class selectors, ID selectors, or pseudo-classes.

> All CSS selectors are case-insensitive. Selectors can also be grouped together to share rules. To group selectors, you just have to split them with commas. Consider the following example:
> ```
> p { color: #ffffff; }
> article { color: #ffffff }
> ```
> Here, the following is the same as the preceding declaration
> ```
> p, article { color: #ffffff }
> ```

The simple selector

The following selectors are all the simple selectors for CSS.

The type selectors

The `type` selectors selects based on the element name:

```
E
ns|E
```

Here, `E` is the element name and `ns` is a namespace.

Description

This is the simplest way to select elements—using their name. For the most part, when using just HTML, you not need to worry about the namespace, as all of the HTML elements are in the default namespace. An asterisk can be used to specify all namespaces, for example, `*|Element`.

When this selector is used, it will match all of the elements in the document. For example, if you have fifteen h2 elements and use a single h2 element, then this rule will match all fifteen.

Here are a few examples of the type selector. The first code sets all the h1 elements' font color to red. The next code applies red as the background color for all p elements:

```
h1 { color: #ff0000; }
p { background: #ff0000; }
```

The universal selector

The asterisk (*) represents any and all qualified elements:

```
*
ns|*
*|*
```

Here, ns is a namespace.

Description

This is essentially a wildcard selector. It will match every element. This is true even when used with other selectors. For example, *.my-class and .my-class are the same.

While you can use it as a single selector to match every element, it is most useful when used with other selectors. Following along with our preceding example, we may want to select any element that is a descendant of an article element. This selector is very explicit and easy to read, take a look at the following syntax:

```
article *
```

Here is an example. The first example uses attribute selectors to select any elements with hreflang in English, and the second example will select all elements in the document:

```
*[hreflang="en"] { display: block; background:url(flag_of_the_UK); }
* { padding: 0; }
```

The attribute selectors

These selectors will match against attributes of an element. There are seven different types of attribute selector and they are as follows:

```
[attribute]
[attribute=value]
[attribute~=value]
[attribute|=value]
[attribute^=value]
[attribute$=value]
[attribute*=value]
```

These selectors are usually preceded by a type selector or universal selector.

Description

This selector is a way to use a regular expression syntax in a selector rule. Each of the selectors will act differently based on the use, so they are listed with the differences here:

- `[attribute]`: This matches an element that has the `[attribute]` attribute, irrespective of the value of the attribute.
- `[=]`: The value has to be an exact match.
- `[~=]`: This is used when the attribute takes a list of values. One of the values in the list must match.
- `[|=]`: This attribute must either be an exact match or the value must begin with the value followed immediately by a `-`.
- `[^=]`: This attribute matches the value that has this prefix.
- `[$=]`: This attribute matches the value that has this suffix.
- `[*=]`: This attribute matches any substring of the value.

The best way to really show the difference between these is to use some examples. We will look at the `lang` and `href` attributes. The examples will be in the same order in which they were introduced.

Here is the HTML file that the examples will be selecting.

```
<span lang="en-us en-gb">Attribute Selector</span>
<span lang="es">selector de atributo</span>
<span lang="de-at de">German (Austria)</span>
<a href="https://example.com">HTTPS</a>
<a href="http://google.com">Google</a>
<a href="http://example.com/example.pdf">Example PDF</a>
```

Using the following, we should have all the spans with a `lang` attribute with a black background, Spanish will be grey, German will be red, English will be blue, anchor elements that have `https` attribute will be yellow, any PDFs will be red, and any anchor to Google will be green. Here are the preceding styles described:

```
span[lang] { background-color: #000000; color: #ffffff; }
span[lang="es"] { color: #808080; }
span[lang~="de-at"] { color: #ff0000; }
span[lang|="en"] { color: #0000ff; }
a[href^="https"] { color: #ffff00; }
a[href$="pdf"] { color: #ff0000; }
a[href*="google"] { color: #00ff00; }
```

The class selectors

This selector will match the HTML elements based on the class attribute of the element.

```
element.class
.class or *.class
element.class.another-class
```

Description

This is the most commonly used selector. Selecting based on the `class` attribute allows you to style elements in an orthogonal manner. Classes can be applied to many different elements and we can style each of those elements in the same manner.

The `class` selector can be stacked so that both classes will have to be present.

Here is some HTML with different elements that have a class attribute:

```
<h1 class="red">Red Text</h1>
<span class="red">Red Text</span>
<span class="green black">Green text, black background</span>
<span class="green">Normal text</span>
```

Here is the CSS to style the HTML:

```
.red { color: #ff0000; }
.green.black { color: #00ff00; background-color: #000000; }
```

When the `red` class is applied to an element, it will change the color of the text to red. The compound green and black will only select elements that have both classes defined.

The ID selectors

This selector will match based on the ID attribute of the element:

```
#id
element#id or *#id
```

Description

The ID attribute should be unique for the document, so the ID selector should only ever target one element. This is in contrast to the class selector, which can be used to select multiple elements. As an example, you can use a class selector to make every image on your page have a certain amount of margin and have a rule that specifically targets just your logo to have a different amount of margin.

Here is an example CSS rule that targets an ID of a logo:

```
#logo { margin: 10px; }
```

Combinators

Combinators are used to select more complex structures. They can help target specific elements or groups of elements that would be difficult to target otherwise.

Descendant combinator

This selector specifies that an element must be contained by another element.

The combinator is the whitespace character. We are explicitly defining it here so that it is clear:

```
selector-a selector-b
```

Description

The two or more statements used in this selector can be any valid selector statement. For example, the first could be a `class` selector followed by a `type` selector. The distance between the selectors does not matter. Each intermediate element will not have to be listed for the selector to work.

The combinator can be stacked. Each statement will have a whitespace character around it. This list of selectors does not need to be all inclusive, but for the selector to match the hierarchy, it does need to exist.

This selector is best used when you only want to style elements in certain situations. The following example highlights this.

In this first example, we will target images that are in an ordered list with the ID of presidents and give them a red border. Here is its HTML code:

```
<ol id="presidents">
  <li><img src="pres01.png" alt="PortraitProtrait of George
  Washington" />George Washington</li>
  <li><img src="pres02.png" alt="PortraitProtrait of John Adams"
  />John Adams</li>
</ol>
<img src="not_pres.png" alt="not a President - no border" />
```

Here is the CSS rule:

```
ol#presidents img { border: 1px solid #ff0000; }
```

Here is an example that demonstrates that there can be many elements between selectors. Here is the very arbitrary HTML.

```
<div class="example">
  I am normal.
  <div>
    <div class="select-me">
      I am red.
      <span class="select-me">I am red as well.</span>
    </div>
  </div>
</div>
```

Here is the CSS rule:

```
.example .select-me { color: #ff0000; }
```

Finally, here is an example of a multiple selector hierarchy, which has the following HTML:

```
<div class="first">Not the target
  <div class="second">Not the target
    <div class="third">I am the target.</div>
  </div>
</div>
```

The CSS rule:

```
.first .second .third { color: #ff0000; }
```

The child combinator

This selector targets a specific child:

```
element-a > element-b
```

Description

This is very similar to the descendant combinatory except for the fact that this only targets a child relationship. The second selector must be a direct descendant of the parent directly contained by the first.

Here is an example that will only target the first span in this HTML:

```
<div>Here is an <span>arbitrary</span>
<p><span>structure.</span></p></div>
```

Here is the CSS rule that only sets the first span's color to red:

```
div > span { color: #ff0000; }
```

The adjacent sibling combinator

This selector targets elements that are next to each other in the hierarchy:

```
element-a + element-b
```

Description

The two elements must have the same parent, and the first element must be immediately followed by the second.

Here is an example that highlights how the selector works. Only the second span will have the rule applied. The final span's preceding sibling is not another span so it is not matched by the selector. Here is the HTML.

```
<p>Here are a few spans in a row: <span>1</span> <span>2</span>
<em>3</em> <span>4</span></p>
```

CSS:

```
span + span { color: #ff0000; }
```

The general sibling combinator

This selector targets any element that has the same parent and follows the first:

```
element-a ~ element-b
```

Description

This is similar to the adjacent sibling combinatory; in that, both elements need the same parent. The difference is that the two elements can be separated by other elements.

Here is an example that shows that both the second and third spans will be targeted even though there is an em element between them. Here is the HTML:

```
<p>Here are a few spans in a row: <span>1</span> <span>2</span>
<em>3</em> <span>4</span></p>
```

Here is the CSS rule:

```
span ~ span { color: #ff0000; }
```

The selector specificity

This is not a selector rule like the others in this section. An element can be targeted by multiple rules, so how do you know which rule takes precedence? This is where specificity comes in. You can calculate which rule will be applied. Here is how it is calculated. Keep in mind that an inline style will trump any selector specificity:

- The number of `ID` selectors in the selector is denoted by a
- The number of `class` selectors, `attribute` selectors, and pseudo-classes in the selector is denoted by b
- The number of `type` selectors and pseudo-elements in the selector is denoted by c
- Any `universal` selectors are ignored

The numbers are then concatenated together. The larger the value, the more precedence the rule has. Let's look at some selector examples. The examples will be composed of the selector and then the calculated value:

- `h1`: a=0 b=0 c=1, 001 or 1
- `h1 span`: a=0 b=0 c=2, 002 or 2
- `h1 p > span`: a=0 b=0 c=3, 003 or 3
- `h1 *[lang="en"]`: a=0 b=1 c=1, 011 or 11
- `h1 p span.green`: a=0 b=1 c=3, 013 or 13
- `h1 p.example span.green`: a=0 b=2 c=3, 023 or 23
- `#title`: a=1 b=0 c=0, 100
- `h1#title`: a=1 b=0 c=1, 101

The easiest way to think about this is that each grouping (a, b, or c) should be a smaller group of elements to choose from. This means that each step has more weight. For example, there can be many instances of `h1` on a page. So, just selecting `h1` is a little ambiguous. Next, we can add a `class`, `attribute`, or pseudo-class selector. This should be a subset of the instances of `h1`. Next, we can search by ID. This carries the most weight because there should only be one in the entire document.

Here is an example HTML that has three headings:

```
<h1>First Heading</h1>
<h1 class="headings"><span>Second Heading</span></h1>
<h1 class="headings" id="third">Third Heading</h1>
```

Here is the CSS rule that will target each heading differently. The first rule targets all the elements, but it has the lowest specificity, the next rule is in the middle, and the last rule only targets one element. In the following example, /* */ denotes text that is a comment:

```
h1 { color: #ff0000; } /* 001 */
h1.headings span { color: #00ff00; } /* 012 */
h1#third { color: #0000ff; } /* 101 */
```

Pseudo-classes

Pseudo-classes are selectors that use information that is outside of the document tree. The information that is not in the attributes of the element. This information can change between visits or even during the visit. Pseudo-classes always have a colon followed by the name of the pseudo-class.

The link pseudo-classes

There are two mutually exclusive link pseudo-classes, namely, :link and :visited.

:link

This selects links that have not been visited. The syntax is as follows:

```
:link
```

Description

This pseudo-class exists on any anchor element that has not been visited. The browser may decide to switch a link back after some time.

Here is an example along with the :visited pseudo-class. Here is its HTML:

```
<a href="#test">Probably not visited</a>
<a href="https://www.google.com">Probably visited</a>
```

Here is the CSS. We can make an assumption that you have visited Google, so the link would likely be green in color:

```
a:link { color: #ff0000; }
a:visited { color: #00ff00; }
```

:visited

This selects links that have been visited. The syntax is as follows:

```
:visited
```

Description

This pseudo-class exists on any anchor element that has been visited.

Here is an example along with the `:link` pseudo-class. Here is its HTML:

```
<a href="#test">Probably not visited</a>
<a href="https://www.google.com">Probably visited</a>
```

Here is the CSS. We can make the same assumption that you have visited Google, so the first link should be red and the second link will be green in color:

```
a:link { color: #ff0000; }
a:visited { color: #00ff00; }
```

User action pseudo-classes

These classes take effect based on actions of the user. These selectors are not mutually exclusive, and an element can have several matches at once.

:active

This is used when the element is being activated:

```
:active
```

Description

The `:active` selector is most commonly used when the mouse button is pressed but not released. This style can be superseded by the other user actions or link pseudo-classes.

Here is an example:

```
<a href="https://www.google.com">Google</a>
```

The link will turn green while you are clicking on it. Here is its CSS:

```
a:active { color: #00ff00; }
```

:focus

This selector targets the element that has to be focused on. The syntax is as follows:

```
:focus
```

Description

An element is considered to have focus when it accepts keyboard input. For example, a text input element that you have either tabbed to or have clicked inside.

Here is a text input example:

```
<input type="text" value="Red when focused">
```

Here is the CSS. This also highlights the fact that you can use a pseudo-class, which allows use of more complex selectors:

```
input[type="text"]:focus { color: #ff0000; }
```

:hover

This selector targets the elements when a user hovers their mouse over an element:

```
:hover
```

Description

This is used when a user has their cursor hovering over an element. Some browsers (a great example being mobile touch devices, such as mobile phones) may not implement this pseudo-class, as there is no way to determine whether a user is hovering over an element.

Here is an example:

```
<span>Hover over me!</span>
```

The text in the span will be red in color when hovered over. Here is its CSS:

```
span:hover { color: #ff0000; }
```

The structural selectors

These selectors allow you to select elements based on the document tree; this is very difficult or impossible to do with other selectors. This only selects nodes that are elements and does not include text that is not inside an element. The numbering is 1-based indexing.

:first-child

This targets an element that is the first child of another element:

```
:first-child
```

Description

This is the same as `:nth-child(1)`. This selector is straightforward, the first child of the element type this is applied to will be selected.

Here is an example that will only select the first paragraph element. Here is the HTML:

```
<p>First paragraph.</p>
<p>Second paragraph.</p>
```

Here is the CSS. This will change the text of the first paragraph red:

```
p:first-child { color: #ff0000; }
```

:first-of-type

This targets the first element type that is a child of another element:

```
:first-of-type
```

Description

The `:first-of-type` attribute is different from `:first-child` because it will not select the element unless it is the first child. This is the same as `:nth-of-type(1)`.

Here is an example that will target the first paragraph element even though it is not the first child. Here is the HTML:

```
<article>
  <h1>Title of Article</h1>
  <p>First paragraph.</p>
  <p>Second paragraph.</p>
</article>
```

Here is the CSS:

```
p:first-of-type { color: #ff0000; }
```

:last-child

This targets an element that is the last child of another element:

```
:last-child
```

Description

This is the same as `:nth-last-child(1)`. This selector is straightforward, the last child of the element type this is applied to will be selected.

Here is an example that will only select the last paragraph element. Here is the HTML:

```
<p>First paragraph.</p>
<p>Second paragraph.</p>
```

Here is the CSS. This will change the color of the second and first paragraph red. This selector works because even on the most basic of pages, the p element is a child of the body element:

```
p:last-child { color: #ff0000; }
```

:last-of-type

This targets the last element type that is a child of another element:

```
:last-of-type
```

Description

The `:last-of-type` attribute is different from `:last-child` because it will not select the element unless it is the first `last-child` attribute. This is the same as `:nth-last-of-type(1)`.

Here is an example that will target the last paragraph element. Here is its HTML:

```
<article>
  <p>First paragraph.</p>
  <p>Second paragraph.</p>
  <a href="#">A link</a>
</article>
```

Here is the CSS:

```
p:last-of-type { color: #ff0000; }
```

:nth-child()

This will divide all of the child elements and select them based on where they exist:

```
:nth-child(an+b)
```

Description

This selector has a parameter that is very expressive in what you can select. This also means that it is more complex than most other CSS rules. Here is the technical specification of the parameter. This selects elements based on its preceding elements.

The parameter can be split into two parts: part a Part b. The part a is an integer that is followed by the character n. Part b has an optional plus or minus sign followed by an integer. The parameter also accepts two keywords: even and odd. Consider *2n+1* for example.

This is much easier to understand when you look at it this way. The first part, an, is what the children are divided by. The 2n value would make groups of two elements and 3n value would make groups of three elements, and so on. The next part +1 will then select that element in the grouping. *2n+1* would select every odd item row because it is targeting the first element in every grouping of two elements. *2n+0* or *2n+2* would select every even item row. The first part, part a, can be omitted, and then it would just select the *n*th child out of the entire group. For example, *:nth-child(5)* would only select the fifth child and no other.

Table rows are a great example of using this selector, so we will target every odd row. Here is the HTML:

```
<table>
  <tr><td>First (will be red)</td></tr>
  <tr><td>Second</td></tr>
  <tr><td>Third (will be red)</td></tr>
</table>
```

Here is the CSS:

```
tr:nth-child(2n+1) { color: #ff0000; }
```

:nth-last-child

This will target the nth element from the end:

```
:nth-last-child(an+b)
```

Description

This selector counts the succeeding elements. The counting logic is the same as it is for :nth-child.

Here is an example using a table. Here is the HTML:

```
<table>
  <tr><td>First</td></tr>
  <tr><td>Second</td></tr>
  <tr><td>Third</td></tr>
  <tr><td>Fourth</td></tr>
</table>
```

The first CSS rule will change the color of every other row to red, but because it counts from the end, the first and third row will be selected. The second CSS rule will only target the last row:

```
tr:nth-last-child(even) { color: #ff0000; }
tr:nth-last-child(-n+1) { color: #ff0000; }
```

See also

The previous section :nth-child.

:nth-last-of-type and :nth-of-type

This selects elements based on their type and where they exist in the document:

```
:nth-last-of-type(an+b)
:nth-of-type(an+b)
```

Description

Like all the other *n*th selectors, this one uses the same logic as :nth-child. The difference nth-of-type being that :nth-last-of-type only groups by elements of the same type.

Here is an example that uses paragraphs and spans:

```
<p>First</p>
<span>First Span</span>
<span>Second Span</span>
<p>Second</p>
<p>Third</p>
```

Here is the CSS. This rule will only target the paragraphs and make the odd ones red:

```
p:nth-of-type(2n+1) { color: #ff0000; }
```

See also

The previous section :nth-child.

:only-child

This targets an element that has no siblings:

```
:only-child
```

Description

This will match when the :only-child attribute is the only child of an element.

Here is an example with two tables, where one has multiple rows and the other has only one:

```
<table>
  <tr><td>First</td></tr>
  <tr><td>Second</td></tr>
  <tr><td>Third</td></tr>
</table>
<table>
  <tr><td>Only</td></tr>
</table>
```

Here is the CSS to target the only row in the second table:

```
tr:only-child { color: #ff0000; }
```

:only-of-type

This targets when there is only one of this element:

```
:only-of-type
```

Description

This will only match when there are no other siblings of the same type under a parent element.

Here is an example that uses arbitrary divisions to create a structure where one paragraph element is the only one of its type. Here is the HTML:

```
<div>
  <p>Only p.</p>
  <div>
    <p>Not the </p>
    <p>only one.</p>
  </div>
</div>
```

Here is the CSS rule that will only target the first paragraph's element:

```
p:only-of-type { color: #ff0000; }
```

Validation

These are pseudo-classes that can be used to target the state of input elements and more.

:checked

This attribute targets the checked radio button or checkbox:

```
:checked
```

Description

Any element that can be toggled on or off can use this selector. As of now, these are radio buttons, checkboxes, and options in a selective list.

Here is an example with a `checkbox` and a `label` value:

```
<input type="checkbox" checked value="check-value" name="test" />
<label for="test">Check me out</label>
```

Here is a CSS rule that will target the label only when the checkbox is checked:

```
input:checked + label { color: #ff0000; }
```

:default

This targets the default element from many similar elements:

```
:default
```

Description

Use this selector to help define the default element from a group of elements. In a form, this would be the default button or the initially selected option from a `select` element.

Here is an example using a form:

```
<form method="post">
  <input type="submit" value="Submit" />
  <input type="reset" value="Reset" />
</form>
```

Here is the CSS. This will only target the submit input as it is the default:

```
:default { color: #ff0000; }
```

:disabled and :enabled

These will target elements based on their enabled state:

```
:disabled
:enabled
```

Description

There is a disabled attribute that is available on interactive elements. Using `:disabled` will target elements where the `:disabled` attribute is present and `:enabled` will do the opposite.

Here is some HTML with two inputs out of which one is disabled:

```
<input type="submit" value="Submit" disabled/>
<input type="reset" value="Reset" />
```

Here is the CSS. The disabled input will have its text color set as red and the other as green:

```
input:disabled { color: #ff0000; }
input:enabled { color: #00ff00; }
```

:empty

This targets elements that have no children:

```
:empty
```

Description

This targets nodes without any children. Children can be any other element including text nodes. This means that even one space will count as a child. However, comments will not count as children.

Here is an example with three `div` tags. The first is empty, the next has text, and the final one has one space in it. Here is the HTML:

```
<div></div>
<div>Not Empty</div>
<div> </div>
```

Here is the CSS. Only the first div will have a red background:

```
div { height: 100px; width: 100px; background-color: #00ff00; }
div:empty { background-color: #ff0000; }
```

:in-range and :out-of-range

These selectors target elements that have a range limitation:

```
:in-range
:out-of-range
```

Description

Some elements now have range limitations that can be applied. When the value is outside of this range, the `:out-of-range` selector will target it, and when the value is within the range, `:in-range` will target it.

Here is an example that uses an input that is the number type:

```
<input type="number" min="1" max="10" value="11" />
<input type="number" min="1" max="10" value="5" />
```

Here is the CSS. The first input will have red text because it is beyond the maximum range and the second will have green text:

```
:in-range {color: #00ff00; }
:out-of-range { color: #ff0000; }
```

:invalid and :valid

The `:invalid` and `:valid` attribute targets an element based on the validity of the data:

```
:invalid
:valid
```

Description

Certain input elements have data validity, a great example being the e-mail element. The selectors select based on whether the data is valid or not. You should note that some elements are always valid, for example, a text input, and some elements will never be targeted by these selectors, for example, a `div` tag.

Here is an example with an e-mail input:

```
<input type="email" value="test@test.com" />
<input type="email" value="not a valid email" />
```

Here is the CSS. The first input will be green as it is valid and the other will be red:

```
:valid {color: #00ff00; }
:invalid { color: #ff0000; }
```

:not or negation

The `:not` attribute negates a selector:

```
:not(selector)
```

Description

The `:not` parameter must be a simple selector and will target the elements where the `:not` parameter is not `true`. This selector does not add to specificity of the rule.

Here is an example using paragraphs:

```
<p>Targeted Element</p>
<p class="not-me">Non targeted element</p>
```

Here is the CSS. Only the first paragraph will be targeted:

```
p:not(.not-me) {color: #ff0000; }
```

:optional and :required

The :optional and :required attributes target elements that are either optional or required, respectively.

```
:optional
:required
```

Description

This is used for any input element that is required or optional.

Here is an example that has two inputs — one that is required and one that is not:

```
<input type="text" value="Required" required />
<input type="text" value="Optional" />
```

Here is the CSS. The required input will have red text and the optional input will have green text:

```
:required { color: #ff0000; }
:optional { color: #00ff00; }
```

:lang()

The :lang() attribute targets based on the language:

```
:lang(language)
```

Description

This selector works differently to the attribute selector; in that, this will target all elements that are in a specific language even if they are not explicitly defined. The attribute selector will only target elements that have a lang attribute.

Here is an example with a span element that does not have a lang attribute, but it is the child of the body which does:

```
<body lang="en-us">
<span>This is English.</span>
</body>
```

Here is the CSS. The first rule will match the element, but the second will not match anything:

```
:lang(en) { color: #ff0000; }
span[lang|=en] { color: #00ff00; }
```

Pseudo-elements

These are selectors that go beyond what is specified in the document. The selectors select things that may not even be elements in the document. Pseudo-elements are not considered part of a simple selector. This means that you cannot use a pseudo-element as part of the :not() selector. Finally, only one pseudo-element can be present per selector.

 Note that all of the pseudo-elements start with a double colon (::). This was introduced in CSS3 to help differentiate between pseudo-classes that have a single colon (:). This is important because in CSS2, pseudo-elements only had the single colon (:). For the most part, you should use the double colon.

::before and ::after

These are used to insert generated content before or after the selected element:

```
::before
::after e
```

Description

This will insert content into the document based on the selector. Whether the content is placed before or after the element targeted depends on the pseudo-element used. Refer to the *Generated content* section to see what you can insert.

Here is an example that uses both ::before and ::after. This will create a turkey sandwich. Here is the HTML.

```
<p class="sandwich">Turkey</p>
```

Here is the CSS that will put a slice of bread before and after the turkey:

```
p.sandwich::before, p.sandwich::after
{ content: ":Slice of Bread:"; }
```

See also

Generated content

::first-letter

This targets the first letter of an element:

```
::first-letter
```

Description

This will select the first letter of an element as long as it does not have any other content before it, for example an `img` element before a character would make `::first-letter` not select the first character. Any punctuation that either precedes or follows the first letter would be included with the first letter. This will select any character, including not just letters but also numbers.

This only applies to block-like containers such as block, `list-item`, `table-cell`, `table-caption`, and `inline-block` elements.

The `::first-letter` pseudo-element will only match if the first letter is on the first formatted line. If there is a line break before the first letter appears, it will not be selected.

Here is an example, which will not select the first letter:

```
<p><br />First letter</p>
```

Here is the CSS:

```
p::first-letter { font-size: 2em; }
```

Here is an example:

```
<p>This is a long line of text that may or may not be broken up
across lines.</p>
```

Here is the CSS. The T in This will be two times the font size of all the other characters:

```
p::first-letter { font-size: 2em; }
```

::first-line

The `::first-line` attribute targets the first line of an element:

```
::first-line
```

Description

This will target the first formatted line of a block-like container such as a `block box`, `inline-block`, `table-caption`, or `table-cell`.

Here is an example, with the following HTML:

```
<p>This is a long line of text that may or may not be broken up
across lines based on the width of the page and the width of the
element it is in.</p>
<p>This is the entire first line.</p>
```

Here is the CSS. This will make the first line, whatever it may be, red:

```
p::first-line { color: #ff0000; }
```

::selection

This targets text highlighted by the user:

```
::selection
```

Description

This pseudo-element allows you to style any text that is highlighted by the user. This pseudo-element does not exist in CSS3, but it is part of the next version. Most browsers will still honor this pseudo-element.

Here is an example:

```
<p>Highlight this to text.</p>
```

Here is the CSS. When the text is selected, the text will be white on a red background:

```
::selection { color: #ffffff; background: #ff0000; }
```

Generated content

This is not a selector, but is used with the pseudo-elements `::before` and `::after`. There are only certain types of content that you can generate. Here is a rundown.

content

This is the content that will be placed either before or after elements:

```
content(none, <string>, <uri>, <counter>, open-quote, close-quote,
no-open-quote, no-close-quote, attr(x))
```

Parameters

Following are the parameters and their description:

- none: This parameter does not generate any content
- normal: This is the default parameter and is the same as none
- <string>: This is any string text content
- <uri>: This will map to a resource, for example, an image
- <counter>: This can be used as either the counter() or counters() function to put a counter before or after each element
- open-quote and close-quote: This is used with the quotes generated content property
- no-open-quote and no-close-quote: This does not add content, but increments or decrements the nesting level of quotes
- attr(x):This returns the value of the attribute of the element this is targeting

Description

This property is used to add content to the document. The output is controlled by the value used. The values can be combined to create more complex content.

A new line can be inserted with the characters \A. Just remember that HTML will ignore a line break by default.

Here are some examples. These will demonstrate how to use many of the content values:

```
<h1>First</h1>
<h1>Second</h1>
<h1 class="test">Attribute</h1>
<h2>Line Break</h2>
<blockquote>Don't quote me on this.</blockquote>
```

Here is the CSS. The h1 elements will have the word "chapter" along with a number before each. The h2 element will have a line break in its content. Finally, the blockquote will have an opening quote and a closing quote:

```
h1 { counter-increment: chapter; }
h1::before { content: "Chapter" counter(chapter) ": " attr(class)
; }
h2::before { content: "New\A Line"; white-space: pre; }
blockquote::before { content: open-quote; }
blockquote::after { content: close-quote; }
```

Quotation marks

Quotation marks specify which characters are used as open and close quotes:

```
quotes: [<string> <string>]+
```

Parameters

<string> <string>: These are pairs of characters that will represent an open and close quote. You can use this multiple times to create levels of quotes.

Description

We can use this property to set which quotation marks are used.

Here is an example that has a nested quote:

```
<blockquote>Don't quote me <blockquote>on</blockquote>
this.</blockquote>
```

The quotation marks are completely arbitrary. Here is the CSS:

```
blockquote { quotes: ":" "!" "&" "*"; }
```

4
CSS Properties – Part 1

CSS properties are characteristics of an element in a markup language (HTML, SVG, XML, and so on) that control their style and/or presentation. These characteristics are part of a constantly evolving standard from the W3C.

A basic example of a CSS property is `border-radius`:

```
input {
  border-radius: 100px;
}
```

There is an incredible number of CSS properties, and learning them all is virtually impossible. Adding more into this mix, there are CSS properties that need to be vendor prefixed (`-webkit-`, `-moz-`, `-ms-`, and so on), making this equation even more complex.

Vendor prefixes are short pieces of CSS that are added to the beginning of the CSS property (and sometimes CSS values too). These pieces of code are directly related to either the company that makes the browser (the "vendor") or to the CSS engine of the browser.

There are four major CSS prefixes: `-webkit-`, `-moz-`, `-ms-` and `-o-`. They are explained here:

- `-webkit-`: This references Safari's engine, Webkit (Google Chrome and Opera used this engine in the past as well)
- `-moz-`: This stands for Mozilla, who creates Firefox
- `-ms-`: This stands for Microsoft, who creates Internet Explorer
- `-o-`: This stands for Opera, but only targets old versions of the browser

Google Chrome and Opera both support the `-webkit-` prefix. However, these two browsers do not use the Webkit engine anymore. Their engine is called Blink and is developed by Google.

A basic example of a prefixed CSS property is `column-gap`:

```
.column {
  -webkit-column-gap: 5px;
  -moz-column-gap: 5px;
  column-gap: 5px;
}
```

Knowing which CSS properties need to be prefixed is futile. That's why it's important to keep a constant eye on `CanIUse.com`. However, it's also important to automate the prefixing process with tools such as `Autoprefixer` or `-prefix-free`, or mixins in preprocessors, and so on.

However, vendor prefixing isn't in the scope of the book, so the properties we'll discuss are absent of any vendor prefixes. If you want to learn more about vendor prefixes, you can visit **Mozilla Developer Network (MDN)** at `http://tiny.cc/mdn-vendor-prefixes`.

Let's get the CSS properties reference rolling.

Animation

Unlike the old days of Flash, where creating animations required third-party applications and plugins, today we can accomplish practically the same things with a lot less overhead, better performance, and greater scalability all through CSS only.

Forget plugins and third-party software! All we need is a text editor, some imagination, and a bit of patience to wrap our heads around some of the animation concepts CSS brings to our plate.

Base markup and CSS

Before we dive into all the animation properties, we will use the following markup and animation structure as our base:

HTML:

```
<div class="element"></div>
```

CSS:

```
.element {
  width: 300px;
  height: 300px;
}
```

```
@keyframes fadingColors {
  0% {
    background: red;
  }
  100% {
    background: black;
  }
}
```

In the examples, we will only see the `.element` rule since the HTML and `@keyframes fadingColors` will remain the same.

 The `@keyframes` declaration block is a custom animation that can be applied to any element. When applied, the element's background will go from red to black.

Ok, let's do this.

animation-name

The `animation-name` CSS property is the name of the `@keyframes` at-rule that we want to execute, and it looks like this:

```
animation-name: fadingColors;
```

Description

In the HTML and CSS base example, our `@keyframes` at-rule had an animation where the background color went from red to black. The name of that animation is `fadingColors`.

So, we can call the animation like this:

CSS:

```
.element {
  width: 300px;
  height: 300px;
  animation-name: fadingColors;
}
```

This is a valid rule using the longhand. There are clearly no issues with it at all. The thing is that the animation won't run unless we add `animation-duration` to it.

animation-duration

The `animation-duration` CSS property defines the amount of time the animation will take to complete a cycle, and it looks like this:

```
animation-duration: 2s;
```

Description

We can specify the units either in seconds using `s` or in milliseconds using `ms`. Specifying a unit is required. Specifying a value of `0s` means that the animation should actually never run.

However, since we do want our animation to run, we do the following:

CSS:

```
.element {
  width: 300px;
  height: 300px;
  animation-name: fadingColors;
  animation-duration: 2s;
}
```

As mentioned earlier, this will make a box go from its red background to black in 2 seconds and then stop.

animation-iteration-count

The `animation-iteration-count` CSS property defines the number of times the animation should be played, and it looks like this:

```
animation-iteration-count: infinite;
```

Description

Here are two values: `infinite` and a *number*, such as 1, 3, or 0.5. Negative numbers are not allowed.

Add the following code to the prior example:

CSS:

```
.element {
  width: 300px;
  height: 300px;
  animation-name: fadingColors;
  animation-duration: 2s;
  animation-iteration-count: infinite;
}
```

This will make a box go from its red background to black, start over again with the red background and go to black, infinitely.

animation-direction

The `animation-direction` CSS property defines the direction in which the animation should play after the cycle, and it looks like this:

```
animation-direction: alternate;
```

Description

There are four values: `normal`, `reverse`, `alternate`, and `alternate-reverse`.

- `normal`: This makes the animation play forward. This is the default value.

- `reverse`: This makes the animation play backward.

- `alternate`: This makes the animation play forward in the first cycle, then backward in the next cycle, then forward again, and so on. In addition, timing functions are affected, so if we have `ease-out`, it gets replaced by `ease-in` when played in reverse.

  We'll look at these timing functions in a minute.

- `alternate-reverse`: This is the same thing as `alternate`, but the animation starts backward, from the end.

In our current example, we have a continuous animation. However, the background color has a "hard stop" when going from black (end of the animation) to red (start of the animation).

Let's create a more "fluid" animation by making the black background fade into red and then red into black without any hard stops. Basically, we are trying to create a "pulse-like" effect:

CSS:

```
.element {
  width: 300px;
  height: 300px;
  animation-name: fadingColors;
  animation-duration: 2s;
  animation-iteration-count: infinite;
  animation-direction: alternate;
}
```

animation-delay

The `animation-delay` CSS property allows us to define when exactly an animation should start. This means that as soon as the animation has been applied to an element, it will obey the delay before it starts running.

It looks like this:

```
animation-delay: 3s;
```

Description

We can specify the units either in seconds using `s` or in milliseconds using `ms`. Specifying a unit is required.

Negative values are allowed. Take into consideration that using negative values means that the animation should start right away, but it will start midway into the animation for the opposite amount of time as the negative value.

Use negative values with caution.

CSS:

```
.element {
  width: 300px;
  height: 300px;
  animation-name: fadingColors;
  animation-duration: 2s;
  animation-iteration-count: infinite;
  animation-direction: alternate;
  animation-delay: 3s;
}
```

This will make the animation start after 3 seconds have passed.

animation-fill-mode

The `animation-fill-mode` CSS property defines which values are applied to an element before and after the animation. Basically, outside the time the animation is being executed.

It looks like this:

```
animation-fill-mode: none;
```

Description

There are four values: none, forwards, backwards, and both.

- none: No styles are applied before or after the animation.

- forwards: The animated element will retain the styles of the last keyframe. This the most used value.

- backwards: The animated element will retain the styles of the first keyframe, and these styles will remain during the animation-delay period. This is very likely the least used value.

- both: The animated element will retain the styles of the first keyframe before starting the animation and the styles of the last keyframe after the animation has finished. In many cases, this is almost the same as using forwards.

The prior properties are better used in animations that have an end and stop. In our example, we're using a fading/pulsating animation, so the best property to use is none.

CSS:

```
.element {
  width: 300px;
  height: 300px;
  animation-name: fadingColors;
  animation-duration: 2s;
  animation-iteration-count: infinite;
  animation-direction: alternate;
  animation-delay: 3s;
  animation-fill-mode: none;
}
```

animation-play-state

The animation-play-state CSS property defines whether an animation is running or paused, and it looks like this:

```
animation-play-state: running;
```

Description

There are two values: running and paused. These values are self-explanatory.

CSS:

```
.element {
  width: 300px;
  height: 300px;
  animation-name: fadingColors;
  animation-duration: 2s;
  animation-iteration-count: infinite;
  animation-direction: alternate;
  animation-delay: 3s;
  animation-fill-mode: none;
  animation-play-state: running;
}
```

In this case, defining `animation-play-state` as `running` is redundant, but I'm listing it for purposes of the example.

animation-timing-function

The `animation-timing-function` CSS property defines how an animation's speed should progress throughout its cycles, and it looks like this:

```
animation-timing-function: ease-out;
```

There are five predefined values, also known as easing functions, for the **Bézier** curve (we'll see what the Bézier curve is in a minute): `ease`, `ease-in`, `ease-out`, `ease-in-out`, and `linear`.

ease

The `ease` function sharply accelerates at the beginning and starts slowing down towards the middle of the cycle, and it looks like this:

```
animation-timing-function: ease;
```

ease-in

The `ease-in` function starts slowly accelerating until the animation sharply ends, and it looks like this:

```
animation-timing-function: ease-in;
```

ease-out

The `ease-out` function starts quickly and gradually slows down towards the end and it looks like this:

```
animation-timing-function: ease-out;
```

ease-in-out

The `ease-in-out` function starts slowly and it gets fast in the middle of the cycle. It then starts slowing down towards the end. And it looks like this:

```
animation-timing-function:ease-in-out;
```

linear

The `linear` function has constant speed. No accelerations of any kind happen. It looks like this:

```
animation-timing-function: linear;
```

Now, the easing functions are built on a curve named the Bézier curve and can be called using the `cubic-bezier()` function or the `steps()` function.

cubic-bezier()

The `cubic-bezier()` function allows us to create custom acceleration curves. Most use cases can benefit from the already defined easing functions we just mentioned (`ease`, `ease-in`, `ease-out`, `ease-in-out` and `linear`), but if you're feeling adventurous, `cubic-bezier()` is your best bet.

Here's what a Bézier curve looks like:

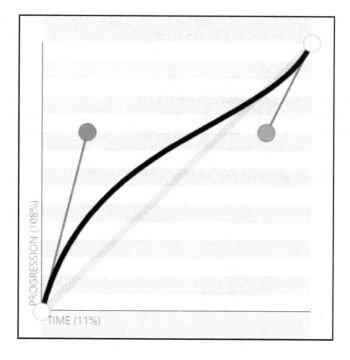

Parameters

The `cubic-bezier()` function takes four parameters as follows:

```
animation-timing-function: cubic-bezier(x1, y1, x2, y2);
```

X and Y represent the *x* and *y* axes. The numbers 1 and 2 after each axis represent the control points. 1 represents the control point starting on the lower left, and 2 represents the control point on the upper right.

Description

Let's represent all five predefined easing functions with the `cubic-bezier()` function:

- ease: `animation-timing-function: cubic-bezier(.25, .1, .25, 1);`
- ease-in: `animation-timing-function: cubic-bezier(.42, 0, 1, 1);`
- ease-out: `animation-timing-function: cubic-bezier(0, 0, .58, 1);`
- ease-in-out: `animation-timing-function: cubic-bezier(.42, 0, .58, 1);`
- linear: `animation-timing-function: cubic-bezier(0, 0, 1, 1);`

I'm not sure about you, but I prefer to use the predefined values.

Now, we can start tweaking and testing each value to the decimal, save it, and wait for the live refresh to do its thing. However, that's too much time wasted testing if you ask me.

 The amazing Lea Verou created the best web app to work with Bézier curves. You can find it at `cubic-bezier.com`. This is by far the easiest way to work with Bézier curves. I highly recommend this tool.

The Bézier curve image showed earlier was taken from the `cubic-bezier.com` website.

Let's add `animation-timing-function` to our example:

CSS:

```
.element {
  width: 300px;
  height: 300px;
  animation-name: fadingColors;
  animation-duration: 2s;
  animation-iteration-count: infinite;
  animation-direction: alternate;
  animation-delay: 3s;
  animation-fill-mode: none;
  animation-play-state: running;
  animation-timing-function: ease-out;
}
```

steps()

The `steps()` timing function isn't very widely used, but knowing how it works is a must if you're into CSS animations.

It looks like this:

```
animation-timing-function: steps(6);
```

This function is very helpful when we want our animation to take a defined number of steps.

After adding a `steps()` function to our current example, it looks like this:

CSS:

```
.element {
  width: 300px;
  height: 300px;
  animation-name: fadingColors;
  animation-duration: 2s;
  animation-iteration-count: infinite;
  animation-direction: alternate;
  animation-delay: 3s;
  animation-fill-mode: none;
  animation-play-state: running;
  animation-timing-function: steps(6);
}
```

This makes the box take six steps to fade from red to black and vice versa.

Parameters

There are two optional parameters that we can use with the `steps()` function: `start` and `end`.

- `start`: This will make the animation run at the beginning of each step. This will make the animation start right away.

- `end`: This will make the animation run at the end of each step. This is the default value if nothing is declared. This will give the animation a short delay before it starts.

Description

After adding a `steps()` function to our current example, it looks like this:

CSS:

```css
.element {
  width: 300px;
  height: 300px;
  animation-name: fadingColors;
  animation-duration: 2s;
  animation-iteration-count: infinite;
  animation-direction: alternate;
  animation-delay: 3s;
  animation-fill-mode: none;
  animation-play-state: running;
  animation-timing-function: steps(6, start);
}
```

Granted, the pulsating effect in our example isn't quite noticeable when we add the `steps()` function. However, you can see it more clearly in this pen from Louis Lazarus when hovering over the boxes, at `http://tiny.cc/steps-timing-function`

Here's an image taken from Stephen Greig's article in *Smashing Magazine, Understanding CSS Timing Functions,* that explains `start` and `end` from the `steps()` function:

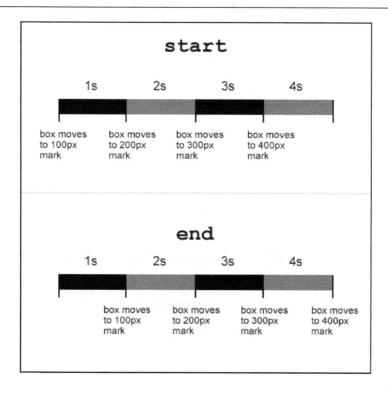

Also, there are two predefined values for the steps() function: step-start and step-end.

- step-start: This is the same thing as steps(1, start). It means that every change happens at the beginning of each interval.

- step-end: This is the same thing as steps(1, end). It means that every change happens at the end of each interval.

CSS:

```
.element {
  width: 300px;
  height: 300px;
  animation-name: fadingColors;
  animation-duration: 2s;
  animation-iteration-count: infinite;
  animation-direction: alternate;
  animation-delay: 3s;
  animation-fill-mode: none;
  animation-play-state: running;
  animation-timing-function: step-end;
}
```

animation

The `animation` CSS property is the shorthand for `animation-name`, `animation-duration`, `animation-timing-function`, `animation-delay`, `animation-iteration-count`, `animation-direction`, `animation-fill-mode`, and `animation-play-state`.

It looks like this:

```
animation: fadingColors 2s;
```

Description

For a simple animation to work, we need at least two properties: `animation-name` and `animation-duration`.

If you feel overwhelmed by all these properties, relax. Let me break them down for you in simple bits.

Using the `animation` longhand, the code would look like this:

CSS:

```
.element {
  width: 300px;
  height: 300px;
  animation-name: fadingColors;
  animation-duration: 2s;
}
```

Using the `animation` shorthand, which is the recommended syntax, the code would look like this:

CSS:

```
.element {
  width: 300px;
  height: 300px;
  animation: fadingColors 2s;
}
```

This will make a box go from its red background to black in 2 seconds, and then stop.

Final CSS code

Let's see how all the animation properties look in one final example showing both the longhand and shorthand styles.

Longhand style

```
.element {
  width: 300px;
  height: 300px;
  animation-name: fadingColors;
  animation-duration: 2s;
  animation-iteration-count: infinite;
  animation-direction: alternate;
  animation-delay: 3s;
  animation-fill-mode: none;
  animation-play-state: running;
  animation-timing-function: ease-out;
}
```

Shorthand style

```
.element {
  width: 300px;
  height: 300px;
  animation: fadingColors 2s infinite alternate 3s none running
  ease-out;
}
```

 The animation-duration property will always be considered first rather than animation-delay. All other properties can appear in any order within the declaration.

Here is a demo in **CodePen**: http://tiny.cc/animation

Background

The CSS background properties handle the display of background effects on HTML elements.

background-attachment

The background-attachment CSS property defines how the background of an element scrolls relative to its containing parent, and it looks like this:

```
background-attachment: fixed;
```

Description

There are three values: `scroll`, `fixed,` and `local`.

- `scroll`: The background does not move within its container
- `fixed`: The background stays fixed to the viewport, no matter what
- `local`: The background scrolls within its container and the viewport

CSS:

```
.scroll {
  background-attachment: scroll;
}
.fixed {
  background-attachment: fixed;
}
.local {
  background-attachment: local;
}
```

Here is a demo in CodePen: `http://tiny.cc/css-background`

background-blend-mode

The `background-blend-mode` CSS property specifies how the background image of an element should blend with its background color, and it looks like this:

```
background-blend-mode: multiply;
```

Description

There are 18 possible blend mode values:

- `color`: Hue and saturation from the top color prevail, but the luminosity of the bottom color is added. Gray levels are preserved.

- `color-burn`: The final color is the result of taking the bottom color and inverting it, dividing the value by the top color, and then inverting that value.

- `color-dodge`: The final color is the result of dividing the bottom color with the inverse of the top one.

- `darken`: The final color is the result of taking the darkest value per color in each channel.

- `difference`: The final color is the result of taking the lighter color and subtracting the darker color of the background image and background color.

- `exclusion`: The result is similar to the `difference`, but with lower contrast.

- `hard-light`: If the bottom color is darker, then the result is `multiply`. However, if the bottom color is lighter, the result is `screen`.

- `hue`: Takes the hue of the top color, and the saturation and luminosity of the bottom color.

- `inherit`: The final color inherits the blend mode of its parent container.

- `initial`: This is the default value without any blending.

- `lighten`: The result is the lightest values per color from each channel.

- `luminosity`: The result is the luminosity of the top color, and the hue and saturation of the bottom one.

- `multiply`: Multiply the top and bottom colors. This is the same effect as printing the colors on a translucent film and laying them one on top of the other.

- `normal`: The final color is the color on top, regardless of the color underneath it.

- `overlay`: The final color is `multiply` if the bottom color is darker. And it would be `screen` if the bottom color is lighter.

- `saturation`: The final color is the saturation of the top color plus the hue and luminosity of the bottom one.

- `screen`: Invert both the top and bottom colors, multiply them, and then invert that final color.

- `soft-light`: Same as `hard-light` attribute but softer, like pointing a diffused light on the final color.

In the following example, we will declare two backgrounds, an image and a color, and then apply a blend mode to them:

CSS with longhand:

```
.element {
  width: 500px;
  height: 500px;
  background-image: url('../images/image.jpg');
  background-color: red;
  background-blend-mode: multiply;
}
```

CSS with shorthand:

```
.element {
  width: 500px;
  height: 500px;
  background-image: url(../images/image.jpg) red;
  background-blend-mode: multiply;
}
```

 Notice that in the second example, the path to the image is not inside quotes. The quotes, single [' '] or double [" "], are optional.

CSS-Tricks has a great Pen showing all these blend modes. However, I forked it to improve a few things on it.

So, check out the CodePen demo with all the blend modes at `http://tiny.cc/background-blend-mode`

background-clip

The `background-clip` CSS property helps define whether an element's background extends below its border or not, and it looks like this:

```
background-clip: border-box;
```

Description

There are four values: `inherit`, `border-box`, `padding-box`, and `content-box`.

inherit

This takes the value from its parent element.

border-box

This makes the background cover the entire container, including the border.

padding-box

This makes the background extend only up to where the border starts.

content-box

This works like `border-box`, but it will take into consideration any padding, thus creating a gap between the border and the background.

CSS:

```
.element {
  background-clip: border-box;
}
```

Here is a demo in CodePen: `http://tiny.cc/background-clip`

background-color

The `background-color` CSS property defines the solid background color of an element, and it looks like this:

```
background-color: red;
```

Description

Also, `transparent` is actually a color in CSS.

 If we wanted to set a gradient background color, we'd have to use the `background-image` property instead. This is because gradients are actually images.

The color value can be defined using any of the following methods:

- Named color
- Hexadecimal
- RGB and RGBa
- HSL and HSLa

CSS:

```
/*Named Color*/
.element {
  background-color: red;
}
/*HEX*/
.element {
  background-color: #f00;
}
/*RGB*/
.element {
  background-color: rgb(255,0,0);
}
```

```
/*RGBa*/
.element {
  /*Background has 50% opacity*/
  background-color: rgba(255, 0, 0, .5);
}
/*HSL*/
.element {
  background-color: hsl(0, 100%, 50%);
}
/*HSLa*/
.element {
  /*Background has 50% opacity*/
  background-color: hsla(0, 100%, 50%, .5);
}
```

background-image

The `background-image` CSS property sets an image or gradient in the background of an element, and it looks like this:

```
background-image: url(../images/background.jpg);
```

Alternatively, it could also look like this:

```
background-image: linear-gradient(red, orange);
```

Description

This property supports the JPG, PNG, GIF, SVG, and WebP image formats.

We can also use the `none` value to declare the absence of an image.

An element can also have several background images in a single declaration.

When it comes to gradients, there are two styles: **Linear** and **Radial**.

Linear

Its syntax is `linear-gradient`. These gradients can go vertical, horizontal, or diagonal.

Radial

Its syntax is `radial-gradient`. These gradients are circular in nature, and by default, they will adapt to an element's dimension. For example, if the element is a perfect square, it would make a perfect circular radial gradient. However, if the element is a rectangle, then the radial gradient would look like an oval.

We can add as many colors in a gradient as we want or need to. Unless it is strictly necessary, I recommend that you steer away from doing so, as it can have a negative impact on browser performance.

Additionally, in order to give us more control over the gradients, we can define where a gradient color stops so that the following one can start. This is called **color stops**. Color stops can be defined in pixels or percentages. Percentages are more commonly used because of their relative nature, which helps maintain the integrity and proportions of the gradients.

CSS:

```css
/*Graphic file*/
.element {
  background-image: url(../images/bg-texture.jpg);
}
/*Multiple images*/
.element {
  background-image:
    url(../images/bg-icon.svg),
    url(../images/bg-texture.jpg);
}
/*Linear gradient*/
.element {
  background-image: linear-gradient(red, orange);
}
/*Linear Gradient with color stops*/
.element {
  background-image: linear-gradient(red 40px, orange 25%, green);
}
/*Radial gradient*/
.element {
  background-image: radial-gradient(red, orange);
}
/*Radial gradient with color stops*/
.element {
  background-image: radial-gradient(red 40px, orange 25%, green);
}
```

background-origin

The `background-origin` CSS property defines how the background gets rendered inside an element, and it looks like this:

```
background-origin: border-box;
```

Description

This property works similarly to the `background-clip` CSS property, except that with `background-origin`, the background is resized instead of clipped.

There are four values: `border-box`, `padding-box`, `content-box`, and `inherit`.

- `border-box`: The background extends all the way to the edge of the container, but under the border
- `padding-box`: The background extends to meet the border edge to edge
- `content-box`: The background is rendered inside the content box
- `inherit`: This is the default value

CSS:

```css
.element {
  background-origin: border-box;
}
```

Here is a demo in CodePen: `http://tiny.cc/background-origin`

background-position

The `background-position` CSS property allows us to place the background (image or gradient) anywhere within its parent container, and it looks like this:

```
background-position: 10px 50%;
```

Description

We can use three different types of values: predefined *keywords*, *percentage*, and *length*.

Predefined keywords

Values such as `left`, `right`, `top`, and `bottom` are the predefined keywords.

Percentages

Values such as 5% and 80%.

Length

Values such as 15px 130px.

This property requires you to declare two values: the first value relates to the *x* axis (horizontal) and the second value to the *y* axis (vertical).

The default value is 0 0; which is exactly the same as left top.

CSS:

```
/*Default values*/
.element {
  background-position: 0 0;
}
/*Keyword values*/
.element {
  background-position: right bottom;
}
/*Percentages values*/
.element {
  background-position: 5% 80%;
}
/*Length values*/
.element {
  background-position: 15px 130px;
}
```

Here is a demo in CodePen: http://tiny.cc/background-position

background-repeat

The background-repeat CSS property has two functions:

1. To define whether a background image is repeated or not
2. To determine how the background image is repeated

It looks like this:

```
background-repeat: no-repeat;
```

Alternatively, it could also look like this:

```
background-repeat-x: repeat;
```

Description

This property only works if `background-image` has been declared.

There are four values: `repeat`, `repeat-x`, `repeat-y`, and `no-repeat`.

- `repeat`: The background image will repeat in both x and y axes. This will completely fill the container. This is the default value.
- `repeat-x`: The background image will only repeat in the x axis, hence, horizontally.
- `repeat-y`: The background image will only repeat in the y axis, hence, vertically.
- `no-repeat`: The background image will not be repeated and will only display one instance of it.

CSS:

```
/*Default value*/
.repeat { background-repeat: repeat; }
/*Repeat horizontally*/
.repeat-x { background-repeat: repeat-x; }
/*Repeat vertically*/
.repeat-y { background-repeat: repeat-y; }
/*No repeat*/
.no-repeat { background-repeat: no-repeat; }
```

Here is a demo in CodePen: `http://tiny.cc/background-repeat`

background-size

The `background-size` CSS property defines the size of the background image, and it looks like this:

```
background-size: contain;
```

Description

There are five values: a *length* value, a *percentage* value, `auto`, `contain`, and `cover`.

Length value

This is when we use one of the following units: px, em, in, mm, cm, vw, and so on.

Percentage value

This is when we use percentages such as 50%, 85%, and so on.

auto

This value scales the image in the corresponding direction (horizontal or vertical) in order to maintain its aspect ratio and not deform it.

contain

This value makes sure the image can be seen completely within its parent container. The image does not bleed on the edges; it's "contained".

cover

This value scales the image and takes the longest dimension (horizontal or vertical). It makes sure that the image completely covers that dimension. Bleeding can occur if the container and the image have different aspect ratios.

When declaring the size of the background, we can use either one or two values. The first value is the *width*, and the second is the *height* of the background image.

Using one value means that the second value is set to auto. When using two values, we are then defining the width and height values of the background image.

We can use any measurement unit we want. Pixels, percentages, and the auto value are the most commonly used though.

We can even combine multiple images in the same container. The background shorthand property is the best way to handle this situation.

CSS:

```
.contain {
  background-size: contain;
}
.cover {
  background-size: cover;
}
.auto {
  background-size: auto;
}
```

```
.multiple {
  background-image:
    url(../images/image-1.jpg),
    url(../images/image-2.jpg);
  background-size: 150px 100px, cover;
}
```

Here is a demo in CodePen: `http://tiny.cc/background-size`

background

The `background` CSS property is the shorthand in which we can list all background values.

I often see many developers write the longhand version of the property to declare a single value, such as a color. Here is an example:

```
background-color: red;
```

Although this is totally fine, I prefer to use the shorthand version for practically everything:

```
background: red;
```

This is a bit more scalable because if we need to add any other values, all we need to do is add the new value to this declaration rather than writing a separate one. However, at the end, it's all a matter of personal style.

CSS:

```
/*BG color*/
.element { background: red; }
/*BG color and image*/
.element { background: url(../images/bg.png) red; }
/*BG color, image and position*/
.element { background: url(../images/bg.png) 50% 50% red; }
/*BG color, image, position and do not repeat*/
.element { background: url(../images/bg.png) 50% 50% red no-
repeat; }
/*BG color, image, position, do not repeat and size*/
.element { background: url(../images/bg.png) 50% 50% / contain red
no-repeat; }
/*BG color, image, position, do not repeat, size and clip*/
.element { background: url(../images/bg.png) 50% 50% / contain red
no-repeat content-box; }
```

```
/*BG color, image, position, do not repeat, size, clip and
attachment*/
.element { background: url(../images/bg.png) 50% 50% / contain red
no-repeat content-box fixed; }
```

Box model

Every element in the web is a square, and as such, it has intrinsic characteristics: width, height, padding, border, and margin. All these characteristics, put together, make the box model.

The almighty box model is one of the most talked about subjects in the CSS industry due to IE6 and IE7 being the most popular browsers back in the day. However, they had major issues interpreting this simple CSS concept. This meant the web designers and developers had to come up with all sorts of tricks to get around such a problem. Those days are now gone, for the most part at least.

Let's move on to the box model properties.

width

The width CSS property specifies the width of an element's content area, and it looks like this:

```
width: 10px;
```

Alternatively, it could also look like this:

```
width: 10px 50px;
```

Description

The content area is inside the padding, border, and margin of the element.

Let's talk about the most used values and keywords: the *length* value, *percentage* value, auto, max-content, min-content, and fit-content.

Length value

This is basically when we use one of the following units: px, em, in, mm, cm, vw, and so on.

Percentage value

This is when we use percentages such as 50%, 85%, and so on.

auto

This is a keyword value that allows the browser to choose the width of the element.

max-content

This is a keyword value that makes the container take the width of its content.

min-content

This is a keyword value that makes the container as small as possible depending on its content.

fit-content

This is a keyword value that makes the container match the width of its content. This works great on containers with unknown or variable width.

You can find more information on MDN at `http://tiny.cc/mdn-width`

CSS:

```
/*max-content*/
.element {
  width: max-content;
}
/*min-content*/
.element {
  width: min-content;
}
/*fit-content*/
.element {
  width: fit-content;
}
```

Here is a demo in CodePen: `http://tiny.cc/width`

height

The `height` CSS property specifies the height of an element's *content area,* and it looks like this:

```
height: 200px;
```

Description

The *content area* is inside the padding, border, and margin of the element.

The most used values are a *length* value, a *percentage* value, and `inherit`.

Length value

This is basically when we use one of the following units: px, em, in, mm, cm, vw, and so on.

Percentage value

This is when we use percentages such as 50%, 85%, and so on.

inherit

With this keyword, the element will inherit its parent container's height.

You can find more information on MDN at `http://tiny.cc/mdn-height`

CSS:

```
/*Length value*/
.element {
  height: 200px;
}
/*Percentage value*/
.element {
  height: 50%;
}
/*Inherit value*/
.element {
  height: inherit;
}
```

padding

The `padding` CSS property creates a space on all four sides of an element on the inside, between its content and the edges, and it looks like this:

```
padding: 10px;
```

Alternatively, it could also look like this:

```
padding: 10px 15px;
```

Description

Borders and margins are outside of the content area and do not get affected by the padding.

The `padding` property is the shorthand for `padding-top`, `padding-right`, `padding-bottom`, and `padding-left`. We can use one, two, three, or all four values.

- **One value**: This means that all four sides have the same value.
- **Two values**: The first value is for Top and Bottom. The second value is for Left and Right.
- **Three values**: The first value is for Top. The second value is for Left and Right. The third value is for Bottom.
- **Four values**: The first value is for Top. The second is for Right. The third is for Bottom. The fourth is for Left.

Negative values are not allowed.

CSS:

```
/*Shorthand, ONE value: all four sides have the same padding*/
.element { padding: 10px; }
/*Shorthand, TWO values: Top & Bottom - Left & Right*/
.element { padding: 10px 15px; }
/*Shorthand, THREE values: Top - Left & Right - Bottom*/
.element { padding: 10px 15px 20px; }
/*Shorthand, FOUR values: Top - Right - Bottom - Left*/
.element { padding: 10px 15px 20px 25px; }
/*Longhand, all values. They can go in any order*/
.element {
  padding-top: 10px;
  padding-right: 15px;
  padding-bottom: 20px;
  padding-left: 25px;
}
```

margin

The `margin` CSS property defines an outside space on one, two, three or all four sides of an element, and it looks like this:

```
margin: 10px;
```

Alternatively, it could also look like this:

```
margin: 10px 15px;
```

Description

The `margin` property is the shorthand for `margin-top`, `margin-right`, `margin-bottom`, and `margin-left`. Just like with `padding`, we can use one, two, three, or all four values.

- **One value**: This means that all four sides have the same padding.
- **Two values**: The first value is for Top and Bottom. The second value is for Left and Right.
- **Three values**: The first value is for Top. The second value is for Left and Right. The third value is for Bottom.
- **Four values**: The first value is for Top. The second is for Right. The third is for Bottom. The fourth value is for Left.

Negative values are allowed.

CSS:

```
/*Shorthand, ONE value: all four sides have the same padding*/
.element { margin: 10px; }
/*Shorthand, TWO values: Top & Bottom - Left & Right*/
.element { margin: 10px 15px; }
/*Shorthand, THREE values: Top - Left & Right - Bottom*/
.element { margin: 10px 15px 20px; }
/*Shorthand, FOUR values: Top - Right - Bottom - Left*/
.element { margin: 10px 15px 20px 25px; }
/*Longhand, all values. They 1can go in any order*/
.element {
  margin-top: 10px;
  margin-right: 15px;
  margin-bottom: 20px;
  margin-left: 25px;
}
```

Collapsing margins

There is a particular behavior with the margins. If two stacked elements have top and bottom margins, the margins are not added. Instead, the larger value is the only one taken into account.

For example, we have an `<h1>` heading and a `<p>` paragraph. The heading has a bottom margin of `20px`, and the paragraph has a top margin of `10px`.

Our senses immediately tell us that the total margin is `30px`, but in reality, because vertical margins collapse, only the largest value is considered, in this case, `20px`.

The reason for this is that many elements, such as headings and paragraphs in our example, have both top and bottom margins. So, having the margins collapse allows the content and layout to maintain consistency and avoid creating undesired extra spacing between stacked elements.

This is also good because it saves us the effort of having to "negate" margins on every stacked element that has top and bottom margins, again, to avoid creating those extra spaces.

The way I see it, is that collapsing margins is an editorial feature of the CSS margin property. I hope that the prior explanations help embrace this behavior.

Here is a demo in CodePen: `http://tiny.cc/collapsing-margins`

border

The `border` CSS property is the shorthand that defines an element's border thickness, style, and color.

The `border` property and all its sister properties (`border-width`, `border-style`, and `border-color`) and variations are self-explanatory, so there's no need for a *Description* section like in prior properties.

The CSS example ahead will help clarify the use of these properties.

border-width

This is the thickness of the border. It can be declared using `px` or `em`, but `px` yields more controllable results.

border-style

This defines the type of line or no line at all. It supports the following values: `dashed`, `dotted`, `double`, `groove`, `hidden`, `inset`, `none`, `outset`, `ridge`, and `solid`.

border-color

This defines the color of the line. It supports all color modes: HEX, RGB, RGBa, HSL, HSLs, and color name.

Keep in mind that all HTML elements are squares, so we can target any side of an element with `border-top-color`, `border-right-color`, `border-bottom-color`, or `border-left-color`.

The order of the values in the shorthand does not affect the output.

In the following example, the top rule in *shorthand syntax* accomplishes exactly the same accomplishment as the bottom rule with the *longhand syntax*:

CSS:

```
/*Shorthand*/
.element-shorthand {
  border: 10px solid green;
}
/*Longhand*/
.element-longhand {
  /*Width*/
  border-top-width: 10px;
  border-right-width: 10px;
  border-bottom-width: 10px;
  border-left-width: 10px;

  /*Style*/
  border-top-style: solid;
  border-right-style: solid;
  border-bottom-style: solid;
  border-left-style: solid;

  /*Color*/
  border-top-color: green;
  border-right-color: green;
  border-bottom-color: green;
  border-left-color: green;
}
```

box-sizing

The `box-sizing` CSS property allows us to change the way browsers understand the box model by default, and it looks like this:

```
box-sizing: border-box;
```

Description

There are two values: `content-box` and `border-box`.

content-box

This is the default value. The padding, border, and margin values are added to the final width and height of the element. This value is rarely used exactly because of the behavior I just described.

border-box

On the other hand, since this value changes the box model, the padding and border are not added to the final width and height of the element but only to the margin.

CSS:

```
/*Padding, border and margin are added to the element's dimensions*/
.element {
  box-sizing: content-box;
}
/*Padding and border are not added to the element's dimensions, only
margin*/
.element {
  box-sizing: border-box;
}
/*Always start your CSS with this rule*/
*, *:before, *:after {
  box-sizing: border-box;
}
```

Here is a demo in CodePen: `http://tiny.cc/box-sizing`

max-height

The `max-height` CSS property defines the maximum height of an element, and it looks like this:

```
max-height: 150px;
```

Description

The max-height attribute overrides the height property. Negative values are not allowed.

The most used values are a *length* value and a *percentage* value.

Length value

This is when we use one of the following units: px, em, in, mm, cm, vw, and so on.

Percentage value

This is when we use percentages such as 50%, 85%, and so on.

You can find more information on MDN at http://tiny.cc/mdn-max-height

CSS:

```
/*Length value*/
.element {
  height: 75px;
  /*This property overrides height*/
  max-height: 150px;
}
/*Percentage value*/
.element {
  max-height: 65%;
}
```

max-width

The max-width CSS property defines the maximum width of an element, and it looks like this:

```
max-width: 75px;
```

Description

The max-width attribute overrides the width property. Negative values are not allowed.

The most used values are a *length* value and a *percentage* value.

Length value

This is when we use one of the following units: px, em, in, mm, cm, vw, and so on.

Percentage value

This is when we use percentages such as 50%, 85%, and so on.

You can find more information on MDN at http://tiny.cc/mdn-max-width

CSS:

```
/*Length value*/
.element {
  width: 150px;
  /*This property overrides width*/
  max-width: 75px;
}
/*Percentage value*/
.element {
  max-width: 65%;
}
```

min-height

The min-height CSS property defines the minimum height of an element, and it looks like this:

```
min-height: 300px;
```

Description

The min-height attribute overrides the height and max-height properties. Negative values are not allowed.

The most used values are a *length* value and a *percentage* value.

Length value

This is when we use one of the following units: px, em, in, mm, cm, vw, and so on.

Percentage value

This is when we use percentages such as 50%, 85%, and so on.

You can find more information on MDN at http://tiny.cc/mdn-min-height

CSS:

```
/*Length value*/
.element {
  height: 75px;
  max-height: 150px;
  /*This property overrides height and max-height*/
  min-height: 300px;
}
/*Percentage value*/
.element {
  min-height: 65%;
}
```

min-width

The `min-width` CSS property defines the minimum width of an element, and it looks like this:

```
min-widht: 300px;
```

Description

The `min-width` attribute overrides the `width` and `max-width` properties.

Negative values are not allowed.

The most used values are a *length* value and a *percentage* value.

Length value

This is when we use one of the following units: `px`, `em`, `in`, `mm`, `cm`, `vw`, and so on.

Percentage value

This is when we use percentages such as `50%`, `85%`, and so on.

You can find more information on MDN at `http://tiny.cc/mdn-min-width`

CSS:

```
/*Length value*/
.element {
  width: 150px;
  max-width: 75px;
```

```
    /*This property overrides width and max-width*/
    min-width: 300px;
}
/*Percentage value*/
.element {
  min-width: 65%;
}
```

object-fit

The `object-fit` CSS property defines how a *replaced element* fits inside its content box, and it looks like this:

```
object-fit: cover;
```

Description

A *replaced element* is an HTML element whose content and dimensions are intrinsic (defined by the element itself) and are not defined by CSS or by its context or surroundings.

Examples of *replaced elements* are `<img>`, `<video>`, `<audio>`, `<canvas>`, `<iframe>`, `<textarea>`, `<object>`, `<input>`, `<button>`, `<br>`, and `<hr>`.

Now, the most important characteristic of replaced elements is that we cannot apply generated content to them via CSS using the `:before` or `:after` pseudo-element selectors.

This property can come in handy when we want a group of thumbnails to have the same width and height, but without distorting the images. However, the images for the thumbnails are uploaded by users, which means that the uploaded images can be of all sizes and different aspect ratios. The `object-fit` CSS property can help us have control of the thumbnails in such a situation.

The content inside the replaced element is centered vertically and horizontally by default. However, the content can be repositioned using the `object-position` property.

There are four keyword values: `contain`, `cover`, `fill`, `none`, and `scale-down`.

contain

The aspect ratio of the content inside the replaced element is preserved. This content is enlarged as much as possible until it reaches its maximum size defined by its width and height. It's possible to see some "unfilled" areas of the element due to preservation of the aspect ratio.

cover

The aspect ratio of the content inside the replaced element is preserved. This content is enlarged as much as possible until it completely fills or "covers" the entire content box.

fill

The aspect ratio of the content inside the replaced element is not necessarily preserved. This means that when filling the entire content box, the content of the replaced element can be stretched or shrunk during the scaling up or scaling down of the content.

none

No resizing is done.

scale-down

This acts as if none or contain were declared. The idea here is that the browser will try to figure out the smallest concrete size of the content inside the replaced element in order to make it fit in its content box while preserving the aspect ratio of the content inside the replaced element.

CSS:

```
img {
  width: 15em;
  height: 25em;
  object-fit: contain;
}
```

Here is a demo in CodePen: http://tiny.cc/object-fit-position

object-position

The object-position CSS property defines the location of the content of the replaced element, and it looks like this:

```
object-position: right bottom;
```

Description

As described in the Tip of the object-fit CSS property, by default, the content of the replaced element is placed in the center of the content box, which is 50% 50%.

Now, this property behaves similarly to the `background-position` CSS property. This means, we can declare either *one* or *two* values.

The values are either *length* or *percentages* of *keyword* values `top`, `right`, `bottom`, or `left`. Negative values are allowed.

CSS:

```
img {
  width: 15em;
  height: 25em;
  object-fit: contain;
  object-position: right bottom;
}
```

Here is a demo in CodePen: `http://tiny.cc/object-fit-position`

Border radius

With this property, we can not only make rounded corners but also circles, ellipses, and other interesting shapes.

I admit that the term "rounded corners" is far less obscure than "border radius".

border-radius

The `border-radius` CSS property allows us to make rounded corners on almost any HTML element, and it looks like this:

```
border-radius: 20px;
```

Description

The `border-radius` attribute is also the shorthand syntax for the `border-top-left-radius`, `border-top-right-radius`, `border-bottom-right-radius`, and `border-bottom-left-radius` properties.

Using either a circle or an ellipse, we can create rounded corners:

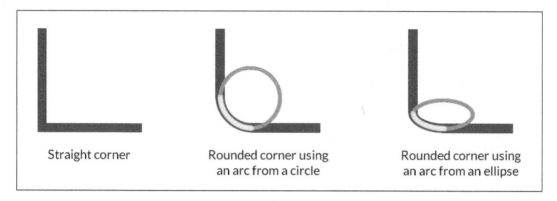

| Straight corner | Rounded corner using an arc from a circle | Rounded corner using an arc from an ellipse |

There are two values: a *length* value and a *percentage* value.

Length value

This is when we use one of the following units: px, em, in, mm, cm, vw, and so on.

Percentage value

This is when we use percentages such as 50%, 85%, and so on.

We can use, one, two, three, or four values in the same declaration. We can also use a slash symbol, "/", to separate groups of values.

Sometimes, the background color or texture "bleeds" over the rounded corners in some browsers. Use background-clip to fix this issue.

CSS:

```
/*Longhand*/
.element {
  border-top-left-radius: 20px;
  border-top-right-radius: 20px;
  border-bottom-right-radius: 20px;
  border-bottom-left-radius: 20px;
}
/*Shorthand*/
.element { border-radius: 20px; }
/*Two values: top-left-and-bottom-right - top-right-and-bottom-
left*/
```

```
.element-1 { border-radius: 70px 7px; }
/*Three values: top-left - top-right-and-bottom-left - bottom-
right*/
.element-2 { border-radius: 70px 7px 20px; }
/*Four values: top-left - top-right - bottom-right - bottom-left*/
.element-3 { border-radius: 70px 7px 20px 150px; }
/*Values divided with a slash "/" symbol */
.element-4 { border-radius: 70px 7px/20px 30px; }
/*Circle*/
.element-5 { border-radius: 200px; }
/*Ellipse*/
.element-6 { height: 100px; border-radius: 100%; }
/*Pill*/
.element-7 { height: 100px; border-radius: 100px; }
/*Half Pill: top-left - top-right - bottom-right - bottom-left*/
.element-8 { height: 100px; border-radius: 100px 0 0 100px; }
```

Here is a demo in CodePen: `http://tiny.cc/css-border-radius`

Unit

CSS unit is a type of data with which we can define measurements, and it looks like this:

```
max-height: 150px;
```

Alternatively, it could also look like this:

```
transform: rotate(45deg);
```

There is no space between the number and the unit.

In most cases, the unit isn't required after the number 0 (zero).

There are several types of length units, such as described in the following explanations.

Relative length units

They are dependent on another element's length (usually, a parent element in the DOM) that relates directly to the element in question. When the other element's length changes, the length of the element in question maintains the defined proportion. In other words, there is no need to declare the length of the child element again.

Description

Relative units are always the best way to go if we want to build scalable systems. Setting values in a single element and then modifying that single element to affect the whole system saves a lot of time and many headaches.

ex

The ex suffix stands for an element's x-height. The ex CSS unit refers to the height of lowercase *x*. This height is dependent on the font. In other words, the heights can be different if we are using Arial than if we are using Verdana, even if the value is the same.

CSS:

```
.element {
  padding: 2ex;
}
```

ch

The ch suffix stands for character. The ch CSS unit refers to the width of the character 0 (zero). This width is dependent on the font. In other words, the widths can be different if we are using Arial than if we are using Verdana, even if the value is the same.

CSS:

```
.element {
  padding: 2ch;
}
```

em

The em suffix stands for the pronunciation of the letter *m*, and it represented the width of the lower case *m* in the print and typography industries. In CSS, the em unit represents a calculation of an element's font-size property.

This unit can be used together with many CSS properties, but the most common use is to define font-size elements.

However, many web designers and developers prefer to use rem units to avoid the inheritance issue em units have in nested elements (3-4 or more levels deep).

CSS:

```
.element {
    font: 1.5em Arial, Helvetica, san-serif;
}
```

rem

The rem suffix stands for the abbreviation of the term *root element*. The rem CSS unit represents the font size of the root element in a markup document. A markup document is not only an HTML document; it can also be an XML, SVG, or other markup-based document.

Granted that in this guide, we are referring to an HTML document, and since this is the case, the root element is the <html> element.

A very common practice is to set the font size on the <html> element to 62.5%. This way, when we're setting our font sizes for other elements, we can still think in pixels, but write in rem units to maintain the relative font size when scaling up or down our document in our responsive projects.

CSS:

```
html {
    font-size: 62.5%;
}
h1 {
    /*It's the same as 22px*/
    font-size: 2.2rem;
}
```

The % sign

The % sign is what it implies, percentage. In CSS em units and percentage units yield the same result. Percentage values, such as any of the other relative units, are dependent on another value, usually that of the parent element.

Like all other relative units, percentages and responsive web design go hand in hand.

CSS:

```
.element {
    margin: 0 1%;
}
```

Viewport-relative length units

These units relate to the viewport. If the viewport's dimensions change, the properties using viewport-relative length values adapt to the new dimensions of the view window.

Description

These units are a godsend in my book. They do what we would expect of fonts in a responsive world: enlarge or shrink according to the width or height of the viewport.

Let's check them out.

vh

The vh suffix stands for *viewport height*. The vh CSS unit relates to the height of the viewport. The value of vh is 1/100th of the height of the viewport.

For example, if we declare the font-size of an element as 1vh, and the browser window is 500px, the font size is then 5px.

CSS:

```
.element {
  font-size: 1vh;
}
```

vw

The vw suffix stands for *viewport width*. The vw CSS unit relates to the width of the viewport. The value of vw is 1/100th of the width of the viewport.

For example, if we declare the font-size of an element as 1vh, and the browser window is 1400px, the font size is then 14px.

CSS:

```
.element {
  font-size: 1vw;
}
```

vmin

The vmin suffix stands for *viewport minimum*. The vmin CSS unit relates to the smallest value of the viewport, of either its height or its width. The value of vmin is 1/100th of the side with the smallest length of the viewport.

For example, if we declare the `font-size` of an element as `1vmin` and the browser's viewport is 600 × 800, the font size is then `6px`.

CSS:

```
.element {
  font-size: 1vmin;
}
```

vmax

The `vmax` suffix stands for viewport maximum. The `vmax` CSS unit relates to the largest value of the viewport, of either its height or its width. The value of `vmax` is 1/100th of the side with the largest length of the viewport.

For example, if we declare the `font-size` of an element as `1vmax`, and the browser's viewport is 600 × 800, the font size is then `8px`.

CSS:

```
.element {
  font-size: 1vmax;
}
```

Absolute length units

These units represent a physical dimension of an element. Some units in CSS come from the printing world, and although it's not common to use them, it's important to know as much as we can about them.

Description

These types of units relate directly to a physical measurement. They work best when the output environment is known, like in print.

The most used absolute unit is the pixel (`px`). A pixel is known to be a single dot on a screen. The thing is that there is no industry standard for the size of that dot.

In other words, a pixel in a standard LED/LCD display (for example, a monitor or a TV) has different sizes than a pixel in a high-density screen. Even the pixel sizes between high-density screens are different.

Let's see what each abbreviation means, and at the end of the section, we'll be able to see a single example with all the units.

cm

The cm suffix stands for *centimeter*.

mm

The mm suffix stands for *millimeter*.

in

The in suffix stands for *inch*.

pc

The pc suffix stands for *pica*.

pt

The pt suffix stands for *point*.

px

The px suffix stands for *pixel*.

CSS:

All the following values represent units that resemble 16px font size, but in different length units.

```
/*Centimeter*/
.element { font-size: .43cm; }
/*Millimeter*/
.element { font-size: 4.3mm; }
/*Inch*/
.element { font-size: .17in; }
/*Pica*/
.element { font-size: 1pc; }
/*Point*/
.element { font-size: 12pt; }
/*Pixel*/
.element { font-size: 16px; }
```

Angle data types

These units represent angle values.

Description

These units are used whenever we want to rotate an element via the `transform` property.

Aside from the `deg` data type, the other angle data type units aren't really that common.

Let's check them out though.

deg

The `deg` suffix stands for *degrees*.

grad

The `grad` suffix stands for *gradients*.

rad

The `rad` suffix stands for *radians*.

turn

The `turn` suffix is not an abbreviation; it's the actual word *turn*. There is one turn in a full circle, so if we're going to make a horizontal rectangle rotate 90 degrees to make it vertical, we would define it as `.25turn`, because it's ¼th of the complete turn.

CSS:

All the following values represent units that resemble a 90-degree turn of an element but in different angle data types:

```
/*Degrees*/
.element { transform: rotate(90deg); }
/*Gradians*/
.element { transform: rotate(100grad); }
/*Radians*/
.element { transform: rotate(89.535rad); }
/*Turn*/
.element { transform: rotate(.25turn); }
```

Resolution units

These units represent the screen density of pixels on any given output or device. Unlike relative and absolute units, it's necessary to add the unit to the value 0 (zero).

Description

Whenever we need to consider density screens, resolution units will do the heavy lifting for us. They are used in media queries.

Let's see how they work.

dpi

The dpi suffix stands for *dots per inch*. Screens contain 72 or 96 dpi, whereas a printed document has much larger dpi. 1 inch = 2.54 cm, so 1dpi≈ 0.39dpcm.

dpcm

The dpcm suffix stands for *dots per centimeter*. 1 inch = 2.54 cm, so 1dpcm≈ 2.54dpi.

dppx

The dppx suffix stands for *dots per pixel*. 1dppx = 96dpi due to the 1:96 fixed ratio of CSS pixels.

CSS:

```
/**@2x pixel ratio**/
/*Dots per inch*/
@media (min-resolution: 192dpi) { ... }
/*Dots per centimeter*/
@media (min-resolution: 75.5906dpcm) { ... }
/*Dots per pixel*/
@media (min-resolution: 2dppx) { ... }
```

Duration units

These units represent the duration of an animation in either seconds or milliseconds.

Description

These units are quite straightforward and are only used in CSS animations.

You may think that because all other units use two, three, or four letters in their abbreviation (px, dip, dpcm, and so on). Always remember: when declaring the seconds unit only one s is used. Using sec or secs is incorrect.

ms

The ms suffix stands for *milliseconds*. 1000ms= 1 second.

s

The s suffix stands for *seconds*. 1s = 1000 milliseconds.

CSS:

```
/*Milliseconds*/
.element { animation-duration: 3ms; }
.element { transition: .003s; }

/*Seconds*/
.element { animation-duration: 3s; }
.element { transition: 3000ms; }
```

Column

CSS columns is the most versatile way to fluidly distribute long strings of content while retaining scalability. If the content grows or is reduced, it would automatically reflow in the available space of the declared columns.

Although not necessarily ideal, actual elements such as DIVs can also be distributed in columns with the CSS columns property.

Let's dive in.

column-count

The column-count CSS property defines the number of columns of an element, and it looks like this:

```
column-count:3;
```

Description

We can use either a *number* value or the keyword `auto`.

When we use the `auto` keyword, we're letting the browser decide how many columns can fit within the available space. This is a very powerful and robust solution for responsive layouts. However, it is required that we declare `column-width` for this to work.

CSS:

```
/*Let the browser decide*/
.element {
  column-count: auto;
  column-width: 200px;
}
/*Specific number of columns*/
.element {
  column-count: 3;
}
```

column-fill

The `column-fill` CSS property controls how the content is assigned across columns, and it looks like this:

```
column-fill: balance;
```

Description

There are two keywords: `auto` and `balance`.

- `auto`: This means that the content is filled sequentially. Basically, as space becomes available, the content will start filling it. This makes the parent container grow vertically by making the columns taller in order to fit the content.

- `balance`: This means that the content will be equally distributed in the available columns. For this to work, we need to declare a height on the parent container. This will make sure that the columns are of the specific height as well. The problem with this is that the content will just keep flowing outside the parent container if the parent container becomes too small.

CSS:

```css
/*Balance*/
.element {
  column-fill: balance;
  column-count: 4;
  height: 400px;
}
/*Auto*/
.element {
  column-fill: auto;
  column-count: 4;
}
```

column-gap

The `column-gap` CSS property defines the space between columns. In editorial terms, this space is the "gutter", and it looks like this:

```css
column-gap: 50px;
```

Description

There are two values: the `auto` keyword and a *length* value.

- `auto`: This is the default value defined by the spec, which is `1em`.

- `Length value`: We define this using `px` or `em`.

CSS:

```css
/*Auto = 1em*/
.element {
  column-gap: auto;
  column-count: 4;
}
/*Length value: px or em*/
.element {
  column-gap: 50px;
  column-count: 4;
}
```

column-rule

The `column-rule` CSS property creates or draws a vertical line that "separates" the columns, and it looks like this:

```
column-rule: 2px solid black;
```

Description

We can define three aspects of the `column-rule` CSS property: the thickness or `width`; the `style`, which are the same styles of the `border-style` property; and `color`.

The `column-rule` CSS property is the shorthand of the following properties:

- `column-rule-width`: This can be just a length value (a number), or we can use any of these keywords: `thin`, `medium`, or `thick`.

- `column-rule-style`: This can be any of the `border-style` values, such as `dotted`, `dashed`, `inset`, and so on.

- `column-rule-color`: This is a color defined in any format: HEX, RGB, or HSL. It also supports alpha channel, so RGBa and HSLa are allowed.

CSS:

```
/*Length, solid line and RGBa*/
.element {
  column-gap: auto;
  column-count: 4;
  column-rule: 2px solid rgba(0, 0, 0, .3);
}
/*Keyword, dotted and color name*/
.element {
  column-gap: 50px;
  column-count: 4;
  column-rule: thick dotted black;
}
```

column-rule-color

The `column-rule-color` CSS property defines the color of the dividing line between columns.

Colors can be defined in any format: HEX, RGB, or HSL. It also supports alpha channel, so RGBa and HSLa are allowed.

CSS:

```
.element {
  column-rule-color: red;
}
```

column-rule-style

The `column-rule-style` CSS property defines the style of the dividing line between columns.

It can be any of the `border-style` values, for example, `dotted`, `dashed`, `inset`, and so on.

CSS:

```
.element {
  column-rule-style: dotted;
}
```

column-rule-width

The `column-rule-width` CSS property defines the thickness (width) of the dividing line between columns.

It can be just a length value (a number), or we can use any of these keywords: `thin`, `medium`, or `thick`.

CSS:

```
.element {
  column-rule-width: 5px;
}
```

column-span

The `column-span` CSS property makes an element that's supposed to behave like a column into an element that spans across all columns. The element is still a "column", but it now expands the full width of the columns, like a block element.

There are two values, `none` and `all`, which are self-explanatory.

CSS:

```
.element {
  column-span: all;
}
```

Here is a demo in CodePen: `http://tiny.cc/column-span`

column-width

The `column-width` CSS property defines the width of the columns.

When we define the width of the columns, the browser will automatically add or remove columns depending on the available space.

For example, if we say our columns are `200px` wide and the parent container is `800px`, then the browser will include three columns (taking into account the default `column-gap` of `1em`). However, if the container is at least `450px` wide, the browser will fit two columns.

CSS:

```
/*em value*/
.element {
  column-width: 10em;
}
/*px value*/
.element {
  column-width: 200px;
}
```

columns

The `columns` CSS property is the shorthand that we can use to set `column-width` and `column-count`.

It can accept either one or two values in the same declaration. The order of the values doesn't matter, but it's a good measure to declare `column-width` first and `column-count` second.

CSS:

```
/*column-width and then column-count*/
.element {
  columns: 300px 2;
}
```

Flexible box (flexbox)

Flexbox is one of the most useful CSS modules when it comes to arranging elements in a container. Flexbox allows elements to grow or shrink, depending on the available space in order to maintain the integrity of layouts.

Using Flexbox is the next step after using float-based layouts, not only because it can be easier to work with and wrap our heads around its concepts, but also because it may result in less markup and CSS.

 A powerful partner to Flexbox is the Grid Layout, which is still in its early stages of development, and browser support is scarce. Since Grid Layout is out of the scope of this section, you can read more on Rachel Andrew's project site, Grid By Example, at http://gridbyexample.com/

Before we dive into the Flexbox properties, the following diagram will help us understand the terminology and orientations:

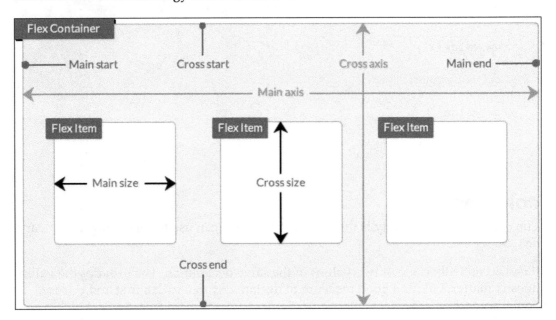

Let's dive into Flexbox properties.

flex-grow

This property defines how much a flex item should grow relative to other flex items via a flex grow factor, and it looks like this:

```
flex--grow: 2;
```

Description

The flex grow factor is a *number* without a unit. Negative values are invalid.

The flex item will grow by the defined grow factor as long as there is space to do so. It can grow on both the main or cross axes, depending on the direction defined by the `flex-direction` property, which we'll talk about in a minute.

CSS:

```
/*First flex item will take 1 unit of the available space*/
.element-1 { flex-grow: 1; }
/*Second and third flex items will take 2 units of the available
space*/
.element-2 { flex-grow: 2; }
.element-3 { flex-grow: 2; }
/*Fourth flex item will take 1 unit of the available space*/
.element-4 { flex-grow: 1; }
```

flex-shrink

This property defines how much a flex item should shrink relative to other flex items via a flex shrink factor, and it looks like this:

```
flex-shrink: 1;
```

Description

The flex shrink factor is a *number* without a unit. Negative values are invalid.

This is used when the sum of all flex items exceeds the size of the flex container. This could be horizontally or vertically (main axis or cross axis). By assigning flex shrink factors to one or multiple flex items, we can make them fit the size of the flex container.

CSS:

```
/*First flex item will take 1 unit of the available space*/
.element-1 { flex-shrink: 1; }
/*Second and third flex items will take 2 units of the available
space*/
.element-2 { flex-shrink: 2; }
.element-3 { flex-shrink: 2; }
/*Fourth flex item will take 1 unit of the available space*/
.element-4 { flex-shrink: 1; }
```

flex-basis

This property defines the initial width of a flex item, and it looks like this:

```
flex-basis: 200px;
```

Description

flex-basis accepts a *length* value with either an absolute or a relative length unit (px, em, %, and so on) or the content keyword.

When using content, the container will adapt to the content inside of it. Negative values are invalid.

CSS:

```
/*Both elements will be 50% wide*/


/*Both elements will be 50% wide*/
.a { flex-grow: 1; }
.b { flex-grow: 1; }

/*First element WILL NOT grow and has a fixed width of 200px if
there's enough space*/
.a {
  flex-grow: 0;
  flex-basis: 200px;
}
/*Second element WILL grow and has a minimum width of 200px if
there's enough space*/
.b {
  flex-grow: 1;
  flex-basis: 200px;
}
```

```
/*First element WILL grow and has a minimum width of 200px if
there's enough space*/
 .a {
  flex-grow: 1;
  flex-basis: 200px;
}
/*Second element:
  - WILL NOT grow
  - WILL shrink if the container is smaller than 400px
  - It has a minimum width of 200px if there's enough space*/
.b {
  flex-grow: 0;
  flex-shrink: 1;
  flex-basis: 200px;
}
```

flex-direction

The flex-direction CSS property defines the direction of the flex items inside a flex container, and it looks like this:

```
flex-direction: column;
```

Description

This property sets the direction in which flex items can be laid out, either horizontal with row or vertical with column.

There are four values: two for horizontal and two for vertical:

row

This lays out the flex items on a horizontal axis. This is the default value.

When flex items are laid out with row, they stack side by side from left to right.

row-reverse

This is the same as row but in reverse. When flex items are laid out with row-reverse, they stack side by side from right to left.

column

This lays out the flex items on a vertical axis.

When flex items are laid out with column, they stack one on top of the other, starting from top to bottom.

column-reverse

This is the same as `column` but in reverse.

When flex items are laid out with `column-reverse`, they stack one on top of the other, starting from bottom to top.

 The `flex-direction` property is applied to the flex container, not the flex items.

CSS:

```
/*Horizontal axis: row*/
.flex-container { flex-direction: row; }
/*Horizontal axis: row-reverse*/
.flex-container { flex-direction: row-reverse; }
/*Vertical axis: column*/
.flex-container { flex-direction: column; }
/*Vertical axis: column*/
.flex-container { flex-direction: column-reverse; }
```

flex-wrap

The `flex-wrap` CSS property defines whether a flex item should wrap or not when the container becomes too small, and it looks like this:

```
flex-wrap: wrap;
```

Description

This property accepts one of three keyword values: `nowrap`, `wrap` and `wrap-reverse`.

nowrap

This is the default value. It tells the flex item to not wrap.

wrap

This tells the flex element to wrap.

wrap-reverse

This tells the flex element to wrap but in reverse.

The `flex-wrap` property is applied to the flex container, not the flex items.

CSS:

```
.flex-container {
  flex-wrap: wrap;
}
```

flex-flow

The `flex-flow` CSS property is the shorthand for the `flex-direction` and `flex-wrap` properties, and it looks like this:

```
flex-flow: row wrap-reverse;
```

Description

We now know that the `flex-direction` property defines the direction of the flex items in either columns or rows.

The `flex-wrap` attribute, on the other hand, defines whether the flex items should wrap or not when the container becomes too small.

We can specify either one or two values. The order doesn't affect the result.

The `flex-direction` attribute can take any of its available values: `row :` (default value), `row-reverse`, `column`, or `column-reverse`.

The `flex-wrap` attribute can take any of its available values as well: `nowrap` (default value), `wrap`, or `wrap-reverse`.

 The `flex-flow` property is applied to the flex container, not the flex items.

CSS:

```
/*Main axis and elements will wrap from bottom to top*/
.flex-container {
  flex-direction: row;
  flex-wrap: wrap-reverse;
}
```

```
/*Above rule is the same as this rule*/
.flex-container { flex-flow: row wrap-reverse; }
/*Main axis and flex items will wrap from top to bottom*/
.flex-container { flex-flow: row-reverse wrap; }
/*Cross axis, wrapping doesn't happen on column layout*/
.flex-container { flex-flow: column; }
```

align-content

The `align-content` CSS property aligns lines inside a flex container as long as there is extra space on the cross axis, and it looks like this:

```
align-content: center;
```

Description

There are six values: `flex-start`, `flex-end`, `center`, `space-around`, `space-between`, and `stretch`.

flex-start

This groups the lines to the start of the container.

flex-end

This groups the lines to the end of the container.

center

This groups the lines to the center of the container.

space-around

This distributes the lines evenly in the container, but the first line is placed at the start of the container and the last line at the end.

space-between

This distributes the lines evenly in the container with an even amount of space between each line.

stretch

This is the default value. The lines will evenly stretch to fill the whole container.

The align-content property is applied to the flex container, not the flex items.

CSS:

```
/*All lines at the top*/
.flex-container { align-content: flex-start; }
/*All lines at the bottom*/
.flex-container { align-content: flex-end; }
/*All lines at the center*/
.flex-container { align-content: center; }
/*Evenly spaced lines. The top one touches the top edge; the
bottom one touches the bottom edge*/
.flex-container { align-content: space-around; }
/*Evenly spaced lines, even the top and bottom ones*/
.flex-container { align-content: space-between; }
/*Lines will stretch to fill all the available space*/
.flex-container { align-content: stretch; }
```

align-items

The align-items CSS property sets the default alignment of the flex elements inside the flex container, and it looks like this:

```
align-items: center;
```

Description

This property accepts five values: flex-start, flex-end, center, baseline, and stretch.

flex-start

This aligns the flex elements to the beginning of the container.

flex-end

This aligns the flex elements to the end of the container.

center

This aligns the flex elements to the center of the container and and at the same time, it aligns them to their center.

baseline

This aligns the flex elements to the text baseline inside each flex element.

stretch

This stretches the flex elements to fill the entire parent container.

 The `align-items` property is applied to the flex container, not the flex items.

CSS:

```
/*Align items to the beginning*/
.flex-container { align-items: flex-start; }
/*Align items to the end*/
.flex-container { align-items: flex-end; }
/*Align items to the center*/
.flex-container { align-items: center; }
/*Align items to their text baseline*/
.flex-container { align-items: baseline; }
/*Make items stretch and fill the parent container*/
.flex-container { align-items: stretch; }
```

align-self

The `align-self` CSS property aligns a specific flex item within its parent container, and it looks like this:

```
align-self: flex-start;
```

Description

This property accepts the exact values as `align-items`, and the results are the same as well: `flex-start`, `flex-end`, `center`, `baseline`, and `stretch`.

flex-start

This aligns the flex element to the beginning of the container.

flex-end

This aligns the flex element to the end of the container.

center

This aligns the flex element to the center of the container.

baseline

This aligns the flex element to the text baseline inside each flex element.

stretch

This stretches the flex elements to fill the entire parent container.

CSS:

```
/*Align the flex item to the top*/
.element { align-self: flex-start; }
/*Align the flex item to the bottom*/
.element { align-self: flex-end; }
/*Align the flex item to the center*/
.element { align-self: center; }
/*Align the flex items to their text baseline*/
.element { align-self: baseline; }
/*Make the flex item stretch*/
.element { align-self: stretch; }
```

order

The order CSS property is used to alter the default order of flex items within the same parent container, and it looks like this:

```
order: 3;
```

Description

By default, flex items appear in the same order they appear in the source (HTML). The order property allows us to alter the display order while maintaining their source order. This property accepts a *number* value without a unit.

The order is defined in a logical way: The lower the number, the more ahead it is in the order. Items that have the same number are laid out according to the source document.

The starting number is 0 (zero), not 1. Negative values are allowed.

CSS:

```
/*The default order of all elements has been altered,
  however, their source order remains the same.*/
.element-1 { order: 3; }
.element-2 { order: 0; }
.element-3 { order: -1; }
.element-4 { order: 2; }
```

justify-content

The justify-content CSS property works only on flex items. It allows the browser to distribute the space in between and around the flex items based on their main axes.

Description

This property supports five keyword values: flex-start, flex-end, center, space-between, and space-around.

flex-start

This is the default value. It groups and positions the elements to the beginning of the container.

flex-end

This groups and positions the elements to the end of the container.

center

This groups and positions the elements to the center of the container.

space-between

This spreads and positions the elements along the container and spaces them evenly.

The first and last flex items are flushed against the left-hand and right-hand sides respectively. In other words, the first and last flex items touch the left and right edges.

space-around

Similar to the `space-between` property, this spreads and positions the elements along the container and spaces them evenly.

However, the first and last flex items do not touch the left and right edges.

CSS:

```
.flex-container {
  display: flex;
  justify-content: space-between;
}
```

flex

The `flex` CSS property is the shorthand in which we can declare the values for `flex-grow`, `flex-shrink`, and `flex-basis`. It's recommended that you follow this order when declaring the values.

CSS:

```
/*Apply flexbox to the parent container*/
.flex-container { display: flex; }
/*Flex items create 4 containers, each of different size.
  Each container grows/shrinks proportional to the
flex growth/shrink factorsand the browser automatically
calculates the flex-basis*/
.element-1 { flex: 1 4 auto; }
.element-2 { flex: 2 3 auto; }
.element-3 { flex: 3 2 auto; }
.element-4 { flex: 4 1 auto; }
```

Summary

And this is how you start the first chapter about CSS Properties! We learned what CSS properties and vendor prefixes are.

Now, with the animation properties clear we can start working on great interactions for our sites and applications. We can also handle all background features, be positioning or even blend modes to create nice visual effects without having to depend on image editors of any kind.

The Box Model concept is something we can tackle easier especially knowing that legacy IE's have less and less impact than before. This is greatly impacted by how we work with CSS units since we need to understand which units work best with different use cases and requirements.

We learned that CSS columns are a great tool to distribute long strings of text. And that the mighty Flexbox is the go-to feature to arrange elements in containers.

Improving our typography and transformations are part of the next chapter, amongst other interesting properties.

Buckle up!

5
CSS Properties – Part 2

Ok, we're through Part 1 of the CSS properties. Indeed, there are many, many more properties to talk about.

Let's now move on to Part 2.

Fonts

In the world of design, fonts are one of the most powerful assets we have, and at the same time, they are one of the most underappreciated ones.

Typography is so powerful that when we use it correctly, we may even get away with not using a single image in our project.

Let's take a look at the CSS font properties, shall we?

font-family

The `font-family` CSS property defines the font we want an element to use, and looks like this:

```
font-family: "Times New Roman", Times, Baskerville, Georgia,
serif;
```

Description

This property can hold one or multiple font names in its declaration. There is no limit as to how many font names it can hold; however, it is not only very unlikely to list more than four or five fonts, but it's also unnecessary.

The font family names are separated by commas. We call this the *font stack*. The browser will read the font stack and use the first one in the stack, if it can't find it or download it, it will move on to the next font family name and so on until it's able to use one from the stack.

There are two types of font family names: family name and generic family name.

Family name

Family names are actually names that represent real fonts, such as Times, Arial, Verdana, Monaco, and so on. They should always be listed before generic family names in the font stack.

Generic family names

These are the only keywords that represent a system font. They are called **fallback** fonts. They should always be listed after the family names in the font stack. Generic family names can be monospace, san-serif, serif, cursive, and fantasy.

> It is not mandatory to use quotes (single or double) when a font family name has multiple words. For example, writing font-family: "Times New Roman", serif; is the same as writing font-family: Times New Roman, serif;. Note that Times New Roman is not quoted in the second example.

CSS:

```
.element {
    font-family: "Times New Roman", Times, Baskerville, Georgia,
    serif;
}
```

font-feature-settings

The font-feature-settings CSS property provides control over typographic properties in OpenType fonts, and looks like this:

```
font-feature-settings: "smcp";
```

Description

The font-feature-settings CSS property allows us to control and use other alternative glyphs that come included in some font files.

An example of an alternate glyph is for example when we type the fractions 1/2 or 1/4 the font actually includes the "small superscript" version like ½ and ¼. Or if we type H_2O it turns into H_2O.

Remember, not all fonts contain special glyphs (font features).

To find out what font features a font file has, you can use any of these two tools:

1. Fontdeck.com (text has link http://fontdeck.com/) - Find the font you want and on the About this typeface, look for the OPENTYPE line, there all the font features will be listed for that specific font.

2. Test OpenType features (text has link http://www.impallari.com/testing/index.php) - Just drag and drop your font file(s) and click on the OpenType Features link on the top left, a large panel will slide where you can select which features to see.

Here are some of the most common feature tags:

- `dlig`: Discretionary ligatures
- `kern`: Kerning
- `liga`: Standard ligatures
- `lnum`: Lining figures
- `onum`: Old style figures
- `tnum`: Tabular figures
- `smcp`: Small capitals
- `ss01, ss02, ss03, ss04... ss20`: Stylistic sets (font-dependent)
- `swsh`: Swash

For more information, check out the MDN website: `http://tiny.cc/mdn-font-feature-settings`

For a complete list of all font features, check the Microsoft site at `http://tiny.cc/msn-font-features-list`

CSS:

```
/*Small capitals*/
.element {
  font-feature-settings: "smcp";
}
```

font-size

The font-size CSS property defines the size of the text of an element, and it looks like this:

```
font-size-settings: "smcp";
```

Description

This property can also be used to change the size of other elements since we can compute the value of em, rem, and ex length units as well.

There are a few different value types that we can use with the font-size CSS property: absolute keywords/size, relative size, length, and percentage.

Absolute keywords/size

The sizes defined relate directly to specific font sizes. They can also be used to set a font size of an element based on the parent element's font size. Values are as follows:

- xx-small
- x-small
- small
- medium (default value)
- large
- x-large
- xx-large

Relative size keywords

These sizes increase or reduce the font size of an element based on the font size of its parent container. The values are:

- smaller
- larger

Length

Negative values are invalid. When using px, the font size is absolute; it's not relative to the font size of the parent container. When using em, ex, and ch, the font size is relative to the font size of the element's parent container. When using rem, the font size is relative to the root element, that is, the <html> element. When using vw, vh, vmax, and vmin the font size is relative to the viewport.

To see all the available values of this attribute, refer to the *Absolute Length Units* section.

The most popular units are:

- px
- em
- rem

Percentage

The percentage attribute refers to the percentage of the parent element's font size. Its unit is %.

CSS:

```
/*Absolute keywords/size*/
.element { font-size: x-small; }
/*Relative size*/
.element { font-size: smaller; }
/*Length value*/
.element { font-size: 18px; }
/*Percentage value*/
.element { font-size: 62.5%; }
```

font-size-adjust

The font-size-adjust CSS property helps us define the aspect ratio of the fonts based on the size difference of the lowercase letter x and upper case letter X, and it looks like this:

```
font-size-adjust: .5";
```

Description

In the font stack, the font sizes can be different from one font to the other, thus the styling of the text can considerably vary from the intended design. With the font-size-adjust CSS property, we can solidly predict that the font sizes are consistent when the browser uses any font from the font stack.

This property accepts a *numeric* value without a unit. It can also accept decimal values.

A great online tool that can do this for us is Fontdeck's font-size-adjust web app: http://fontdeck.com/support/fontsizeadjust.

 Although Firefox is the only one that supports the font-size-adjust property at the time of writing this section, I decided to still include it because it will be of great value once other browsers start supporting it.

CSS:

```
.element {
  font-size-adjust: .5;
}
```

font-stretch

The font-stretch CSS property allows us to select a condensed, normal, or expanded face from the font family in question, and it looks like this:

```
font-stretch: condensed;
```

Description

The font-stretch property doesn't just *stretch* the font to whatever we tell it to. It looks for an actual face inside the font file that matches the declared style; or at that is as close as possible.

This property supports the following values:

- ultra-condensed
- extra-condensed
- condensed
- semi-condensed
- normal

- semi-expanded
- expanded
- extra-expanded
- ultra-expanded

CSS:

```
.element {
  font-stretch: condensed;
}
```

font-style

The `font-style` CSS property specifies the font style of an element, and it looks like this:

```
font-style: italic;
```

Description

The `font-style` property accepts the following values: `normal`, `italic`, and `oblique`.

Let's clear up the difference between `italic` and `oblique`.

According to the spec:

> *"Italic forms are generally cursive in nature, while oblique faces are typically sloped versions of the regular face."*

This means that when we declare the font style `italic`, the browser will look for the italic face of the font and use that face. A good example of this is the typeface *Georgia*; when we use the `italic` property, we can clearly see that it's an actual italicized face rather than making the normal face oblique.

Oblique makes the Normal face slanted or inclined in order to *simulate* italics.

CSS:

```
.element {
  font-style: italic;
}
```

font-variant

The `font-variant` CSS property turns the targeted text into small caps and it looks like this:

```
font-variant: small-caps;
```

Description

The `font-variant` property is considered a shorthand in CSS3 and has been extended with new values, which developers rarely use.

One thing to note is that if the text is already in all caps and we apply the `small-caps` property to it, the text will not change; it will continue to be in all caps.

The most used values are: `normal` and `small-caps`. Some of the additional values in CSS3 are `small-caps`, `all-small-caps`, `petite-caps`, `all-petite-caps`, `unicase`, and `titling-caps`.

For more information, check out the MDN website: `http://tiny.cc/mdn-font-variant`

CSS:

```
.element {
  font-variant: small-caps;
}
```

font-variant-ligatures

The `font-variant-ligatures` CSS property defines ligatures in text, which specify how glyphs are combined in order to produce a more harmonic text, and it looks like this:

```
font-variantligatures: discretionary-ligatures;
```

Description

The `font-variant-ligatures` are common in OpenType fonts.

The `font-variant-ligatures` property uses the following values: `common-ligatures`, `no-common-ligatures`, `discretionary-ligatures`, `no-discretionary-ligatures`, `historical-ligatures`, `no-historical-ligatures`, `contextual`, `no-contextual`, and `contextual`.

For more information, check out the MDN website: `http://tiny.cc/mdnfont-variant-ligatures`

CSS:

```
.element {
  font-variant-ligatures: discretionary-ligatures;
}
```

font-weight

The `font-weight` CSS property defines the thickness (weight) of the font, and it looks like this:

```
font-weight: bold;
```

Description

This property accepts two types of values: a *numeric* value and a *keyword* value.

Numeric values

This property accepts numeric values such as 100, 200, 300, 400, 500, 600, 700, 800 and 900.

Keyword values

This property also accepts keyword values such as `normal`, `bold`, `bolder`, and `lighter`.

 The `normal` keyword is the same as 400 numeric value and the `bold` keyword is the same as 700.

One thing to note is that the keywords `bolder` and `lighter` are dependent on the parent element's font weight.

CSS:

```
/*Numeric value*/
.element { font-weight: 200; }
/*Keyword value*/
.element { font-weight: bold; }
```

font

The `font` CSS property is the shorthand for the `font-style`, `font-variant`, `font-weight`, `font-size`, `line-height`, and `font-family` properties, and it looks like this:

```
font: italic small-caps bold 18px/2 "Times New Roman", Times,
Baskerville, Georgia, serif;
```

Description

There are a few things to consider when using the `font` shorthand in order for it to work:

- At least the `font-size` and `font-family` properties need to be declared
- If any of the preceding two properties are omitted, the declaration will be ignored
- If any more than these two properties are going to be declared, it's mandatory to adhere to the following order:
  - `font-style`
  - `font-variant`
  - `font-weight`
  - `font-size`
  - `line-height`
  - `font-family`

 When declaring the `line-height` value in the shorthand, it always has to go after the `font-size` property separated with a slash "/" character, for example, `.element { font: 12px/1.6 Arial; }`.

- **CSS:**
```
/*All font properties in a single declaration*/
.element { font: italic small-caps bold 18px/2 "Times New Roman",
Times, Baskerville, Georgia, serif; }
/*font-style*/
.element { font-style: italic; }
/*font-variant*/
.element { font-variant: small-caps; }
/*font-weight*/
.element { font-weight: bold; }
/*font-size*/
```

```
.element { font-size: 18px; }
/*line-height*/
.element { line-height: 2; }
/*font-family*/
.element { font-family: "Times New Roman", Times, Baskerville,
Georgia, serif; }
```

Transform

CSS transforms have gained such popularity that it's rare not to see some sort of transformation in a website nowadays — from button shapes and animations to layouts.

Let's dig in.

transform

The `transform` CSS property allows us to scale, rotate, skew, and translate elements in 2D and 3D spaces, and it looks like this:

```
transform: translate(-10px, 10%);
```

Description

This property supports the following values: `scale()`, `skewX()` and `skewY()`, `translate()`, `rotate()`, `matrix()`, and `perspective()`.

Note that X-axis equals *horizontal* and Y-axis equals *vertical*.

 An easy way to remember which axis is which is by saying this: "*x is a cross so the x-axis is across*". `http://tiny.cc/xy-axis`

scale()

The `scale()` function scales an element. It's also the shorthand for `scaleX()` and `scaleY()` functions. It accepts a *numeric* value without a unit. The *numeric* value represents the proportion in which the element will be scaled. For example, 2 means that the element will be scaled to twice its size. Negative values are valid.

skew()

The skew() function tilts the element. If a single value is declared, then it will only tilt the element on the *x* axis. If two values are declared, then the element is tilted on both the *x* and *y* axes. The skew() function accepts a *numeric* value followed by the deg, grad, rad, or turn units. However, the deg unit is the most commonly used unit. Negative values are valid.

skewX() and skewY()

The skewX() and skewY() functions tilts the element only horizontally or vertically.

translate()

The translate() function alters the location of an element. If a single value is declared, then it will only translate the element on the X-axis. If two values are declared, then the element is translated in both the X and Y-axis. Negative values are valid.

translateX() and translateY()

The translateX() and translateY() functions alters the location either horizontally or vertically.

rotate()

The rotate() function rotates an element around a fixed point in a 2D space. It accepts a *numeric* value followed by the deg, grad, rad, or turn units. The deg unit is the most common though. Negative values are valid.

matrix()

The matrix() function is shorthand for all transformation values since they can be combined here. Granted the complexity of the matrix() function, this requires a solid understanding of math.

perspective()

This value gives a 3D perspective to the element; once the perspective is set, we can then use any of the other values. The element in question will react in a 3D plane. It accepts a *numeric* value with a *length* unit.

The explanation of the advanced mathematics of the `matrix()` function are out of scope of this book. However, for very detailed explanations, you can refer to either of these two articles:

- *Understanding the CSS Transforms Matrix* by Tiffany Brown at `http://tiny.cc/css-matrix-1`

- *The CSS3 matrix() Transform for the Mathematically Challenged* by Zoltan Hawryluk at `http://tiny.cc/css-matrix-2`

CSS:

```
/*Scale the same value in both X an Y-axis*/
.element { transform: scale(1.1); }
/*Scale different values for X and Y-axis*/
.element { transform: scale(1.1, 1.5); }
/*Tilt the element on X-axis only*/
.element { transform: skew(10deg); }
/*Tilt the element on both X and Y-axis*/
.element { transform: skew(10deg, -20deg); }
/*Move the element 10px to the right*/
.element { transform: translate(10px); }
/*Move the element 10px to the right and 10% down*/
.element { transform: translate(-10px, 10%); }
/*Rotate in a 2D plane*/
.element { transform: rotate(10deg); }
/*Matrix*/
.element { transform: matrix(2, 2, 1, 2, 0, 0); }
/*Add perspective to the element to make it rotate in a 3D plane*/
.element { transform: perspective(100px) rotateX(40deg); }
```

transform-origin

The `transform-origin` CSS property allows us to change the point of origin of the transformed element, and it looks like this:

```
transform-origin: 50px;
```

Description

The `transform-origin` property only works if the `transform` property is declared.

2D transformations can affect the x and y axes. 3D transformations can change these two as well as the z axis.

For a 2D transformation, up to two values can be declared; the first one is the X axis (horizontal) and the second the Y axis (vertical).

3D transformations can take up to three values that represent the X, Y, and Z axes.

The keywords that are accepted in this property are: top, right, bottom, left, and center.

CSS:

```
/*Single value affects both X and Y-axis*/
.element {
  transform: scale(2, 4);
  transform-origin: 50px;
}
/*Two values one for each axis*/
.element {
  transform: scale(2, 4);
  transform-origin: 50px -100px;
}
/*Keyword value*/
.element {
  transform: scale(2, 4);
  transform-origin: bottom;
}
/*Length and keyword values*/
.element {
  transform: scale(2, 4);
  transform-origin: 50px bottom;
}
/*Both keyword values*/
.element {
  transform: scale(2, 4);
  transform-origin: right bottom;
}
```

transform-style

The transform-style CSS property defines whether an element is positioned in a 3D space or 2D space (flat), and it looks like this:

```
transform-style: preserve-3d;
```

Description

This property takes only two values: `flat` and `preserve-3d`.

When the `preserve-3d` property is applied, the elements' stack on the *z* axis can be altered via the `translate()` function, thus the elements can appear in different planes regardless of the order in which they appear in the source HTML.

When the `flat` property is applied, the elements obey the order in which they appear in the source HTML.

> Note that this property is applied to the parent element, not the child elements.

CSS:

```css
/*Perspective*/
.parent-container {
  transform-style: preserve-3d;
  perspective: 500px;
}
.element-1 {
  transform: translateZ(1px) rotateX(60deg);
}
.element-2 {
  transform: translateZ(-2px);
}
```

Transition

CSS transitions allow us to have very granular control over our animations.

Let's take a look at these properties.

transition

The `transition` CSS property is the shorthand for all transition properties: `transition-delay`, `transition-duration`, `transition-property`, and `transition-timing-function`. It looks like this:

```css
transition: width 400ms ease-out 1s;
```

Description

This property lets us define the transition between two states of an element via the
:hover or :active pseudo-classes.

One thing to consider is that the order in which these properties appear doesn't
matter. However, since transition-delay and transition-duration use the
same value unit, transition-delay will always be considered first, followed by
transition-duration.

CSS:

```
/*Shorthand with all properties in a single declaration*/
.element {
  width: 100px;
  /*property - duration - timing function - delay*/
  transition: width 400ms ease-out 1s;
}
/*Longhand. Each property is declared separately*/
.element {
  transition-property: width;
  transition-duration: 400ms;
  transition-timing-function: ease-out;
  transition-delay: 1s;
}
.element:hover {
  width: 300px;
}
```

transition-delay

The transition-delay CSS property allows us to set a *timer*. When the timer
reaches zero, the transition begins. It looks like this:

```
transition-delay: 1s;
```

Description

This property accepts a *numeric* value followed by either s or ms, which stand for
seconds and *milliseconds*, respectively.

CSS:

```
.element {
  transition-delay: 1s;
}
```

transition-duration

The `transition-duration` CSS property allows us to define how long a transition should take from start to end. This is also called a **cycle,** and it looks like this:

```
transition-duration: 400ms;
```

Description

The `transition-duration` property accepts a *numeric* value followed by either `s` or `ms`, which stand for seconds and milliseconds, respectively.

CSS:

```
.element {
    transition-duration: 400ms;
}
```

transition-property

The `transition-property` CSS property specifies which CSS property or properties will be transitioned.

Not all properties are animatable though. The W3C has a nice list of animatable CSS properties, which can be found at `http://tiny.cc/w3c-animatable-css-props`

Description

The `transition-property` CSS property accepts the following values:

- `none`: This means that no transitions will take place
- `all`: This means that all properties will be transitioned
- `Property name`: This means that the specified property or properties will be transitioned

CSS:

```
.element {
    transition-property: width;
}
```

transition-timing-function

The `transition-timing-function` CSS property defines how an animation's speed should progress throughout its cycles.

Both the `transition-timing-function` and `animation-timing-function` properties accept the same five predefined values, which are also known as easing functions for the **Bézier** curve: `ease`, `ease-in`, `ease-out`, `ease-in-out`, and `linear`.

Refer to the *animation-timing-function* section for a detailed explanation of all the values.

CSS:

```
.element {
  transition-timing-function: ease-out;
}
```

Positioning

Positioning elements is something we spend a lot of our time on when building sites and applications, so having a good understanding of how to place an element on a layout is crucial, especially when an element can have different positions depending on the available space.

Let's see what positioning is all about.

position

The `position` CSS property defines the location of an element.

Description

There are five keyword values for the `position` property: `static`, `absolute`, `relative`, `fixed`, and `sticky`.

static

This is the default value of the `position` property. The element stays in the flow of the document and appears in the actual location where it's located in the markup.

absolute

The element is removed from the document flow and it's positioned in relation to its closest relative positioned ancestor element.

relative

The element does not change positions unless one or several properties of `top`, `right`, `bottom`, or `left` are declared. It also creates a *reference position* for `absolute` positioned child elements.

fixed

The element is removed from the document flow just like the `absolute` positioned elements. However, unlike the `absolute` positioned elements, which are relative to an ancestor element, the `fixed` elements are always relative to the document.

sticky

This value is a mix between the `relative` and `fixed` positions. The element is treated as `relative` until a specific point or threshold is met, at which point the element is then treated as `fixed`. At the time of writing this, only Firefox supports this property.

CSS:

```
/*Position relative*/
.element {
  position: relative;
}
/*When the element hits the top of the viewport, it will stay fixed at
20px from the top*/
.element {
  position: sticky;
  top: 20px;
}
```

top

The `top` CSS property is closely tied to the `position` property.

This property specifies the distance of an element from the top of its current location if the element has `position: relative;` declared or from the top of its nearest ancestor when the ancestor has `position: relative;` and the element has `position: absolute;` declared.

If none of the ancestors have `position: relative;` declared, the absolute positioned element will traverse the DOM until it reaches the `<body>` tag, at which point it will position itself at the top of the page regardless of its location in the source HTML.

Negative values are valid.

Description

It supports the following values:

- `auto`: The `auto` keyword is the default value. The browser calculates the top position.

- `Length value`: For the length value, we use one of the following units: `px`, `em`, `in`, `mm`, `cm`, `vw`, and so on.

- `Percentage value`: For the percentage value, we use percentages like `50%`, `85%`, and so on.

CSS:

```
/*auto*/
.element { top: auto; }
/*Length value*/
.element { top: 20px; }
/*Percentage value*/
.element { top: 15%; }
```

bottom

The `bottom` CSS property is closely tied to the `position` property.

This property specifies the distance of an element from the bottom of its current location if the element itself has `position: relative;` declared or from the bottom of its nearest ancestor when the ancestor has `position: relative;` and the element has `position: absolute;` declared.

If none of the ancestors have `position: relative;` declared, the absolute positioned element will traverse the DOM until it reaches the `<body>` tag, at which point it will position itself at the bottom of the page regardless of its location in the source HTML.

Negative values are valid.

Description

It supports the following values:

- `auto`: The auto keyword is the default value for the `bottom` property. The browser calculates the top position.

- `Length value`: For the length value, we use one of the following units: `px`, `em`, `in`, `mm`, `cm`, `vw`, and so on.

- Percentage value: For the percentage value, we use percentages like 50%, 85%, and so on.

CSS:

```
/*auto*/
.element { bottom: auto; }
/*Length value*/
.element { bottom: 20px; }
/*Percentage value*/
.element { bottom: 15%; }
```

left

The left CSS property is closely tied to the position property.

This property specifies the distance of an element from the left of its current location if the element has position: relative; declared or from the left of its nearest ancestor when the ancestor has position: relative; and the element has position: absolute; declared.

If none of the ancestors have position: relative; declared, the absolute positioned element will traverse the DOM until it reaches the <body> tag, at which point it will position itself at the left of the page regardless of its location in the source HTML.

Negative values are valid.

Description

The left property supports the following values:

- auto: The auto keyword is the default value for the left property. The browser calculates the top position.
- Length value: For the length value, we use one of the following units: px, em, in, mm, cm, vw, and so on.
- Percentage value: For the percentage value, we use percentages like 50%, 85%, and so on.

CSS:

```
/*auto*/
.element { left: auto; }
/*Length value*/
.element { left: 20px; }
/*Percentage value*/
.element { left: 15%; }
```

right

The `right` CSS property is closely tied to the `position` property.

This property specifies the distance of an element from the right of its current location if the element has `position: relative;` declared or from the right of its nearest ancestor when the ancestor has `position: relative;` and the element has `position: absolute;` declared.

If none of the ancestors have `position: relative;` declared, the absolute positioned element will traverse the DOM until it reaches the `<body>` tag, at which point it will position itself at the right of the page regardless of its location in the source HTML.

Negative values are valid.

Description

It supports the following values:

- `auto`: The `auto` keyword is the default value for the `right` property. The browser calculates the top position.

- `Length value`: For the length value, we use one of the following units: px, em, in, mm, cm, vw, and so on.

- `Percentage value`: For the percentage value, we use percentages like 50%, 85%, and so on.

CSS:

```
/*auto*/
.element { right: auto; }
/*Length value*/
.element { right: 20px; }
/*Percentage value*/
.element { right: 15%; }
```

vertical-align

The `vertical-align` CSS property controls the vertical positioning of an element in order to align it to another element(s) next to it.

Description

It accepts the following values:

- `baseline`: This is the default value. It aligns the elements to the bottom, exactly at the last line of text regardless of the elements' line height. In other words, it aligns the last line of text to baselines of the elements.

- `bottom`: This aligns the elements' containers to the bottom. The text and line height of the elements are not considered, only the elements' containers to the bottom.

- `Length value`: For the length value, we use one of the following units: `px`, `em`, `in`, `mm`, `cm`, `vw`, and so on. Negative values are valid.

- `middle`: This aligns the elements to their horizontal center based on their vertical midpoint.

- `Percentage value`: For the percentage value, we use percentages like `50%`, `85%`, and so on. Negative values are valid.

- `sub`: This aligns the element to the subscript baseline of the parent container.

- `super`: This aligns the element to the superscript baseline of the parent container.

- `top`: This aligns the elements' containers to the top. The text and line height of the elements are not considered.

- `text-bottom`: This aligns the elements to the bottom based on the parent's text baseline. The line height of the elements is not considered, only the bottom of their containers is considered.

- `text-top`: This aligns the elements to the top based on the parent's text baseline. The line height of the elements is not considered, but the top of their containers is.

Text

Typography is an incredibly powerful design feature and, in reality, styling text with CSS is actually simple.

Let's see how.

color

The `color` CSS property defines the color of the text and looks like this:

```
color: red;
```

Alternatively, it can look like this:

```
color: #f00;
```

Description

The `color` property supports all color modes, HEX, RGB, RGBa, HSL, HSLs, and *color name.*

CSS:

```
/*Color Name*/
.element { color: red; }
/*HEX*/
.element { color: #f00; }
/*RGB*/
.element { color: rgb(255, 0, 0); }
/*RGBa - Color has 50% opacity*/
.element { color: rgba(255, 0, 0, .5); }
/*HSL*/
.element { color: hsl(0, 100%, 50%); }
/*HSLa - Color has 50% opacity*/
.element { color: hsla(0, 100%, 50%, .5); }
```

text-align

The `text-align` CSS property defines the alignment of the text, and it looks like this:

```
text-align: center;
```

Description

The text can be centered, left-aligned, right-aligned, and fully-justified.

The `text-align` property only works on inline elements. If this property is applied to a block-level element, it will not work on the element itself, but it will work on its content.

CSS:

```
/*Centered text*/
.element { text-align: center; }
/*Left aligned text*/
.element { text-align: left; }
/*Right aligned text*/
.element { text-align: right; }
/*Fully justified text*/
.element { text-align: justify; }
```

text-decoration

The text-decoration CSS property defines several formatting features for the text, and it looks like this:

```
text-decoration: underline;
```

Description

The text-decoration property accepts the following keyword values: underline, overline, line-through, none, and blink.

This property is also the shorthand for the text-decoration-line, text-decoration-color, and text-decoration-style properties.

It can accept one, two, or three values in the same declaration if used as a shorthand.

CSS:

```
/*Line above the text*/
.element { text-decoration: overline; }
/*Line under the text*/
.element { text-decoration: underline; }
/*Line across the text*/
.element { text-decoration: line-through; }
/*No underline*/
.element { text-decoration: none; }
/*Blinking text*/
.element { text-decoration: blink; }
/*Shorthand*/

/*Two values*/
.element { text-decoration: underline wavy; }
/*Three values*/
.element { text-decoration: overline dashed yellow; }
```

text-decoration-line

The `text-decoration-line` CSS property defines the type of decoration line that a text can have, and it looks like this:

```
text-decoration-line: overline;
```

Description

The `text-decoration-line` property accepts one, two, or three values in a single declaration. The keyword values are the same as in the `text-decoration` property: `underline`, `overline`, `line-through`, `none`, and `blink`.

CSS:

```
/*One value*/
.element { text-decoration-line: overline; }
/*Two values*/
.element { text-decoration-line: overline underline; }
/*Three values*/
.element { text-decoration-line: overline underline blink; }
```

text-decoration-color

The `text-decoration-color` CSS property defines the type of color the `text-decoration` property can have, and it looks like this:

```
text-decoration-color: red;
```

Description

It supports all color modes: HEX, RGB, RGBa, HSL, HSLs, and *color name*.

CSS:

```
/*Color Name*/
.element { text-decoration-color: red; }
/*HEX*/
.element { text-decoration-color: #f00; }
/*RGB*/
.element { text-decoration-color: rgb(255, 0, 0); }
/*RGBa - Color has 50% opacity*/
.element { text-decoration-color: rgba(255, 0, 0, .5); }
/*HSL*/
.element { text-decoration-color: hsl(0, 100%, 50%); }
/*HSLa - Color has 50% opacity*/
.element { text-decoration-color: hsla(0, 100%, 50%, .5); }
```

text-decoration-style

The `text-decoration-style` CSS property defines the type of line the `text-decoration` property can have, and it looks like this:

```
text-decoration-style: dotted;
```

Description

The `text-decoration-style` property supports the following keyword values: `dashed`, `dotted`, `double`, `solid`, and `wavy`.

CSS:

```
.element {
  text-decoration-style: wavy;
}
```

text-indent

The `text-indent` CSS property defines the space to the left (indentation) of the first line of text in an element, and it looks like this:

```
text-indent: red;
```

Description

It accepts `length` and `percentage` values. Negative values are valid.

CSS:

```
.element {
  text-indent: 50px;
}
```

text-overflow

The `text-overflow` CSS property defines how text that is *bleeding* outside of a container should be clipped, and it looks like this:

```
text-overflow: ellipsis;
```

Description

For this property to work, two other properties should have to be declared: `overflow: hidden;` and `white-space: nowrap;`.

There are two keyword values: `clip` and `ellipsis`.

clip

This cuts the text exactly at the edge of its parent container. This may cause the last character to be clipped at any point showing only a portion of it.

ellipsis

This adds an ellipsis character "…" at the end of the line of text.

CSS:

```
.element {
  white-space: nowrap;
  overflow: hidden;
  text-overflow: ellipsis;
}
```

text-rendering

The `text-rendering` CSS property allows us to define the quality of the text over speed/performance and it looks like this:

```
text-rendering: optimizeLegibility;
```

Description

Depending on the font, when this property is applied, we can see benefits like better kerning and better ligatures.

However, since this CSS property is actually an SVG property and is not part of any CSS standard, browsers and operating systems apply this property at their own discretion, which in turn may not yield the desired improvements from one browser and/or platform to another.

In addition to this, some small screen devices have serious performance issues when they encounter the `text-rendering` CSS property, especially older iOS and Android devices.

Use the text-rendering CSS property with extreme caution and make sure you run all pertinent tests.

This property supports four values: auto, optimizeSpeed, optimizeLegibility, and geometricPrecision.

auto

This is the default value. The browser tries to make the best educated guess as to how to render the text in order to optimize for speed, legibility, and geometric precision.

Remember, each browser interprets this property differently.

optimizeSpeed

The browser favors rendering speed over legibility and geometric detail. It disables kerning and ligatures.

optimizeLegibility

The browser favors legibility over rendering speed and geometric detail. It enables kerning and some optional ligatures. Keep in mind that if the browser tries to use any kerning and ligatures, this information needs to be contained in the font file, otherwise we won't see the effects of such features.

geometricPrecision

The browser favors geometric detail over legibility and rendering speed. This property helps when scaling fonts.

For example, the kerning in some fonts does not scale correctly, so when we apply this value, the browser is capable of keeping the text looking nice.

CSS:

```
.element {
  text-rendering: geometricPrecision;
}
```

text-shadow

The `text-shadow` CSS property applies a drop shadow to the text, and it looks like this:

```
text-shadow: 5px -2vw .2cm black;
```

Description

This property can accept two, three, or four values in the same declaration. The first length value in the declaration will always be for the `x-offset` value and the second length value for the `y-offset` value.

These are the four values it supports: `x-offset`, `y-offset`, `color`, and `blur`.

- `x-offset`: This sets the horizontal distance of the shadow from the text. It's declared as a length value (`px`, `em`, `in`, `mm`, `cm`, `vw`, and so on). Negative values are valid. This value is mandatory.

- `y-offset`: This sets the vertical distance of the shadow from the text. It's declared as a length value (`px`, `em`, `in`, `mm`, `cm`, `vw`, and so on). Negative values are valid. This value is mandatory.

- `color`: This is the color of the text shadow. It supports all color modes: HEX, RGB, RGBa, HSL, HSLs, and *color name*. This value is optional. If it is not specified, the default color will be the same color as the text itself.

- `blur`: This is the **smudge** effect. It's declared as a length value (`px`, `em`, `in`, `mm`, `cm`, `vw`, and so on). It supports all color modes: HEX, RGB, RGBa, HSL, HSLs, and *color name*. This value is optional. If it is not specified, the default value is zero (`0`).

CSS:

```
/*2 values: x-offset and y-offset*/
.element { text-shadow: 5px 10px; }
/*3 values: x-offset, y-offset and blur. Color value defaults to
the font color*/
.element { text-shadow: 5px 2vw 5px; }
/*4 values: x-offset, y-offset, blur and color name*/
.element { text-shadow: 5px -2vw .2cm black; }
```

text-transform

The `text-transform` CSS property controls the capitalization of text, and it looks like this:

```
text-transform: capitalize;
```

Description

The `text-transform` property supports the following four keyword values: `none`, `capitalize`, `uppercase`, and `lowercase`.

- `none`: This is the default value. No capitalization should be applied to the element.
- `capitalize`: This capitalizes the first letter of each word. This property is smart enough to ignore any special characters or symbols at the beginning of the line and capitalize the first letter of the first word.
- `uppercase`: This changes all the text to upper case/capitals. This property can also ignore special characters or symbols at the beginning of the line.
- `lowercase`: This makes all the text lowercase. This property can also ignore special characters or symbols at the beginning of the line.

text-underline-position

The `text-underline-position` CSS property defines the location of the underline on elements that have the `text-decoration` property declared, and it looks like this:

```
text-underline-position: left;
```

Description

The `text-underline-position` property supports four keyword values: `auto`, `left`, `right`, and `under`.

auto

This is the default value. This property allows the browser to decide where to place the underline, whether at the base line of the text or below it.

left

This is only for vertical writing modes. It places the underline to the left of the text.

right

This is only for vertical writing modes. It places the underline to the right of the text.

under

This value places the underline below the base line of the text, so it won't cross any descender (it supports values like q, p, y, and so on). This is helpful in text that has mathematical and chemical formulas that use a lot of subscripts, so the underline doesn't interfere with certain characters and make such formulas confusing or difficult to read.

CSS:

```
.element {
  text-underline-position: left;
}
```

direction

The direction CSS property sets the direction of the text. Left to right for western languages and other similar languages and right to left for languages like Arabic or Hebrew. It looks like this:

```
direction: rtl;
```

Description

The text direction is typically defined in the HTML via the dir attribute rather than via CSS.

The direction CSS property is not inherited by table cells. So, in addition to this, it's recommended to set the direction of the text via the dir attribute in the HTML document to maintain complete cascading support if the CSS files do not load.

This property accepts two keyword values, ltr and rtl, which mean *left to right* and *right to left*.

CSS:

```
.element {
  direction: rtl;
}
```

Tables

Tables, tables, tables! Together with images, HTML tables are the black sheep of web design.

Regardless of being the black sheep, the power of tables is amazing. And if there's an HTML element that does its job well, very well, it's tables.

Let's dig in.

table-layout

The `table-layout` CSS property allows us to define the how HTML tables are laid out on the document, and it looks like this:

```
table-layout: fixed;
```

Description

There are two keyword values: `auto` and `fixed`.

- `auto`: This is the default value. Tables are automatically laid out by the browser this way without declaring anything in the CSS. The table cells adapt to the content inside of them; the behavior of table can sometimes be unpredictable.
- `fixed`: By declaring the width of the table cells from the first row, the rendering of the entire table can be actually faster; anything we do to improve performance is big win for everyone.

Since the table cells have a fixed width, depending on the data in the cells, some information can overflow the cells. Using a combination of the `overflow` properties and `text-overflow: ellipsis;` we can fix the issue.

CSS:

```
table {
  table-layout: fixed;
}
```

border-collapse

The `border-collapse` CSS property tells the table cells to stay separated or get close together (collapse), and it looks like this:

```
border-collapse: collapse;
```

Description

This property supports two keyword values: `separate` and `collapse`.

- `separate`: This is the default value. There is a space between the table cells, and each cell has its own border.

- `collapse`: This value brings the cells together, thus the space is lost and the cells share borders.

CSS:

```
table {
  border-collapse: collapse;
}
```

border-spacing

The `border-spacing` CSS property creates a space between the table cells, and it looks like this:

```
border-spacing: 10px;
```

Description

The `border-spacing` property only works when the `border-collapse: separate;` declaration is present.

CSS:

```
table {
  border-collapse: separate;
  border-spacing: 10px;
}
```

empty-cells

The `empty-cells` CSS property allows us to define how browsers should render borders and backgrounds on cells that have no content in them, and it looks like this:

```
empty-cells: hide;
```

Description

The `empty-cells` property supports two keyword values: `show` and `hide`, which determine whether the borders and background should, or should not, be rendered.

CSS:

```
table {
  empty-cells: hide;
}
```

caption-side

The `caption-side` CSS property defines the location of the table caption, and it looks like this:

```
caption-side: bottom;
```

Description

It supports two keyword values: `top` and `bottom`.

In CSS 2, other keyword values, such as `left` and `right`, were supported, but they were dropped in CSS 2.1.

CSS:

```
caption {
  caption-side: bottom;
}
```

Words and paragraphs

Continuing with typography features, we now enter the word and paragraph properties.

Let's get going.

hyphens

The hyphens CSS property tells the browser how to handle hyphenation when text lines wrap, and it looks like this:

```
hyphens: auto;
```

Description

We can control when to hyphenate and whether to allow it or let it happen under certain conditions.

Hyphenation is language dependent. The language in a document is defined by the lang attribute; browsers will hyphenate if they support the language and a proper hyphenation dictionary is available. Each browser supports hyphenation differently.

 Ensure that the lang attribute is declared either globally on the <html> tag or on the specific element whose content should be hyphenated.

This property supports three keyword values: none, manual, and auto.

- none: Text lines are not broken at line breaks even if there are characters suggesting where a line break should be introduced. Lines will only break on whitespace.

- manual: Text lines are broken at line breaks where there are characters that suggest a line break.

- auto: The browser makes the decision to introduce line breaks as it seem necessary. It bases its decisions on either the presence of hyphenation characters or by language-specific information.

Unicode characters to suggest line break opportunities

There are two Unicode characters that we can use to manually set a potential line break in the text:

```
U+2010 (HYPHEN)
```

This character is called a **hard** hyphen. It's an actual hyphen "-" and it's visible in the text. The browser may or may not break the line on that specific character.

```
U+00AD (SHY)
```

This character is called a **soft** hyphen. Although it is present in the markup, it is not rendered in the text. However, the browser *sees* this character and, if it can use it to create a line break, it will. To insert a soft hyphen, we use ­.

CSS:

```
.element {
  hyphens: auto;
}
```

word-break

The `word-break` CSS property is used to specify whether line breaks should happen within words instead of breaking the lines on a hyphen or a space between words, and it looks like this:

```
word-break: break-all;
```

Description

The `word-break` property is very helpful in situations where a long string, such as a URL, is wider than its parent container, thus disrupting the layout or bleeding off the side. Applying the `word-break` property makes the URL break somewhere along the string.

This property supports three keyword values: `normal`, `break-all`, and `keep-all`.

normal

This is the default value. Line breaks will happen based on default line breaking rules.

break-all

This allows line breaks to happen anywhere, including between two letters.

keep-all

This affects CJK (Chinese, Japanese, and Korean) text only. Here, text words are not broken.

CSS:

```
.element {
  word-break: break-all;
}
```

word-spacing

The `word-spacing` CSS property controls the space between words, and it looks like this:

```
word-spacing: .2em;
```

Description

It supports the following values: a `normal` value, a `length` value and a `percentage` value.

normal

This is the default value. It's defined by the current font or the browser itself, and it resets to the default spacing.

Length value

We use one of the following units when we use a length value: px, em, in, mm, cm, vw, and so on

Percentage value

For a percentage value, we use percentages like 50%, 85%, and so on.

CSS:

```
.element {
  word-spacing: .2em;
}
```

word-wrap

The word-wrap CSS property allows long words to break at an arbitrary point if there are no suggested break points in the long word in question, and it looks like this:

```
empty-cells: hide;
```

Description

This property supports two keyword values: normal and break-word.

- normal: It makes long words break at normal break points
- break-word: It indicates that otherwise unbreakable words can now break at an arbitrary point

CSS:

```
.element {
  word-wrap: break-word;
}
```

line-height

The line-height CSS property defines the distance between lines of text. In typography, the line height is called **leading**.

Description

It supports the following values: a normal value, a number value, a length value, and a percentage value.

- normal: This is the default value. The line height is defined by the browser.
- Number value: This is a number without any unit. This is the recommended method. The reason a unitless value is recommended is because this value can cascade into child elements. Child elements can then scale their line height based on their font size.
- Length value: We use one of the following units when we use the length value: px, em, in, mm, cm, vw, and so on. We can use decimals as well.
- Percentage value: For the percentage value, we use percentages like 50%, 85%, and so on.

CSS:

```
.element {
  line-height: 1.6;
}
```

orphans

Let's understand the term **orphans** first. Orphans are the lines of a paragraph left in the previous page when a block of text is split over two pages. In the Web world, this is seen in text that spans several columns, where the first line of a paragraph is left on the previous column.

From an editorial standpoint, this is very bad. The recommended treatment of orphans is to leave at least three lines on the previous page or column. The more lines, the better.

The orphans CSS property controls the number of lines left on the previous page, and it looks like this:

```
orphans: 3;
```

Description

This property is very useful in print stylesheets, but it can also work when using CSS columns.

It supports a *numeric* value without a unit. This numeric value defines the number of lines left on the previous page or column.

CSS:

```
/*Print stylesheet*/
@media print {
  .element {
    orphans: 3;
  }
}
/*Screen stylesheet*/
.element {
  orphans: 4;
}
```

quotes

The `quotes` CSS property controls the types of quotation marks to use, and it looks like this:

```
quotes: """ """ "'" "'";
```

Description

Quotation marks are added via the `:before` and `:after` pseudo-elements.

The simplest way to add quotation marks is to let the browser do it using the `content` property and the `open-quote` and `close-quote` values: `content: open-quote;` and `content: close-quote;`.

We can also declare the types of quotes we want to use and not let the browser decide. We'll see this in the following CSS example.

Quotes always start and end with a double-character symbol, either " " or, for example, « » in French. But, if there's a nested quote, this nested quote uses a single-character symbol, either ' ' or, for example, ‹ › in French.

This property supports two values: `none` and a `[string string]` value.

none

No quotation marks are generated when using the `content` property.

[string string +] value

Each `string` represents a pair of quotes. The first `string` represents the outer level quotation marks and the second `string` represents the nested level quotation marks.

The + sign means that we can add deeper levels of nested quotation marks, but it's not really necessary, two levels should work for most cases.

Taking into account these considerations, we can then create the following quotation marks with the `quotes` property:

```
CSS:/*Quotation marks inserted by the browser " " and ' '*/
p:before { content: open-quote; }
p:after { content: close-quote; }
/*Custom declared quotation marks*/
p { quotes: """ """ "'" "'"; }
/*French quotation marks*/
p { quotes: "«" "»" "‹" "›"; }
```

widows

Let's clarify the term **widows** first. Widows are the lines of a paragraph that appear on the next page when a block of text is split over two pages. In the Web world, this is seen in text that spans several columns, where the last line of a paragraph appears on the next column.

From an editorial standpoint, this is very bad. The recommended treatment of widows is to leave at least three lines on the next page or column. The more lines, the better.

The `widows` CSS property controls the number of lines that will appear on the next page, and it looks like this:

```
widows: 3;
```

Description

The `widows` property is very useful in print stylesheets, but it can also work when using CSS columns.

It supports a *numeric* value without a unit. This numeric value defines the amount of lines that will appear on the next page or column.

CSS:

```
/*Print stylesheet*/
@media print {
  .element {
    widows: 3;
  }
}
/*Screen stylesheet*/
.element {
  widows: 4;
}
```

writing-mode

The `writing-mode` CSS property defines the direction in which lines of text or even block-level elements are laid out, either vertically or horizontally, and it looks like this:

```
writing-mode: vertical-rl;
```

Description

This property supports three keyword values: `horizontal-tb`, `vertical-rl`, and `vertical-lr`.

horizontal-tb

This means *horizontal, from top to bottom*. The content flows from left to right, top to bottom.

vertical-rl

This means *vertical, from right to left*. The content is turned 90 degrees and flows vertically.

To understand this better, think of this: tilt your head to the right shoulder, at this point, you will be able to read the text flow from top (which was to the right before tilting your head) to bottom (which was to the left before tilting your head).

vertical-lr

This means *vertical, from left to right*. The content is turned 90 degrees and flows vertically.

However, unlike `vertical-rl`, when you tilt your head over your right shoulder, the content flows from bottom (which was to the left before tilting your head) to top (which was to the right before tilting your head), and the text lines are inverted.

CSS:

```
.element {
  writing-mode: vertical-rl;
}
```

letter-spacing

The `letter-spacing` CSS property defines the space between the characters in a line of text, and it looks like this:

```
letter-spacing: 5px;
```

Description

The `letter-spacing` property supports the keyword values: `normal` and `length`.

Negative values are valid.

Unless you understand the legibility and design implications, the default letter spacing in most fonts is ideal and should rarely be changed.

CSS:

```
.element {
  letter-spacing: 5px;
}
```

white-space

The `white-space` CSS property defines how the whitespace inside an element is going to be treated, and it looks like this:

```
white-space: pre-wrap;
```

Description

This property supports five keyword values: `normal`, `nowrap`, `pre`, `pre-wrap`, and `pre-line`.

normal

This is the default value. If we have two or more spaces together, they will collapse into a single space. This is the normal behavior of HTML documents. It will wrap the text where necessary.

nowrap

Multiple spaces will collapse into a single space, and the line will never wrap except if there's a `<br>` tag in the markup.

pre

It's the same as the HTML element `<pre>`, which means **preformatted**. This value will honor all spaces in the text, but will not wrap it unless there's a `<br>` tag in the markup, just like `nowrap` does. This value is great to display short chunks of code.

pre-wrap

This value honors all the spaces and will wrap the text where necessary. This value is great to display long chunks of code.

pre-line

This value collapses multiple spaces into a single space and will wrap the text where necessary.

tab-size

The `tab-size` CSS property allows us to define the number of spaces the tab character can have.

As we saw in the prior `white-space` property description, multiple spaces are collapsed into a single space by default. Therefore, this property will only work on elements that are inside a `<pre>` tag or, have one of the `white-space` properties that honor multiple spaces, `pre` and `pre-wrap`.

This property is great for displaying code.

The default number of spaces the tab character has is 8. But we, web designers and developers, are picky and like either four spaces or sometimes two. With the `tab-size` property, we can modify that default value to anything we want.

Description

The `tab-size` property supports two values: A `numeric` value and a `length` value.

- **Numeric value**: It's just a number without a unit. Negative values are not valid.
- **Length value**: We use one of the following units when we use the length value: px, em, in, mm, cm, vw, and so on.

CSS:

```
pre {
  white-space: pre-wrap;
  tab-size: 4;
}
```

Paging

Although we build sites and applications for the Web, sometimes what we make is also printed.

The following properties will help us make our content more presentable and better handled across pages when printed.

Let's check out these paging properties.

page-break-after

The `page-break-after` CSS property defines where the page breaks after a specific element, and it looks like this:

```
page-break-after: always;
```

Description

What this means is that when a new page break is created, a new page will be printed.

It works only on block-level elements. Also, since this property is used for printing, it's common to see it inside an `@print` media query.

This property supports five keyword values: `always`, `auto`, `avoid`, `left`, and `right`.

- `always`: This value will force a page break after the element.
- `auto`: This is the default value. It creates automatic page breaks.
- `avoid`: This will not allow any page breaks after the element, if possible.
- `left`: This will force one or two page breaks after the element in order to make the following page a left-side page.
- `right`: This will force one or two page breaks after the element in order to make the following page a right-side page.

CSS:

```
@media print {
  .element {
    page-break-after: always;
  }
}
```

page-break-before

The `page-break-before` CSS property works similar to the `page-break-after` CSS property. However, it defines where the page breaks before a specific element, and it looks like this:

```
page-break-before: always;
```

Description

When a new page break is created, a new page will be printed.

It works only on block-level elements. Also, since this property is used for printing, it's common to see it inside an @print media query.

This property supports the same five keyword values as the page-break-before property: always, auto, avoid, left, and right.

Refer to the page-break-before CSS property section for the description of each keyword value.

CSS:

```
@media print {
  .element {
    page-break-before: always;
  }
}
```

page-break-inside

The page-break-inside CSS property also works similar to the page-break-before and page-break-after properties. However, it defines where the page breaks inside a specific element, and it looks like this:

```
page-break-inside: avoid;
```

Description

What this means is that when a new page break is created, a new page will be printed.

This property supports only two keyword values, though: auto and avoid.

- auto: This is the default value. It creates automatic page breaks.
- avoid: This will not allow any page breaks inside the element, if possible.

CSS:

```
@media print {
  .element {wdwqd
    page-break-before: avoid;
  }
}
```

6
CSS Properties – Part 3

Now that we're done with Part 2 of the CSS properties, let's end strongly with Part 3.

Let's do this.

Page box

The page box is a square/rectangular area built out of two parts: the *page area* and the *margin area*.

The page area is where the content sits and all elements are laid out. The margin area sits around the page area and is transparent. If we add a background color to the page area, it will cover the page area and the margin area.

The size of the page box cannot be modified. But if we plan to modify some of the page box properties, we need to include them in an @page rule.

Let's check it out.

bleed

The bleed CSS property is also called the *CSS at-rule descriptor*. It defines how much a page should "*overflow*" or bleed outside the page box. This property only works if marks have been enabled using the marks property, which we'll see next.

Description

The `bleed` property only supports a length value: px, em, in, mm, cm, vw, and so on.

CSS:

```
@page {
  bleed: 5mm;
}
```

marks

The `marks` CSS property, also called a *CSS at-rule descriptor*, defines the types of mark that should be rendered and printed outside the page box.

Since the marks are printed outside the page box, the pages need to be a bit larger in order to have the space to print the marks.

Description

The `marks` property supports three keyword values: crop, cross, and none.

- `crop`: Crop marks define where the page should be cut
- `cross`: Cross marks are used to align the pages
- `none`: Marks will not be displayed

CSS:

```
@page {
  marks: crop cross;
}
```

List

CSS lists are one of the most versatile elements of web design. Aside from being used for making, well, lists, they are also used for navigation, layouts, slideshows, carousels, and so on.

Let's see some of their properties.

list-style

The list-style CSS property is shorthand for the list-style-type, list-style-image, and list-style-position properties. These properties are actually the values that the list-style CSS property supports. We'll see all these properties next.

Description

The list-style property supports one, two, or three values, in any order. If a value isn't declared, it will use its default value.

CSS:

```
/*Default values*/
ul { list-style: disc outside none; }
/*One value, the other two are default*/
ul { list-style: circle; }
/*Two values, the other one is defaults*/
ul { list-style: lower-roman inside; }
/*Three values*/
ul { list-style: decimal outside url(../images/list-bullet.png); }
```

list-style-type

The list-style-type CSS property defines the type of graphic or marker (also called **bullet**) the list will use. The color of the marker is determined by the color of the text of the element it's applied to.

Description

The list-style-type property supports many values, but we'll list 15 of the most commonly used ones: armenian, circle, decimal, decimal-leading-zero, disc, georgian, lower-alpha, lower-greek, lower-latin, lower-roman, none, square, upper-alpha, upper-latin, and upper-roman.

Here's a screenshot with all values except the none value:

armenian	lower-greek
Ա Բ Գ	α, β, γ
circle	lower-latin
○ ○ ○	a, b, c
decimal	lower-roman
1, 2, 3	i, ii, iii
decimal-leading-zero	square
01, 02, 03	■ ■ ■
disc	upper-alpha
● ● ●	A, B, C
georgian	upper-latin
ა ბ გ	A, B, C
lower-alpha	upper-roman
a, b, c	I, II, III

CSS:

```
/*Style: 01, 02, 03...*/
ul { list-style-type: decimal-leading-zero; }
/*Style: α, β, γ...*/
ul { list-style-type: lower-greek; }
/*Style: A, B, C...*/
ul { list-style-type: upper-latin; }
```

list-style-position

The list-style-position CSS property defines the location of the marker.

Description

The list-style-position property supports two keyword values: inside and outside.

inside

When the inside value is applied, the marker will appear inside the text. If there's a line that wraps, the marker will be flushed to the left and not "*sticking out*" like in traditional lists.

outside

The default value is outside. When this value is applied (or not, since it's the default), the marker will appear outside the text. If there's a line that wraps, the marker will be outside the text block. It will "*stick out*" just like in traditional lists.

CSS:

```
ul {
    list-style-position: inside;
}
```

list-style-image

The list-style-image CSS property allows us to replace the default markers with a custom image.

Description

The list-style-image property supports one keyword value and one function: none and url().

- none: No image is used to replace the marker
- url(): It's used to define the path to the image that will replace the marker

CSS:

```
ul {
    list-style-image: url(../images/list-bullet.png);
}
```

Here's a demo in CodePen with all HTML lists: http://tiny.cc/html-lists

Counter

Traditional lists via the <ul>, <ol>, <dl> tags aren't too versatile when it comes to styling the markers. Sometimes, we have to rely on extra markup to accomplish some minimal custom styling.

CSS counters, on the other hand, take styling lists (or any element for that matter) to a whole new level of customization and styling.

Granted, CSS counters rely not only on the properties we're going to see next, but also on the content property and the :before pseudo-element.

Let's check out the properties that make CSS counters so great.

counter-reset

The `counter-reset` CSS property resets the counter by giving it a name, and it looks like this:

```
counter-reset: basic-counter;
```

Description

The `counter-reset` property serves two purposes: resets the counter and defines a name for the counter. The name is later used by the `counter-increment` and `counter()`/`counters()` functions that we'll see later.

I have to admit that the term "`counter-reset`" isn't as intuitive as it should be if it's used to set a name for the counter. Something like "`counter-name`" would be more suitable if you ask me.

This property supports two values: a *name* and a *number*.

We can reference multiple counter resets in the same declaration.

name

We need to give the reset counter a name. This value is required. It can be any name but it needs to adhere to the following conditions:

- It can start with a letter, an underscore "_", or a hyphen "-"
- It can start with a hyphen "-" character but cannot have two consecutive hyphens at the beginning of the name
- The name cannot be just a hyphen"-"; at least one more character is required, but it can't be a number since it would be interpreted as "minus 1" (-1)
- It cannot start with a number or a special character like #, $, !, and so on

number

It's the number that the counter is reset to. The default value is 0 (zero) if no value is declared.

This value is optional unless we want to start the list from a number different than 1. Pay close attention to this value, because the first number in the list is not the number declared in this value.

If we set the value to 1, the list starts at 2. If we leave the value empty, it defaults to 0 (zero) and the list starts at 1. Negative values are valid.

CSS:

```
/*Define a name and counter reset to 0*/
ul { counter-reset: basic-counter; }
/*The counter will start at 3*/
ul { counter-reset: basic-counter 2; }
/*Multiple counters in a single declaration*/
ul { counter-reset: basic-counter-A, basic-counter-B 2; }
```

counter-increment

The counter-increment CSS property increments the value of one or more counters, and it looks like this:

```
counter-increment: basic-counter 2;
```

Description

This property is used with the counter-reset CSS property. This is because the name specified in the counter-reset property is used in the counter-increment CSS property.

As a refresher, remember that the counter name will also be used by the counter()/counters() function.

We can declare multiple counter increments in the same declaration. Multiple counters are separated by a space. This property supports two values: A *name* and a *number*.

name

It can be any name but it needs to adhere to the following conditions:

- It can start with a letter, an underscore "_", or a hyphen "-"
- It can start with a hyphen "-" character but not have two consecutive hyphens at the beginning of the name
- The name cannot be just the hyphen"-"; at least one more character is required, but it can't be a number since it would be interpreted as "minus 1" (-1).
- It cannot start with a number or a special character like #, $, !, and so on.

number

This is the number that the counter is reset to. The default value is 0 (zero) if no value is declared. This value is optional unless we want to start the list from a number different than 1.

Now, the number value defines the amount of increments each counter will have. For example, if we declare 2, then the counter will be 2, 4, 6, and so on. If we declare 3, then the counter will be 3, 6, 9, and so on.

If we do not declare a value, the default increment will be by 1, as in 1, 2, 3, and so on.

Negative values are valid. If we declare -2, then the counter will be -2, -4, -6, and so on.

CSS:

```
/*First, define a name and counter reset to 0 with counter-reset*/
ul { counter-reset: basic-counter; }
/*Then, invoke the counter name and increment every element by 2 (2,
4, 6, and so on.)*/
ul li { counter-increment: basic-counter 2; }
/*Multiple counters*/
ul li { counter-increment: basic-counter 2 roman-numeral-counter;
}
```

Here is a demo in CodePen: http://tiny.cc/css-counters

Drop shadows

There are three ways to create the effect of depth: using lights, shadows, or both.

Let's see how we create box shadows for our containers.

box-shadow

The box-shadow CSS property creates one or several shadows on an element, and it looks like this:

```
box-shadow: 10px 10px 13px 5px rgba(0, 0, 0, .5) inset;
```

Description

The box-shadow property supports three, four, five, or six values in the same declaration: four *length* values, one *color* value, and the *keyword* inset.

Length values

We use one of the following units when we use the length values: px, em, in, mm, cm, vw, and so on.

The four length values are as follows:

- The first value is for the horizontal offset of the shadow. Negative values are valid. This value is required.

- The second value is for the vertical offset of the shadow. Negative values are valid. This value is required.

- The third value is for the blur radius of the shadow. The larger the value, the more spread the shadow becomes, but also more translucent. Negative values are not valid. This value is required.

- The fourth value is for the size of the shadow (or "spread radius"). Negative values are valid. This value is optional.

Color value

This is the fifth value in the list. It supports all color modes: HEX, RGB, RGBa, HSL, HSLs, and *color name*.

This value is optional. If no color is specified, it's up to the browser to decide which color to use. Some browsers may not even display a shadow at all without a color value.

The *color* value can go either at the beginning or at the end of the declaration but never between the length values; otherwise, the box-shadow property won't work.

inset

The sixth value in the list is inset. It creates the shadow inside the container, like a background. However, if there is actually a background color or image, the inset shadow will sit on top of it but under the content without affecting the layout of the child elements of the container.

This value is optional. If this value is not declared, the shadow defaults to displaying the shadow outside the element.

This value can go either at the beginning or at the end of the declaration but never between the length values; otherwise, the box-shadow property won't work.

CSS:

```
/*Left 10px, top 10px, blur 13px, spread 5px, RGBa mode, inside
the element*/
.element {
  box-shadow: 10px 10px 13px 5px rgba(0, 0, 0, .5) inset;
}
```

Display and visibility

Display properties are some of the most widely used CSS features in web design and development.

Let's check them out.

all

The all CSS property resets an element's properties to its default values, and it looks like this:

```
all: initial;
```

Description

The only properties that are not reset are the direction and unicode-bidi properties, which control text direction. This is important because text direction is required to understand the content. If these properties were reset by the all property, then text would run the opposite way it's supposed to, disrupting the message completely.

This property supports three keyword values: `initial`, `inherit`, and `unset`.

- `initial`: This changes all the properties of the element or the element's parent to their initial values.

- `inherit`: This changes all the properties of the element or the element's parent to their parent values.

- `unset`: This changes all the properties of the element or the element's parent to their parent values if those properties are inheritable, otherwise it will change them to their initial value.

CSS:

```
/*Change an element's properties to their initial value*/
.element { all: initial; }
/*Inherit all the initial properties of the parent container*/
.element { all: inherit; }
/*Change the parent's properties to its parent values if
inheritable*/
.parent-container { all: unset; }
```

clear

The `clear` CSS property specifies which side of an element, or both, should not *float*, and it looks like this:

```
clear: both;
```

Description

When the `clear` property is used, it clears the specific box in question, not its child elements. If we wanted to clear its child elements, we'd have to declare the `clear` property on them.

When dealing with float-based grids, this property is crucial to the layout. That is because floated elements are taken out of the document flow. Thus, their parent container will not take them into account and its height isn't determined by those floated elements anymore.

So, adding a clearing declaration (with the display and content properties) to the parent's :after pseudo element "*tells*" the parent element to consider the floated elements and thus the parent container's height is now determined by the tallest floating child element. Let's take a look at the following image:

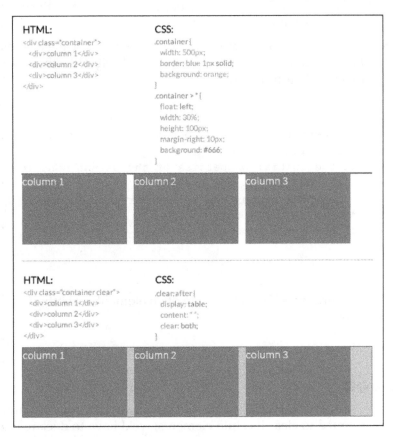

Here is a demo in CodePen: http://tiny.cc/clearing-floats

The clear CSS property supports four values: left, right, both, and none.

- left: It means that floated elements to the left are not allowed.
- right: It means that floated elements to the right are not allowed.
- both: It means that floated elements, both left and right, are not allowed.
- none: This is the default value. No clearing is performed and floating elements to both sides are allowed.

CSS:

```
/*Float an element to the left*/
.element-a { float: left; }
/*Float an element to the right*/
.element-b { float: right; }
/*Clear the floats on the parent container*/
.parent-container:after {
  content: '';
  display: table;
  clear: both;
}
```

display

The display CSS property defines how an element (box) should be or should not be displayed on a page. It looks like this:

```
display: block;
```

Description

This property accepts about 25 keyword values; some of them are very obscure and rarely used. Let's focus on the 15 most relevant ones:

- block
- flex
- grid
- inline
- inline-block
- inline-flex
- none
- table
- table-cell
- table-column
- table-column-group
- table-footer-group
- table-header-group
- table-row
- table-row-group

- `block`: Makes an element be displayed as a block-level element, like a `<div>` tag or an `<h1>` element.

- `flex`: Makes an element be displayed as a block-level element and lays out its content based on the `Flexbox` model.

- `grid`: Makes an element be displayed as a block-level element and lays out its content based on the `Grid` model.

- `inline`: Makes an element be displayed as an inline-level element, like a link `<a>` element.

- `inline-block`: Makes an element be displayed as an `inline-block` element, like a list `<li>` element.

- `inline-flex`: Makes an element be displayed as an inline element and lays out its content based on the `Flexbox` model.

- `none`: Hides the element from rendering in the browser. The element still exists in the markup though. When this value is applied to an element, the browser does not render the element and all its children.

Table-related values

In the following list, all the `table-related` values are mapped to an HTML element. So when any of those values are applied to an element, they make that element behave as a `table-related` element. Let's take a look at the attributes:

- table = `<table>`
- table-cell = `<td>`
- table-column = `<col>`
- table-column-group = `<colgroup>`
- table-footer-group = `<tfoot>`
- table-header-group = `<thead>`
- table-row = `<tr>`
- table-row-group = `<tbody>`

Visit MDN for a list of all the display values: `http://tiny.cc/mdn-display`

CSS:

```
/*Make an element display like a block level element*/
.element { display: block; }
/*Make an element display like a <table> element*/
.element { display: table; }
/*Make an element display like an inline-block element - <li>*/
.element { display: inline-block; }
/*Hide an element an its children*/
.element { display: none; }
```

opacity

The opacity CSS property defines the transparency (opacity) of an element, and it looks like this:

```
opacity: .55;
```

Description

When the opacity property is applied to an element, the element itself and its children are affected.

This property supports a *numeric* value ranging from 0.0 (zero) to 1.0, which is the default value. A value of 0 is completely transparent, as in 0 percent opaque, and 1 is 100 percent opaque, no transparency whatsoever. Decimal numbers are allowed.

This property behaves the same as the alpha channel value used in the RGBa and HSLa color modes.

CSS:

```
/*Make an element 55% opaque. This affects its children as well*/
.element { opacity: .55; }
/*Makes shadow 20% opaque. Same effect as in RGBa and HSLa color
modes.*/
.element { box-shadow: 0 0 5px rgba(0, 0, 0, .2); }
```

filter

The `filter` CSS property allows us to apply visual effects to an `img` element or to the `background` or `border` properties, and it looks like this:

```
filter: blur(10px);
```

Description

A few examples of CSS filters are blur, turning a color image into grayscale or sepia, or changing its opacity.

> This `filter` property is not the same as Microsoft's proprietary `filter` property that only IE supports. Unlike Microsoft's proprietary filters, which are not part of a standard, this CSS `filter` property is part of a work in progress of the W3C.

This property supports 11 values. These values are called CSS functions. Multiple functions can be declared in the same selector, separated by a space.

Let's see the list:

- `blur()`
- `brightness()`
- `contrast()`
- `drop-shadow()`
- `grayscale()`
- `hue-rotate()`
- `invert()`
- `opacity()`
- `saturate()`
- `sepia()`
- `url()`

blur()

This gives a **smudge** effect. Values are declared as *length* values (`px`, `em`, `in`, `mm`, `cm`, `vw` and so on). The higher the value, the more intense the blur effect is (and vice versa).

Percentage and negative values are not allowed, but decimal values are allowed.

brightness()

This modifies the illumination of an image. Values are declared as either a *percentage* or a *number* without a unit, for example, 10% and 0.5%.

A value of 100% leaves the element unchanged, and a value of 0% makes the element completely black. Values over 100% are allowed and create a more intense effect. There is no limit to the value.

Then, a value of 1 leaves the element unchanged; a value of 0 makes the element completely black. Values over 1 are allowed and create a more intense effect. There is no limit to the value. Negative values are not valid.

contrast()

This modifies the contrast of an element. Values are declared as either a *percentage* or a *number* without a unit, for example, 10% and 0.5%.

A value of 100% leaves the element unchanged, and a value of 0% makes the element completely black. Values over 100% are allowed and create a more intense effect. There is no limit to the value.

Then, a value of 1 leaves the element unchanged; a value of 0 makes the element completely black. Values over 1 are allowed and create a more intense effect. There is no limit to the value. Negative values are not valid, and decimal values are allowed.

drop-shadow()

This adds a shadow under the element.

This function works almost exactly the same way as the `box-shadow` property with two differences: the `drop-shadow()` function doesn't support the `spread-radius` attribute or the `inset` values.

Please refer to the `box-shadow` property for a detailed description of all the values.

Additionally, some browsers actually provide hardware acceleration when using this function, which eventually improves performance. You know how it goes, anything we can do to improve performance is always a+1.

grayscale()

This converts an element to grayscale. Values are declared as either a *percentage* or a *number* without a unit, for example, 10% and 0.5%.

A value of 0% leaves the element unchanged; a value of 100% makes the element grayscale. Values over 100% are not allowed.

A value of 0 leaves the element unchanged, and a value of 1 makes the element grayscale. Values over 1 are not allowed. Negative values are not valid, and decimal values are allowed.

hue-rotate()

This applies a hue rotation to the element. It accepts an *angle* value.

The angle value defines the degrees around the color wheel the element sample will be modified to. There isn't a maximum value, however, if the value is larger than 360deg, the rotation will just go around. For example, if we declare 380deg, that would the same as 20deg.

invert()

The invert() function inverts the color of the element. If used in an image, it makes the image look like a film negative.

A value of 100% completely inverts the element's color; a value of 0% leaves the element unchanged. Values over 100% are not allowed.

A value of 1 completely inverts the element's color, and a value of 0 leaves the element unchanged. Values over 1 are not allowed.

Negative values are not valid, and decimal values are allowed.

opacity()

It defines the transparency (opacity) of an element. When this function is applied to an element, the element itself and its children are affected.

This function supports a numeric value ranging from 0 (zero) to 1, which is the default value. A value of 0 is completely transparent, as in 0% opaque, and 1 is 100% opaque, no transparency whatsoever.

Negative values are not valid, and decimal values are allowed.

saturate()

It affects the saturation levels of an element. Values are declared as either a *percentage* or a *number* without a unit, for example, 10% and 0.5%.

The default saturation value of an element is 100%, or 1 if using a unitless number.

A value of 0% completely desaturates the element (it removes all color leaving the element in grayscale); a value of 100% leaves the element unchanged. Values over 100% are allowed, creating a more intense effect.

A value of 0 completely desaturates the element (it removes all color leaving the element in grayscale), and a value of 1 leaves the element unchanged. Values over 1 are allowed, creating a more intense effect.

sepia()

This converts an element to sepia—think of a grayscale image but in shades of brown.

A value of 100% completely turns the element to sepia; a value of 0% leaves the element unchanged. Values over 100% are not allowed.

A value of 1 completely turns the element to sepia; a value of 0 leaves the element unchanged. Values over 1 are not allowed. Negative values are not valid.

url()

It takes the location of an XML file with an SVG filter to be applied to the element. The URL may include an anchor to a specific filter element in the SVG.

CSS:

```
/*Blur*/
.element { filter: blur(10px); }
/*Brightness*/
.element { filter: brightness(20%); }
/*Contrast*/
.element { filter: contrast(10); }
/*Drop shadow*/
.element { filter: drop-shadow(5px 5px 3px rgba(0, 0, 0, .5)); }
/*Grayscale*/
.element { filter: grayscale(.8); }
/*Hue rotation*/
.element { filter: hue-rotate(80deg); }
/*Invert*/
.element { filter: invert(1); }
/*Opacity*/
.element { filter: opacity(.2); }
/*Saturation*/
.element { filter: saturate(300%); }
/*Sepia*/
.element { filter: sepia(100%); }
/*URL*/
.element { filter: url(/images/file.svg#blur); }
/*Multiple filters for a single element*/
.element { filter: sepia(100%) saturate(200%) hue-rotate(50deg); }
```

overflow

The `overflow` CSS property defines how a block level element should handle content that "*bleeds*" (overflows) outside its boundaries, and it looks like this:

```
overflow: auto;
```

Description

A peculiarity of the `overflow` property is that it is used to clear floats and make the parent container expand vertically to wrap the floating elements. This is accomplished by using any of the following values except `visible`.

However, a word of caution. When using the prior technique since it can have unforeseen effects. For example, if a child element has a `box-shadow`, the shadow could be clipped/hidden.

In order for content to overflow, the parent container needs to have a fixed height or the content needs to have a `white-space: nowrap;` declaration applied to it.

This property supports four keyword values: `auto`, `hidden`, `scroll`, and `visible`.

- `auto`: This creates horizontal and vertical scrollbars only if necessary. In other words, if the content overflows the container in any direction, the browser will create scrollbars in one or both axes.
- `hidden`: This will clip/hide the content that's outside of the element. No scrollbars are generated. This value is very popular when clearing floats. Again, be careful when using this value.
- `scroll`: This creates horizontal and vertical scrollbars even if the content isn't overflowing the container.
- `visible`: This is the default value. No content is clipped/hidden and no scrollbars are generated.

CSS:

```css
/*Scroll bars are generated if the content needs them*/
.element {
  white-space: nowrap;
  overflow: auto;
}
/*Clearing floats. Be careful with this technique*/
.parent-container { overflow: hidden; }
```

overflow-x

The overflow-x CSS property behaves the same as the overflow property, and it looks like this:

```
overflow-x: auto;
```

Description

The difference is that the overflow-x property handles the overflow on the *X* axis (horizontally). Please refer to the description of overflow, since the values are the same.

CSS:

```css
.element {
  white-space: nowrap;
  overflow-x: auto;
}
```

overflow-y

The overflow-y CSS property behaves like the overflow property, and it looks like this:

```
overflow-y: auto;
```

Description

The difference is that the overflow-y property handles the overflow on the *Y* axis (vertically). Please refer to the prior description of overflow, since the values are the same.

CSS:

```css
.element {
  height: 100px;
  overflow-y: auto;
}
```

visibility

The `visibility` CSS property defines whether an element is visible or not, and it looks like this:

```
visibility: hidden;
```

Description

The `visibility` property is similar to `display: none;` in terms of hiding an element; the difference is that when hiding an element with the `visibility` property, the space the element occupies still affects the layout. It's just *"invisible"*. With `display: none;`, it's like the element doesn't even exist.

The `visibility` CSS property is not inheritable; in other words, we can still make the child elements visible even if their parent container is not. It can also be used to hide rows and columns in tables.

This property supports three different keyword values: `collapse`, `hidden`, and `visible`.

- `collapse`: This is used only on table elements to remove rows or columns. However, the collapsed/hidden elements still affect the layout since they are still taking up their space. If this value is used in other elements than a table elements, they will be treated as if the value `hidden` is being used.

- `hidden`: This is used to visually hide an element. However, any hidden elements still affect the layout because they are still taking up their space.

- `visible`: This is the default value. It makes an element visible.

CSS:

```
/*Hide an element*/
.element { visibility: hidden; }
/*Parent container visible while child heading is visible*/
.parent-container { visibility: hidden; }
.parent-container h1 { visibility: visible; }
/*Hide table elements*/
tr { visibility: collapse; }
tfoot { visibility: collapse; }
```

z-index

The z-index CSS property defines the stacking order of elements. Think of it in this way: elements sometimes overlap, like a stack of poker cards on a table. The card sitting at the top of the stack has the highest z-index, the card sitting at the bottom has the lowest z-index.

For this property to work, the element has to have a position property declared with any value different from static.

Description

The z-index property accepts two values: a *number* and a *keyword* value.

- **Number value**: This is also called an "**integer**". It's just a number without a unit.

- **auto**: This is the default value. The stacking order of elements is the same as their parent.

CSS:

```
/*Set all cards to relative position so z-index can work*/
.card { position: relative; }
/*The Ace card sits on top of the pile*/
.card.ace { z-index: 2; }
/*The Five card sits at the bottom of the pile*/
.card.five { z-index: 0; }
/*The Queen card sits in between the Ace and the Five*/
.card.queen { z-index: 1; }
```

Masking and clipping

These two features allow us to hide parts of an element in order to show a background image or color, or to give an element a special shape. Both terms can be a bit confusing, so let's see a brief description of each:

- **Clipping** is done with vectors or paths since this CSS feature was taken from the SVG specification. It creates a solid edge between the element and its background.

- **Masking**, on the other hand, uses images/bitmaps. With images, we can have "*feathered*" or blurred edges, whereas with clipping we have straight edges.

Let's check these properties out.

mask

The mask CSS property is the shorthand for the mask-clip, mask-composite, mask-image, mask-mode, mask-origin, mask-position, mask-repeat, and mask-size properties. We'll see each of these in more detail later. The mask property looks like this:

```
mask: url(../images/mask.png) 50% 50% / contain no-repeat border-box;
```

Description

A group of all the prior properties is called a "*mask layer*".

It's recommended to use the shorthand syntax over individual specific properties, since the shorthand resets undeclared properties to their initial values. This is helpful because it makes it easier to override values later in the cascade, thus avoiding specificity issues and potential use of the !important directive.

Additionally, mask-clip and mask-origin use a geometry value. If we declare only one value, then both properties will use that value. With two values, mask-clip will use the first one and mask-origin will use the second one.

As I mentioned before, CSS masks use images, which means that we can reference a bitmap/raster file with a transparency or a background gradient with the linear-gradient() CSS function. We can even create a mask by referencing several images in the same declaration.

There are two types of mask: *alpha* masks and *luminance* masks. We'll see what each of these types of mask are later.

CSS:

```
/*Mask referencing a bitmap file.
We are specifying: mask-image mask-position / mask-size mask-repeat mask-clip
*/
.element {
  mask: url(../images/mask.png) 50% 50% / contain no-repeat
  border-box;
}
/*Mask using the CSS linear-gradient property*/
.element {
  mask: linear-gradient(black 5%, transparent);
}
```

```
/*Mask created by declaring multiple masks*/
.element {
  mask:
    url(../images/mask.png) 50% 50% / contain no-repeat border-
    box,
    linear-gradient(white 5%, transparent);
}
```

mask-clip

The mask-clip CSS property determines the area of the element that will be affected by the mask, and it looks like this:

```
mask-clip: padding-box;
```

Description

This property is similar to the background-clip CSS property. Refer to *Chapter 4, CSS Properties – Part 1*, for more information.

Multiple comma-separated keyword values can be present in the same declaration. Each value represents its corresponding image in the comma-separated values of the mask-image property.

It supports four keyword values: border-box, content-box, padding-box, and no-clip.

- border-box: This is the default value. If the element has any borders, they are seen through the mask.

- content-box: Only the parts of the element that are inside its *content* area are visible through the mask.

- padding-box: If the element has any padding, it will be seen through the mask.

- no-clip: The content is not *clipped*.

CSS:

```
/*Padding box clipping*/
.element { mask-clip: padding-box; }
/*Multiple values*/
.element { mask-clip: padding-box, border-box; }
```

mask-composite

The `mask-composite` CSS property defines how multiple masks with different shapes are combined or *composited* to form a single mask, and it looks like this:

```
mask-composite: intersect;
```

Description

The `mask-composite` property works when `mask-image` is used and at least two mask images are declared. Multiple comma-separated keyword values can be present in the same declaration. Each value represents its corresponding image in the comma-separates values of the `mask-image` property.

The `mask-composite` CSS property supports four keyword values: `add`, `subtract`, `exclude`, and `intersect`.

For example, picture part of triangle over part of a circle, where the triangle is on top and the circle below; the different types of *composite* make different shapes of masks:

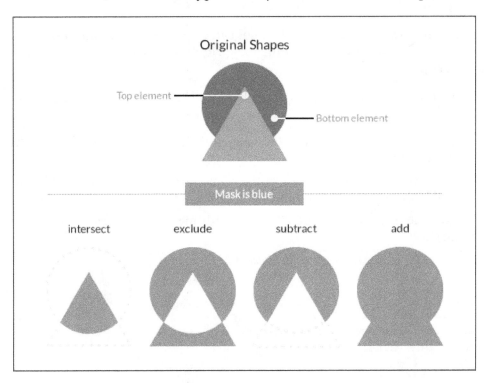

- intersect: The shape of the mask is where the triangle and the circle overlap, or *intersect*. The rest of the shape is discarded.

- exclude: The part where the triangle and the circle intersect is discarded, and the rest of the elements is what makes the mask.

- subtract: Since the triangle is on top, it will *trim* or *crop* the circle, thus leaving a **Pac-Man** shape mask.

- add: The triangle is fused to the circle creating a single shape that will be used as the mask.

CSS:

```
/*Intersect the masks*/
.element { mask-composite: intersect; }
/*Multiple values*/
.element { mask-composite: intersect, exclude; }
```

mask-image

The mask-image CSS property defines the image or images to be used as mask layers on any given element, and it looks like this:

```
mask-composite: intersect;
```

Description

The mask-image property may also refer to <mask> elements in an SVG file. Multiple values are comma-separated. The images can be bitmap files, SVGs, and even CSS gradients that are images as well.

CSS:

```
/*Mask referencing a bitmap*/
.element { mask-image: url(../images/mask.png); }
/*Mask using a CSS gradient*/
.element { mask-image: linear-gradient(black 5%, transparent); }
/*Mask referencing an SVG <mask>*/
.element { mask-image: url(../images/file.svg#mask); }
/*Multiple values*/
.element { mask-image: url(../images/mask.png), linear-
gradient(black 5%, transparent); }
```

mask-mode

The `mask-mode` CSS property defines whether the mask layer is an `alpha` mask or a `luminance` mask. These terms are the actual keyword values, and it looks like this:

```
mask-mode: alpha;
```

Description

Multiple comma-separated keyword values can be present in the same declaration. Each value represents its corresponding image in the comma-separates values of the `mask-image` property.

Alpha masks

Alpha masks use the *alpha channel* of the image. Whatever is transparent will be covered; whatever is opaque will show. Of course, a semi-transparent area on the image is partially covered.

Luminance masks

Luminance masks uses the *luminance values* of the image. Whatever is *white* on the image being used as mask will show. Whatever is black is hidden. Gray areas partially cover the image.

CSS:

```
/*Alpha mask*/
.element { mask-mode: alpha; }
/*Multiple values*/
.element { mask-mode: alpha, luminance; }
```

mask-origin

The `mask-origin` CSS property defines the location or position of the mask layer in relation to the element's box starting at the top left corner, and it looks like this:

```
mask-mode: alpha;
```

Description

The `mask-origin` property works in a similar way to the `background-origin` property. Refer to *Chapter 4, CSS Properties – Part 1*, for more information.

Now, this property can be used in both HTML and SVG elements. However, there are some keyword values that apply to one that won't work on the other.

Multiple comma-separated keyword values can be present in the same declaration. Each value represents its corresponding image in the comma-separates values of the `mask-image` property.

The HTML keyword values are `border-box`, `padding-box`, `margin-box`, and `content-box`.

The SVG keyword values are `view-box`, `fill-box`, and `stroke-box`.

- `border-box`: The origin starts at the top left corner of the border box. It will include the border and any padding (if any is declared) when applying the mask, but it will not go beyond that border.
- `padding-box`: The origin starts at the top-left corner of the padding box. It will include the padding when applying the mask, but it will not include any borders if any are declared.
- `margin-box`: The origin starts at the top-left corner of the margin box. It will include the margin, the border, and the padding when applying the mask.
- `content-box`: The origin starts at the top-left corner of the content box. It will include only the *content* area. No margins, padding, or borders are taken into consideration.
- `view-box`: It uses the closest SVG viewport as a reference box.
- `fill-box`: The position of the mask is relative to the *object bounding box*.
- `stroke-box`: The position of the mask is relative to the *stroke bounding box*.

CSS:

```
/*Content box origin; the mask will exclude borders and paddings*/
.element { mask-origin: content-box; }
/*Multiple values*/
.element { mask-origin: border-box, padding-box; }
```

mask-position

The `mask-position` CSS property defines the starting position of the mask, and it looks like this:

```
mask-position: right top;
```

Description

This property works similar to the `background-position` property. Refer to *Chapter 4, CSS Properties – Part 1*, for more information.

Multiple comma-separated keyword values can be present in the same declaration. Each value represents its corresponding image in the comma-separates values of the `mask-image` property.

The `mask-position` CSS property supports several types of values: four *keyword* values, `top`, `right`, `bottom`, and `left`; a *length* value, `px`, `em`, `in`, `mm`, `cm`, `vw`, and so on; and a *percentage* value such as 50%, 85%, and so on.

CSS:

```
/*Keyword values*/
.element { mask-position: right top; }
/*Length and Percentage values*/
.element { mask-position: 50px 25%; }
/*Multiple values*/
.element { mask-position: right top, 50% 50%; }
```

mask-repeat

The `mask-repeat` CSS property defines whether a mask layer is repeated or not, and it looks like this:

```
mask-repeat: space;
```

Description

This property works in a similar way to the `background-repeat` property. Refer to *Chapter 4, CSS Properties – Part 1*, for more information.

Multiple comma-separated keyword values can be present in the same declaration. Each value represents its corresponding image in the comma-separates values of the `mask-image` property.

It supports six keyword values: `repeat`, `no-repeat`, `repeat-x`, `repeat-y`, `space`, and `round`.

- `repeat`: The mask will be repeated on both the *X* and *Y* axes. This is the default value.
- `no-repeat`: The mask is not repeated on any axis. The mask image is displayed only once.
- `repeat-x`: The mask is repeated on the *X* axis (horizontally).
- `repeat-y`: The mask is repeated on the *Y* axis (vertically).
- `space`: The mask is repeated as many times as possible without being clipped or cut in both the *X* and *Y* axes.

- round: Similar to the space value, the difference is that the mask images are rescaled in order to fit the specified direction.

CSS:

```
/*Space out the mask without clipping it*/
.element { mask-repeat: space; }
/*Repeat the mask in the X-axis (horizontally)*/
.element { mask-repeat: repeat-x; }
/*Multiple values*/
.element { mask-repeat: space, repeat-x; }
```

mask-size

The mask-size CSS property defines the dimensions or size of a mask image, and it looks like this:

```
mask-size: contain;
```

Description

The mask-size property works similar to the background-size property. Refer to *Chapter 4, CSS Properties – Part 1,* for more information.

Multiple comma-separated keyword values can be present in the same declaration. Each value represents its corresponding image in the comma-separates values of the mask-image property.

The mask-position CSS property supports several types of value: a *length* value, a *percentage* value, and three *keyword* values.

- Length value: This is when we use one of the following units: px, em, in, mm, cm, vw, and so on.

- Percentage value: This is when we use percentages such as 50%, 85%, and so on.

- contain: This scales the image mask without distorting its aspect ratio to fit the maximum width or height of the element.

- cover: This scales the image mask and distorts it if necessary in order to fit the maximum width or height of the element. If the image mask is larger on its width or height, it will get clipped.

- auto: This scales the image mask to the actual size of the image's intrinsic proportions without distorting it.

CSS:

```
.element {
  mask-size: contain;
}
```

mask-type

The `mask-type` CSS property is specifically for SVG files. It specifies if an SVG `<mask>` element is an *alpha* or a *luminance* mask.

For the definitions of *alpha* and *luminance* masks, refer to the `mask-mode` property.

mask-border

The `mask-border` CSS property is the shorthand for the `mask-border-source`, `mask-border-mode`, `mask-border-slice`, `mask-border-width`, `mask-border-outset`, and `mask-border-repeat` properties. It looks like this:

```
mask-border: url(../images/border-image-mask.png) 15 / 15px
stretch and so on;
```

Description

Using the shorthand is recommended because any values that are not declared are set to their initial values, thus making it easier to override down the road, minimizing the use of the `!important` directive.

CSS:

```
.element {
  mask-border: url(../images/border-image-mask.png) 15 / 15px
  stretch;
}
```

mask-border-source

The `mask-border-source` CSS property defines an image that is to be used in the `border-image` declaration.

CSS:

```
/*Border image referencing a bitmap file*/
.element { mask-border-image: url(../images/border-image-
mask.png); }
/*Border image using a CSS gradient*/
.element { mask-border-image: linear-gradient(red, transparent); }
```

mask-border-mode

The mask-border-mode CSS property defines whether the image used for the mask is an *alpha* mask or a *luminance* mask.

For the definitions of *alpha* and *luminance* masks, refer to the mask-mode property.

CSS:

```
.element {
  mask-border-mode: luminance;
}
```

mask-border-slice

The mask-border-slice CSS property is used to **slice** the image into nine parts, and it looks like this:

```
mask-border-slice: 40;
```

Description

Think of this example: take a square image and trace two vertical lines and then two horizontal lines. We end up with nine parts, like **Tic-Tac-Toe**, on top of the image.

This property supports one, two, three, or four keyword offset values: top, right, bottom, left, and fill. These values, except fill, can be declared using either a *number* value without a unit or a *percentage* value using 50%, 85%, and so on.

If one value is declared, all four sides take that value. If two values are declared, the first value is for the top and bottom sides, and the second value for the left and right sides. If three values are declared, then the first value is for the top side, the second value is for the left and right sides, and the third for the bottom side. If four values are declared, they correspond to top, right, bottom, and left sides.

When declaring a unitless value with a bitmap image mask, the value is interpreted as if it were pixels.

fill

By default, the center of the image mask is discarded and treated as empty. If this value is present, the center will be taken into account and will become part of the mask.

CSS:

```
/*All sides are offset by 40*/
.element { mask-border-slice: 40; }
/*Top & bottom and left & right values*/
.element { mask-border-slice: 20% 30%; }
/*Make the center of the image part of the mask with top & bottom,
and left & right offsets*/
.element { mask-border-slice: fill 40 25; }
```

mask-border-width

The `mask-border-width` CSS property scales the mask image slices created by the `mask-border-slices` property, and it looks like this:

```
mask-border-width: auto;
```

Description

This `mask-border-width` property supports one, two, three, or four keyword offset values: `top`, `right`, `bottom`, `left`, and `auto`. These values, except `auto`, can be declared using either a *number* value without a unit, or a *percentage* value such as 50%, 85%, and so on.

If one value is declared, all four sides take that value. If two values are declared, the first value is for the top and bottom sides, and the second value for the left and right sides. If three values are declared, then the first value is for the top side, the second value is for the left and right sides, and the third for the bottom side. If four values are declared, they correspond to top, right, bottom and left sides.

auto

It makes the mask border use the intrinsic width or height of the image slice. The browser is the one that decides if it needs to use this intrinsic width or height or not.

CSS:

```
.element {
  mask-border-width: auto;
}
```

mask-border-outset

The `mask-border-outset` CSS property defines the amount the border mask image area extends beyond its border box, and it looks like this:

```
mask-border-outset: 10px;
```

Description

This property supports one, two, three, or four keyword outset values: `top`, `right`, `bottom`, and `left`. These values can be declared using either a *number* value without a unit, or a *length* value using `px`, `em`, `in`, `mm`, `cm`, `vw`, and so on. The *number* value without a unit is a multiplier of the `border-width` property of the element.

If one value is declared, all four sides take that value. If two values are declared, the first value is for the top and bottom sides, and the second value for the left and right sides. If three values are declared, then the first value is for the top side, the second value is for the left and right sides, and the third for the bottom side. If four values are declared, they correspond to the top, right, bottom and left sides.

CSS:

```
/*All four sides have the same value*/
.element { mask-border-outset: 10px; }
/*Top & bottom and left & right values*/
.element { mask-border-outset: 2 6; }
/*Top, left & right, and bottom values*/
.element { mask-border-outset: 5 20px 2; }
```

mask-border-repeat

The `mask-border-repeat` CSS property defines how the image mask for all four sides and the center are scaled and tiled (repeated) around the element, and it looks like this:

```
mask-border-repeat: repeat;
```

Description

The `mask-border-repeat` property supports one or two keyword values. The values are: `repeat`, `round`, `stretch` and `space`.

repeat

The mask border image is tiled (repeated). Under certain circumstances, the image mask can be clipped on the edges showing only part of it.

round

This works in a similar way to `repeat`; the difference is that the image mask is scaled to fit exactly in the allotted distance without clipping the image mask.

stretch

This is the default value. The image mask is stretched to completely fill the area.

space

Similar to `repeat`, but the difference is that if the area isn't filled with complete image masks, it will distribute the space around the tiles.

CSS:

```
.element {
  mask-border-repeat: repeat;
}
```

clip-path

The `clip-path` CSS property is used to partially or fully hide parts of an element and it looks like this:

```
clip-path: url(..images/file.svg#clipping-path);
```

Description

We can say that clip-path is a form of *masking*. The difference is that clipping uses a vector graphic to do the clipping, rather than a bitmap/raster image.

This vector graphic can be a *basic shape* or an *SVG path*.

Note: The clip CSS property is now deprecated due to poor features and limitations with SVGs. The current and widely supported clip-path property is part of the SVG specification, and it's been adopted by the CSS masking module.

The clip-path CSS property combined with the shape-outside property can create amazing layouts. With this combination, we can make a paragraph "*curve*" around a clipped element whose basic shape is also a curve or circle.

This property supports four values: three *functions*: url(), a *shape*, a *geometry box*, and one *keyword* value none.

url()

This CSS function points to an SVG clipPath element that will be used as the clipping path.

CSS:

```
/*Clipping path referenced from an external SVG file*/
.element { clip-path: url(..images/file.svg#clipping-path); }
/*Clipping path referenced from an embedded SVG*/
.element { clip-path: url(#clipping-path); }
```

circle()

This CSS function declares a circle as a clipping path. This function accepts two arguments: a *shape radius* and a *position*.

- **Shape radius**: It defines the radius of the circle. It supports a *length*, a *percentage*, and two *keyword* values. Negative values are not allowed.

  The two keyword values are: closest-side or farthest-side.

  - closest-side: This is the default value. If this value is not declared, the browser will take the length from the center of the circle to its closest side, and create a circle based on that distance. With this, the circle never bleeds or overflows the content, it's always complete.

- ○ `farthest-side`: This value will create a circle by taking the length from the center to the farthest side. This means that if the element has a side that is longer than the other, the circle will bleed or overflow on the opposite sides.

- **Position**: It defines the location of the circle. The position value is preceded by the `at` word. If this value is not declared, the circle will be positioned at the center of the element. The values for this argument are the same as those of the `background-position` property.

CSS:

```
/*Circle 150px wide and tall with location*/
.element { clip-path: circle(150px at 0 50%); }
/*Circle without location is centered on the element*/
.element { clip-path: circle(150px); }
/*Circle defaults to closest-side and is centered on the element*/
.element { clip-path: circle(); }
```

ellipse()

This CSS function declares an ellipse as a clipping path. It takes the same arguments as the `circle()` function; the only difference is that it accepts two radii values, rx and ry, for the shape radius instead of one. rx represents the X axis and ry the Y axis.

CSS:

```
/*Ellipse with location*/
.element { clip-path: ellipse(200px 100px at 0 50%); }
/*Ellipse without location is centered*/
.element { clip-path: ellipse(200px 100px); }
/*No value makes an ellipse that is as wide an tall as the
element*/
.element { clip-path: ellipse(); }
```

inset()

This CSS function defines a rectangle shape inside the element. It can take one, two, three, or four offset values. The syntax is the same as the syntax of the `margin` property.

It supports a *length* and a *percentage* value.

Additionally, the `inset()` function also supports a `border-radius` value, which is optional. This value must be preceded by the term `round` before any *length* or *percentages* are declared.

CSS:

```
/*Inset clip path where all four offset sides have the same
distance*/
.element { clip-path: inset(20px); }
/*Inset clip path with border-radius declared*/
.element { clip-path: inset(5% 20px 10% 40px round 20px); }
```

polygon()

This CSS function is used to declare more various types of shapes, usually irregular ones that are different from a square, a circle or an ellipse.

Coordinate pairs are used to declare the points of the polygon; each pair specifies the position of a point. The first argument represents the X-position and the second argument, the Y-position coordinates. The first and last coordinate points are closed automatically by the browser. The coordinate values are comma-separated and support a *length* or a *percentage* value.

Now, creating polygons by hand is not only a major undertaking but it could be very time consuming. The best solution is to use a tool for the creation process:

- Bennet Feely's *Clippy* (`http://bennettfeely.com/clippy/`)
- *Clip Path Generator* (`http://cssplant.com/clip-path-generator`)

CSS:

```
/*This polygon has 3 pairs of coordinates so it creates a
triangle-shaped clipping path*/
.element { clip-path: polygon(0 0, 0 100%, 100% 0); }
/*Custom polygon (a star) from Bennett Feely's, Clippy tool*/
.element { clip-path: polygon(50% 0%, 63% 38%, 100% 38%, 69% 59%,
82% 100%, 50% 75%, 18% 100%, 31% 59%, 0% 38%, 37% 38%); }
```

none

There is no clipping path that gets created.

Image rendering and orientation

Making sure images display correctly is not only a designer's responsibility, we as web designers and developers also have a say in how images behave and display under particular circumstances.

Let's see how to change the orientation and rendering quality of images with CSS.

image-orientation

The `image-orientation` CSS property defines the rotation that we can apply to an image, and it looks like this:

```
image-orientation: flip;
```

Description

Many images contain information about the settings used to take a picture, such as ISO speed, aperture, shutter speed, camera model, white balance, date and time, and so on. This information is called **EXIF Data**, and CSS uses this data for image orientation purposes. It also supports one or two values in a single declaration.

The `image-orientation` property supports two keyword values and an *angle* value: `from-image`, `flip`, and an *angle* value.

- `from-image`: The image is rotated using the EXIF Data contained in the image.
- `flip`: The image is flipped horizontally; it's reflected. This value should go after the *angle* value.
- `Angle value`: This defines the rotation applied to the image. It uses a number followed by the `deg` unit. This value should go before the `flip` keyword value.

CSS:

```
/*Flip the image horizontally*/
img { image-orientation: flip; }
/*Rotate the image 180 degrees and flip it horizontally*/
img { image-orientation: 180deg flip; }
/*Follow the orientation from the EXIF information in the image*/
img { image-orientation: from-image; }
```

image-rendering

The `image-rendering` CSS property defines what type of algorithm the browser should use to render scaled images, and it looks like this:

```
image-rendering: pixelated;
```

Description

The `image-rendering` CSS property works for either downscaled or upscaled images. This property supports three keyword values: `auto`, `crisp-edges`, and `pixelated`.

- `auto`: This is the default value. When an image is either scaled up or down, this property *smooths* or blurs the image in order to preserve the best appearance possible. However, sometimes this may produce undesired results, depending on the type of image.

- `crisp-edges`: This property does not apply any smoothing or blurring to the image. It preservers its contrast, edges, and color. This property was exclusively created for pixel art.

- `pixelated`: This property only works on images that have been scaled up via the **nearest neighbor** algorithm, which makes the image look like it was made with large pixels. This is useful when scaling up *checkered* patterns like a chessboard, a checkerboard, or QR codes.

CSS:

```
/*Good for checkered patterns or QR codes*/
img { image-rendering: pixelated; }
/*Exclusively for pixel art*/
img { image-rendering: crisp-edges; }
```

User interface

The following properties are directly tied to UX Design but on the frontend. Addressing the following properties from the beginning of any build can go a long way.

Let's check them out.

cursor

The `cursor` CSS property defines the style of the pointer, and it looks like this:

```
cursor: pointer;
```

Description

The `cursor` property is meant to work only in the hover state; this property is not meant to replace the styling of the pointer in its *normal* state.

All operating system have many types of cursors for all types of behaviors, so whenever we need a certain action a cursor for it may already exist.

We can also use custom cursors. Keep in mind the following notes:

- It's recommended that the image of the cursor is 32 x 32 pixels.
- It's required to declare a built-in cursor to act as a fallback in case the custom image(s) doesn't load.
- Legacy versions of IE require an absolute path to the image of the custom cursor.
- We can use `.cur` or `.png` files for custom cursors. However, legacy IEs only support the `.cur` extension.

The `cursor` CSS property can accept one or multiple values in the same declaration.

This property supports the following values: a URL, X and Y coordinates, and 32 keyword values.

A URL (or URI)

The URL is used for custom cursors. It's the path to the image. Several URLs can be defined in the same declaration. Thus, several custom cursors can be used. If declaring more than one URL, the values are comma-separated.

It's mandatory that after the declaration of the URL, a native non-URL value should be declared. This is so if everything else fails, the user can still use the pointer. This value is optional.

X and Y coordinates

The X and Y coordinates are used to align the custom cursor with the right hotspot. These coordinates are just two numbers without a unit and separated only by a space.

Negative numbers are not allowed and the values range from 0 to 32.

32 keyword values

The keyword values use the operating system or browser native cursors. There's practically a cursor for any pointer action.

Here's a list of the 32 keyword values:

- `alias`
- `all-scroll`
- `auto`
- `cell`
- `col-resize`
- `context-menu`
- `copy`
- `crosshair`
- `default`
- `e-resize`
- `ew-resize`
- `help`
- `move`
- `n-resize`
- `ne-resize`
- `nesw-resize`
- `no-drop`
- `none`
- `not-allowed`
- `ns-resize`
- `nw-resize`
- `nwse-resize`
- `pointer`
- `progress`
- `row-resize`
- `s-resize`
- `se-resize`
- `sw-resize`
- `text`
- `vertical-text`
- `w-resize`
- `wait`

Some of the most commonly used values are default, move, pointer, and text:

- default: This sets the default pointer. This is the arrow pointer we all know.
- move: This sets the *move* pointer. It looks like a large plus sign with arrows on all four ends.
- pointer: This sets the pointer to the "hand" icon.
- text: This sets the *text* pointer. It usually looks like a serif capital "I" but taller.

See all cursors in action here: http://tiny.cc/cursor

CSS:

```
/*Custom cursor with absolute path and coordinates*/
.element { cursor: url(/images/cursor.cur) 10 10, default; }
/*Multiple custom cursors with coordinates*/
.element { cursor: url(/images/cursor-1.png) 5 5, url(/images/
cursor-2.png) 0 0, default; }
/*Assign a pointer on the <button> and <select> elements*/
button,
select { cursor: pointer; }
```

pointer-events

The pointer-events CSS property controls when an element in the document can become a target of mouse/touch events, and it looks like this:

```
pointer-events: none;
```

Description

One particularity of pointer-events is as shown in the following example: say we have two containers where they considerably overlap. If we apply pointer-events: none; to the element on top, the clicking/tapping goes through that element and targets the content in the bottom one. Basically, we can select the content on the bottom element even if we're clicking/tapping on the element on top.

This property supports ten keyword values. However, only two are related to HTML; all the rest are part of the SVG specification, which is out of the scope of this guide.

Those HTML-related values are none and auto.

none

No mouse/touch events will act on the element. However, if the element has descendants with `pointer-events` set to a different value, those descendent elements will trigger mouse events.

auto

This is the default value. This acts as if no `pointer-events` were declared.

More info on MDN can be found here: `http://tiny.cc/mdn-pointer-events`

CSS:

```
/*Clicking/tapping on the element won't work*/
.element { pointer-events: none; }
/*Restore the default clicking/tapping behavior to the element*/
.element { pointer-events: auto; }
```

outline

The `outline` CSS property creates a border around an element to provide a visual cue that it's active or has gained focus.

This property is the shorthand for the `outline-color`, `outline-width` and `outline-style` properties. For convenience, it's recommended to always use this shorthand rather than separate properties when declaring `outline`.

The difference between `outline` and `border` is that `outline` doesn't take up space; it's created on top of the content, so the layout is never affected by it.

However, declaring the `outline` values is exactly the same as declaring the `border` values.

Description

The `outline` CSS property supports three values represented in longhand properties: the *color*, the *width*, and the *style*. All three values are required and can appear in any order in the declaration.

- `color`: This is mapped to the `outline-color` property. It's the color of the outline. It supports all color modes: HEX, RGB, RGBa, HSL, HSLs, and color name.

- `width`: This is mapped to the `outline-width` property. It's the thickness of the outline. It supports any length value, such as px, em, in, mm, cm, vw, and so on. Percentage values are not valid.

- style: This is mapped to the outline-style property. It's the type of line to be used. It takes the same values as border: dashed, dotted, double, groove, hidden, inset, none, outset, ridge, and solid.

CSS:

```
.element {
  outline: dotted 2px rgba(0, 0, 0, .5);
}
```

3-Dimensional

The power of CSS is mind-boggling; not only can we do amazing animations just with CSS, but CSS can also handle three-dimensional designs.

Let's check out the properties that allows us to do so.

perspective

The perspective CSS property defines the distance between the screen and the user in the Z axis, and it looks like this:

```
perspective: 300px;
```

Description

Keep in mind that the perspective property is applied to the parent element in order to enable a 3D canvas or space in which its child elements will move.

This property accepts a keyword value, normal, and a *length* value.

normal

No perspective is defined on the parent element.

Length value

This is when we use one of the following units: px, em, in, mm, cm, vw, and so on.

The lower the value, the closer the elements will move in the Z axis. Thus, the perspective is more pronounced. With higher values, the perspective effect is less intense.

CSS:

```
/*Enable perspective for child elements by applying it on the
parent container*/
.parent-container { perspective: 300px; }
/*Child element will move in a 3D plane*/
.parent-container .element { transform: rotateX(170deg); }
```

perspective-origin

The perspective-origin CSS property defines the origin of the X and Y axis of an element in a 3D space, and it looks like this:

```
Perspective-origin: 24% center;
```

Description

This is what is known as the **vanishing point** used by the perspective property. The perspective-origin property supports a combination of three types of value: a *length* value, a *percentage* value, and five keyword values in both X and Y axes.

Length value

This is when we use one of the following units: px, em, in, mm, cm, vw, and so on.

Percentage value

This is when we use percentages like 50%, 85%, and so on.

Keyword values

The five keyword values are top, right, bottom, left, and center.

CSS:

Adding to the prior CSS from the perspective example:

```
/*Enable perspective for child elements by applying it on the
parent container*/
/*The origin of the perspective X and Y-axis*/
.parent-container {
  perspective: 300px;
  perspective-origin: 24% center;
}
/*Child element will move in a 3D plane*/
.parent-container .element { transform: rotateX(170deg); }
```

backface-visibility

The `backface-visibility` CSS property defines whether the rear face of an element that's facing the viewer is visible or not, and it looks like this:

```
backface-visibility: hidden;
```

Description

The `backface-visibility` property supports two self-explanatory keyword values: `visible` and `hidden`.

CSS:

```
And finalizing the prior example from the perspective-origin
example:
/*Enable perspective for child elements by applying it on the
parent container*/
/*The origin of the perspective X and Y-axis*/
.parent-container {
  perspective: 300px;
  perspective-origin: 24% center;
}
/*Child element will move in a 3D plane*/
/*The backside of the element will not be visible*/
.parent-container .element {
  transform: rotateX(170deg);
  backface-visibility: hidden;
}
```

Summary

And this is it for the CSS Properties chapters, quite a ride eh?

In this final chapter we learned how to work with the Page Box's properties like bleed and marks for printing. We also learned that HTML lists are used for many other things like menus, navigation, slideshow, and so on, amongst other things like CSS counters and how to create custom styles for list marks.

Creating the effect of depth with drop shadows is quite easy with the `box-shadow` property. Just don't overdo it. Then we learned about display and visibility, one of the most important features of CSS. In this section we learned how to clear floating elements as well in addition to applying filters to images and elements alike.

Masking and clipping elements isn't so difficult after all, we can use either bitmaps or vectors depending on our specific circumstances. This led us to understand better how to work with images and their orientation.

Then we talked about some User Interface features like creating custom cursors or adapting the default cursor to change depending on its context.

And finally we learned about the 3D properties like `perspective` and `backface-visiblity` that allow us to do pretty cool things with CSS only.

The following chapter about CSS functions is going to take what we've seen so far to a new level of possibilities.

Let's fly.

7
CSS Functions

CSS functions are used for many things in CSS. They can be used to create special types of processes such as creating animations or use custom fonts, or create visual effects like transparencies or transforming elements in both two-dimensional and three-dimensional planes.

Let's see what CSS functions are all about.

Filter

CSS filters allow us to manipulate the color of an element in different ways.

brightness()

The `brightness()` CSS function is used with the `filter` property, and it looks like this:

```
filter: brightness(20%);
```

Description

The `brightness()` function modifies the illumination of an image. Values are declared as either a *percentage* or a *number* without a unit, for example, `10%` and `0.5`

A value of `100%` leaves the element unchanged; a value of `0%` makes the element completely black. Values over `100%` are allowed and create a more intense effect. There is no limit to the value.

A value of `1` leaves the element unchanged; a value of `0` makes the element completely black. Values over `1` are allowed and create a more intense effect. There is no limit to the value. Also, negative values are not valid for either the percentage of the number.

CSS:

```
.element {
  filter: brightness(20%);
}
```

contrast()

The contrast() CSS function is used with the filter property, and it looks like this:

```
filter: contrast(10);
```

Description

The contrast() function modifies the contrast of an element. Values are declared as either a *percentage* or a *number* without a unit, for example, 10% and 0.5.

A value of 100% leaves the element unchanged; a value of 0% makes the element completely black. Values over 100% are allowed and create a more intense effect. There is no limit to the value.

A value of 1 leaves the element unchanged; a value of 0 makes the element completely black. Values over 1 are allowed and create a more intense effect. There is no limit to the value. Also, negative values are not valid and decimal values are allowed for both.

CSS:

```
.element {
  filter: contrast(10);
}
```

grayscale()

The grayscale() CSS function is used with the filter property, and it looks like this:

```
filter: grayscale(.8);
```

Description

The grayscale() function converts an element to shades of black. Values are declared as either a *percentage* or a *number* without a unit, for example, 10% and 0.5.

A value of 0% leaves the element unchanged; a value of 100% makes the element grayscale. Values over 100% are not allowed.

A value of 0 leaves the element unchanged; a value of 1 makes the element grayscale. Values over 1 are not allowed. Also, negative values are not valid for either. Decimal values are allowed

invert()

The invert() CSS function is used with the filter property, and it looks like this:

```
filter: invert(1);
```

Description

The invert() function inverts the color of the element. If used in an image, it makes the image look like a film negative.

A value of 100% completely inverts the element's color; a value of 0% leaves the element unchanged. Values over 100% are not allowed.

A value of 1 completely inverts the element's color; a value of 0 leaves the element unchanged. Values over 1 are not allowed. Also, negative values are not valid. Decimal values are allowed for both.

hue-rotate()

The hue-rotate() CSS function is used with the filter property, and it looks like this:

```
filter: hue-rotate(80deg);
```

Description

The hue-rotate() function applies a hue rotation to the element. It accepts an *angle* value.

The angle value defines the degrees around the color wheel that the element sample will be modified to.

There is no maximum value. However, if the value is larger than 360deg, the rotation will just go around. For example, if we declare 380deg, that would the same as 20deg.

blur()

The `blur()` CSS function is used with the `filter` property, and it looks like this:

```
filter: blur(10px);
```

Description

The `blur()` function gives the *smudge* effect. Values are declared as *length* values (px, em, in, mm, cm, vw and so on). The higher the value, the more intense the blur effect is, and vice versa.

Percentage and negative values are not allowed, but decimal values are.

saturate()

The `saturate()` CSS function is used with the `filter` property, and it looks like this:

```
filter: saturate(300%);
```

Description

It affects the saturation levels of an element. Values are declared as either a *percentage* or a *number* without a unit, for example, `10%` and `0.5`

The default saturation value of an element is `100%`, or `1` if using a unitless number.

A value of `0%` completely desaturates the element (it removes all color leaving the element in grayscale); a value of `100%` leaves the element unchanged. Values over `100%` are allowed creating a more intense effect.

A value of `0` completely desaturates the element (it removes all color leaving the element in grayscale); a value of `1` leaves the element unchanged. Values over `1` are allowed creating a more intense effect.

sepia()

The `sepia()` CSS function is used with the `filter` property, and it looks like this:

```
filter: sepia(100%);
```

Description

The `sepia()` function converts an element to sepia. Think of a grayscale image but in shades of brown.

A value of `100%` completely turns the element to sepia; a value of `0%` leaves the element unchanged. Values over `100%` are not allowed.

A value of `1` completely turns the element to sepia; a value of `0` leaves the element unchanged. Values over `1` are not allowed.

Also, for both, negative values are not valid.

Transforms

CSS transforms have gained such popularity that it's rare not to see some sort of transformation in a website nowadays, for example, button shapes, animations, and layouts.

Let's see the transformation CSS functions.

matrix()

The `matrix()` CSS function is used with the `transform` property, and it looks like this:

```
matrix(0.5, 0, 0.0881635, 0.5, 0, 0);
```

Description

The `matrix()` function is the shorthand for all transformation properties, since they can be combined here. This function is used to define a two-dimensional transformation matrix.

This function requires a solid understanding of math, but in reality this function isn't something to be done by hand. Instead, we can use a tool like Eric Meyer's and Aaron Gustafson's *The Matrix Resolutions* (`http://tiny.cc/eric-meyer-matrix`).

The explanation of the advanced mathematics of the `matrix()` function are beyond the scope of this book. However, for very detailed explanations you can refer to any of these two articles:

- *Understanding the CSS Transforms Matrix* by Tiffany Brown (`http://tiny.cc/css-matrix-1`)
- *The CSS3 matrix() Transform for the Mathematically Challenged* by Zoltan Hawryluk (`http://tiny.cc/css-matrix-2`)

CSS:

```
/*This*/
.element { transform: skew(10deg) scale(.5); }
/*Is the same as this*/
.element { transform: matrix(0.5, 0, 0.0881635, 0.5, 0, 0); }
```

matrix3d()

The `matrix3d()` CSS function is used with the `transform` property, and it looks like this:

```
matrix3d(0.852825, 0.195593, -0.484183, 0, 0.0958426, 0.852825,
0.513326, 0, 0.513326, -0.484183, 0.708564, 0, 0.948667, 1.04842,
0.0291436, 1);
```

Description

Just like the two-dimensional `matrix()` function, the `matrix3d()` function is a shorthand, but this one is for all transform 3D properties in a 4 x 4 grid.

This function requires a solid understanding of math, but in reality this function isn't something to be done by hand. Instead, we can use a tool like Eric Meyer and Aaron Gustafson's *The Matrix Resolutions* (`http://tiny.cc/eric-meyer-matrix`).

CSS:

```
/*This*/
.element { transform: rotate3d(10, 10, 1, 45deg) translate3d(1px,
1px, 0); }
/*Is the same as this*/
.element { transform: matrix3d(0.852825, 0.195593, -0.484183, 0,
0.0958426, 0.852825, 0.513326, 0, 0.513326, -0.484183, 0.708564,
0, 0.948667, 1.04842, 0.0291436, 1); }
```

rotate()

The `rotate()` CSS function is used with the `transform` property, and it looks like this:

```
rotate(10deg);
```

Description

The `rotate()` function rotates an element around a fixed point in a two-dimensional space. It accepts an *angle* value using the `deg`, `grad`, `rad`, or `turn` units. The `deg` unit is most commonly used. Negative values are valid.

CSS:

```
.element {
  transform: rotate(10deg);
}
```

rotate3d()

The `rotate3d()` CSS function is used with the `transform` property, and it looks like this:

```
rotate3d(1, 2, 1, 10deg);
```

Description

The `rotate3d()` function rotates an element around a fixed position in a three-dimensional plane via the X, Y, and Z axes. It accepts four values: three unitless *number* values that correspond to the X, Y, and Z axes, and an *angle* value that defines the amount of rotation.

Positive values rotate the element clockwise in the corresponding axis. Negative values rotate the element counter-clockwise.

CSS:

```
.element {
  transform: rotate3d(1, 2, .5, 10deg);
}
```

rotateX()

The `rotateX()` CSS function is used with the `transform` property, and it looks like this:

```
transform: rotateX(25deg);
```

The previous code is similar to the following code:

```
transform: rotate3d(1, 0, 0, 25deg);
```

Description

The `rotateX()` function rotates an element on the X axes in a three-dimensional plane. It accepts an *angle* value.

Positive values rotate the element clockwise. Negative values rotate the element counter-clockwise.

CSS:

```
/*This*/
.element { transform: rotateX(25deg); }
/*Is the same as this*/
.element { transform: rotate3d(1, 0, 0, 25deg); }
```

rotateY()

The `rotateY()` CSS function is used with the `transform` property, and it looks like this:

```
transform: rotateY(75deg);
```

The previous line is the same as this:

```
transform: rotate3d(0, 1, 0, 75deg);
```

Description

The `rotateY()` function rotates an element on the Y axes in a three-dimensional plane. It accepts an *angle* value.

Positive values rotate the element clockwise. Negative values rotate the element counter-clockwise.

CSS:

```
/*This*/
.element { transform: rotateY(75deg); }
/*Is the same as this*/
.element { transform: rotate3d(0, 1, 0, 75deg); }
```

rotateZ()

The `rotateY()` CSS function is used with the `transform` property, and it looks like this:

```
transform: rotateZ(33deg);
```

Which is the same as this:

```
transform: rotate3d(0, 0, 1, 33deg);
```

Description

The `rotateY()` function rotates an element on the Z axes in a three-dimensional plane. It accepts an *angle* value.

Positive values rotate the element clockwise. Negative values rotate the element counter-clockwise.

CSS:

```
/*This*/
.element { transform: rotateZ(33deg); }
/*Is the same as this*/
.element { transform: rotate3d(0, 0, 1, 33deg); }
```

scale()

The `scale()` CSS function is used with the `transform` property, and it looks like this:

```
.element { transform: scale(2); }
```

Or:

```
.element { transform: scale(2, 3); }
```

Description

The `scale()` function changes the size of an element in a two-dimensional plane to make it larger or smaller. It supports one or two unitless *number* values, where the second value is optional. The number indicates the number of times the element should be scaled. For example, a value of 2 means the element is scaled (enlarged) 200%; a value of 0.5 means the element should be scaled (reduced) to 50%.

The first value represents a horizontal scale and the second a vertical scale. If a single value is declared, it means that both orientations will use the same value.

Negative values are allowed. However, when negative values are used, the element is flipped.

 When an element is scaled, it *does not* affect the layout; it will simply overlap or appear below other elements depending on the source order.

CSS:

```
/*Element is flipped in both directions and scaled to 200% its
size*/
.element { transform: scale(-2); }
/*Element is scaled to 200% horizontally and 300% vertically*/
.element { transform: scale(2, 3); }
```

scale3d()

The `scaled3d()` CSS function is used with the `transform` property, and it looks like this:

```
transform: scale3d(2, 2, 2);
```

Description

The `scaled3d()` function changes the size of an element in a three-dimensional plane via the X, Y, and Z axes to make it larger or smaller.

It supports three unitless *number* values which are required. Negative values are allowed. However, when negative values are used, the element is flipped.

CSS:

```
/*The element is twice the size*/
.element { transform: scale3d(2, 2, 2); }
/*Flipped element in both X and Y-axis while scaled to 300%, and
200% on the Z-axis*/
.element { transform: scale3d(-3, -3, 2); }
```

scaleX()

The `scaleX()` CSS function is used with the `transform` property, and it looks like this:

```
transform: scaleX(-2);
```

Description

The `scaleX()` function changes the size of an element on the *X* axes in a two-dimensional plane. It supports a unitless *number* value.

Negative values are allowed. However, the element is flipped when negative values are used.

CSS:

```
.element {
  transform: scaleX(-2);
}
```

scaleY()

The `scaleY()` CSS function is used with the `transform` property, and it looks like this:

```
transform: scaleY(4);
```

Description

The `scaleY()` function changes the size of an element on the *Y* axes in a two-dimensional plane. It supports a unitless *number* value.

Negative values are allowed. However, the element is flipped when negative values are used.

CSS:

```
.element {
  transform: scaleY(4);
}
```

scaleZ()

The `scaleZ()` CSS function is used with the `transform` property, and it looks like this:

```
transform: scaleZ(3);
```

Description

The `scaleZ()` function changes the size of an element on the *Y* axes in a two-dimensional plane. It supports a unitless *number* value.

Negative values are allowed. However, the element is flipped when negative values are used.

CSS:

```
.element {
  transform: scaleY(4);
}
```

skew()

The `skew()` CSS function is used with the `transform` property, and it looks like this:

```
transform: skew(20deg);
```

Or you can also use the following code:

```
transform: skew(20deg, 25deg);
```

Description

The `skew()` function skews or *tilts* an element on the *X* axes or both the *X* and the *Y* axes on a two-dimensional plane. For example, a parallelogram is a skewed rectangle.

It supports one or two *angle* values: the first one corresponds to the *X* axes and the second one to the *Y* axes. If only one value is declared, the element is skewed only on the *X* axes. Negative values are allowed.

It's recommended that you use either the `skewX()` or `skewY()` functions rather than `skew()`, because `skew()` has been removed from the spec (although most browsers still support it).

CSS:

```
/*One value only affects the element on the X-axis*/
.element { transform: skew(20deg); }
/*Two values affects the element on both X and Y-axis*/
.element { transform: skew(20deg, 25deg); }
```

skewX()

The `@skewX()` CSS function is used with the `transform` property, and it looks like this:

```
transform: skewX(40deg);
```

Description

The @skewX() function skews or *tilts* an element on the X axes on a two-dimensional plane.

It supports one *angle* value. Negative values are allowed.

CSS:

```
.element {
  transform: skewX(40deg);
}
```

skewY()

The @skewY() CSS function is used with the transform property, and it looks like this:

```
transform: skewY(36deg);
```

Description

The @skewY() function skews or *tilts* an element on the Y axes in a two-dimensional plane.

It supports one *angle* value. Negative values are allowed.

CSS:

```
.element {
  transform: skewY(36deg);
}
```

steps()

The steps() timing function is used with the transition-timing-function or the animation-timing-function properties, and it looks like this:

```
transition-timing-function: steps(3);
animation-timing-function: steps(3);
```

Description

The `steps()` timing function divides the transition or the animation into intervals of equal sizes. We can also specify if the steps of transition or animation happen at the `start` or the `end` of the interval. The `end` value is the default in case no argument is declared.

It supports one *numeric* value, or one *numeric* value and an optional value of either `start` or `end`.

The best way to understand how `start` or `end` works is with an example: the animation will begin right away when using `start`, and it will be delayed a bit when using `end`.

CSS:

```
/*The transition is divided in 3 equal size intervals*/
.element { transition-timing-function: steps(3); }
/*The transition is divided in 3 equal size intervals but it will
delay a bit before it starts*/
.element { transition-timing-function: steps(3, end); }
```

translate()

The `translate()` CSS function is used with the `transform` property, and it looks like this:

```
transform: translate(20px);
```

Or like this:

```
transform: translate(20px, -50%);
```

Description

The `translate()` function affects the position of an element on the X axes or both the X and the Y axes on a two-dimensional plane.

It supports both *length* and *percentage* values. Negative values are allowed. It supports one or two *length* and *percentage* values; the first one corresponds to the X-axis and the second one to the Y-axis. If only one value is declared, the element is moved only on the X-axis. Negative values are allowed.

CSS:

```
/*One value, the element is moved on the X-axis only*/
.element { transform: translate(20px); }
/*Two values, the element is moved on the X and Y-axis*/
.element { transform: translate(20px, -50%); }
```

translate3d()

The `translate3d()` CSS function is used with the `transform` property and the `perspective` function, and it looks like this:

```
transform: perspective(100px)  translate3d(75px, 75px, -200px);
```

Description

The `translate3d()` function is used to move an element on the X, Y, and Z axes on a three-dimensional plane.

It supports both *length* and *percentage* values. Negative values are allowed.

In order to be able to see this function work, we need to give the element in question a three-dimensional plane with the `perspective` function, otherwise the `translate3d()` declaration will have no effect.

CSS:

```
.element {
  transform: perspective(100px) translate3d(75px, 75px, -200px);
}
```

translateX()

The `translateX()` CSS function is used with the `transform` property, and it looks like this:

```
transform: translateX(99%);
```

Description

The `translateX()` function is used to move an element on the X axes in a two-dimensional plane.

It supports both *length* and *percentage* values. Negative values are allowed.

CSS:

```
.element {
  transform: translateX(99%);
}
```

translateY()

The `translateY()` CSS function is used with the `transform` property, and it looks like this:

```
transform: translateY(55px);
```

Description

This is used to move an element on the Y axes in a two-dimensional plane. It supports both *length* and *percentage* values. Negative values are allowed.

CSS:

```
.element {
  transform: translateY(55px);
}
```

translateZ()

The `translateZ()` CSS function is used with the `transform` property and with the `perspective` function, and it looks like this:

```
transform: perspective(100px) translateZ(77px);
```

Description

This is used to move an element on the Z axes on a three-dimensional plane. It supports both *length* and *percentage* values. Negative values are allowed.

In order to be able to see this function work, we need to give the element in question a three-dimensional plane with the `perspective` function; otherwise, the `translateZ()` declaration will have no effect.

CSS:

```
.element {
  transform: perspective(100px) translateZ(77px);
}
```

Colors

Colors can make or break a design, there are many ways to go about creating palettes and all that good stuff.

Let's take a look at *HSL(a)* and *RGB(a)*.

hsl() and hsla()

The `hsl()` and `hsla()` CSS functional notations set the color in HSL/HSLa formats, and they look like this:

```
background-color: hsl(10, 20%, 30%);
background-color: hsla(10, 20%, 30%, .5);
```

Description

HSL stands for **Hue, Saturation, and Lightness** (or Luminance). The **a** stands for **Alpha**, which is the alpha channel, with which we declare the transparency of the color.

The `hsl()` function supports three or four values separated by commas. The first value is the hue, which is the base color. This is declared with a unitless *number*. This number represents an angle in degrees (*10 = 10°*) in the color wheel from 0 to 360. So, 0 and 360 are Red, 90 is Yellow-Green, 180 is Cyan, and 270 is Blue-Magenta.

The second value is the saturation, which is basically the amount of the base color. This is declared with a *percentage* value. `0%` means there is no base color at all and it shows gray. `100%` means the base color is full.

The third value is the lightness, also known as luminance. This is basically the brightness of the base color. `0%` means there is no lightness, hence it's black. `100%` is full lightness, hence it looks white. `50%` means the base color is full.

The fourth value is the alpha channel. This is the transparency of the color. It's declared with a unitless *numeric* decimal value from `0` to `1`. Complete transparent is `0`, and `1` is fully opaque.

The great advantage that HSL color naming system has over RGB is that it is more intuitive. Once we choose a base color, we can easily create a palette based on that color by only changing the saturation and lightness values.

You can see the HSL color wheel in CodePen: `http://tiny.cc/hsl-color-wheel`

CSS:

```
/*HSL*/
.element { background-color: hsl(240, 100%, 50%); }
/*HSLa*/
.element { background-color: hsla(10, 20%, 30%, .5); }
```

rgb() and rgba()

The rgb() and rgba() CSS functional notations set the color in RGB/RGBa formats, and they look like this:

```
background-color: rgb(240, 100, 50);
background-color: rgba(10, 20, 30, .5);
```

Description

RGB stands for **Red, Green and Blue**. The *a* stands for **Alpha**, which is the alpha channel with which we declare the transparency of the color.

This supports three or four unitless *numeric* values separated by commas, or three *percentage* values and one unitless *numeric* value. The last value is for the alpha channel.

The *numeric* values range from 0 to 255. The *percentage* values range from 0% to 100%. For example, we can represent the color green as rgb(0, 255, 0) or rgb(0, 100%, 0).

As I just mentioned, the fourth value is the alpha channel. This is the transparency of the color. It's declared with a unitless *numeric* decimal value from 0 to 1. Complete transparent is 0, and 1 is fully opaque.

CSS:

```
/*RGB*/
.element { background-color: rgb(240, 100, 50); }
/*RGBa*/
.element { background-color: rgba(10, 20, 30, .5); }
```

Gradients

For those who didn't know, CSS gradients are actually images. But these images are created by the browser the moment it sees a gradient color declared. The thing with these images is that they are created on the fly and do not cause any HTTP requests.

CSS gradients are so powerful that we can not only create gradients in any direction and various shapes, but we can also create amazing patterns.

With this being said, Lea Verou has an amazing library of CSS patterns created with gradients everyone reading this book should bookmark. Check it out here: `http://tiny.cc/leave-verou-css3-patterns`

Let's see how to create gradients in CSS.

linear-gradient()

The `linear-gradient()` CSS function creates a gradient that transitions from one color to another in a *line*. It looks like this in its simplest form:

```
background-image: linear-gradient(red, blue);
```

Description

We can create linear gradients that obey practically any direction called the *gradient line*: left to right, right to left, top to bottom, bottom to top, diagonal, and at any degree in a 360° radius.

If no direction for the gradient line is specified, the default value is from top to bottom.

Any amount of colors can be declared in the gradient line. Technically speaking, there's no limit, but from a design standpoint we should always try to keep it simple. At least two color values are required.

The `linear-gradient()` function supports all color modes: HEX, RGB, RGBa, HSL, HSLa, and *color name*.

Direction

We can also declare the direction of the gradient line via an *angle* value or four *keyword* values: `to top`, `to bottom`, `to left`, and `to right`.

- `to top`: The gradient will start at the bottom and end at the top
- `to bottom`: The gradient will start at the top and end at the bottom
- `to left`: The gradient will start at the right and end at the left
- `to right`: The gradient will start at the left and end at the right

The *angle* value is defined at the beginning of the declaration and can range from 0 to 360. Larger values wrap around the circumference.

Color stops

We can also define where a color *stops* in the gradient. A color stop is a combination of a *color* value followed by a *stop position*, which is optional.

Stop positions can be declared in any *length* value or a *percentage* value and go after the color value.

 Percentage values are more commonly used due to the fact that they can scale with the element. Pixel values are fine too, but they just don't have the same versatility as relative units.

Color stops are very flexible because they allow us to make solid transitions between colors. This is great for making patterns or other types of graphics that require solid color transitions, like country flags.

When the *stop positions* aren't declared, the browser distributes the gradient colors evenly along the gradient line.

CSS:

```
/*Basic gradient. Colors are distributed evenly along the gradient
line*/
.element { background-image: linear-gradient(red, blue); }
/*Gradient goes from right to left and starts with color red*/
.element { background-image: linear-gradient(to left, red, blue); }
/*Gradient line is diagonal; inclined 170 degrees*/
.element { background-image: linear-gradient(170deg, red, blue); }
/*Gradient with stop positions in percentages*/
.element { background-image: linear-gradient(red 50%, blue 75%); }
/*Gradient with stop positions in pixels*/
.element { background-image: linear-gradient(red 100px, blue
150px); }
/*Colombian flag (yellow, blue and red bands) made with solid
color transitions using stop positions*/
.element { background-image: linear-gradient(#fcd116 50%, #003893
50%, #003893 75%, #ce1126 75%); }
```

radial-gradient()

The `radial-gradient()` CSS function creates a gradient that transitions from one color to another but in circular or elliptical form, and it looks like this in its simplest form:

```
background-image: radial-gradient(orange, green);
```

Description

There are three parts to a radial gradient: its *center*, its *ending shape*, and *color stops*.

The *center* defines the location in the element from which the radial gradient will start; a radial gradient doesn't have to start at the center of an element. The *ending shape* defines if the radial gradient is going to be a circle or an ellipse. The ellipse shape is the default shape if the `circle` keyword isn't declared. The *color stops* are the colors that make the gradient and, if declared, any *stop positions* which are optional. Remember that stop positions can be declared in any *length* value or a *percentage* value and go after the color value.

At least two colors are required to make a radial gradient, or *any* gradient for that matter.

Position

We can define where the center of the radial gradient is located within the element. As I mentioned before, the default position is at the center of the element.

To declare a specific position we use the keyword `at` and define the X and Y axes coordinates. This value should go before any color value is declared but after the *ending shape*.

The X and Y axes coordinates can be declared in any *length* value, a *percentage* value or any of the keyword values, `top`, `right`, `bottom`, and `left`. This is pretty much the same way we declare the `background-position` on an element.

The position requires an *ending shape* to be declared, either `circle` or `ellipse`; otherwise, the declaration is invalid.

Sizing

We can also change the size of the radial gradient. The *size* of the gradient is declared before the *position* but it can go before or after the *ending shape*. It can take one or two values for *width* and *height*. If one value is declared it will be used for both.

The size can be defined with a *length* value, a *percentage* value, or one of four *keyword values*: `closest-corner`, `farthest-corner`, `closest-side`, and `farthest-side`.

- `closest-corner`: The size of the gradient depends on the corner that is closest to the center.
- `farthest-corner`: The size of the gradient depends on the corner that is farthest from the center.

- closest-side: The size of the gradient depends on the side that is closest to the center.

- farthest-side: The size of the gradient depends on the side that is farthest from the center.

CSS:

```
/*Basic gradient. Colors are distributed evenly in the ellipse*/
.element { background-image: radial-gradient(red, blue); }
/*Ending shape declared as circle*/
.element { background-image: radial-gradient(circle, red, blue); }
/*Position declared (only one value). Gradient will start at the
left and center*/
.element { background-image: radial-gradient(circle at left, red,
blue); }
/*Position declared (two values)*/
.element { background-image: radial-gradient(circle at left top,
red, blue); }
/*Position declared with percentages. An ending shape value is
required*/
.element { background-image: radial-gradient(circle at 25% 75%,
red, blue); }
/*Size of the gradient declared in pixels*/
.element { background-image: radial-gradient(100px 50px ellipse at
25% 75%, red, blue); }
/*Size of the gradient relative to the farthest side of the
element. Ending shape can be after or before size*/
.element { background-image: radial-gradient(circle farthest-side
at 25% 75%, red, blue); }
```

repeating-linear-gradient()

The repeating-linear-gradient() CSS function is used to repeat a gradient image, and it looks like this:

```
background-image: repeating-linear-gradient(orange 50px, green
75px);
```

Description

The repeating-linear-gradient() function uses the same syntax and values as the linear-gradient() CSS function, so please refer to that function for a detailed explanation of all the available values.

In order for the `repeating-linear-gradient()` function to work, we need to define *stop positions* on the colors. Otherwise, the repeated gradient will look as if we're just using `linear-gradient()`.

CSS:

```
/*Basic repeating linear gradient*/
.element { background-image: repeating-linear-gradient(orange
50px, green 75px); }
/*Repeating gradient goes from right to left and starts with color
orange*/
.element { background-image: repeating-linear-gradient(to left,
orange 50px, green 75px); }
/*Repeating gradient line is diagonal; inclined 170 degrees*/
.element { background-image: repeating-linear-gradient(170deg,
orange 50px, green 75px); }
/*Repeating gradient with stop positions in percentages*/
.element { background-image: repeating-linear-gradient(orange 25%,
green 50%); }
```

repeating-radial-gradient()

The `repeating-radial-gradient()` CSS function is used to repeat a gradient image, and it looks like this:

```
background-image: repeating-radial-gradient(navy 50px, gray 75px);
```

Description

The `repeating-radial-gradient()` function uses the same syntax and values as the `radial-gradient()` CSS function, so please refer to that function for a detailed explanation of all the available values.

In order for the `repeating-radial-gradient()` function to work, we need to define *stop positions* on the colors. Otherwise, the repeated gradient will look as if we're just using `radial-gradient()`.

CSS:

```
/*Basic repeating linear gradient*/
.element { background-image: repeating-radial-gradient(navy 50px,
gray 75px); }
/*Ending shape declared as circle*/
.element { background-image: repeating-radial-gradient(circle,
navy 50px, gray 75px); }
```

```
/*Position declared (only one value). Gradient will start at the
left and center*/
.element { background-image: repeating-radial-gradient(circle at
left, navy 50px, gray 75px); }
/*Position declared (two values)*/
.element { background-image: repeating-radial-gradient(circle at
left top, navy 50px, gray 75px); }
/*Position declared with percentages. Defaults to ellipse shape
unless 'circle' is specified*/
.element { background-image: repeating-radial-gradient(at 25% 75%,
navy 50px, gray 75px); }
/*Size of the gradient declared in pixels*/
.element { background-image: repeating-radial-gradient(200px 25px
at 25% 75%, navy 50px, gray 75px); }
/*Size of the gradient relative to the farthest side of the
element. Ending shape can be after or before size*/
.element { background-image: repeating-radial-gradient(circle
farthest-side at 25% 75%, navy 50px, gray 75px); }
```

Values

The following CSS functions allow us to declare many custom values for various results. Let's check them out.

attr()

The attr() CSS function allows us to target the value of any HTML attribute and use in CSS, and it looks like this:

```
attr(href);
```

Description

The term **attr** is the abbreviation of the word **attribute**. This CSS function targets an *HTML attribute* and uses its value to accomplish different things via CSS.

In CSS, the attr() function is most commonly used with the content property together with the :after CSS pseudo-element to inject content into the document, but in reality the attr() function can be used with *any* other CSS property.

In HTML, it's very common to use the attr() CSS function to target the HTML5 data- or the href attributes. The attr() function can be used to target *any* HTML attribute.

In CSS3 the syntax of the attr() CSS function is a bit different. It accepts not only an attribute value but it also accepts two more arguments, a *type-or-unit* argument and an *attribute fallback* argument. The *type-or-unit* argument is optional. It tells the browser which type of attribute is in order to interpret its value. The *attribute fallback* argument defines a fallback value in case something goes wrong during the parsing of the main attribute of the element.

> The new CSS3 syntax that includes the *type-or-unit* and the *attribute fallback* arguments is not stable and it may potentially be dropped from the spec. Do your research before deciding to use the new syntax.

A good practice for printing web documents is to print the URL next to the linked element. Another common practice is to use a combination of the attr() CSS function with the content property and the HTML5 data- attribute in responsive tables to inject the content of a cell (usually a heading) next to their corresponding value via CSS, thus saving space.

CSS:

```css
/*Print the links from the content*/
@media print {
    main a[href]:after {
        content: attr(href);
    }
}
```

Responsive Table

When the viewport width is 640px or less, the table will become responsive. This is accomplished by combining the use of the attr() CSS function with the content property and the HTML5 data- attribute.

HTML:

```html
<table>
  <tr class="headings">
    <th>Plan</th>
    <th>Price</th>
    <th>Duration</th>
  </tr>
  <tr>
    <td data-label="Plan:">Silver</td>
    <td data-label="Price:">$50</td>
```

```
      <td data-label="Duration:">3 months</td>
   </tr>
</table>
```

CSS:

```css
/*40em = 640÷16*/
@media (max-width:40em) {
  /*Behave like a "row"*/
  td, tr {
    display: block;
  }
  /*Hide the headings but not with display: none; for
  accessibility*/
  .headings {
    position: absolute;
    top: -100%;
    left: -100%;
    overflow: hidden;
  }
  /*Inject the content from the data-label attribute*/
  td:before {
    content: attr(data-label);
    display: inline-block;
    width: 70px;
    padding-right: 5px;
    white-space: nowrap;
    text-align: right;
    font-weight: bold;
  }
}
```

calc()

The calc() CSS function allows us to perform mathematical calculations, and it looks like this:

```css
width: calc(100% / 2 + 25px);
```

Or like this:

```css
padding: calc(5 * 2px - .25em);
```

Description

We can perform those calculations with addition (+), subtraction (-), division (/), and multiplication (*). It's commonly used to calculate relative values for `width` and `height`, but as you saw, we can use this function with any CSS property.

A few things to consider are that a space is required before and after the addition (+) and subtraction (-) operators, otherwise a subtraction, for example, can be considered to have a negative value, for example, `calc(2.5em -5px)`. This `calc()` function is invalid since the second value is considered a negative value. Space is required after the subtraction (-) operator. However, the division (/) and multiplication (*) operators don't require the spaces.

Now, when doing a division (/), the value on the right *must* be a *number* value. For a multiplication (*) operation, at least one of the values *must* be *number* value as well.

CSS:

```
/* The element's width is half its intrinsic width plus 25px*/
.element { width: calc(100% / 2 + 25px); }
/*The element's padding is 10px minus .25em of the result*/
.element { padding: calc(5 * 2px - .25em); }
```

url()

The `url()` CSS function is used to point to an external resource, and it looks like this:

```
background-image: url(..images/sprite.png);
```

Description

The `url()` function uses the URL value to point or link to a resource. **URL** stands for **Uniform Resource Locator**.

This function is commonly used with the `background` or `background-image` properties, but it can be used with any of the properties that take a URL as a value, like `@font-face`, `list-style`, `cursor`, and so on.

The URL can be quoted using single (' ') or double quotes (" "), or not quoted at all. However, there can't be any combinations of quote styles such as starting with a single quote and ending with a double quote.

Also, double quotes inside a URL that uses single quotes and single quotes inside a URL that uses double quotes *must* be escaped with a backslash (\). Otherwise, it will break the URL.

The URL pointing to the resource can be either absolute or relative. If it's relative, it's relative to the location of the style sheet in the folder structure, not the webpage itself.

The url() CSS function also supports Data URI's, which is basically the code of an image. So instead of pointing the selector to download an image in the /images folder, we can embed the actual image in the CSS.

Be careful with this because although we are reducing an HTTP request (and that's a *huge* win), we might be making the CSS file larger and a bit harder to maintain if the image changes. There can also be potential performance and render-blocking issues.

For more information about Data URIs, you can read this great article by Nicholas Zakas: *Data URIs Explained* (https://www.nczonline.net/blog/2009/10/27/data-uris-explained/).

CSS:

```css
/*Colombian flag icon as Data URI. No quotes in URL*/
.element { background:
url(data:image/png;base64,iVBORw0KGgoAAAANSUhEUgAAABAAAAALCAYAAAB2
4g05AAAABHNCSVQICAgIfAhkiAAAAlwSFlzAAALEgAACxIB0t1+/AAAABx0RVh0U2
9mdHdhcmUAQWRvYmUgRmlyZXdvcmtzIENTNui8sowAAAAkSURBVCiRY3y7leE/AwWA
iRLNw8QARgbO40M8EBnvMgz1dAAAkeoGYBluZXgAAAAASUVORK5CYII=) #ccc no-
repeat center; }

/*Custom cursor. Single quotes in URL*/
.element { cursor: url('../images/cursor.cur') 10 10, default; }

/*Web font. Double quotes in URL*/
@font-face {
  font-family: Franchise;
  src: url("../fonts/franchise.woff") format("woff");
}
```

cubic-bezier()

The cubic-bezier() function allows us to create custom acceleration curves, and it looks like this:

```css
animation-timing-function: cubic-bezier(.42, 0, 1, 1);
```

Description

The `cubic-bezier()` function is used with the `animation-timing-function` and the `transition-timing-function` CSS properties. Most use cases can benefit from the already defined easing functions we mentioned in *Chapter 4, CSS Properties – Part 1*, (ease, `ease-in`, `ease-out`, `ease-in-out`, and `linear`); if you're feeling adventurous, `cubic-bezier()` is your best bet.

Refer to the `animation-timing-function` CSS property in *Chapter 4, CSS Properties – Part 1*, to see what a **Bézier** curve looks like. The `cubic-bezier()` function takes four parameters in the form of:

```
animation-timing-function: cubic-bezier(a, b, a, b);
```

Let's represent all five predefined easing functions with the `cubic-bezier()` function:

- ease: animation-timing-function: cubic-bezier(.25, .1, .25, 1);
- ease-in: animation-timing-function: cubic-bezier(.42, 0, 1, 1);
- ease-out: animation-timing-function: cubic-bezier(0, 0, .58, 1);
- ease-in-out: animation-timing-function: cubic-bezier(.42, 0, .58, 1);
- linear: animation-timing-function: cubic-bezier(0, 0, 1, 1);

I'm not sure about you, but I prefer to use the predefined values.

Now, we can start tweaking and testing each value to the decimal, save, and wait for the live refresh to do its thing. But that's too much wasted time testing if you ask me.

The amazing Lea Verou created the best web app to work with Bézier curves: www. cubic-bezier.com. This is by far the easiest way to work with Bézier curves. I highly recommend this tool.

The Bézier curve image showed previously was taken from the www.cubic-bezier. com website.

CSS:

```
.element {
  width: 300px;
  height: 300px;
  animation: fadingColors 2s infinite alternate 3s none running
  cubic-bezier(.42, 0, 1, 1);
}
```

Miscellaneous

The following CSS functions have no specific category, so we grouped them here in a miscellaneous section.

Let's see what we have.

drop-shadow()

The `drop-shadow()` CSS function works with the `filter` property adds a shadow under the element, and it looks like this:

```
drop-shadow(5px 5px 3px rgba(0, 0, 0, .5));
```

Description

The `drop-shadow()` function works almost exactly the same way as the `box-shadow` property with two differences: the `drop-shadow()` function doesn't support the `spread-radius` or the `inset` values.

Please refer to the `box-shadow` property for a detailed description of all the values. Additionally, some browsers actually provide hardware acceleration when using this function, which eventually improves performance. You know how it goes; anything we can do to improve performance is always a +1.

CSS:

```
.element {
  filter: drop-shadow(5px 5px 3px rgba(0, 0, 0, .5));
}
```

element()

The `element()` CSS function allows us to use any HTML element as a background for another HTML element, and it looks like this:

```
background: element(#other-element);
```

Description

Use cases for the `element()` function are rare, but nonetheless it is available to us (granted, browser support isn't ideal yet).

CSS:

```
.element {
  background: element(#other-element);
}
```

image()

The `image()` CSS function allows us to target an image file to be used as background, and it looks like this:

```
image(../images/sprite.png);
```

Description

The `image()` function is practically the same as the `url()` function and it's considered to be more flexible and ideal to declare background images rather than using the commonly known `url()` function. However, the `image()` CSS function is at risk from being dropped from the spec due to lack of browser support.

CSS:

```
.element {
  background-image: image(../images/sprite.png);
}
```

opacity()

The `opacity()` CSS function works with the `filter` property. It defines the transparency (opacity) of an element, and it looks like this:

```
filter: opacity(.2);
```

Description

When this function is applied to an element, the element itself and its children are affected. This function supports a numeric value ranging from `0` (zero) to `1` which is the default value. A value of `0` is completely transparent, as in `0%` opaque, and `1` is `100%` opaque, no transparency whatsoever. Decimal numbers are allowed but negative values are not.

CSS:

```
.element {
  filter: opacity(.2);
}
```

perspective()

The perspective() CSS function is used with the transform CSS property, and it looks like this:

```
perspective(300px);
```

Description

This value gives three-dimensional perspective to the element. The element in question will react in a three-dimensional plane.

This function works similarly to the perspective property, and the difference is that the perspective() function is used to give perspective to a single element. Hence, it's applied to the *element itself*. The perspective property is good for giving perspective to several elements at once, hence it is applied to the parent element instead.

For example, if we apply the perspective() function to every element on a list, each element will have its own vanishing point. But if we apply the perspective property to the parent container of that list, all elements will share the same vanishing point.

The perspective() function on its own doesn't do much, so in order to see it in action we must combine it with any of the other transform functions like rotate(), rotateX(), or rotateY().

It accepts a *numeric* value with a *length* unit. Negative values are not allowed. The value defines the distance of the Z axes from the user.

The higher the value, the less intense the perspective. This is because the element is farther away from us. However, the lower the value, the more pronounced the perspective looks. This is because the element is closer to us.

CSS:

```
.element {
  transform: perspective(300px) rotateY(45deg);
}
```

rect()

The rect() CSS function is used to create a rectangle-shaped clipping mask with the clip property, and it looks like this:

```
clip: rect(0, 100px, 200px, 0);
```

The clip CSS property is now deprecated due to poor features and limitations with SVGs. The current and widely supported clip-path property is part of the SVG specification and it has been adopted by the CSS Masking module.

Description

This function *only* works with the clip property, and as I mentioned, this property is now deprecated. Also, this CSS function *does not* work with the more modern clip-path CSS property, so the recommendation is to use the inset() CSS function instead.

Refer to the inset() CSS function in *Chapter 6, CSS Properties – Part 3*.

At-rules

CSS *at-rules* start with the @ character and are followed by a keyword or identifier. They always have to end with a semicolon (;) character.

Some of the most popular at-rules are @font-face, which is used to declare custom fonts; @import that is used to import external CSS files (not recommended by the way for performance reasons), and it is also used in some CSS preprocessors to bring external partial files that will eventually get compiled into a single CSS file (recommended method); @media is used to declare media queries in our responsive projects or print style sheets and so on; @keyframes is used to create animations and so on.

At-rules, let's see where they're *at*.

@charset

The @charset() at-rule defines the character encoding to be used by a style sheet, and it looks like this:

```
@charset "UTF-8";
```

Description

We rarely need to define the character encoding in a style sheet as long as it's defined in the HTML. When the browser detects the character encoding in the HTML, it implies that it's the same character encoding for the CSS file(s).

If you like to declare the character encoding in your CSS files, that's fine too. If you plan to use this in a style sheet, it should be the first thing at the top of the file. It cannot have a space character before the @ symbol, or a blank line above it. The *character encoding name* should always be inside quotes, either single (' ') or double quotes (" ").

CSS:

```
/*Correct character encoding directive*/
@charset "UTF-8";
/*Character encoding of the CSS is set to Latin-9 (Western
European languages, with Euro sign)*/
@charset 'iso-8859-15';
/*This is invalid, there is a space before the @ symbol*/
 @charset "UTF-8";
/*This is invalid, character encoding name should be inside single
[''] or double quotes [""]*/
@charset UTF-8;
```

@document()

The @document() at-rule allows to define styles that only apply to a certain pages of a site, and it looks like this in one of its forms:

```
@document url('http://website.com/page.html') { ... }
```

Description

There are four CSS functions that are exclusive to the @document() at-rule: url(), url-prefix(), domain(), and regexp(" "). Multiple functions can be defined in a single declaration.

The values inside the functions can either be declared without quotation marks, or use single (' ') or double quotes (" "). Only the regexp("") function requires the use of double quotes (" ").

- url(): This restricts the styles to a document that matches the URL
- url-prefix(): This restricts the styles to a document that start with the specified URL
- domain(): This restricts the styles to a document's specific domain
- regexp(""): This restricts the styles to a document that match the regular expression

CSS:

```
/*url() function*/
@document url('http://website.com/page.html') { ... }
/*url-prefix() function*/
@document url-prefix("http://website.com/about/") { ... }
/*domain() function*/
@document domain(website.com) { ... }
/*regexp() function*/
@document regexp("https:.*")
/*Multiple functions in a single declaration*/
@document url('http://website.com/page.html') { ... },
  url-prefix("http://website.com/about/") { ... },
  domain(website.com) { ... },
  regexp("https:.*") { ... }
```

@font-face

The @font-face() at-rule is used to define custom fonts to use on a document, and it looks like this in its simplest form:

```
@font-face {
  font-family: Franchise;
  src: url("../fonts/franchise.woff") format("woff");
}
```

Description

The @font-face() at-rule has been around for actually more years than many believe, so our buddy IE6 supports this function. With the @font-face() at-rule, we can target custom font files to use on a website/webapp and extend the design and branding possibilities way beyond system fonts.

One peculiarity of custom fonts is that different versions of each browser support one format but not another or even has its own proprietary font format.

Paul Irish's article *Bulletproof @font-face Syntax*, where the *smiley face* technique originated, is a must-read @font-face article for all web designers and developers (http://tiny.cc/paul-irish-font-face).

The five font formats we need to account for are: WOFF/WOFF2, EOT, TTF, OTF, and SVG.

WOFF/WOFF2

WOFF stands for **Web Open Font Format** and was created by Mozilla. The WOFF format is a *wrapper* for OTF/TTF font formats and it provides better font data compression than any other format, thus making the file(s) smaller.

WOFF2 is basically WOFF on steroids. It provides even more compression, about 30 percent in average and in some cases up to 50 percent more.

All modern browsers support these two formats.

EOT

EOT stands for **Embedded Open Type** and was created by Microsoft. Only old versions of IE (IE6 to IE8) require the use of this font format. No other browsers support this format, so if we don't need to support legacy browsers, we do not need to declare a link to this font format in the `@font-face()` at-rule declaration.

OTF and TTF

OTF and **TTF** stand for **OpenType Font** and **TrueType Font**. These font formats are cross-platform compatible and include advanced layout features and information for expert typographic control. OTF is a newer format and has a few more features than TTF, such as small caps, ligatures, fractions, and so on.

SVG

SVG stands for **Scalable Vector Graphic**. An SVG *font file* doesn't really have a font; it has vector representations of the font. This type of font file is used when old iOS devices need to be supported. However, if this type of font is not declared, the old iOS device will simply use a system font instead, which if you ask me, I'm totally fine with.

The values inside the `@font-face` brackets are called the **font descriptors**. In it, we can declare several values: `font-family`, `src`, `font-variant`, `font-stretch`, `font-style`, `font-weight`, and `unicode-range`.

font-family

This is a required value. It defines the name of the font to be used in the style sheet.

src

This is a required value. It defines the location or URL of the font file(s). Multiple URLs can be defined in the same `src` declaration block to account for the different types of fonts that each browser supports. However, legacy IEs choke when it finds multiple URLs in the same `src` declaration block, so an independent `src` declaration block needs to be declared if support for legacy IEs is required.

In addition to targeting external files with URLs, we can also target locally installed files with the `local()` function.

font-variant

The `font-variant` CSS property turns the targeted text into small caps. In CSS3, it's considered a shorthand and has been extended with new values, which developers rarely use. Refer to *Chapter 5*, *CSS Properties – Part 2*, for more information.

font-stretch

The `font-stretch` CSS property allows us to select a *condensed*, *normal*, or *expanded* face from the font family in question. Refer to *Chapter 5*, *CSS Properties – Part 2*, for more information.

font-weight

The `font-weight` CSS property defines the thickness (weight) of the font. Refer to *Chapter 5*, *CSS Properties – Part 2*, for more information.

unicode-range

The `unicode-range` CSS property descriptor defines a specific range of characters or glyphs that should be downloaded from a font declared in a `@font-face` declaration. This is helpful, for example, when working on a site with different languages. By declaring `unicode-range`, the browser only downloads the specific characters of that language for that page, thus saving bandwidth and optimizing performance.

This property is rarely used.

Google fonts

We can't talk about `@font-face` without talking about **Google Fonts**. Google Fonts is a free web font service that allows us to practically skip all the manual work of creating `@font-face` declaration block in our CSS files by giving us an HTML `<link>` that points to the font(s) we selected.

Check out Google Fonts at `http://tiny.cc/google-fonts`

HTML:

```html
<!-- Google Fonts link snippet -->
<link href='https://fonts.googleapis.com/css?family=Roboto'
rel='stylesheet' type='text/css'>
```

CSS:

```css
/*Full descriptive @font-face declaration*/
@font-face {
  font-family: Roboto;
    /*IE9 Compat Modes*/
  src: url("../fonts/roboto.eot");
    /*Locally installed font file*/
  src: local("roboto"),
    /*IE6-IE8*/
    url("../fonts/roboto.eot?#iefix") format("embedded-
    opentype"),
    /*Modern Browsers*/
    url("../fonts/roboto.woff2") format("woff2"),
    url("../fonts/roboto.woff") format("woff"),
    /*Safari, Android, iOS*/
    url("../fonts/roboto.ttf") format("truetype"),
    /*Old iOS devices*/
    url("../fonts/roboto.svg#roboto") format("svg");
  /*Unicode range*/
  unicode-range: U+0400-045F, U+0490-0491, U+04B0-04B1, U+2116;
  /*Font properties*/
  font-weight: normal;
  font-style: normal;
}

/*Recommended @font-face syntax*/
@font-face {
  font-family: Roboto;
  src: url("../fonts/roboto.woff2") format("woff2"),
       url("../fonts/roboto.woff") format("woff");
  font-weight: normal;
  font-style: normal;
}

/*Usage*/
.element {
  font-family: Roboto, Arial, Helvetica, san-serif;
}
```

@import

The `@import()` at-rule is used to import a style sheet into another, and it looks like this:

```css
@import "other-style-sheet.css";
```

Description

The previous example targets another style sheet with a `string` value. But style sheets can also be imported using the `url()` function.

The `@import` rules should always precede any other rules except the `@charset` rule, otherwise, it will be ignored by the browser.

One thing to take into consideration is cascading. Imported style sheets cascade in the order they are imported. There is also a way to specify the media a specific imported style sheet is for via media queries. If more than one media query is declared, it needs to be separated by commas.

 It's a known fact that using `@import` has a negative impact on performance due to sequential downloading instead of parallel downloads and multiple HTTP requests. Read more about this issue on Steve Souders' article *Don't Use @import* at `http://tiny.cc/steve-souders-avoidimport`

CSS:

```css
/*Import a style sheet in the same directory*/
@import "other-style-sheet.css";
/*Import a style sheet from a relative path*/
@import url(../other-stylesheets/other-style-sheet.css);
/*Import a style sheet with an absolute path*/
@import url(http://website.com/other-stylesheets/other-style-
sheet.css);
/*Define a print style sheet with the 'print' media query*/
@import "print.css" print;
/*Declare multiple media queries*/
@import "screen.css" screen, projection;
/*Use more a commonly known media query*/
@import url("portrait.css") screen and (orientation: portrait);
```

@keyframes

The `@keyframes()` at-rule is used to list CSS properties to be animated, and it looks like this:

```css
@keyframes animationName {
  from {
    /*Animation properties START here*/
  }
  to {
```

```
        /*Animation properties END here*/
    }
}
```

Description

The animation created with the @keyframes at-rule only runs for one cycle. If we want the animation to play over and over, ease-in, ease-out, or show other behavior, we need to declare those properties in the element itself, outside the @keyframes at-rule.

Please refer to the Animation section in *Chapter 4, CSS Properties – Part 1,* for detailed explanations of those CSS properties.

The animation's name (also called an **identifier**) always comes after the @keyframes keyword separated by a space. This animation name will later be referenced with the animation-name or animation shorthand CSS properties.

The beginning and end of an animation can be declared with the two *selector keywords* from and to, or with two *keyframe selectors* 0% and 100%. Negative values are not allowed.

Obviously, we can declare intermediate waypoints but we can only do this using *keyframe selectors*. There is no limit to the amount of properties that can be declared in the @keyframes at-rule. However, some browsers animate properties that the spec says can't be animated, while others follow the spec correctly. Granted, the spec is unclear about some of the definitions, so make sure to run proper tests.

Now the difference between using @keyframes at-rule and the transition property is that with the @keyframes at-rule we have the power of defining what happens in the middle waypoints rather than letting the browser figure it out for us.

Basically, if we have a simple animation, we can just use the transition property. If we have somewhat more complex and elaborate animations, use @keyframes.

CSS:

```
@keyframes diamond {
  from {
    top: 0;
    left: 0;
  }
  25% {
    top: 200px;
    left: -200px;
  }
  50% {
```

```
      top: 400px;
      left: 0;
  }
  75% {
      top: 200px;
      left: 200px;
  }
  to {
      top: 0;
      left: 0;
  }
}

.element {
  position: relative;
  animation: diamond 3s infinite ease-in-out;
}
```

@media

The `@media()` at-rule allows us to define a set of CSS styles that apply to a certain media type, and it looks like this:

```
@media (min-width: 40em) { ... }
```

You can use the preceding code or the following code as well:

```
@media print { ... }
```

Description

This piece of CSS allows us to declare any set of styles to a specific media type.

The two types of directives that come after the `@media()` at-rule, for example, `print` and `screen` and even `(min-width: 40em)` or `(max-width: 40em)`, and they are called **media queries**.

The keywords (`print` and `screen`) are called **media types**. And the ones that test specific features of a **User Agent (UA)** or display are called **media features**.

Media types

Media types are case-sensitive. There are 10 media types that we can use with the `@media()` at-rule:

- `all`: This is meant to work on all devices
- `braille`: This is meant to work with braille tactile-feedback devices
- `embossed`: This is meant to work on braille printers
- `handheld`: This is meant to work with handled "mobile" devices
- `print`: This is meant to work for printing documents
- `projection`: This is meant to work with projectors
- `screen`: This is meant to work with computer screens of all sizes
- `speech`: This is meant to work with speech synthesizers
- `tty`: This is meant to work with teletypes
- `tv`: This is meant to work with televisions

CSS:

```css
/*Viewport width media query*/
@media (min-width: 40em) {
  header { background: red; }
}
/*Print media query*/
@media print {
  *, *:before, *:after { background-image: none; }
}
```

@namespace

The `@namespace()` at-rule is used to define the XML namespaces in a style sheet, and it looks like this:

```css
@namespace url(http://www.w3.org/1999/xhtml);
```

You can use the preceding code or the following code as well:

```css
@namespace svg url(http://www.w3.org/2000/svg);
```

Description

We use the @namespace() at-rule in a CSS document when we need to use selectors that apply or target certain elements in a specific namespace. For example, we can have an embedded SVG file in our HTML document. The thing is that SVGs share common elements with HTML and XML, such as the <a> element. So instead of creating a separate style sheet to target the SVG elements, we can declare an SVG namespace with the @namespace() at-rule to target the <a> elements within the same HTML document, thus we only have to work in one style sheet rather than two (or more).

Now, the @namespace() at-rule is mostly used for legacy XHTML documents where it's necessary to declare a namespace in the <html> element:

```
<html xmlns="http://www.w3.org/1999/xhtml" xml:lang="en" lang="en">
```

With the xmlns directive in place, we can now declare the namespaces in our CSS. Finally, we can then target the <a> elements in the SVG block without affecting the HTML <a> elements.

The URLs are merely to make the markup more readable and easier to understand when someone is reading through it.

XHTML:

```
<!DOCTYPE html PUBLIC "-//W3C//DTD XHTML 1.0 Strict//EN"
"http://www.w3.org/TR/xhtml1/DTD/xhtml1-strict.dtd">
<html xmlns="http://www.w3.org/1999/xhtml" xml:lang="en" lang="en">
```

CSS:

```
@namespace "http://www.w3.org/1999/xhtml";
@namespace svg "http://www.w3.org/2000/svg";

svg|a {
  background: orange;
}
```

@page

The @page() at-rule is used to modify certain properties of a page to get it ready for printing, and it looks like this:

```
@page {
  margin: 2cm;
}
```

Description

When using the @page() at-rule, only a few properties of the page can be changed: margins, widows, orphans, and *page breaks*. Declaring any other types of properties will be ignored.

We can also declare if we want to target *only the first page, all the left pages only,* or *all the right pages only* with the :first, :left and :right pseudo-classes. The @page() at-rule is most commonly used to change the margins.

CSS:

```
/*Affects all pages*/
@page {
  margin: 2cm;
}
/*Affects all left pages only*/
@page :left {
  margin: .8in;
  orphans: 3;
}
/*Affects all right pages only*/
@page :right {
  margin: 15mm;
}
```

@supports

The @supports() at-rule is used to detect a *feature* on a browser, and it looks like this:

```
@supports (display: flex) { ... }
```

Description

Feature detection is something that's usually done with polyfills like **Modernizr**. With the @supports() at-rule, we can accomplish similar results via CSS only.

In order for this function to work properly, we need to specify a *property* and a *value*. There are three keyword operators that we can use with the @supports() at-rule: not, and and or.

The not operator

Just like we can check for features that the browser supports, we can also check for features that the browser *does not* support using the not operator.

The and operator

The and operator allows us to check for multiple CSS properties in the same declaration.

The or operator

A good example of this operator is when we need to check for a vendor-prefixed CSS property in case we need to support legacy browsers. When using this operator, if one of the expressions is true, it will make all other expressions valid as well. Additionally, we can also combine operators when necessary.

CSS:

```css
/*Detect a feature that is supported*/
@supports (transform: translateX(-50%)) {
  .element {
    transform: translateY(-50%)
  }
}
/*Detect a feature that is NOT supported*/
@supports not (transform: translateX(-50%)) {
  .element {
    margin-left: 120px;
  }
}
/*Detect multiple features*/
@supports (transform: translateX(-50%)) and (display: flex) {
  .element {
    transform: translateY(-50%);
    justify-content: space-between;
  }
}
/*Detect at least one feature*/
@supports (-webkit-box-pack: justify) or (-webkit-justify-content:
space-between) or (-ms-flex-pack: justify) or (justify-content:
space-between) {
  .element {
    justify-content: space-between;
  }
}
/*Combining conditions*/
@supports (transform: translateX(-50%)) and ( (-webkit-justify-
content: space-between) or (justify-content: space-between) ) {
  transform: translateY(-50%);
  justify-content: space-between;
}
```

Global CSS keyword values

The following list of keyword values is ubiquitous to web designers and developers, but have you ever wondered what exactly they mean and do?

auto

The `auto` CSS keyword value tells the browser to automatically compute the CSS property's value, and it looks like this:

```
margin: auto;
```

The term **auto** is short for **automatic**. It's not the same as saying 100% because 100% is an actual defined value; `auto` is calculated by the browser.

One of the most common locations to see the keyword `auto` applied is when centering an element horizontally with the `margin` CSS property.

CSS:

```
.element {
  margin: auto;
}
```

I've seen most people use `margin: 0 auto;` to center an element. This is fine, but the value zero (0) can be omitted. `margin: auto;` is enough and yields the same result.

inherit

The `inherit` CSS keyword value makes an element derive/inherit the values of its parent container.

CSS:

```
/*All <h1>'s are red*/
h1 { color: red; }
/*All text in .element is blue*/
.element { color: blue; }
/*Make all <h1>'s inside .element blue*/
.element h1 { color: inherit; }
```

initial

The `initial` CSS keyword value sets the CSS property to its default value as per the CSS spec.

CSS:

```
/*All <h1>'s are red*/
h1 { color: red; }
/*Set the color of all <h1>'s inside .element to the default
(black)*/
.element h1 { color: initial; }
```

none

The `none` CSS keyword value defines the lack of a specific styling.

CSS:

```
.element {
  border: none;
}
```

normal

The `normal` CSS keyword value defines a *standard* value.

CSS:

```
.element {
  font-weight: normal;
}
```

unset

The `unset` CSS keyword is the combination of the `inherit` and `initial` keywords, and it looks like this:

```
color: unset;
```

By combining the `inherit` and `initial` keywords, the `unset` CSS keyword value resets the value of a property.

If an element is inheriting values from its parent container and the unset keyword is declared, then the property's value is reset to the parent container's value (since it's inheriting). But if an element has no parent container and the unset keyword is declared, then its property's value is reset to the default value as per the spec (since it's not inheriting).

CSS:

```
/*All <h1>'s are set to the default color per the spec*/
h1 { color: unset; }
/*All <h1>'s are set to the default color of the parent*/
.element { color: green; }
.element h1 { color: unset; }
```

revert

The revert CSS keyword value is like an *undo* in CSS as it returns the cascade to a previous state and resets the property to the default value defined by the *user agent*. It looks like this:

```
display: revert;
```

This is different from the initial CSS keyword because revert rolls back the cascade and resets the value as per the user agent's *style sheet* value. With initial the value is reset to its default value as per the specification.

For example, the spec says that the default value of display is inline. However, most UAs assign a default value of display: block; to <div>, or display: table; to <table>.

CSS:

```
/*Default value per the spec*/
display: inline;
/*Default value per the UA style sheet*/
div { display: block; }
/*Style defined by the developer/designer*/
.element { display: inline-block; }
/*Style sheet is rolled back and DIV behaves as display: block;*/
div.element { display: revert; }
```

Summary

This conclude the chapters about CSS, pretty interesting stuff eh?

We learned about CSS Filters and how we can modify elements' colors without having to rely on image editing tools. This also applies to CSS Transforms because we can modify the shape and orientation of elements', at least to some extent, quite easily with CSS only.

At the same time we learned about the different ways we can create colors in CSS, and that HSL mode is more intuitive and versatile than any other color mode.

Calculating and declaring different values with the `attr()` or `calc()` functions opens new possibilities in our CSS toolbox, for example, how to make responsive tables.

We now know that to improve performance with drop shadows we can use the `drop-shadow()` function; or to modify the transparency of an element we can use the `opacity()` function; or the perspective of an element with the `perspective()` function.

At-rules now make more sense I'm sure. Additionally, we addressed the different font formats and learned that if we don't need to support legacy IEs we can just use WOFF and WOFF2.

And finally, we got clarification on the all the global CSS keyword values like auto or inherit that we use all the time and never really question what they are and how they work.

Note that you don't have to know and remember all the CSS functions, you need to know where to look — this book.

8

JavaScript Implementations, Syntax Basics, and Variable Types

JavaScript (JS) is a programming language mostly used to produce dynamic and user-interactive webpages. A huge number of websites and all the latest Internet browsers (clients) use and support JavaScript. It is a part of the stack of technologies that every web developer must learn; these include HTML (the content), CSS (the presentation of content), and JS (behavior of the content when a user interacts with the webpage).

Previously, the use of JavaScript was just limited to input validations. For example, it can produce an error message if the user enters invalid information or tries to submit a form with missing information. Now, JS is acknowledged as a fully-fledged programming language that is capable of manipulating with complex calculations and deals with all aspects of a client window. JS enhances the webpage by making it more interactive. For instance, a page with scattered thumbnails can be converted into a pretty stylish image gallery, content of the website can be loaded without forcing the client to reload it over and over, different sorts of error handling can be done in a nice way, user polls can be created and their results can be viewed on a website, and playing with HTML elements on the go and much more is made possible by the power of JavaScript.

JavaScript is quick — real quick. It responds instantly to user actions, such as clicking, double-clicking, resizing, dragging, scrolling, and so on. JavaScript has a syntax that is similar to that of the Java language. The name *JavaScript* causes confusion for many people. Only the syntax of JS resembles the syntax of the Java language. Otherwise, it has nothing to do with the Java programming language at all.

The following are some of the key differences between Java (programming language) and JS (scripting language):

- JavaScript is embedded into HTML and runs in a browser, while Java requires a **Java Virtual Machine (JVM)** for its execution; however, Java applets can run in browsers.

- JavaScript is known as a client-side language as it runs in the browser on the client end, but now, Node.js is the gateway of JS to the server end. On the other hand, Java runs on the web server, for example, **Apache Tomcat**.

- JavaScript is usually interpreted by the client, while Java is compiled and then executed by a JVM.

- JavaScript was created by **Netscape** (now Mozilla) while Java was developed by **Sun Microsystems** (now Oracle).

History of JavaScript

Brendan Eich of Netscape (now Mozilla) developed JavaScript in 1995. Originally, it was named as **Mocha**, later its name was changed to **Livescript**, and finally it was renamed to JavaScript. After its launch, Microsoft introduced **Jscript** — their own version of JavaScript that was included in Internet Explorer. Netscape submitted JavaScript to **European Computer Manufacturers Association(ECMA)** for standardization and specification. The standardized version was named **ECMAScript**. ECMAScript is a trademarked scripting language specification standardized by ECMA International.

The ECMAScript V5 introduced a new mode called the **strict mode**; this brought forward better and thorough error checking to avoid constructs that cause errors. Many ambiguities from the third version were removed and real-world implementations were added.

The ECMAScriptV6 added plenty of new syntax for writing complex programs. It introduced classes and modules extending the semantics from V5. Iterators were also added in this version along with many Python-styled semantics, including proxies, arrow functions, generators and generator expressions, maps, sets, and so on.

Evolution of JavaScript

After the standardization of JavaScript as ECMAScript, the next step was to have complete control over **Document Object Model (DOM)**.

The HTML is parsed into DOM by the web browser's DOM API. DOM is the client understanding of the webpage. All the elements/nodes are converted into a tree-like structure known as **DOM Tree**. The members of this tree can be manipulated on the fly using different methods such as `getElementById()` and `getElementsByName()`. The HTML source we see in developer tools, such as **Inspect Element**, **Fire Bug**, and so on are DOM View. These development tools also help a lot to modify our DOM instantly.

Later, **Asynchronous JavaScript and XML (AJAX)** was introduced to make asynchronous applications. The data was sent to and received from the web server without reloading or refreshing the whole DOM Tree (asynchronously).

As JavaScript advanced, different JS libraries were developed to ease DOM manipulation. Some of the popular libraries are jQuery, Prototype, and Mootools. The primary feature of these libraries is to handle DOM manipulations, animations, and AJAX. The most famous and widely used JS library is jQuery. Furthermore, a server-side version of JavaScript was developed and named **Node.js**.

In this book, you will learn about JavaScript, its history, and its evolution. You will learn about its implementations and syntax. Function references and complete examples for how to use it in different cases are also provided.

JavaScript implementations

As JavaScript and ECMA Script are used in similar context, JavaScript has much more to offer than ECMAScript. It is implemented in the following three parts:

- Core JavaScript (ECMAScript)
- Document Object Model (DOM)
- Browser Object Model (BOM)

Core JavaScript (ECMAScript)

JavaScript supports mobile devices as well as desktop computers; this feature makes it a cross-platform scripting language. However, it is not much useful if used alone, which is why it is used along with server-side languages to make powerful and interactive applications. It can be easily integrated within a web browser environment, enabling users to have complete control over the browser's objects and events.

The core capabilities of JavaScript are also called ECMAScript. ECMAScript is not actually browser-dependent or environment-dependent. It is a set of core language elements that are used in different environments such as **ScriptEase** and **Flash Action Script**. Hence, we can say that ECMA Script contains definitions for the following:

- Language syntax
- Keywords/reserved words
- Data types
- Statements
- Operators
- Control structures
- Objects (for example, array, date, math and so on)

Therefore, ECMAScript defines all of the functions, methods, properties, and objects of a scripting language. Other scripting languages such as JavaScript are implementations of ECMAScript.

ECMAScript is implemented differently in various browsers, after which DOM and BOM are included.

Document object model (DOM)

DOM is an **Application Programming Interface(API)** for HTML and XML documents. It is a logical structure of the web document. It is a hierarchical tree view of the nodes that are present in the document. The browser translates the document into DOM and only understands it. DOM enables developers to take control over the nodes and to make changes to the document on the fly.

For instance, this is a simple webpage:

```
<html>
  <head>
    <title>My Web Document</title>
  </head>
  <body>
    <p>Javascript Reference!<p>
  </body>
</html>
```

Browser object model (BOM)

While DOM deals with the document, **Browser Object Model** (**BOM**) deals with the browser window. BOM enables programmers to perform several actions on the browser window, which is not directly related to and has no impact on the HTML document itself. BOM also deals with the browser objects, such as history, screen, navigator, and location.

 BOM is implemented differently in different clients.

Client-side JavaScript

JavaScript is primarily known as a client-side scripting language. Any language that is used to write programs or scripts that are executed in a client (any web browser such as Internet Explorer, Safari, Google Chrome, Mozilla Firefox, Opera, and so on) is called a **client-side scripting language**. These scripts make your HTML look interactive and dynamic. JavaScript enables user to interact with the web page's content and the client window itself.

Adding JavaScript into a web page

Mostly, JavaScript code is embedded into the HTML within the `<script>` tags and can be viewed by viewing the source of the page. A good practice to embed JavaScript into your page is to place all the scripts in a separate file (a JavaScript file having the `.js` file extension). Then, this file can be included on the page. When the page is interpreted, it will be treated the same as if it was embedded on the same page.

The JavaScript files must be of a .js extension.

Since, the client is expecting HTML all the time, anything else such as styles or scripts have to be enclosed in their specific tags; for example:

```
<style>
  /* all css code */
</style>
<script>
  //all scripts
</script>
```

The JavaScript interpreter is evoked as soon as the browser's rendering engine discovers any <script> tag.

Most of the time, JavaScript lies within the <head> tags of the web document:

```
<html>
  <head>
    <title>My First JavaScript Example</title>
    <script type="text/javascript">
      alert("Hello earthlings!");
    </script>
  </head>
  <body>
  </body>
</html>
```

The type attribute specifies that the code enclosed within these <script> tags is plain code written in JavaScript. It is not compulsory to mention the type attribute. The preceding code can be written without it as well and will work exactly the same.

Although <script>tags can be placed anywhere within an HTML document, another good practice is to place it at the end of the document before closing the</body> tag so that all the pages are loaded before any script executes.

Loading external JavaScript files

Just like external CSS files are included into the web page, JavaScript can also be included into the webpage from external JavaScript files. Let's take a look at the following HTML code:

```
<html>
  <head>
    <title> My First JavaScript Example </title>
    <script src="external_javascript_Planets.js"></script>
  </head>
  <body>
  </body>
</html>
```

The `src` attribute is very similar to that used in the image `<img>` tags. It just mentions the reference path to the external JavaScript files, which are later included into the page. Do not add any other JavaScript code into the `<script>` tags, which import external JS files. If needed, place another `<script>` tag.

Multiple external JS files can also be included, as follows:

```
<html>
  <head>
    <title> My First JavaScript Example </title>
    <script src="external_javascript_Moon.js"></script>
    <script src="external_javascript_Sun.js"></script>
    <script src="external_javascript)Stars.js"></script>
  </head>
  <body>
  </body>
</html>
```

> In cases where external JavaScript libraries, such as jQuery and MooTools are used, the order in which the files are included has to be taken care of.

Writing our first program in JavaScript

Don't worry; it is not at all an alien language. It is a high-level language and can be understood very easily as its statements, keywords, and other syntax is based on basic English. The simplest way to learn any programming language is to jump into it and play with its code. To get your feet wet in JavaScript, we will write a very basic JavaScript program.

Prerequisites

The following are the prerequisites that are required to write our first JavaScript program:

- A web browser
- A text/code editor
- A web document

How to do it

1. Create a `index.html` file in any code editor you are comfortable with. Copy and paste the following code into your document. It is a simple HTML code:

```html
<html>
  <head>
    <title> My First JavaScript Example </title>
  </head>
  <body>
    <h1>The Planetary System</h1>
  </body>
</html>
```

2. Create a `<script>` tag after a `<title>` tag before closing the`</head>` tag in the head section:

```html
<html>
  <head>
    <title> My First JavaScript Example </title>
    <script type="text/javascript"></script>
  </head>
  <body>
    <h1>The Planetary System</h1>
  </body>
</html>
```

3. Insert `alert("hello world"); document.write('<h2>This text has been added by JavaScript!</h2>');` within the script tags.

4. The `alert` attribute is a JavaScript function that creates a popup with the message written inside the quotes and parentheses. The message is treated as a string passed to the alert function. Similarly, `document.write` is a JavaScript function that outputs the given string on the webpage.

```
<html>
  <head>
    <title> My First JavaScript Example </title>
    <script type="text/javascript">
      alert("Hello Earthlings");
      document.write('<h2>Greetings from Mars!</h2>');
    </script>
  </head>
  <body>
    <h1>The Planetary System</h1>
  </body>
</html>
```

5. Double-click on the `index.html` file to execute and open it in the browser. A popup will appear with an alert message.

Click on **OK** to close the alert box and the webpage will be displayed.

This was your first step into the world of JavaScript, although it was very basic and did not show the real power of JavaScript. We will be practicing advanced JavaScript code in the chapters that follow.

Server-side JavaScript

The server is responsible for serving web pages in programming languages. The client sends a request to the server with a command, and the server responds to that client request. Server-side programming is the name given to programs that run on the server. We will study this in further detail in *Chapter 11, Extending JavaScript and ECMA Script 6.*

The term *server-side* means that the control over webpages is handled by web servers rather than web pages. Web crossing runs that script and sends information in the form of HTML to each user's browsers.

Rhino and **Node** are both commonly used to create servers. Server-side scripting is not downloaded to client's browser.

Server side

Server side refers to operations that are performed by the server in a client–server relationship in a computer networking. The term *server side* can also be understood as anything outside of the browser.

Client side

Anything that is at *client side* means that it is running inside the web browser.

Scripting with Rhino

Rhino is a JavaScript engine/interpreter developed and written in the Java language and managed by the Mozilla foundation (`http://www.mozilla.org/rhino`) as open source software. It enables and allows JavaScript program elements to access the complete Java API.

Description

Rhino is a JavaScript open source implementation written in pure Java. Rhino is used to provide scripting to end users. Basically, Rhino converts JavaScript scripts into classes. It is used for server-side programming in JavaScript.

MDN mentions the following: "Scripting Java has many uses. It allows us to write powerful scripts quickly by making use of the many Java libraries available." More information on things such as the `this` statement would extend the general statement and give some insight into the `this` statement's implementation and its purpose.

We can use Rhino scripting as a shell for acting like a debugger. This shell runs code in a batch mode. Batch mode refers to batch processing, which means automated processing without human intervention. Batch is the opposite of interactive.

Being open source, Rhino is a free program provided by Mozilla and can be downloaded from `http://www.mozilla.org/rhino`. Rhino is distributed as a JAR file. To start it with a command line, you can execute the Rhino JAR on a file from the command-line interface:

```
java -jar rhino1_7R3/js.jar programfiles.js
```

The 1.7R2 version of Rhino uses ECMAScript 3, while the 1.7R3 version of Rhino partially uses ECMAScript 5. The latest stable release of Rhino is 1.7R5, which was released on January 29, 2015.

Here are a few functions with their usage and description:

Function	Usage	Description
print	print(x)	This is a global print function that prints to the console
version	version(170)	This is used to tell Rhino that we want the JS 1.7 features
load	load(file1,file2…)	This loads and executes one or more files of JavaScript code
readFile	readFile(file)	This reads a text file and returns its contents as a string
readUrl	readUrl(url)	This reads the textual contents of a URL and returns the output as a string
spawn	spawn(f)	This runs f() or load and executes the f file in a new thread
runCommand	runCommand(cmd, [args..])	This runs a system command with zero or more command-line args
quit	quit()	This makes Rhino exit

Here is a simple example that displays the message in the strNote string:

```
Dim strNote
strNote = "Welcome to Rhino"
Rhino.printstrNote
```

You can find some more useful scripts at http://www.rhinoscript.org/.

Node.js

Node.js is an implementation of JavaScript that allows JavaScript to run outside the browser and perform OS-based and network-based tasks. It is a runtime interface for JavaScript.

Node uses Google V8, which implements ECMAScript 5 standards, meaning that there is not much difference between the syntax of JavaScript and Node. For example, if you want to print out "Hello World" in the console, you will write the following:

```
console.log("Hello from Mars!"); //This is same for JavaScript as
well.
```

Description

Node.js is a super fast interface that runs on the Google Chrome V8 engine. Node.js is easy to use, fast, and scalable. Like JavaScript client-side programming, Node.js provides abstraction. So, by this abstraction, Node.js can handle a huge amount of code.

Here is an example or server-side coding in Node.js:

```
var http=require("http");
http.createServer(function(request,response){
  response.writeHead(200,{"content-type":" text/plain"});
  response.write("Hello from Mars!");
  response.end();
}).listen(8080)
```

The language syntax

The language syntax is basically a means of communication. In a programming language, it's a formal way of communicating with algorithms, from both algorithms to programmer and programmer to machine. This is because a machine works on given instructions.

These instructions are meant to be written in a specific format, so that a machine could understand and compile it properly. That specific format is defined by some general rules of a programming language, known as language syntax.

A computer contains a list of instructions to be executed. Every computer language has different syntax and rules. To use different languages, we must have knowledge of their language syntax, such as the following:

- Syntax (a set of symbols and rules)
- Semantics (for transforming term to term)
- Pragmatics (the particular construct of a language)

Similarly, other languages in JavaScript have a unique syntax. JavaScript is not a language of Java; these are two different languages and the syntaxes for both languages are different. JavaScript is a powerful and expressive language. JavaScript's statements are separated by a semicolon at the end.

The JavaScript language syntax is much easy for beginners who have an idea of object-oriented programming. JavaScript is contained between the `<scripts>`...`</script>` tags. These are treated as HTML tags in any web browser.

You can place your JavaScript code anywhere on your webpage, but I prefer the way of defining your script using the `<head>` tag. So, the structure of your script will be as follows:

```
<head>
  <script>
      ............. . .
  </script>
</head>
```

Basically, the `<script>` tag when written writing `<head>` tag, tells the browser that this scripts need to be executed first when the web page loads. Although, its a good practice to include javaScript is to place it at the bottom of a web page. There are two important attributes of this `script` tag.

Language

The `language` attribute will tell which language attribute you are using; typically, it's JavaScript. It is the default value if the attribute is absent.

Type

The `type` attribute is the same as the preceding explanation. This is not a required attribute. Its value is set as `text/javascript,` which shows that this scripting language is in use.

```
<script language=" javascript" type="text/javascript">
  .Script code.
</script>
```

The character set

A character set is basically a list of characters recognized by computer hardware and software. It is represented by a number. Earlier ASCII was used as standard character set encoding for web pages. There were lots of character encoding problems that were almost solved after the arrival of HTML5 and XML. JavaScript provides support for different types of languages and their characters. The character set attribute shows the character encoding in external files. For HTML5, there is a default character set encoding is UTF-8.

There are some common values of character set encoding such as the following:

- **ISO-8859-1**: This is used to encode the Latin alphabet
- **UTF-8**: This is used for Unicode encoding that is compatible with ASCII

For example, if your frontend page is in Spanish, and you do not use the character set property in your page, then it will not show some special characters in Spanish clearly. For this, you must declare a character set property in the top `<head>` tag of your page, as follows:

```
<meta charset="utf-8">?
```

For this, you can also change your web server's configuration to serve as UTF-8. Alternatively, we can send a content-type header to our server-side script.

In JavaScript, the `charset` property returns the character encoding of the current document. The syntax for reading the `characterSet` property from the document is `document.characterSet;`.

We can define the `characterSet` attribute in the `<script>` tag in the parent page of our website, as follows:

```
<script type="text/javascript"charset="utf-8"></script>
```

Another way is to add the UTF-8 character set into the server configuration file (`.htaccess`), as follows:
AddCharset UTF-8
So, character set encoding will apply to all JavaScript pages in your application.

Case sensitivity

HTML is not a case-sensitive language, but XML and JavaScript are case sensitive languages.

Description

JavaScript is a case-sensitive language. Case sensitivity in JavaScript does not only apply to variable names but also to JavaScript keywords and JavaScript's event handlers. For example, if you have the `firstname` and `firstName` variables, then these will be two different variables. In JavaScript, while calling a function, you must write its name exactly the same way as it was defined, matching the letter case.

A popular convention also used in JavaScript's primitive methods is to use camel case, in which a phrase is written with the first letter of the first word in lowercase and every successive word has an uppercase first letter, which makes it easier to read.

Examples of some functions are as follows:

- `toUpper();`
- `toArray();`

 Keywords in JavaScript are all in lowercase such as `while`, `for`, `if`, and so on.

JavaScript has functions that are built into the language; they take strings and transform them to the uppercase or lowercase. This can make handling strings easier to manipulate when the input has varying cases. The following are the two parameters the functions can take:

- `.toUpperCase()`
- `.toLowerCase()`

The `.toUppercase()` function will convert letters into uppercase and the `.toLowerCase()` function will convert letters into lowercase. These are the built-in and case-sensitive functions of JavaScript.

Whitespaces and line breaks

Whitespaces and line breaks are used to format and indent code in a neat and consistent manner so that the code becomes readable and easy to understand.

Description

Spaces, Tabs, New lines which are not a part of a string are called whitespaces. JavaScript removes whitespaces and line breaks between tokens in the programs, Spaces and Line breaks that are a part of a string are not removed when script is executed.

In any text, there are three types of line breaks:`\r\n` or as `\r` or `\n`.

These line breaks occur in different types of operating systems:

- `\r\n` is usually created on Windows
- `\n` is usually created on OS X

If you want to remove line breaks from any text, then we must deal with all types of line breaks because the text could be from these three sources Windows, Linux, and Mac.

We have several methods to remove line breaks from any text. For example, we have the following:

```
varabc = abc.replace(/(\r\n|\n|\r)/gm,"");
```

In this code, we have used a regular expression for removing line breaks from our text. This will remove line breaks \r\n, then \n, and finally \r. We used the suffix gm at the end of the regular expression because m shows that line breaks should be removed from all the text and g shows that it should be done more than once.

Regular expressions are discussed in detail in *Chapter 8, JavaScript Expressions, Operators, Statements, and Arrays.*

Now, there are some spaces between texts; you can remove these whitespaces using JavaScript. There are different functions of JavaScript for removing all leading spaces from a string; you can use the following:

```
str = str.replace(/^\s+|\s+$/g,'');
```

This piece of code uses a regular expression, which checks multiple occurrences of white spaces at beginning and end of string.

The g in this regular expression shows that the global search should be performed while checking the text. There are more methods, such as the following:

- The string.replace() function is used to replace all leading whitespaces with an empty string
- The str.trim() function is used to remove spaces from both sides of a string

The Unicode escape sequence

Every Unicode escape sequence consists of six characters with a much defined syntax: four characters following\u. Smaller code is accompanied by leading zeroes but the length of the sequence is maintained. For example, \u00a9 has two leading zeros. Similarly, the copyright symbol can be represented as\u00A9.

Any character with a code point that is less than 65536 can be escaped using the hexadecimal value of its code point, prefixed with\u.

A code point (also known as **character code**) is a numerical representation of a specific Unicode character.

Description

The JavaScript Unicode escape sequence allows you to place special characters in a string. Browsers that support JavaScript can use the escape function.

To add the next line within the same string, we can use \n. Let's take a look at the following code:

```
alert("Welcome to JavaScript. \n We hope you love it!")
```

To add quotes within a string, we can use something like this:

```
var myquote="Jinnah said \"Impossible is a word unknown to me.\""
```

This Unicode escape sequence starts with a backslash (\) followed by characters. This backslash is the escape sequence character. To insert a backslash itself, just add another backslash "\" before the next one. Also called double backslash (\\).

You can specify a Unicode character by \uaaaa, where aaaa is a hexadecimal number. So a Unicode escape character can represent a 16-bit character.

A Unicode escape sequence represents a Unicode sequence, as follows:

- A backslash (\)
- A character (u)
- A hexadecimal number (0-9)(a-f)

For example, the word cat will be represented as\u732b.

A Unicode escape sequence can also be used in comments and literals. Consider the following example:

```
var x = "http\\u00253A\\u00252F\\u00252Fexample.com";
```

 The hexadecimal part of this kind of a character escape is case-insensitive, which means \u041a and \u041A are equivalent.

You can also represent an escape sequence to represent a Unicode character ["\ u03b1"] as ["a"].The Unicode escape for the character é, for example, is \u00E9, and the following two JavaScript strings are identical:

```
"cafn" === "caf\u00e9" // => true
```

The == operator tries to convert the values to the same type before testing if they're the same; whereas, === does not do this. It requires objects to be of the same type to be equal.

Here are some examples of the escape sequence for some characters:

Unicode	Escape sequence	Meaning
\u000B	\v	Vertical tab
\u000A	\n	New line
\u0009	\t	White spaces
\u000C	\f	Form field
\u000D	\r	Line terminator
\u0020		Whitespace

Normalization

The Unicode standard (which can be found at http://unicode.org/standard/ standard.html) defines the most acceptable pattern of encoding characters and the normalization method. Javascript presupposes that the code it is reading and interpreting has all the Unicode representations normalized. ECMAScript V6 has a string prototype function (string.prototype.normalize()) to fix any unaddressed encodings.

 ECMAScript 6 introduces String.prototype.normalize(), which takes care of Unicode normalization.

Identifiers

Identifiers are used to give names to functions and variables. There are certain rules for these identifiers and these rules are the same for all programming languages. Identifiers can contain letters and a digest of the complete Unicode character set. These JavaScript identifiers include variables, objects, functions, properties, methods, events, and so on.

Here are the rules for identifiers:

- Identifiers cannot start with a number
- Identifiers can contain numbers, letters, underscore, and the dollar sign ($)
- It can be of any length
- These are case-sensitive
- We must not use reserved words for identifiers

We can also use Unicode characters as identifiers. Unicode escape sequences such as \uaaaa, can also be used as identifiers. We must avoid using global methods or properties as identifiers.

A best practice while writing identifiers is to use one word and use camel case. Consider the following example:

- myNote
- myNewNotebook
- $sum

The `var` variable is a valid identifier name, but it is an invalid identifier because of the reserved word. If you use a valid identifier, then your browser will handle it correctly; however, if you use an invalid identifier, your browser will show a warning recognizing it as a bug.

Reserved keywords

Reserved words are keywords in JavaScript. There are some words that cannot be used as a function or a variable name. These reserved words are also identifiers. These reserved words are reserved for JavaScript engine. If you use these reserved words as a function, variable, or a method name, then your browser will show a warning and your script may fail.

Reserved words are basically keywords that have special meaning in JavaScript, for example, `break`, `case`, `do`, `delete`, `else`, and so on.

There are three types of reserved words:

- Protected reserved words
- New reserved word
- Future reserved words

Protected reserved words

Protected reserved words cannot be used as a variable or a function name. If we use these, then there will be a compilation error in it. Here are a few protected reserved words:

Break	case	catch
class	const	Continue
Debugger	Default	Delete
do	Else	Export
Extends	False	If
Import	in	var

New reserved words

JavaScript also released new keywords, and these reserved words have a special meaning for the current version of JavaScript. These reserved keywords can also be used as identifiers. Once you declare it as an identifier, then it will forget that it was a keyword. Here are some examples of new reserved keywords:

Abstract	Boolean	byte
char	enum	final
doubke	implements	int
interface	internal	long
set	short	static
uint	ulong	ushort

Future reserved words

Future reserved words are proposed for future extensions of JavaScript. These are also used as an identifier in the current version of JavaScript. When you choose a word as an identifier, it is also important to note whether it is already the name of JavaScript reserved keyword. Here are some examples of future reserved words:

asset	event
namespace	require
transient	violate
ensure	goto
native	synchronized
use	Invariant

Comments

In any programming language, comments are used to make your code readable. In JavaScript, comments are used to explain JavaScript code.

Another use of comments is to write them to add hints, suggestions, and warnings into our JavaScript code, so if someone other than the developer wants to change or modify your script, they can easily modify it. Use of comments in a script is considered as a best practice. Comments are also used to disable the execution of some parts of code. In debugging, comments are very helpful, so it is a valuable debugging tool for developers.

There are three different types of comments you can put into your JavaScript script:

- Multiple-line comments
- One-line comments
- The HTML comment opening sequence

Multiple-line comments

We can write multiple lines between the comment boundaries; this block of code will not be executed:

```
/* this is a comment */
```

One-line comments

Adding two forward slashes in the beginning of the line comments it. The text between // and the end of the line is commented and will not be compiled. Double forward slash is used to comment one line at a time:

```
// this is comment
```

The HTML comment opening sequence

JavaScript treats the HTML comment's opening sequence, that is, <!-- as // comment. It does not recognize the closing sequence of HTML comment, that is, --> HTML styled comments are not usually used within JavaScript code blocks as // is much handy. It is recommended not to use HTML comments in JS as that was an old practice. They were used to hide incompatible JavaScript code from old browsers.

Literals

Literals are used to represent values for the different data structures in JavaScript; for example:

- 3.14
- to be or not to be

In the following sections, we will cover the literal types for JavaScript.

Object literals

An object literal is used to hold values in an object.

Description

An object literal holds pairs of comma-separated lists of property names and associated values, and they are enclosed within { }. It is possible for an object literal to have no values as well. In an object literal, each name:value pair is separated by a comma.

Here is an example of an object literal:

```
varbookObj={
  bookName="The Kite Runner",
  CoverImage="KiteRunner1.png",
  Author="KhaledHoesenni",
  bookCategory ="Bestseller"
};
```

Array literals

An array literal contains a list of expressions that represent an array element.

Description

Array literals contain values inside an array. They are placed inside array brackets [] and each element is separated by a comma (,). Just like an object literal, an array can be empty and contain 0 elements. When you create an array literal it is specified values as its element and its length is specified as a number of arguments of this array. Here is an example of an array literal:

```
var Planets= ["Earth", "Neptune", "Saturn", "Mars"];
```

Boolean literals

As the name suggests, a Boolean literal has Boolean values, so its value is either true or false.

Integers

Integer literals must contain values that are only integers.

Description

In JavaScript, an integer literal must contain a digit from 0 to 9. Commas and brackets are not allowed in integer literals. Integers can be negative or positive. If there is no sign present then it is consider as positive.

Floating point literals

A floating point literal is used to contain floating numbers—numbers that have a decimal point, fraction, or exponent.

Description

Examples of floating point literals are as follows:

```
22.56
-26.35689
18.4e2 //Equivalent to [18.4 x 10^2]
-17.22E3 //Equivalent to [17.22 x 10^-3]
```

String literals

String literals, as the name suggests, hold only string values, that is, values placed inside a pair of quotation marks.

Description

A string literal contains characters placed inside quotation marks. You can also create a null string to not contain anything. Two or more strings can be joined together using the + sign. Special characters can be inserted in the string. A few special characters are \n, \r, \b, \t, to name a few.

A few examples of string examples are as follows:

```
strFirstName= "Jamie";
strLastName="Down";
strMarksObtained="200";
strClassesJoined="Microprocessors, "+ "Microcontrollers";
strAddress= "Michigan University \n United States";
```

Statements

JavaScript also supports a set of statements used to identify a set of instructions and carry out tasks. There are different types of statements in JavaScript such as if, for, while, and so on. The basic purpose of using these statements is to evaluate or check whether certain conditions are being met. These statements are common for all programming languages.

Conditional statements

As the name suggests, conditional statements are based on conditions and the if and then rule. For example, "if you work hard, you will get rewarded". Here, working hard is the condition of getting rewarded.

Consider the following example:

```
if (age < 20 && age > 12) {
  person = "Teen ager";
}
else {
  person = "Not a Teenager";
}
```

The loop statement

In a loop statement, a condition is provided within a set of parentheses. If the condition evaluates to `true`, then the loop will continue working, and if the condition equates to `false`, the program will jump to the next line after the loop. An exception is the `do while` loop, which will always execute at least once. There are different types of loops in programming languages; they are as follows:

- The for loops
- The `for/in` loops
- The `while` loops
- The `do/while` loops

Here is an example that shows how the `while` loop is used:

```
var number = "";
var n = 0;
while (n < 10) {
  number += "\nThe number is " + n;
  n++;
}
console.log(number);
```

Loops are covered in more detail in *Chapter 8, JavaScript Expressions, Operators, Statements, and Arrays.*

Object manipulation statements

Object manipulation statements in JavaScript are used to access the object's properties and methods at runtime to perform certain functions. JavaScript uses the `for...in` and `with` statements to manipulate objects.

Here is an example that shows how the object car can be manipulated:

```
<script type="text/javascript">
  var x;
  var car = new Object();
  car.brand = "Porche";
  car.model = "2014";
  car.colour = "Black";
  for (x in car) {
    console,log(x + " --- " + car[x] + "<br />");
  }
</script>
```

Output:

```
brand — Porche
model — 2014
color — Black
```

Exception handling statements

The `try`, `catch`, `throw`, and `finally` statements are used in JavaScript exception handling. Let's take a look at the following description:

- The `try` statement tests code for errors.

- The `catch` statement usually follows the `try` statement and catches and handles the error found in the `try` block.

- The `throw` statement creates custom errors or alerts.

- The `finally` statement executes code after `try` and `catch`, regardless of the result. Usually, this block of code is used to clean up and release resources.

Here is an example showing how exceptions are handled using the `try` and `catch` block:

```html
<!DOCTYPE html>
<html>

  <head>

    <script type="text/javascript">
      <!--
        function Calculate() {
          x = document.getElementById("Val1").value;
          y = document.getElementById("Val2").value;

          try{
            if ( x == 0 ||y==0 ) {
            throw("Divide by zero error." );
          }
          else {
            var a = x / y;
            alert("The answer is: " + a );
          }

          catch ( err ) {
```

```
            alert("Error: " + err );
        }
      }
    //-->
  </script>

</head>

<body>
  <form>
    <p>Enter first value</p>

    <input id="Val1" type="text">
    <p>Enter second value</p>

    <input id="Val2" type="text">
    <p><input type="button" value="Calculate"
    onclick="Calculate();" /></p>
  </form>

</body>
</html>
```

Optional semicolon

Semicolons in JavaScript are used to separate statements from each other. Let's say, if you have two different statements and you just write them, then it will not be understandable. So, JavaScript uses semicolons to separate statements. It will make your code clear and meaningful. If you do not use semicolon in JavaScript, then it will make your statements complex, meaning that the end of one of your statements could be the start of your statement.

 Placing semicolons in your code can help you prevent a lot of errors. Absence of semicolons, from your code block will treat it as a single line of code when compiled resulting in several errors.

JavaScript does not consider a line break as a semicolon. Here is an example of the use of semicolons in JavaScript:

```
a=10;
b=20;
a=10; b=20;
```

A semicolon in JavaScript is not a terminator; these are just separators used to separate statements.

JavaScript automatically inserts a semicolon at the end of your statement. You should not put a semicolon after the closing curly bracket. Similarly, at times, putting a semicolon after round brackets `()` is also a bad idea, and importantly, the code will not run.

If there is a `for` loop in your script, then put a semicolon after the first and second statements and don't put a semicolon after third statement. It will produce a syntax error. For example, if you have a `for` loop like this:

```
for(i=0;i<5;i++;){}
```

The preceding code will give you a syntax error. The right way of doing this is as follows:

```
for(i=0;i<5;i++){}
```

Here are some rules for semicolons:

- Insert a semicolon when an assignment operator is used
- Insert a semicolon after rite operand of assignment operator
- Insert a semicolon after a closing round bracket of a function
- Insert a semicolon after keywords
- When you declare a variable insert a semicolon

Data type

A computer works on a set of given instructions; it cannot differentiate between a number and a character. For example, if you write some numbers, such as 12345, and some character, abcsd, it cannot tell integers from characters. So, data types are used for this. The datatype tells which type of data is being used or referenced in a statement.

In all programming languages (C, C++, Java, JavaScript), data types are used. Every data type has a specific function of storing data. Many classical computer programming languages require you to specify the data type when you declare a data object. JavaScript does not have this requirement. Similarly, some databases require declaration of the data types for storing data.

JavaScript is a dynamic language. This means that if you declare an object, then its data type can be changed dynamically, for example:

```
var a=16;
a="abc";
a=true;
```

In the first statement, the data type is an integer; in the second statement, the data type is a character; and in third statement, the data type is a Boolean. So, in JavaScript, the data type dynamically changes while the program is being processed.

There are six major data types defined in ECMAScript standard.

- Null
- Undefined
- Boolean
- String
- Symbol
- Number

 JavaScript considers integer values and floating point values to be the same. It doesn't distinguish between the two. All numbers in JavaScript are represented as floating point type values.

Here, Null and undefined are trivial data types in JavaScript because each of these defines single values. JavaScript also supports a composite data type, which is known as the object. Objects in JavaScript are treated as an associative array.

Functions in JavaScript are also treated as objects. So, functions can also be stored as a variable.

The typeof operator

Operators are used to find the type of a JavaScript variable. For example, you have two numbers variables, as follows:

```
5+1=6
```

Here, 5 and 1 are operands and + is an operator.

The syntax of this operator is as follows:

```
Typeof (operand)
```

Description

The Typeof operator is a unary operator; it returns a string that indicates the typeof expressions. The `typeof` operator returns information as a string. There are six possible values that can be returned as a string. They are `string`, `number`, `object`, `function`, `Boolean`, and `undefined`.

Here are some examples of the `typeof` operator:

- `typeof("5"+"1")`: This will return a string
- `typeof(5+1)`: This will return a number
- `typeof(5+"1")`: This will return a string
- `typeof(5*"1")`: This will return a number

 The `typeof` operator is not a function. Operands are written in round brackets, so it looks like a function, but these are not functions. When you use the `typeofnull` operator, it returns an object.

The undefined type

In JavaScript, an empty variable or a variable without values has an undefined value. And, `typeof` is also undefined. If you want to empty a variable, you can assign it an undefined value; for example:

```
var employee = undefined;
```

Description

In JavaScript, `undefined` is a property of the `global` object. This means that the value is undefined and we declare it in the global scope of the browser.

There are basically three `property` attributes of `undefined`:

- Writeable
- Enumerable
- Configurable

These three `property` attributes show that, for modern browsers, these properties are not writeable, enumerable, and configurable. And, we should avoid overriding these properties. The `undefined` type is a primitive type in JavaScript.

The Undefined type shows that a variable has not been assigned a value. All browsers, such as Firefox, Google Chrome, Opera, and Safari, support the undefined property according to ECMAScript.

Undefined is a built-in type in the JavaScript library. Every type of function for which the value is not defined is consider as an undefined type. For example, if you have a function without the return statement, the result of that function will be considered as undefined.

Being a property of a global object, its value is initially undefined. We can access it as a global variable, although it's a global property. A simple idea of an undefined type is when a variable is not defined in your script, but it does exist and you are considering it as a global variable.

Whenever a function executes in a script, and it finishes executing without returning a value, then it returns the undefined type, for example:

```
var abc,
f1=function(){}
f2=function() {
  var hello;
  return hello;
}
typeof(abc) ; // undefined
typeof(f1); // function
typeof(f2); // function
```

Here, in this example, the variable abc is defined but no value has been assigned to it. Notice that undefined type is a primitive property of a object declared in a global scope. Here, defining it as a global object does not mean that it cannot be redefined. It can be redefined according to ECMAScript. So, undefined is not a reserved word; it can be used as a variable name in other scopes outside of its global scope.

When you use comparison operators, you can also declare the undefined type there to know whether a variable has a value or not.

The null type

In JavaScript, null shows an empty value.

Here is the syntax:

```
varabc; // Here abc does not exist and it has been not
initialized

varabc=null; // Here abc exist but it does not has a value or a
type
```

Description

The data type of `null` is an object in JavaScript. `Null` shows that value does not exist in the script. When you want to empty a value, you declare it as a `null`. `Null` can be expected in places where we are expecting some values, but we find nothing.

 There is a big difference between the `null` and `undefined` type. The data type of `null` is an object and the data type of `undefined` is undefined. In the `identity` operator, `null` cannot be undefined, but in the `equality` operator, `null` can be undefined. This is because the `equality` operator will cast the value on the left to the same type before making a comparison.

Undefined means a variable is declared but values is not assigned. For instance, `var abc`:

```
console.log(abc); //undefined
console.log(typeof abc); //undefinednull  is an empty value. It can
be assigned to a variable which means variable is defined and an empty
value has been assigned to it. For instance,var abc = null;
console.log(abc); //null
console.log(typeof abc); //returns object
```

Consider the following example:

```
Null===undefined;
//It's a false because identity operator always verify data type
//equality

Null==undefined; //It's true because of equality operator
```

"You may wonder why the typeof operator returns object for a value that is null. This was actually an error in the original JavaScript implementation that was then copied in ECMAScript. Today, it is rationalized that null is considered a placeholder for an object, even though, technically, it is a primitive value."

- Professional JS For Web Developers, Wrox Press

The number type

There is only one type of number in JavaScript. Numbers can be written with or without decimals. Much larger or smaller numbers can be written with scientific notation.

Description

Unlike other programming languages where we have several numeric data types like integer, float, double, and so on. JavaScript has a Number data type for all numeric values. JavaScript has three symbolic values for this type: infinity, and NaN (not a valid number). NaN defined in the number type in JavaScript shows that it is a reserved word, and its value is not a number in reality.

> There is no difference between an integer and a floating point value in JavaScript.

Integer values can be positive numbers, 0, or negative numbers. They can be of any base number like base 10, 16, or 8. But mostly, in JavaScript, numbers are written to base 10. To check the largest or smallest number representable or available in JavaScript, you can use constants of maximum and minimum values:

```
Number.maxValue
Number.minValue
```

> In Firefox or Chrome, it is `Number.MAX_VALUE`.

In the number type, you only check a number that has two representations, for example, if you have the number 0, then it has two representations—one is -0 and the other is +0. JavaScript numbers can be written with or without a decimal point; for example:

```
A non- decimal number
var a=10
A number with decimal
var b=10.0123
```

If the number is too large or too short, then we use a scientific notation's exponent for it. Consider the following example:

```
If we have a number 100000000
var a=1000e5
And 0.00111
var b=111e-5
```

The limit is `1e+21` (the console displays a scientific notation from the power of 10).

> In other programming languages, we can define numbers as `float`, `integer`, `long`, and `short`. But, in JavaScript, there is only one data type for numbers, that is, `numbers`. These numbers follow the IEEE standard and also these numbers are double-point precision.

The Boolean type

In programming languages, the `Boolean` type works on the Boolean logic in which variables return results as `true` or `false`. These `true` and `false` are basically literals. The Boolean logic is used usually in comparison operators, for example, lesser or greater than, and so on.

Any variable can be assigned a `Boolean` value written as `true` or `false` in lower case.

Description

In JavaScript, when you declare a `Boolean` data type to a variable, then the variable should not have any quote. Here is how you should use boolean assignment: `var abc = "true"; //string assignment` and `var abc = true; //boolean assignment`. The `Boolean` variables are also used in the `if`, `if` then `else`, and `while` loop.

Here is an example showing how Boolean variables are used:

```
var x=true;
if(x==true) {
   document.write("this true");
}
```

The `Boolean` operators are also used when there is a lack of or presence of a value. For example, if we have a checkbox in our script, then its value is present or not depending on whether it is checked or not.

In other data types, there is an unlimited number of values a variable can take, but for the `Boolean` data types, there are only two—`true` and `false`. This data type is usually used when we have a controlled structure such as a comparison, the `if else` loop, and the `while` loop. These are controlled structures. The `If` and `else` statement performs one action if the value is `true`; otherwise, it will perform another action, that is, `false`.

You can also use the `Boolean` data type as a comparative expression. A comparative expression is an expression that evaluates `0`, `null`, and `undefined` as `false` and other values as `true`. Consider the following example:

```
C=A+B
```

In this example, the result of `A+B` is stored in `C` first and then this expression is evaluated. If you want to check that the `C` value is equal to `A+B`, then you must use the comparison operator for this, as follows:

```
C==A+B
```

The string type

In JavaScript, anything that is written between quotes is treated as a string. Double or single quotes can be used.

Strings literals can be defined in two ways. One way is to write a string in double quotes and the other way is to write a string in single quotes.

 There is no special type of representation of a single character in JavaScript. If you want to represent a single character in JavaScript, then you must define a single character string, for example, the character a. An empty string is a zero length string, for example "".

Description

In JavaScript, the text data is represented in the form of the `string` data type. In programming languages, string is a combination of characters and numbers. A JavaScript string is an ordered sequence of zero or more characters.

The restriction for writing these strings is that you must use the same quotation mark at the beginning and end. This means that a string that starts with a single quote must end with a single quote, and the same rule applies for double quotation marks. Consider the following example:

```
var x="xyz" //double quotes
var y='xyz' //single quotes
var z="" //empty string
```

If there is a problem in a string and it cannot show some characters. For a representation of these characters, there is a technique in JavaScript—we define the escape sequence for this. This means that the character which we cannot write directly is written using an escape sequence. For example, if we want to insert a quotation mark within a string, we can do it by preceding quotation mark with a backslash. It is known as escaping the quotation mark. Similarly, string literals are unable to represent nonprinting characters such as tab, new line, and so on.

An escape sequence is a combination of characters starting with a backslash. Some escape sequences are as follows:

- \b: BackspaceDeletes the previous character and moves cursor one space backwards.
- \n: New lineEnds the current line and moves the cursor to a new line. If used in the middle of a string it will move the text after \n to new line.
- \f: Form feedIt is a page-break ASCII control character. It tells printer to continue printing on new page.
- \v: Vertical tabIt was used to control the vertical movement on page. It is rarely used now.
- \t: Horizontal tab control the insertion of text horizontally on page. It is inserted usually using the *Tab* key on the keyboard.
- \" : Double QuotesA double quotes is preceded with a backslash to insert it within a string.
- \' : Single QuotesA single quotes is preceded with a backslash to insert it within a string.
- \\: Backslash to insert a backslash within a string we escape it with another backslash.

Here is an example of this:

```
var abc = "hello \n Morning"
```

Its output will be as follows:

```
Hello
Morning
```

The object type

Object is a sequence of primitive and, sometimes, reference data types stored as name-value pairs.

The syntax is as follows:

```
varsomeObj= {property:value};
```

Description

In JavaScript, objects are written into curly brackets. Each item of an object is called a **property**. Property values can be defined as any valid data type as well as functions or methods. Consider the following example:

```
varobj= {book_name:"xyz", Author:"abc"};
```

We can say that the object is a list of items, and each item in the list has some method and function stored as its name-value pair:

In JavaScript, everything is like an object, for example:

- Regular expressions are objects
- Numbers are objects
- Strings are objects
- Mathematical notations are objects
- Arrays and functions are objects
- Objects are objects

The property name of any item can be a string or number. When a property is a number, then the way of writing this property is different; we will write it as follows:

```
var age = {"30": "abc"};
```

In JavaScript, objects are used to store data and for writing your own custom methods and functions. Primitive values are, for example, `null`, `undefined`, `true`, and `false else`.

Object properties are basically variables that are used in methods and function internally. They can also be global variables for the whole page. There is a difference between a method and a function. A function is a standalone unit of an object, but a method is attached to an object and it is used with `this` keyword:

```
Document.write ("hello world");
```

Variable, scope, and memory

When we describe a variable in JavaScript, there is no limit to how much data this variable holds. The maximum is described by the browser's capacity depending on how much data it can hold. Let's take a look the following code:

```
var abc="xyz";
```

We can define a variable in JavaScript using the var keyword. We can define the value of a variable immediately or later. A variable that we define outside the boundary of a function is a global variable.

 Creating too many global variables in JavaScript is a very bad approach. The major reason why global variables are discouraged in JavaScript is because in JavaScript, all the code shares a single global namespace, also JavaScript has implied global variables, that is, variables that are not explicitly declared in local scope are automatically included with global namespaces. Relying too much on global variables can result in conflicts between various scripts on the same page.

Every function in a script can access a global variable. When you define a variable in a function, then its scope is inside that function. Let's take a look at the following code snippet:

```
Function abc() {
    var xyz="abc";
}
```

 The scope of a global variable never stops during the execution of the whole page even it is not needed.

If you fail to write var inside the function, then this variable is considered as a global variable. If you define a variable with the same global variable name, then it will be considered as a global variable.

JavaScript dynamically allocates memory to variables. When the scope of these variables is dereferenced or finished, it is automatically removed from the memory by the garbage collector. So, its disadvantage is that the unwanted variables remain in the memory.

There are two ways to save memory:

- Using the function scope
- Dereferencing these variables manually

The use of the function scope is more appropriate as variables get dereferenced when the function ends, thus saving memory:

```
(Function (window, document, undefined) {
  varabc="abc";
}
(window, document);
```

Variable declaration

JavaScript variables can be identified by unique names. These unique names are known as **identifiers**. Variables in JavaScript are used to store information. Identifiers can be of any length and size, for example, a, b, myName.

When you declare a variable in JavaScript, the machine will save it in the memory so that you can store or retrieve data from memory when needed. Variable names should be unique in the script.

The rules to declare variable names in JavaScript are the same as those for identifiers, as discussed previously.

When a code starts its execution, it first processes the variable declaration. These variables can be declared globally as well as within a function. We can declare multiple comma-separated variables, for example:

```
var myName,myAddress,myContact;
```

When we store data into a variable, this process is called **variable initialization**. We can initialize a variable at the time of its creation or later when we want to use it, for example:

```
var a=1;
var b=2;
var c;
c=a+b;
```

Here, in this example, the variable a stores the value 1, and b stores 2, and then we create the variable c and define its value later.

The variable scope

A variable scope is a frame where a variable exists in a program. We can define a scope of a variable in a program. Basically, the scope is a set of methods, functions, and objects that we have access to.

There are two scopes of variables in JavaScript:

- Local scope variables
- Global scope variables

Local scope variables

A variable when defined inside a function is called a local scope variable, as this variable can only be accessed into this function. Function variables will be local to this variable.

Description

For a variable, which is defined in the local scope, a variable of the same name can be used in a different function. When a function starts, the local variable is created and when the function ends, the local variable is deleted. In JavaScript, always declare variables before using them; failing to do this will throw some exceptions. In a function, if you have a local and a global variable with the same name, then the local variable will get priority over the global variable. So, avoid using the same variable name. Let's take a look at the following code snippet:

```
function xyz() {
  varabc="xyz";
  document.write(abc);
}
```

Global scope variables

A global variable can be declared anywhere in a JavaScript program. They can be accessed from everywhere. A global scope variable remains in the memory throughout the execution of scripts on the page. This results in memory depletion.

Description

Basically, global variables are window objects. Global variables are generally defined outside of the function and all functions in a webpage can access this global variable. If you give some value to a variable which is not declared, then this variable will be considered as a global variable. When you close a web page, the global variable will be deleted. For frontend developers in HTML, the window object is a global variable.

```
var abc="xyx";
functionmy Function() {
  //some code
}
```

Primitive and reference values

There are two types of values a variable can have:

- Primitive type values
- Reference type values

Primitive type values

Generally objects are aggregated from properties and those properties can be used to reference the object. Primitive (value, data type) is not an object and has no methods associated to it.

Description

In JavaScript, there are five types of the primitive type: `string`, `number`, `null`, `undefined`, and `Boolean`. A primitive value is stored directly in the stack. These values are stored in the same location from which they are accessed. Because of its fixed size, it can be easily manipulated.

Reference type values

Reference type values are specialized objects similar to arrays and functions stored in a heap. A pointer is used to locate their location into the memory.

Description

In JavaScript, a variable holding a reference type value is stored in the heap memory. These objects cannot be easily manipulated because they contain arbitrary elements and properties. When a reference value is passed to a function, the function modifies its values or contents, and that change can be seen by the object, which calls the function and other functions that have references to the object.

The execution context and scope

The scope and context are not the same things. Every function in JavaScript has a scope and a context. When we declare a function in JavaScript, this function can be accessed in different and various contexts and scopes. JavaScript follows design patterns for scopes and context.

The main difference between a scope and context is that scope is function based and context is object based. The scope is used to access a function when it is invoked. Whereas the context is used with the `this` keyword, so it is basically a reference type.

The scope is associated with the execution context when the execution context starts. There is a chain of scope with it, for example:

```
function first() {
  second();
  function second() {
    third();
    function third() {
      fourth();
      function fourth() {
        // do something
      }
    }
  }
}
first();
```

In JavaScript, the environment in which the code is executed is classified into the following:

- Global code
- Function code
- Eval code

The global code

The global code is a default environment where the code is executed for the first time, that is, the external `.js` files and local inline code are loaded.

The function code

The function code is the environment in which flow control enters the function body during the code execution. Every return from the function exits the current execution context.

The eval code

The code is supplied to built-in `eval` functions. The `eval` code calls the context and creates an execution context.

For example:

```
var eval_context = { a: 10, b: 20, c: 30 };
function test() {
   console.log(this);
}
function evalInContext() {
   console.log(this);        // { a: 10, b: 20, c: 30 }
   eval("test()");       // { a: 10, b: 20, c: 30 } inside test()
}
evalInContext.call(eval_context);
```

In this example you call the function with the context you want and run `eval` within that function.

Garbage collection

There is no separate memory management in JavaScript. A browser decides when a cleanup is needed. Garbage collection is basically knowing if the variables are still being used or will be used in future throughout the program execution and if not collect and remove them. In simple words, the track of reference made to an object is kept in background. once it becomes idle or reaches zero it can be collected by the GC.

We can clean memory manually, but in some cases, there is no need for manual memory cleaning. We cannot force JavaScript to clean memory because this task is done on runtime by the garbage collector. Some heavy applications, such as computer games, require a lot of memory and slowdown your system; so, in this case, it only depends on your code and how you structured your application code for use of computer memory.

You can structure your code by following these steps:

Objects

When you declare an object, try to reuse that object by deleting its properties and restoring it to an empty object such as{}. This process is known as recycling the objects. When an object is created for the first time (new foo();), memory is allocated to it. So, if an object is already declared, we can reuse it in our script.

Arrays

When you use an array in your script, clear that array after using it. Assigning [] to an array is often used as a shorthand to clear it, but it actually creates a new empty array and garbages the old one. You can set the array length to 0, (arr.length = 0;); this will also clear the array but while reusing the same array object.

Functions

When you need to call a function more than one time, then you can optimize our code by assigning a permanent variable to the function rather than calling it again and again.

9

JavaScript Expressions, Operators, Statements, and Arrays

JavaScript is the most commonly used web programming language and is very popular among developers around the world. This chapter will cover most of the expressions, operators, statements, and arrays used in this language.

Expressions

A valid unit of code required to resolve a value is known as an **expression**. It is a set of literals, operators, variables, and expressions required to evaluate a value. This value can be a string or any logical value. An expression results in a value that can be written wherever a value is expected. There are two types of expressions:

- An expression that assigns a value to a variable
- An expression that has a value

Consider the following example:

```
var A = 2;
```

In the preceding example, a value is assigned to variable A, and for assigning that value to the variable, we use an assignment operator. Now consider another example:

```
2+3;
```

In this example, no value is assigned to a variable; however, it evaluates the result of 2+3 as 5. The operator used in this expression is known as an **addition operator**.

Expressions in JavaScript can be broadly classified into three types:

- **Arithmetic**: These evaluate numbers. This means that these expressions perform mathematical calculations between values.

- **Logical**: These are used to evaluate and give the result in the form of true or false.

- **String**: These are used to evaluate strings.

> There is another type of expression known as a **conditional expression**. These expressions are usually used in the if-else and loop conditions. These conditional expressions evaluate the result in the form of true or false and have only two values True and False. If the first condition is true, then it will evaluate first, otherwise it will evaluate second, for example:
>
> ```
> int age = 20;
> var flag;
> if (age<18) {
>    flag=true;
> }
> else {
>    flag=false;
> }
> ```

Primary expressions

In JavaScript, primary expressions are basic keywords and they are special objects, identifiers, and literals, which do not need any further evaluation to resolve their value. They may also be the result of another expression that is surrounded by brackets.

For example, this and function are keywords and these are primary expressions in JavaScript. The this keyword always returns a value whenever it enters an execution context. Identifiers are also primary expressions, and they refer to a function or an object.

There are four types of literals, as primary expressions:

- **Boolean literals**: These contain `1`/`0` or `true`/`false`
- **Null literals**: These contain a `null` value
- **Undefined literals**: These contain any type of data type
- **String literals**: These contain a string of characters

Object initializer

In JavaScript, an object initializer is used to initialize an object. It is an expression known as an **object initializer**. Every object in JavaScript is an entity that has a type. Every object has some property associated with it. There are functions associated with objects and these functions are called **methods**. Objects properties are basically JavaScript variables. A property associated with an object tells you about the object's characteristics.

Object properties can belong to primitive data types such as `int` or other data types such as `char`. An object can have an empty property as well. We can create an object with an empty property, as follows:

```
var xyz={};
```

In these curly brackets, you can easily and quickly create objects. These are comma-separated name-value pairs. The object initializer is basically used to create a new object. These object initializers are called **object literals**.

> In JavaScript, the property name and object name are case sensitive, so when you create an object, this should be kept in mind.

An object initializer creates an object with a literal notation, for example:

```
var studentInfo =  {  age:24, Name:"Ali" };
```

This is covered in more detail in *Chapter 8, JavaScript Object-Oriented Programming*.

The function definition expression

Functions in JavaScript are defined with a function keyword. Expressions are defined on these functions. They are used to declare a function or function expression. You can define a function anywhere in your script. Functions use expressions to define their prototype.

There are many ways to define a function in JavaScript, for example, we have the following:

- The function declaration
- The function expression

The function declaration

When a browser thinks of executing a script, a function declaration is a pre-executed stage. A function can be declared anywhere in your code:

```
function greetings() {
   alert("Happy New Year");
}
greetings();
```

The function expression

When a function takes the form of an expression, it is called a **function expression**. This expression can be a large expression, meaning that the function declaration requires several expressions. The function that is assigned with a function expression can be named or can be without a name. This is commonly referred to as an anonymous function. It is a first-class value, which means that it allows passing values in the function as parameters.

Consider the following example:

```
var abc=function() {
   return 1;
};

 var xyz=function foo() {
   return 2;
};
```

A function value can also be assigned to another function parameter. In this way, a function value is passed to another function parameter as a pass-by-value.

```
var f = function f ( function foo() );
```

A function in JavaScript is also a regular value. If you do not want your variables to be set in the global scope, then put these variables into a function. We do this because it's not always a good choice to set a global variable, as it can be accessed by any function anywhere in the program, which may alter the value of the variable and overwrite the original value that was supposed to be used. Functions are generally written inside brackets because JavaScript allows expressions to be all in the same space.

The property access expression

In JavaScript, to access a value of an object or value of an array element, we use the property access operation. There are two ways of writing the property access expression to access values from these expressions:

- Bracket notation
- Dot notation

The bracket notation

A bracket notation is also known as an array notation. The syntax for writing a bracket notation is as follows:

```
get=abc[xyz];
abc[xyz]=set;
get = abc [1]; // get value at array abc index 1
```

The dot notation

A dot notation is also known as an object notation. The syntax for writing a dot notation is as follows:

```
document.write ("hello world");
```

The invocation expression

In JavaScript, an invocation expression is used to execute or invoke a function or an expression. When a function invocation starts, it first evaluates its expression and then its arguments. Here are the two targets on an invocation expression:

- The invocation target
- The optional argument list

Invocation target

An invocation target followed by an open bracket then a target list and then a closing bracket target list must be classified as a method or object. There are two types of argument lists:

- Positional arguments
- Named arguments

Positional arguments are expressions and named arguments are identifiers. Here is an example of an invocation expression:

```
Function.getvalue(5);
Math.max(2,3);
```

Named arguments are the arguments that are passed with its name.

The optional argument list

Variable is assigned a value that is passed as a parameter to the function. If the value is not passed, a default value is assigned to the variable:

```
function add(a, b) {
  b = typeof b !== 'undefined' ?  b : 0; // if b not defined set
  it to 0
  return a+b;
}

add(10); // returns 10
```

The object creation expression

In JavaScript, this expression is used to create an object using the constructor method. This method is used to initialize an object's properties. This method first creates new objects and then initializes the objects using object initializer methods in JavaScript. The constructors that are used to initialize the object do not return any value, and this value becomes the value of the object. Consider the following example:

```
New myObj();
```

Evaluation expression

The evaluation expression is used to evaluate a string. This is a property of the global object in JavaScript. When it evaluates a string, it gives a value as the output.

The Eval() function is used in JavaScript to get a value. In this function, we do the following:

- As the input, we pass one argument
- If it does not return a value, then it means that there is an error in the code, and it will send an exception

```
var x = 10;
console.log(eval("x * 5")); //50
```

There are two ways you can invoke an eval() function:

- Direct: Calls a function directly named 'eval'. Direct eval() executes code in its local scope. For example:

```
var abc = 'global scope';
    function directEval() {
        'use strict';
        var abc = 'local scope';
        console.log(eval('abc')); // local scope
    }
```

- Indirect: By calling it through call() function, method of window or by storing it with a different name and calling from there, etc. Indirect eval() executes code in its global scope. For example:

```
var abc = 'global scope';
    function indirectEval() {
        'use strict';
        var abc = 'local scope';
        // eval via call()
```

```
console.log(eval.call(null, 'abc')); // global scope
console.log(window.eval('abc')); // global scope
console.log((1, eval)('abc')); // global scope
// eval with a different name
var abceval = eval;
console.log(abceval('abc')); // global scope
var obj = { eval: eval };
console.log(obj.eval('abc')); // global scope
}
```

Operators

In programming languages, operators are operations to be performed on operands. Basically, operators are symbols used to perform various operations. Consider the following example:

```
9 + 11 = 20
```

In the preceding example, 9 and 11 are operands and + is the additional operator.

Overview

Like other languages, in JavaScript, there are several operators to perform an operation, such as addition, multiplication, subtraction, and so on.

In JavaScript, there are different operators such as:

- The logical operator
- The bitwise operator
- The conditional operator
- The arithmetic operator
- The assignment operator

Binary operator

As the name suggests, binary operators require two operands; for example:

```
A + B
```

Here, A and B are operands and + is the operator to perform addition between them.

Unary operator

In programming languages, unary operators have just one operand and operator with them, for example:

```
A++;
```

This can also be written as:

```
++A;
```

 A++ is a post increment operator. It will first evaluate A and then increment it; whereas, ++A is a pre-increment operator. It increments the value of A and then evaluates the expression.

Ternary operator

The ternary operators require three operands to perform different operations; for example:

```
<condition> ? <true>: <false>;
```

In the preceding statement, ? is the ternary operator.

Arithmetic operators

In programming languages, arithmetic operators are use to perform arithmetic operations on values and variables. The basic arithmetic operations are as follows:

- +: Addition
- -: Subtraction
- *: Multiplication
- /: Division
- %: Modulus operator
- ++: Increment operator
- --: Decrement operator

These operators perform operations on numeric operands and return a result as a numeric value.

In JavaScript, operators are the same as those in other programming languages; for example, if you want to perform division between variables, then you will write the expression as follows:

```
var a=2;
a=(2+a)*1/a;// a=2
console.log(a); // prints 2
```

 In JavaScript, arithmetic operators are the most useful and powerful operators.

The + operator

The + operator performs an addition of two or more numbers.

Returns

The + operator returns the addition of the numbers.

Parameter

The + operator does not have any parameters.

Description

The + operator is used to add two numbers or two variables in which numbers are stored.

For example:

```
var a = 3;
var b = 4;
var c = a + b;
Document.Write("The value of c is " + c);
Document.Write(3+1);
```

The output of this will be:

```
The value of c is 7
4
```

This operator can also be used to append or concat two strings; for example:

```
document.write("Apple "+"Banana");
```

The output will be as follows:

```
Apple Banana
```

The - operator

The - operator performs a subtraction between two numbers.

Returns

The result of the - operator returns subtraction between two numbers.

Parameter

The - operator has no parameters.

Description

The - operator is used to subtract two numbers or two variables in which numbers are stored.

Consider the following example:

```
var a = 6;
var b = 4;
var c = a - b;
Document.Write("The value of c is " + c);
Document.Write(3-1);
```

The output of this will be as follows:

```
The value of c is 2
2
```

The * operator

The * operator performs a multiplication between two or more numbers.

Returns

The result of the multiplication between the numbers.

Parameter

There are no parameters.

Description

This operator is used to multiply two or more numbers or two or more variables in which numbers are stored.

Consider the following example:

```
var a = 3;
var b = 4;
var c = a * b;
Document.Write("The value of c is " + c);
Document.Write(3*1);
```

The output of this will be as follows:

```
The value of c is 12
3
```

The / operator

The / operator performs a division between two numbers.

Returns

The result of the division between the numbers.

Parameter

There are no parameters.

Description

This is also called the **remainder operator**, since the value returned is not an absolute value (in that, it retains the sign of the first operand, not the second).

Consider the following example:

```
var a = 5;
var b = 2;
var c = a % b;
Document.Write("The value of c is " + c);
Document.Write(10%3);
```

The output will be as follows:

```
The value of c is 1
1
```

The % operator

The % modulus operator is used to calculate the remainder.

Returns

The result of the multiplication between the numbers.

Parameter

There are no parameters.

Description

This operator is used to multiply two or more numbers or two or more variables in which numbers are stored.

Consider the following example:

```
var a = 3;
var b = 4;
var c = a * b;
Document.Write("The value of c is " + c);
Document.Write(3*1);
```

The output will be as follows:

```
The value of c is 12
3
```

The ++ Operator

The ++ operator is used to increment a value.

Returns

The result is the incremented value.

Parameter

There are no parameters.

Description

Increment. the value and stores the value in itself.

Consider the following example:

```
I = 0; // I contains 0
I++; // this line is equivalent to I = I + 1
```

The output of this will be:

```
I = 1
```

The -- Operator

The -- operator is used to decrement a value.

Returns

The result is the decremented value.

Parameter

There are no parameters.

Description

The -- operator decrements the value and stores the value in itself.

For example:

```
I = 0; // I contains 0
I--; // this line is equivalent to I = I - 1
```

The output will be as follows:

```
I = - 1
```

Logical operators

In programming languages, logical operators are Boolean operators. These operators work on Boolean logic. Like other languages, JavaScript works on Boolean evaluation. These Boolean operators always return a Boolean value. There are two possible results of any logical operator:

- True
- False

The following are the logical operators used in programming languages as well as JavaScript:

- Logical AND (&&)
- Logical OR(||)
- Logical NOT(!)

 Arithmetic operators get priority over logical operators.

Let's say, if there is an expression and there are logical and arithmetic operators in it, then the arithmetic operators will be evaluated first because of their higher priority. Logical operators work from left to right.

Logical operations are applicable on everything. A non-Boolean value can result in a Boolean value after evaluation.

The && Operator

The && operator is the translation of the English word "and". For example, if we have to write apples and oranges, we write *apples && oranges*.

Returns

This returns the most specific value on an operand; if a non-Boolean value is used, then a non-Boolean value is returned.

Parameter

We normally write an expression or a condition that is to be evaluated separated by the '&&' sign.

Description

This is called the **AND** operator.

Here is an example of the && operator:

```
var a= true && true; // it will be true
var b=true && false;//it will be false
```

The || Operator

This operator is the translation of the English word "or". For example, if we have to write apples or oranges, we write *apples || oranges*.

Returns

This returns the most specific value on an operand; if a non-Boolean value is used, then a non-Boolean value is returned.

Parameter

We normally write an expression or a condition that is to be evaluated separated by the '||' sign.

Description

This is called the **OR** operator.

Here is an example of the || operator:

```
var a= true  ||  true; // it will be true
var b=true  ||  false;// it will be true
```

The ! Operator

This is the NOT operator. NOT operator evaluates if the values are not equal to each other. For instance:

```
if(abc != 0){
 //if abc is not equal to 0 run this block
}else{
 //if abc = 0 then run this block
}
```

Returns

Boolean value.

Parameter

null

Description

This is called as the **NOT** operator.

Here is an example of the ! operator:

```
var a=!false //it will print true
var b=!true //it will print false
```

In JavaScript, these logical operators are used in conditional statements and in the `while` loop.

Assignment operators

In JavaScript, assignment operators are used to assign values to variables. The assignment operator = assigns the value of the operand on it right to the operand on its left. For instance, abc = xyz, here xyz is right operand whose value is being assigned to abc, which is the left operand. An assignment operator can assign the value of a single variable to multiple variables. In the following sections, we will discuss the assignment operators in JavaScript.

The = operator

The = operator is used to assign the value to a variable.

Returns

There are no parameters but it is used between two or more operands.

Parameters

There are no parameters.

Description

This is the simplest of all assignment operators and is used commonly. It assigns the value of the right side operand to the left side operand.

Consider the following example:

```
var x=2;
console.log("The value of x is " + x);
```

The output of this will be:

```
The value of x is 2
```

The += operator

This operator is known as addition assignment operator.

Returns

This adds the value to the variable and returns the result of the addition.

Parameters

There are no parameters.

Description

The addition assignment operator is used to add a value to a variable and assign the value to another or the same variable in the same operation.

Consider the following example:

```
var abc = 2;
abc += 10;
console.log(abc); //12
```

This is short hand of writing abc = abc + 10.

The -= operator

This operator is known as subtraction assignment operator.

Returns

This operator subtracts the given value from the variable and returns the result of the subtraction.

Parameters

There are no parameters.

Description

The -= operator is used to subtract a value from a variable and assign the given value to another or the same variable in the same operation.

Consider the following example:

```
var abc = 10;
abc -= 2;
console.log(abc); //8
```

This is short hand of writing abc = abc - 2.

The *= Operator

This operator is known as multiplication assignment operator.

Returns

This multiplies the variable and the value and returns the result of the multiplication.

Parameters

There are no parameters.

Description

This operator is used to multiply a value with a variable and assign the value to another or the same variable in the same operation.

Consider the following example:

```
var abc = 5;
abc *= 5;
console.log(abc); //25
```

This is short hand of writing abc = abc * 5.

The /= Operator

This operator is known as division assignment operator.

Returns

It divides the variable with the value of right operand and assign it to the variable.

Parameters

There are no parameters.

Description

This operator is used to divide a variable with the value and assign the result to the variable.

Consider the following example:

```
var abc = 5;
abc /= 5;
console.log(abc); //1
```

This is short hand of writing abc = abc / 5.

The %= Operator

The %= operator is also called remainder assignment operator.

Parameters

The %= operator takes a null parameter.

Returns

The %= operator returns the remainder.

Description

It divides the variable with the value of right operand and assigns the remainder value it to the variable. For example:

```
var abc = 10;
abc %= 3;
console.log(abc); //1
```

This is short hand of writing abc = abc % 3.

> This is an experimental technology, part of the ECMAScript 2016 (ES7) proposal.

Exponentiation assignment (**=)

This operator returns the result of raising power of left operand to the value of second operand.

```
var abc = 5;
abc **= 2;
console.log(abc); //25
```

This is short hand of writing abc = abc ** 2.

Relational operators

In programming languages, relational operators are also known as comparison operators. These operators show the relative order of two values. These comparison operators are covered in the following sections.

The < operator

The < (Less Than) operator operator is used to compare the values on both sides of the expression and check whether the value of the left-hand side is less than the value on the right-hand side of the operator.

Returns

If the preceding condition is true, then expression returns `true` else `false`.

Parameter

Here, both the operands must be numbers or both must be strings.

Description

This is also known as the **less than** operator.

A simple example of the usage of this operator is as follows:

```
if(2<3) { //returns true
   //block of code
}
```

The <= Operator

The `<=` operator is used to compare the values on both sides of the expression and check whether the value on the left-hand side is less than or equal to the value on the right-hand side of the operator.

Returns

If the preceding condition is true, then it returns the Boolean value `true`, otherwise it returns `false`.

Parameter

Here, both the operands must be numbers or both must be strings.

Description

This is also known as the **less than or equal to** operator.

A simple example of the usage of this is as follows:

```
if(2 <= 3) { //returns true
   //block of code
}
```

The > Operator

The `>` operator is used to compare the values on both sides of the expression and check whether the value on the left-hand side is greater than the value on the right-hand side of the operator.

Returns

If the preceding condition is true, then it returns the Boolean value `true`, otherwise it returns `false`.

Parameter

Here, both the operands must be numbers or both must be strings.

Description

This is also known as the **greater than** operator.

A simple example of the usage of this is as follows:

```
if(2>3) { //returns false
  //block of code
}
```

The >= Operator

The `>=` operator is used to compare the values on both the sides of the expression and check whether the value on the left-hand side is greater than or equal to the value on the right-hand side of the operator.

Returns

If the preceding condition is true, then it returns the Boolean value `true`, otherwise it returns `false`.

Parameter

Here, both the operands must be numbers or both must be strings.

Description

This is also known as the **greater than or equal to** operator.

A simple example of the usage of this is as follows:

```
if(3 >= 3) { //returns true
  //block of code
}
```

The != Operator

The != operator is used to compare the values on both the sides of the expression and check whether the value on the left-hand side is not equal to the value on the right-hand side of the operator.

Returns

If the preceding condition is true, then it returns the Boolean value true, otherwise it returns false.

Parameter

Here, both the operands must be numbers or both must be strings.

Description

This is also known as the **not equal to** operator.

A simple example of the usage of this is as follows:

```
if(2!=3) { //returns true
  //block of code
}
```

The == Operator

The == operator is used to compare the values on both sides of the expression and check whether the value of the left-hand side is equal to the value on the right-hand side of the operator.

Returns

If the preceding condition is true, then it returns the Boolean value true, otherwise it returns false.

Parameter

Here, both the operands must be numbers or both must be strings.

Description

This is also known as the **Equal To** operator.

A simple example of the usage of this is as follows:

```
if(2==3) { //returns false
  //block of code
}
```

The === Operator

The === operator is used to compare the values on both sides of the expression and see if the value of the left is equal to the value on the right of the operator and to also check if both the operands are of the same datatype.

Returns

If the preceding condition is true, then it returns the Boolean value `true`, otherwise it returns `false`.

Parameter

The === operator takes parameter `null`.

Description

This is also known as the **equal value and equal type** operator.

A simple example of the usage of this is as follows:

```
if(3 === 3) { //returns true
  //block of code
}
if(3 === "3") { //returns false
  //block of code
}
```

Statements

JavaScript works on sets of statements. These statements have an appropriate syntax where the syntax depends on what the statements contain. A statement can have multiple lines in it. Basically, a statement is a set of instructions given to a computer browser to execute JavaScript code. A statement can return a value that is terminated with a semicolon. A statement can be a call for a certain action, for example:

```
Document.Write("hello world");
```

The preceding statement calls the in-built `Write()` function and prints the message **hello world** on the screen.

We can write multiple statements in one line separated by a semicolon; for example:

```
var a=20; var b=2;var c=a*b; document.write(c);
```

A statement can also be terminated with a line break, for example:

```
var a=20;
Document.Write(a);
```

Each statement in JavaScript runs one by one in order of the given instructions in the JavaScript program.

Expression statements

In JavaScript, there is a difference between a statement and an expression. Whenever a value is expected in your script or code, an expression produces that value using a statement.

An expression is made of literals, variables, operators, and methods. The data type of the returned value depends on the variable used in the expression. We can create a compound expression from a smaller expression's group depending on their data type.

```
x = Math.PI;
 cx = Math.cos(x);
 alert("cos(" + x + ") = " + cx);
```

Statements are basically actions performed in scripts, for example, loops and `if-else` are statements in JavaScript. Wherever JavaScript expects a statement and you can also write an expression, is called an expression statement. It fulfills purpose of both statement and expression. But this can not be reversed. We can not write a statement where JavaScript is expecting an expression. For instance, if statement can not be used as an argument to a function.

To prevent this from happening JavaScript doesn't allow us to use function expressions and object literals as statements, that is, **expression statement** should not start with:

- Curly brace
- Keyword function

Compound empty statements

A compound statement is a set of statements written in curly brackets and all these statements are separated by a semicolon. It combines multiple statements in a program into a single statement. A compound statement is also known as a **block statement**.

This type of statement is usually used with conditional statements such as `if`, `else`, `for`, `while` loop, and so on. Consider the following example:

```
if(x<10) //  if x is less than 10 then x is incremented {
   x++;
}
```

An empty statement is the opposite of a compound statement. There is no statement in an empty statement but just a semicolon. This semicolon means that no statement will be executed. Usually, empty statements are used when you need to put comments in your code. Consider the following example:

```
for(i=0; i<10; i++)
{} /*  Empty  */
```

Declaration statements

This statement is use to declare a variable or a function in JavaScript.

function

In JavaScript, the `function` keyword is used to declare a function in a program.

Here is a simple example where the `myFunction` function is declared:

```
function myFunction() {
   //block of code
}
```

var

In JavaScript, to declare a variable, we use the `var` keyword. We need to declare a variable before using it.

Consider the following example:

```
var a =5;
var b = 23.5;
var c = "Good morning";
```

Here is an example of both `var` and `function`:

```
var a=2;
var b=3;
function Addition(x,y) {
   return x+y;
```

```
}
var c= Addition(a,b)
Document.Write("The value of c is " + c)
```

The output of the preceding code will be as follows:

```
The value of c is 5
```

Conditional statements

In JavaScript, when we want to perform different actions for different statements, we use a conditional statement. These are a set of commands to perform different actions on different conditions. In JavaScript, there are three types of conditional statements, which are as follows:

- if
- else
- switch

Basically, these statements show the flow of your code. Conditional statements control the flow of your program, that is, which action will be perform on which condition.

Consider an example where you have an e-commerce website and you want to display an offer label on a product when there is special offer on it. In such a scenario, you can place the appropriate code inside conditional statements.

If statements

In programming languages, the `if` statement is a control statement. An `if` statement has two important parts:

- A condition
- A code to perform the action

In JavaScript and other languages, the `if` statement makes decisions based on the variable and type of data. For example, if you write a script asking to be notified on your birthday, then when the time arrives, the message "**It's your birthday today**" will be displayed.

The `if` statement is only executed when the condition is `true`. If the expression is `false`, then it will not execute.

Syntax

Here is the syntax for an if statement in JavaScript:

```
if(condition) {
  // block of code
}
```

Example

For example, in JavaScript, we can write an if statement code as follows:

```
var cAge=25;
If (cAge>18) {
  document.write ("You must have CNIC");
}// if age is above 18 it displays that you must have a CNIC
```

Else if statements

In JavaScript, there may be some situations when we require to make a decision based on different possibilities. The else if statement will only be executed when the previous statement is false and its condition is true. There are two major points of the else if statement, they are as follows:

- There should be an if statement before any else if statement
- You may use as many else if statements as desired, but at the end, you must have an else statement.

Syntax

Here is the syntax for a simple if statement in JavaScript:

```
if(condition 1) {
  // block of code
}
else if(condition 2) {
  //block of code
}
else {
  //  block of code
}
```

In the preceding syntax, two conditions can be checked for their validity.

Here is the syntax for a slightly more complex `else if` statement in JavaScript:

```
if(condition 1) {
  // block of code
}
else if(condition 2) {
  // block of code
}
else if(condition 3) {
  // block of code
}
else {
  // block of code
}
```

In the preceding syntax, three conditions can be checked for their validity.

Example

For example, if you have a web page and you want to check who is accessing that web page. You will put two custom messages in your script inside the `Else if` statement. You will write these as follows:

```
var person="Manager";
If(person=="Admin") {
  Document.Write("I am visiting it");
}
Else if(person=="Manager") {
  Document.Write("I am accessing it");
}
Else {
  document.write("hello kitty");
}
```

The `Else if` statement is one of the most advanced forms of statements in JavaScript. It makes a decision after checking all the `if` conditions. It is just a type of complex statement where every `if` is a part of an `else` statement. All conditions must be `true` within the parenthesis following the `else if` keyword. If any of the conditions are `false`, then the `else` part will be executed.

Switch statement

In programming languages, the `switch` statement execution depends only on the value of the expression. There are lists of cases against which checks are done. The checks are done sequentially; JavaScript interpreter checks the first case and its condition to check whether it is `true` or not. Similarly, checks are done for all case statements to check whether their conditions are `true` and to find a break statement. When the interpreter encounters the break statement, it exits the `switch` loop. The break statement is meant to ensure that the `switch` statement returns control to the calling function once one case is executed, interpreter does not forward the control to the next applicable case.

Syntax

Here is the syntax for a simple `switch` statement in JavaScript:

```
switch(condition/expression)
  case expression 1:
    //block of code
  break;
  case expression 2:
    //block of code
  break;

  case expression 3:
    //block of code
  break;

  default:
    //block of code
  break;
```

Example

Following is an example of a valid `switch` statement:

```
Switch (personName)
  case "Jack":
    alert("my name is Jack");
  Break;
  case "Ahmed":
    alert("my name is Ahmed");
  break;
  default:
    alert("my name is Talha");
  break;
```

If the preceding code does not find a matching case then it executes the default statement. Basically a `switch` statement is an expression which evaluates different statements in order to execute some code based on some conditions.

Loops

In programming languages, loops are used to execute a block of code a number of times, depending on a condition. For example, if you have a statement and you want to execute it over and over, you just put it in a loop. Loops are basically used for repetitive tasks.

Another specific example of a loop is that if you want to traverse an array to find a specific number, you have to iterate through array elements. Each iteration will get the next array index.

There are four types of loops in JavaScript, they are as follows:

- `for`
- `while`
- `do-WHILE`
- `for-in`

For repetitive tasks we put a set of instructions in a loop. To control the number of times a loop executes, we use control variables in a loop for incrementing or decrementing value of an iterator or counter variable, which will repeat the block of code. You can also use the `break` and `continuous` statements in a loop.

For loop

The `for` loops are used to loop through or execute a block of code, until a condition returns a `false` result. In a `for` loop, we mention how many times the script should perform. For example, you might want to execute your script 12 times.

Syntax

A `for` loop in JavaScript is the same as in other languages, such as C, C++, and Python. The `for` loop syntax has three important parts:

- **Initialization**: This is where loop initializes the counter variable. This is the first statement when a loop starts its execution.
- **Condition**: This is an expression to be evaluated before every loop iteration. If the condition is satisfied and is `true`, we enter the loop; otherwise, if the condition is not satisfied and the condition returns `false`, then we exit the `for` loop.

- **Increment/Decrement**: This is used for iteration and for increasing or decreasing the counter variable value. This is an update statement where increment or decrement is executed.

```
for (initialization; condition; increment / decrement) {
  //code block
}
```

Example

Consider the following example of a basic counter code in JavaScript:

```
var i; // declares the variable i
for(i=1; i < 5 ; i++) {
  Document.Write("basic counter:"+i);
  Document.Write("<br/>");
}
```

The output will be as follows:

```
Basic counter:1
Basic counter:2
Basic counter:3
Basic counter:4
```

While loop

This is also a commonly used loop in JavaScript. The `while` loop executes a block of statements repeatedly as long as its condition is `true`. The loop exits when the condition becomes `false`.

Syntax

Here is the syntax for a `while` loop in JavaScript:

```
while (condition expression) {
  // code block
}
```

There are two parts of a `while` loop:

- The condition statement
- The `while` loop code written in curly brackets

The `while` loop conditions have to be met in order for the loop to work. If the condition breaks, then the loop breaks.

Example

Here is an example of the while loop, which will print numbers from 1 to 4:

```
var count= 0;
While(count<5) {
   Document.Write("count");
   Document.Write("<br/>");
   count++;
}
```

The output will be as follows:

```
1
2
3
4
```

Do while loop

The do while loop is also known as a **post-test loop** because it first executes the statement and then checks the condition. If the condition is true, then it will enter the loop, and if the condition is false, it will break out from the loop.

Syntax

Here is the syntax for the do while loop in JavaScript:

```
Do {
   //statement
}
While(condition);
```

There are two important parts of the do while loop:

- A statement
- A condition

The do while loop is similar to the while loop, but it checks the condition at the end of the loop. The do while loop executes the specified statement at least once before checking the condition.

Example

Here is an example of the do while loop that prints the values 1 to 5:

```
var i=1;
Do {
  document.write("The value of i is " + i + "</br>");
  i++;
}
While(i<6);
```

The output will be as follows:

```
The value of i is 1
The value of i is 2
The value of i is 3
The value of i is 4
The value of i is 5
```

The do while loop can be used where we need to execute the loop at least once, irrespective of whether or not the condition is met.

For in loop

There is another type on loop used in JavaScript that is known as the for in loop. This loop is used for object properties in JavaScript. In this loop, one property of the object is assigned to a variable name.

Syntax

Here is a syntax for the for in loop in JavaScript:

```
For (property in object) {
  //code block
}
```

Example

Here is an example of the for in loop:

```
var I;
For (I is navigator) {
  Document.Write(i);
}
Document.Write("The loop ends here");
```

Jumps and labeled statements

In JavaScript, the `jump` statements are used to force the flow of execution to jump to another condition in the script. Basically, it is used to terminate iterative statements. There are two types of `jump` statements in JavaScript:

- Break
- Continue

These statements are used when you immediately leave a loop or when you want to jump to another condition due to a condition in a code.

Break statement

In JavaScript, a `break` statement is used with a `switch` statement. It is used to exit a loop or a condition earlier than planned. Break statements are also used in the `for` loop and the `while` loop.

Syntax

Here is the syntax for the `break` statement in JavaScript:

```
Any loop(condition) {
  //block of code that will be executed
  break;
  //block of code that won't get executed
}
```

Example

Consider the following simple example:

```
var i=1;
While(i<10) {
  if(i==3) {
    Document.Write("Breaking from if loop");
    Break;
  }
  Document.Write("The value of i is " + i);
  i+=2;
}
```

The output will be as follows:

```
The value of i is 1
Breaking from if loop
The value of i is 3
```

Continue statement

The keyword `continue` will skip the current iteration.

Syntax

Here is the syntax for the `continue` statement in JavaScript:

```
Any loop(condition) {
  //block of code that will be executed
  Any loop (condition) {
    //block of code that will be executed
    continue;
    block of code that wont be executed
  }
  //block of code  that will be executed
}
```

Example

Consider the following simple example:

```
var i=1;
While(i<5) {
  if(i==3) //skip the iteration {
    Document.Write("Continue statement encountered");
    continue;
  }
  Document.Write("The value of i is " + i);
  i=i+2;
}
```

The output will be as follows:

```
The value of i is 1
Continue statement encountered
```

Return statement

In JavaScript, a `return` statement is used to return a value from a function. After returning the value, it stops the function execution. Every function and statement returns a value. If no return statement is provided, undefined value is returned instead.

Syntax

Here is the syntax for the `return` statement in JavaScript:

```
function myfunc(x, y) {
  //some block of code
  return x;
}
Document.Write("The result is " + myfunc(2, 3));
```

Example

Consider the following simple example showing the working of a `return` statement:

```
Function multiply(a,b) {
  return a*B;
}
var mul=multiply(2,3);
Document.Write("The result is "+ mul);
```

The output will be as follows:

```
The result is 6
```

Throw statement

A `throw` statement is used to create a user-defined error condition for the `try` and `catch` block. These errors are also called **exceptions**. We can create our own exceptions in a code script.

Syntax

Here is the syntax for the `throw` statement in JavaScript:

```
try {
  //block of code
  throw "error";
  //block of code
}
catch(error) {
  //block of code
}
```

Example

Let's take a look at the following code snippet:

```
Try {
  document.write( "hello world);//the code will throw an error due
  to the missing "
}
Catch(error) {
  Error.messageTxt;
}
```

Try catch finally statement

In a `try` statement we write the code that needs error testing when it is being executed. In a `catch` block, you write code to handle errors occurring in the `try` block. When you write code inside the `try` block, you must write a `catch` block to handle any error that might occur in the the `try` block. The `finally` statement executes when the `try` and `catch` statements are executed successfully.

Syntax

The syntax for a `try`, `catch`, and `finally` block is as shown in the following code snippet:

```
Try {//generate exception}
Catch {//error handling code}
Finally {//block of code which runs after try and catch}
```

Arrays

Arrays are use to store ordered collections of data. If we have multiple items, then we can use arrays to store these values. Array prototype methods are used to perform mutation operations in JavaScript. There is no fixed length of an array. An array can contain multiple value types and the number of items can be mutated at any point after initialization.

Array types

There are two array types in JavaScript:

- **Nominal type**: This type of array has a unique identity.
- **Structure type**: This array type looks like an interface; it is also known as duck type. It uses a specific implementation of a behavior.

Sparse array

In programming languages, a sparse array denotes an array that has the same values such as 0 or null. There is a large number of zeroes in an array storage, which occurs in a sparse array. In a sparse array, indexes do not start from 0. In a sparse array, lengths of the elements are less than the length of the property.

In JavaScript, the length property is not the actual amount of elements in the array, it is last *index+1*. So, in case of a sparse array, this is crucial to deal with the blank indexes. Consider the following example:

```
var person=[];
Person[1]="Ali";
Person[20]="Ahmed";
Alert(person.length);// it will be 21 length
```

Array type object

Some objects in JavaScript look like an array, but in reality, they are not arrays. They are known as **array-like** objects.

An array-like object:

- **Has**: This tells you the number of elements an object has
- **Does not have**: These are array methods such as indexOf, push, and forEach

Strings as an array

There are some strings in JavaScript that behave like an array. If we make a string like an array, then it will only be treated as an array. There are some methods in arrays such as push(), reverse(), and so on, which do not work on strings.

Creating arrays

In JavaScript, there are two ways to create arrays:

- Using an array initializer
- Using an array constructor

You can use either of these two methods.

We have a comma-separated string in brackets in an array initializer; for example:

```
var students= ["Ali","Ahmed","Amina"];
```

In JavaScript, you can also create an array using an array constructor using a new keyword, which creates an array and assigns values to it; for example:

```
var students=new Array ("Ali,"Ahmed","Amina");
```

 The array initializer method is a quick and good way of initializing an array because its execution speed is higher than that of the constructor method. If you do not pass any argument in an array constructor, then it will set its length to zero.

Array initializer

Arrays are used to store ordered collections of data in a single variable. It means that when you want to store a list of items then you should use an array. Before using an array in your program you need to first initialize it.

In an array initializer, there are comma separated lists of items stored in a variable, for example:

```
var a1=[];
var a2=[2];
var a3=[1,2,3];
var a4=['hi', [2]];
```

 When you initialize an array using an array initializer, the type does not have to be the same for all items. Also, arrays can have zero length.

Array constructor

There are three different ways in which you can use an array constructor. Their syntax is as follows:

```
var a1=new array(); // new empty array
var a2=new array(2); // new array of size 2
var a3= new array(1,2,3); // new array containing 1, 2, 3
```

If you call an array constructor without argument it will set its length to zero.

If an array constructor has only one argument then this argument will initialize its new length.

If you call an array with two or more elements, the the argument will initialize an array with size equal to the number of parameters.

Reading and writing array elements

To read and write elements from an array we use square brackets [ ]. It works as accessing object properties. Inside the brackets there should be a non-negative number. The syntax for both reading and writing in an array is the same. Values are also indexed in an array. You read values index by index. The array's reference should be on left side of bracket.

Consider the following example:

```
var obj=["abc"];
var start=obj[0]; //its is for reading

Document.Write(start);

var obj[1]="hello";
i="world";
Obj[i]="hello world";//writing
Document.Write(obj[i]);
```

The output of this would be as follows:

```
Hello world
```

Multidimensional arrays in JavaScript

Like other programming languages, you can also create multidimensional arrays in JavaScript. Their syntax is same as in other languages. In multidimensional arrays you create arrays within arrays of nested array loops.

You can create an array by adding more arrays for each dimension you need. Creating a multidimensional array is useful when you need to cover the whole storage with information. If most of your data is sparse, meaning if array is empty, then a better technique to store the information is using an associative array. Here is an example of creating a multidimensional array in JavaScript:

```
var a=5;
var b=2;
var c=new array();
For(i=0;i<5;i++) {
  C[i]=new array();
  for For(j=0;j<5;j++)
  c[i][j];  }}
}
```

Properties in an array

An array has a prototype, length, and a constructor as its properties.

Length

In JavaScript, the array length property returns the number of elements in an array.

Returns

This returns an integer value of 32 bit.

Description

We can also use an array length property when we want to empty an array at any time. When you increase the length of any array, it will not increase the number of elements in it. We can set or return the length of any array using the array length property.

Consider the following example:

```
var num=new Array[1,2,3];
Document. write (num.length);
```

The output will be as follows:

```
3
```

Constructor

An array contractor is used to initialize an array. An array can contain zero or more elements and has the following syntax where array elements are separated by a comma inside square brackets.

```
var fruits = ["Apple", "Banana"];
```

Prototype

All array instances inherit from `Array.prototype`. The prototype constructor of an array allows to add new methods and properties to the `Array()` object.

```
Array.prototype is an array itself.
Array.isArray(Array.prototype); // true
```

You can find detailed information on how to make these changes at MDN (`https://developer.mozilla.org/en-US/docs/Web/JavaScript/Reference/Global_Objects/Array/prototype`).

Array methods

There are several methods that can be performed on arrays to obtain different results. Some of these methods are defined in the following sections.

concat()

The concat() method performs concatenation between two arrays.

Returns

The concat() method returns the concatenated array.

Parameter

The concat() method takes a string to concatenate with.

Description

This takes two arrays and joins them.

```
var alpha = ['a', 'b', 'c'],
var numeric = [1, 2, 3];
var alphaNumeric = alpha.concat(numeric);
console.log(alphaNumeric); // Result: ['a', 'b', 'c', 1, 2, 3]
```

every()

The every() method tests a function for every array element.

Returns

The every() method returns a Boolean true or false.

Parameter

A call back function to be applied on every element of the array.

Description

If every element in an array provides the testing function, then it returns true.

```
function isBigEnough(element, index, array) {
  return element >= 10;
}
[12, 5, 8, 130, 44].every(isBigEnough);   // false
[12, 54, 18, 130, 44].every(isBigEnough); // true
```

foreach()

The `foreach()` method executes a function passed as a parameter for every element of the array.

Returns

The output of each function.

Parameter

A call back function to be called for every element of the array.

Description

The `foreach()` method calls the functions of each element:

```
function logArrayElements(element, index, array) {
  console.log('a[' + index + '] = ' + element);
}

// Note elision, there is no member at 2 so it isn't visited
[2, 5, , 9].forEach(logArrayElements);
// logs:
// a[0] = 2
// a[1] = 5
// a[3] = 9
```

join()

This joins all elements into a string.

Returns

A joined string.

Parameter

`Null` or a separator to place between array elements.

Description

It joins all elements into a string.

```
var a = ['One', 'Two', 'Three'];
var var1 = a.join();       // assigns 'One,Two,Three' to var1
var var2 = a.join(', ');   // assigns 'One, Two, Three' to var2
var var3 = a.join(' + ');  // assigns 'One + Two + Three' to var3
var var4 = a.join('');     // assigns 'OneTwoThree' to var4
```

pop()

The pop() method removes the last element of an array, just like a stack.

Returns

The pop() method returns a null parameter.

Parameter

The pop() method takes the null parameter.

Description

It removes the last element of an array, just like a stack.

```
var myColours = ['Yellow', 'Black', 'Blue', 'Green'];
console.log(myColours); // ['Yellow', 'Black', 'Blue', 'Green']
var popped = myColours.pop();
console.log(myColours); // ['Yellow', 'Black', 'Blue' ]
console.log(popped); // 'Green'
```

push()

It adds elements on the last index on an array.

Returns

null.

Parameter

null.

Description

This adds elements at the last index on an array.

```
var sports = ['cricket', 'baseball'];
var total = sports.push('football');

console.log(sports); // ['cricket', 'baseball', 'football']
console.log(total);  // 3
```

indexOf()

The indexOf() method returns the first index of an array.

Returns

The indexOf() method returns an index.

Parameter

The indexOf() method takes an array element as a parameter.

Description

It returns the first index of an array.

```
var array = [2, 5, 9];
array.indexOf(9);      // 2
array.indexOf(7);      // -1 if not found
```

lastIndexOf()

The lastIndexOf() method returns the last index at which a given element is found inside an array.

Returns

It returns the last index of an array.

Parameter

An array element.

Description

```
var array = [2, 5, 9, 2];
array.indexOf(2);      // 3
array.indexOf(7);      // -1 if not found
```

reverse()

The reverse() method reverses the order of all the elements in an array.

Returns

The array.

Parameter

null.

Description

The `reverse()` method reverses the order of the elements in an array. The first element becomes the last element and so on.

```
var myArray = ['one', 'two', 'three'];
myArray.reverse();

console.log(myArray) // ['three', 'two', 'one']
```

shift()

In an array, the `shift()` method removes the very first element and returns that element.

Returns

`null`.

Parameter

`null`.

Description

In an array, it removes the very first element and returns the removed element.

```
var myColours = ['Yellow', 'Black', 'Blue', 'Green'];
console.log(myColours); // ['Yellow', 'Black', 'Blue', 'Green']
var shifted = myColours.shift();
console.log(myColours); // ['Black', 'Blue', 'Green']
console.log(shifted); // 'Green'
```

unshift()

This method adds a new element at the beginning of the array and returns the new array length.

Returns

The new length of the array.

Parameter

The element(s) to add in the array.

Description

This method adds a new element at the beginning of the array and returns the new array length:

```
var arr = [1, 2, 3];
arr.unshift(0); // arr is [0, 1, 2, 3]
```

slice()

The `slice()` method slices an array into a new array.

Returns

The new sliced array.

Parameter

The indices of elements to slice.

Description

This method slices an array into a new array:

```
var fruits = ['Banana', 'Orange', 'Lemon', 'Apple', 'Mango'];
var citrus = fruits.slice(1, 3);

// citrus contains ['Orange','Lemon']
```

splice()

The `splice()` method is also used to add new elements to an array by removing existing elements.

Returns

The new spliced array.

Parameter

The indices of elements to remove and the elements to add.

Description

This method is also used to add new elements to an array by removing existing elements:

```
var myCars = ['Audi', 'BMW', 'Ferrari', 'Volkswagen'];

// removes 0 elements from index 2, and inserts 'Toyota'
var removed = myCars.splice(2, 0, 'Toyota');
// myCars is ['Audi', 'BMW', 'Toyota', 'Volkswagen']
// removed is [], no elements removed
```

sort()

This sorts an array alphabetically.

Returns

null.

Parameter

null.

Description

Called as an array method, this sorts an array alphabetically (unicode characters) and will not work well with numbers:

```
var fruit = ['cherries', 'apples', 'bananas'];
fruit.sort(); // ['apples', 'bananas', 'cherries']
```

toString()

The toString() method converts the object into a string.

Returns

The toString() method returns a string.

Parameter

The toString() method takes a null parameter.

Description

Converts the array object into a string with its elements separated by commas character.

```
var monthNames = ['Jan', 'Feb', 'Mar', 'Apr'];
var myVar = monthNames.toString(); // 'Jan,Feb,Mar,Apr' to myVar.
```

ECMA5 Array methods

New array methods were added into the ECMA5 script, which is also known as **arrays extras**. These are nine new methods. These methods perform common operations working with arrays. These new methods are covered in the following sections.

array.prototype.map()

The map() method creates a new array on the result values from each iteration.

Returns

A modified array.

Parameters

A callback function.

Description

It loops through an array, running a function, and creates a new array based on the return values from each iteration. It takes the same arguments as the forEach() method.

Here is a simple example:

```
var numbers = [1, 4, 9];
var roots = numbers.map(Math.sqrt);
```

The roots are now as follows:

```
[1, 2, 3]
```

array.prototype.filter()

The filter() function creates a new or modified array that consist of values that are processed by the function.

Returns

A modified array.

Parameters

A callback function.

Description

It creates a new array of only those elements that returned `true` to their callbacks.

Here is a simple example:

```
function isBigEnough(value) {
  return value >= 10;
}
var filtered = [12, 5, 8, 130, 44].filter(isBigEnough);
```

The output is as follows:

```
[12, 130, 44]
```

array.prototype.reduce()

The `reduce()` function simultaneously applies a function to two values of the array to reduce them to a single value. The direction of selection of values is from left to right.

Returns

A modified array.

Parameters

A callback function.

Description

The `array.prototype.reduce()` method is used to accumulate all values in an array to a single value by the operations performed in the callback function.

Here is a simple example:

```
[0, 1, 2, 3, 4].reduce(function(previousValue, currentValue,
index, array) {
  return previousValue + currentValue;
});
```

The callbacks are executed as follows:

	previousValue	currentValue	index	array	return value
First call	0	1	1	[0, 1, 2, 3, 4]	1
Second call	1	2	2	[0, 1, 2, 3, 4]	3
Third call	3	3	3	[0, 1, 2, 3, 4]	6
Fourth call	6	4	4	[0, 1, 2, 3, 4]	10

array.prototype.forEach()

The `array.prototype.forEach()` method executes a function passed as a parameter for every element of the array.

Returns

The output of each function.

Parameter

A callback function to be called for every element of the array.

Description

The `array.prototype.forEach()` method calls functions of each element. Here is a simple example:

```
function logArrayElements(element, index, array) {
   console.log('a[' + index + '] = ' + element);
}

// Note elision, there is no member at 2 so it isn't visited
[2, 5, , 9].forEach(logArrayElements);
// logs:
// a[0] = 2
// a[1] = 5
// a[3] = 9
```

array.prototype.indexOf()

The `array.prototype.indexOf()` method returns the first index of an array.

Returns

An index.

Parameter

An array element.

Description

The `array.prototype.indexOf()` method returns the first index of an array. Here is a simple example:

```
var array = [2, 5, 9];
array.indexOf(9);      // 2
array.indexOf(7);      // -1 if not found
```

array.prototype.lastIndexOf()

The `array.prototype.lastIndexOf()` method returns the last index at which a given element is found inside an array.

Returns

It returns the last index of an array.

Parameter

An array element.

Description

As stated in the preceding descriptions, the `array.prototype.lastIndexOf()` function will return the last index of the specified element if found within the array. Here is a simple example:

```
var array = [2, 5, 9, 2];
array.indexOf(2);      // 3
array.indexOf(7);      // -1 if not found
```

array.prototype.every()

The `array.prototype.every()` method tests a function for every array element.

Returns

A Boolean `true` or `false`.

Parameter

A callback function to be applied on every element of the array.

Description

If every element in an array provides the testing function, then it returns `true`. Here is a simple example:

```
function isBigEnough(element, index, array) {
   return element >= 10;
}
[12, 5, 8, 130, 44].every(isBigEnough);   // false
[12, 54, 18, 130, 44].every(isBigEnough); // true
```

array.prototype.some()

This method tests if any element passes the test implemented by the provided function.

Returns

A Boolean `True` or `False`.

Parameters

A callback function.

Description

The `array.prototype.some()` method is similar to `Array.prototype.every()`, but here the condition is that at least one callback should return `true`.

A simple example is as follows:

```
function isBiggerThan10(element, index, array) {
   return element > 10;
}
[2, 5, 8, 1, 4].some(isBiggerThan10);   // false
[12, 5, 8, 1, 4].some(isBiggerThan10); // true
```

array.prototype.reduceRight()

The `array.prototype.reduceRight()` method applies a function simultaneously against two values of the array (from right to left) so as to reduce them to a single value.

Returns

A modified array.

Parameters

A callback function.

Description

This is exactly the same as reduce, but it starts from right and moves toward the left while accumulating the values.

Here is a simple example:

```
var total = [0, 1, 2, 3].reduceRight(function(a, b) {
    return a + b;
});
```

This returns the sum as 6.

10
JavaScript Object-Oriented Programming

JavaScript is an object-oriented programming language. In **object-oriented programming (OOP)** languages, we use the concept of objects rather than actions to develop applications. In the past, JavaScript had no real foundation and was just a basic language. JavaScript is not a fully OOP-based language like JAVA, C#, and other programming languages, but it still has many OOP features.

There are many features in JavaScript where code is reused. So, rather than using procedural concepts in JavaScript, we use object-oriented programming techniques. There are four basic principles of object-oriented programming.

Polymorphism

Since JavaScript is a dynamic language, it supports **polymorphism**. Polymorphism can be understood as the ability of an object to be different at different times. For example, a shape can be a square, a rectangle, or a circle.

Encapsulation

This feature is also supported in JavaScript. It means protecting parts of code from external use. It protects part of the code that does not concern the end user but is important for running an application, such as in an application that stores passwords. Users don't have to know how their passwords are encrypted. Hence, this code is encapsulated.

Inheritance

In JavaScript, inheritance can be used to derive properties of parent objects to their child objects and have some unique attributes for themselves as well. For example, a square and a triangle may inherit their stroke or fill from a `shape` object and, at the same time, have a number of vertices unique to themselves.

Abstraction

Abstraction is not natively supported in JavaScript, but there are methods through which this can be achieved, using a combination of polymorphism and inheritance.

Objects

Objects are the basic key to understand object-oriented programming. Programming objects are just like real-world objects. Look around, you'll see many objects. Your car, mobile phone, desk, laptop, pet dog, and DVD player are all objects.

All objects have two characteristics: properties and methods.

A mobile has properties (color, screen size, height, and weight) and methods (make calls, send SMSs, receive calls, and transfer files).

A car has properties (color, height, gearbox, wheels, engine, brakes, and steering) and methods (start engine, steer, change gear, apply brake, stop, and crash).

Just like these real-world examples, the objects in OOP have the same characteristics. So, an object, in terms of programming, can have properties (variables in any programming language) and methods (functions in any programming language). Hence, we can define an object as *"an entity or a thing that has some properties and methods associated with it. An object can be individually selected and manipulated"*.

All generic properties and methods are combined into a template called a **class**. A class is then used as a template to instantiate single or multiple objects. In JavaScript, there are many built-in objects, such as Maths, Dates, Regular Expressions, Arrays, and so on.

Creating objects

In JavaScript, we can create objects in three different ways:

- Using object literals
- Using new keywords
- Using the `object.create()` method (ECMAScript 5)

Object literals

This is the simplest way to create an object. An object can be both created and defined in one statement using an object literal. An object literal is a comma-separated list of `name:value` (like year:1990, age:25) pairs enclosed within curly brackets.

Here is an example:

```
var car= {
  model:"2014",
  company:"Honda",
  color:"White"
};
```

In the preceding example, we have created a `car` object with four properties or attributes.

```
var empty = {}
```

On the other hand, this piece of code creates an object with no properties.

The new keyword

The new keyword is used to create and initialize a new object. The new keyword is always followed by a function call. This function is known as a constructor, which initializes the newly created object. JavaScript contains built-in constructors for the native types.

Here is an example:

```
var car = new Object();
car.model = "2014";
car.company = "Honda";
car.colour = "White";
```

The preceding example also creates a new `car` object with four properties:

```
varempty = new Object();      // An empty object, same as {}.
vararr = new Array();         // An empty array, same as [].
varcurrdate = new Date();     // Current Date.
varregex = new RegExp("JavaScript"); // A pattern matching object.
```

The object.create() method

The `object.create()` method was originally defined in ECMAScript 5. It is also used to create an object. The first argument passed to this method is the prototype of that object. The second argument is optional. It describes the object's properties.

Here is an example:

```
// obj1 inherits properties model, company and colour.
varcar =
Object.create({model:"2014",company:"Honda",colour:"White"});

// car inherits no properties or methods.
varcar = Object.create(null);
```

`Null` can be passed if the object does not have any prototype. However, this object will not inherit anything:

```
// car is same as {} or new Object().
varcar = Object.create(Object.prototype);
```

Design patterns

To write scalable code, we need to track down the recurring sections in our code and to optimize them in a way that it's easy to maintain the code. Design patterns help us in doing this.

In a book, *Addison-Wesley Professional* by *Erich Gamma, John Vlissides, Ralph Johnson,* and *Richard Helm*; First edition (November 10, 1994), Design Patterns are defined as:

> *A design pattern names, abstracts, and identifies the key aspects of a common design structure that make it useful for creating a reusable object-oriented design. The design pattern identifies the participating classes and their instances, their roles and collaborations, and the distribution of responsibilities.*

Each design pattern focuses on a particular object-oriented design problem or issue. It describes when it applies, whether or not it can be applied in view of other design constraints, and the consequences and trade-offs of its use. Since we must eventually implement our designs, a design pattern also provides sample code to illustrate an implementation.

Although design patterns describe object-oriented designs, they are based on practical solutions that have been implemented in mainstream object-oriented programming languages.

Developers usually question whether there is any best design pattern to implement in their workflow.

Actually, no single design pattern is perfect for all scenarios. Each and every web application that is developed has its own needs. We have to see which pattern will add value to our application if implemented, because all design patterns serve different solutions.

So, once we have a good understanding of design patterns, it will be easier for us to integrate a pattern into our application architecture. Design patterns are classified into three categories: creational, structural, and behavioral.

- **Creational design patterns**: Constructor, factory, prototype, and singleton are examples of creational design patterns
- **Structural design patterns**: Decorator, façade, and flyweight are example of structural design patterns
- **Behavioral design patterns**: Observer and mediator are examples of such patterns

Constructor pattern

Constructors are special methods used to initialize objects. They may accept arguments, which are then used to set values to member properties and methods when the object is created. Native constructors, such as arrays and objects, are present inside JavaScript as native functions. We can also create custom constructors that define properties and methods for our custom object.

Description

In the `constructor` method, we create an object using the `new` keyword. In this method, we define properties and methods with the `this` keyword. Properties are defined after the = sign. When you define each property, you must place a semicolon at the end. When you use the `this` method in your script, you need to first initialize the object and then use it in your code:

Simple constructors

A constructor is considered to be the most suitable way to implement an instance. The `new` keyword tells JavaScript that we would like that function to act like a constructor and to create an instance also called `object`. Within a constructor, the `this` keyword is used to reference the new object.

Prototype constructors

Prototype is a property of functions in JavaScript. Whenever a `constructor` function is invoked to create a new object, all of the characteristics of that constructor's prototype are then associated to the new object.

Module pattern

Modules are an essential part of any well-constructed web application. They are independent blocks linked with each other in a neat, understandable and well-organized way. In other words, they give the program a structure and also provide encapsulation.

Description

Modules can be implemented in several ways in JavaScript. We will be discussing two of them here:

- Object literal notation
- The module pattern

Object literal notation

As we have read earlier, object literals are a list of `name:value` pairs separated by commas enclosed inside curly braces { }. Names can be identifiers or strings followed by a colon. Make sure there is no comma after the last `name:value` pair; otherwise, it may result in some unexpected errors:

```
varObjectLiteral = {
  variableKey: Value,
```

```
  functionKey: function() {
    //...
  }
};
```

We do not have to instantiate object literals with the `new` keyword.

Care should be taken to see that the keyword `new` is not used at the start of the statement. This is because the opening curly bracket could be interpreted as the start of a code block.

We can add new members from the outside object as follows:

```
myModule.property = 'someValue';
```

Using modules can help in hiding data members (encapsulation) and managing code in an organized way.

The module pattern

In conventional software engineering, the module pattern provides public and private access to classes, methods, and variables. The focus of the module pattern is to reduce the use of global variables, minimizing the conflicts inside the code throughout the application.

This is the most famous and commonly used design pattern that is implemented in large JavaScript frameworks and extension libraries such as **jQuery**, **ExtJS**, **YUI**, and **DoJo**.

Here is an example of the module pattern that makes use of a shared private cache. This method enables us to create objects using shared storage that will, in return, optimize performance because the functions are only created one time in the start. The mixin uses the function reference to call them rather than creating a new instance of that function every time it needs them.

Here are a few advantages and disadvantages of the module pattern:

Advantages:

- This pattern has a cleaner approach for developers
- It supports encapsulation
- There is less global namespace cluttering
- This supports localized functions and variables with closures

Disadvantages:

- As the public and private members are accessed in a different manner, when there is a need to change visibility of a specific member we would have to change it everywhere the object was being used

- Private members cannot be accessed from new methods that are added to objects afterwards

- Private members cannot be extended easily

The revealing module pattern

This pattern is almost identical to the module pattern. The only difference is that, in this pattern, all members are kept private until they are explicitly called, usually by an object literal returned by the closure from which it is defined.

Description

Christian Heilmann engineered this pattern. He disliked the fact that we had to switch to object literal notation for the objects that we want to keep public. There was another drawback: we had to repeat the name of main object if we had to access public variables from one method into an other or call public methods.

In this pattern, we define all functions and variables as private and, at the end of module, return an anonymous object along with the pointers to the private functions and variables we would like to expose as public.

Here are a few advantages and disadvantages of the revealing module pattern:

Advantages:

- Cleaner approach for developers
- Supports encapsulation
- Less global namespace cluttering
- Localized functions and variables with closures
- More consist script syntax
- Explicit definition of public functions and variables
- Increased readability

Disadvantages:

- Private members are inaccessible
- It's difficult to patch public functions and variables that are referred to by some private members

The singleton pattern

This pattern ensures that only one instance of a class is created and provides a global access point to the object.

Description

The singleton pattern is implemented by creating a class with a method whose object can only be created if it doesn't exist already. If the object already existed, the reference will be returned to that object.

It is recommended to delay the initialization of singletons in cases where they require some information that might not be available at the time of initialization. Hence, they are different from static classes or objects.

Here are a few advantages and disadvantages of the singleton pattern:

Advantages:

- Optimized memory usage
- Single global point of access
- Delayed initialization, which prevents instantiation until it is required

Disadvantages:

- There is no reset option once it is instantiated.
- Unit testing is difficult because when we reference a singleton class that exists outside of the class under test, then we do not have a true unit test. Instead of what should have been a single unit test of the target class, we end up testing the target class and the singleton together.
- It may introduce hidden dependencies.

The observer pattern

The observer pattern is such that if one object changes state all others are notified and can update automatically. Thus this pattern defines a one-to-many dependency relationship between objects.

Description

In the observer pattern, an object (also called a subject/publisher) is connected to multiple other objects that are dependent on our subject. These depending objects are called **observers/subscribers**.

The subject broadcasts a notification whenever a change in state occurs. All observers receive the notification and update them accordingly.

The book, *Design Patterns: Elements of Reusable Object-Oriented Software*, describes the observer pattern as follows:

> "*One or more observers are interested in the state of a subject and register their interest with the subject by attaching themselves. When something changes in our subject that the observer may be interested in, a notify message is sent which calls the update method in each observer. When the observer is no longer interested in the subject's state, they can simply detach themselves.*"

Here are a few advantages and disadvantages of the observer pattern:

Advantages:

- Requires a deeper understanding of various components in the system and their relationship with each other
- Helps in pointing out dependencies
- Helps in disintegrating objects into smaller reusable components

Disadvantages:

- Application integrity check can become difficult
- Switching an observer from one subject to another can be tough

The mediator pattern

As the name suggests, a mediator is a person who assists in negotiations between two or more conflicting parties.

In terms of software engineering, mediator comes under the behavioral design pattern category. The pattern enables us to implement a single object through which different components of an application communicate.

Description

The mediator pattern promotes loose coupling by ensuring that, instead of objects interacting with each other directly, they communicate across a central point.

Let's take a real-world example to understand it in a better way. Consider an airport traffic-control system. The control tower acts as a mediator, while all other planes are communicating with the control tower and waiting for the notifications to land or to take off. They do not contact each other but just with the control tower. The role of the control tower is very essential and central. Hence, it an important key for this system.

Similarly, the mediator is as important in this pattern.

When we call mediator's subscribe method, we pass in a callback, and the mediator queues up these callbacks for when the given event is fired and subsequently the decoupled object's callback is fired. Mediator triggers the signal for the object to fire, allowing the object to be decoupled from any others.

Here are a few advantages and disadvantages of the mediator pattern:

Advantages:

- Removes many-to-many relationships
- Establishes many-to-one relationship
- Help us to figure out dependencies
- Helps in disintegrating objects to promote smaller reusable components

Disadvantages:

- Introduces a single point of failure
- Performance issues may arise when too many modules try to communicate back and forth

The prototype pattern

In the prototype pattern, objects are created on the template of the existing object through cloning.

Description

This pattern focuses on creating an object that can be used as a template/blueprint for other objects through prototypal inheritance. JavaScript has native support for prototypal inheritance. Therefore, it's easy to work in this pattern.

Here are a few advantages and disadvantages of the prototype pattern:

Advantages:

- Suitable for applications where object creation is in focus
- Better performance as new objects inherit features from the prototype

Disadvantages:

- Overkill for an application that has very few objects or prototypes

Command pattern

In this pattern, commands are encapsulated as objects.

Description

Command objects allow loosely coupled systems to separate objects that issue requests from the objects that process requests. These requests are known as **events** and the code that processes these requests is called an event handler.

In simpler words, we can say that the main purpose of the command pattern is separating the features of giving out commands from executing commands and delegating this feature to a different object. Practically, command objects bind an action to the object that will invoke the action. They always include a function such as `run()` or `execute()`. One of the biggest advantages of this pattern is that command objects with the same interface can be easily interchanged whenever needed.

Advantages:

- The command pattern makes it easier to construct general components that have to execute/delegate/sequence method calls
- Command objects with same interface can be interchanged whenever needed
- It allows bookkeeping about command executions, without interference from the client

Disadvantages:

- It significantly increases the number of classes for each command

It is useful while creating structures where generation and execution of requests do not depend on each other. We can say that a command instance can be instantiated by the client and run later by the **invoker**. The client and invoker may not know anything about each other.

This pattern is scalable as we can add new commands without changing any existing code.

The facade pattern

A façade is a front layer that is presented to and is visible to the world. Behind it lies all the complexity and unpresentable objects.

Description

The façade pattern is a structural pattern that enables us to hide the backend complexities under an interface. This pattern increases usability of the application modules. Internal features and methods are not exposed directly to developers, but they can interact with them through this façade. This pattern makes your application secure.

jQuery is an example of a JavaScript library that uses the façade pattern.

Whenever we use jQuery's `$(this).animate()` or `$(this).css()` function, we are using a façade. Similarly, `$(document).ready()` implements a façade.

The core jQuery attributes should be considered intermediate abstractions. The more immediate burden to developers is the DOM API and facades are what make the jQuery library so easy to use.

The `ready()` function has lots of complexities at the backend. jQuery simplifies browser inconsistency to ensure that `ready()` is invoked at the appropriate time.

However, we only see a façade or a simple interface layer.

Here are a few advantages and disadvantages of the facade pattern:

Advantages:

- Improves a web application's security
- Compatible with other patterns
- Easier to patch internal modules
- Easier to implement
- Provides a simpler public interface
- Being used in other JavaScript frameworks, such as jQuery

Disadvantages:

- No proven disadvantages

The factory pattern

Just like other creational design patterns, the factory pattern also focuses on object creation. However, it differs in the way that it does not require a constructor method to create objects.

Description

The factory pattern provides an interface for object creation where we specify the type of factory object we need to create. Subclasses are allowed to decide which class will be instantiated so that they can specify which type of factory object will be created. Factory pattern is very extensible. Factory methods are used when collection of objects are being maintained. These collection of objects are different but still have many common methods and properties.

In this pattern, we do not use the new keyword to create an object.

Let's take a real-time example that will clarify this pattern:

Suppose there is a garment factory. We need to create a type of garment. Instead of creating this object directly using the new keyword, we will request a factory object for a new garment. We tell the factory which type of object is needed (a shirt, jeans, coat, a scarf, and so on). It instantiates that class and returns the object for our further usage.

ExtJS is a JavaScript library that uses this pattern. Methods for creating objects can be categorized and further sub classed.

Here are a few advantages and disadvantages of the factory pattern:

Advantages:

- Object creation is much easier through an interface class, which does the process for us
- Good for creating objects based on different scenarios
- Practical for similar instantiating objects
- Creating objects through one instance is simplified

Disadvantages:

- Difficult to test object-creation process as it's hidden behind factory methods

The mixin pattern

In OOP, mixins are classes that can be inherited by a subclass or a group of subclasses for functionality reuse.

Description

Subclassing means to inherit properties for our new object from a super or base class object.

For instance, there is an `apple` class that is able to extend from another class, `fruit`. Here, `fruit` is a superclass, while `apple` is a subclass of `fruit`. All objects of `apple` inherit properties from `fruit`. However, `apple` is able to define its own methods and override those defined by `fruit`.

If `apple` needs to call an overridden method in `fruit`, it's called method chaining.

If `apple` needs to call `fruit`'s constructor, it's called **constructor chaining**.

Mixins let other objects inherit their functionality with a very minimal level of complexity. This pattern allows us to share functionalities from many mixins through multiple inheritance.

Here are a few advantages and disadvantages of the mixin pattern:

Advantages:

This pattern helps in decreasing function duplication and promotes reuse of functions. In applications where functionality is shared across the system, we can put the shared functions in mixins and focus on the rest of the distinct functionality in our system.

Disadvantages:

Keeping functionality in the object prototype may result in prototype pollution and may confuse tracking the origin of our functions. This may cause problems in large-scale applications.

Example:

```
// Detailed explanation of Mixin Design Pattern in JavaScript can be
found here: http://addyosmani.com/resources/essentialjsdesignpatterns/
book/#mixinpatternjavascript

/* Car Class */
var Car = function(settings) {
    this.model = settings.model || 'no model provided';
    this.colour = settings.colour || 'no colour provided';
};

/* Mixin Class */
var Mixin = function(){};
Mixin.prototype = {
    driveForward: function() {
        console.log('drive forward');
    },
    driveBackward: function() {
        console.log('drive backward');
    }
};

/* Augment existing class with a method from another class */
function augment(receivingClass, givingClass) {
    /* only provide certain methods */
    if(arguments[2]) {
        var i, len = arguments.length;
        for (i=2; i<len; i++) {
            receivingClass.prototype[arguments[i]] = givingClass.
prototype[arguments[i]];
        }
    }
    /* provide all methods */
    else {
        var methodName;
        for (methodName in givingClass.prototype) {
            /* check to make sure the receiving class doesn't have a
method of the same name as the one currently being processed */
            if (!receivingClass.prototype[methodName]) {
```

```
                     receivingClass.prototype[methodName] = givingClass.
prototype[methodName];
                }
            }
        }
}

/* Augment the Car class to have the methods 'driveForward' and
'driveBackward' */
augment(Car, Mixin, 'driveForward', 'driveBackward');

/* Create a new Car */
var vehicle = new Car({model:'Ford Escort', colour:'blue'});

/* Test to make sure we now have access to the methods */
vehicle.driveForward();
vehicle.driveBackward();
```

Property getter and setter

In programming languages, getting and setting properties are used to `get` and `set` the values of an object. The `getter` method is used to get values of properties and the `setter` method is used to set values of properties.

There are two property accessors in JavaScript:

* getter
* setter

Description

* The `getter` and `setter` are methods that help us access and manipulate the data within an object very easily. They can help us build shortcuts to access concealed information. The `getter` and `setter` methods work in such a way that they bind objects with a function so that they look like normal object properties.

* `getter`: This method is a special kind of property accessor. When you want to access a property, the value is generated dynamically. Here is an example:

  ```
  Obj.getButtonColor();
  ```

* `setter`: This method is used to set properties. It passes a value as an argument and the returned value of the function is set to the property. Here is an example:

  ```
  Obj.setButtonColor(value);
  ```

Deleting properties

Just like we can add properties to objects, JavaScript allows us to remove object properties as well.

Description

The `delete` operator is used to delete a property of an object. It deletes properties from the local version. The scope of a property can be reassigned to another variable on the same scope. In JavaScript, the `delete` operator always returns a Boolean value. Using this keyword, you cannot delete objects declared with the `var` keyword.

Let's assume we have an object like this:

```
varauthor = {
   "name":"talha",
   "age":"24"
};
```

We wish to remove the `age` property so that we can have a final object that looks like this:

```
{
   "name":"talha"
};
```

Enter the following command:

```
deleteauthor.age;
```

You can also use this command to achieve the same result:

```
delete author["age"];
```

Testing properties

One of the common tests performed by developers on an object is to check whether an object has a specific property or not. There are different ways to check whether an object has a given property.

Description

In JavaScript, there are two methods for property testing:

- `hasOwnProperty`: This method is used to check whether an object has its own property or not. If the property is inherited from anywhere, then it will return `false`:

  ```
  For example:
    samantha = new girls();
    samantha.eyecolor = 'brown';

  o.hasOwnProperty('eyecolor');    // returns true
  ```

- `propertyIsEnumerable`: This method returns `true`, only if `hasOwnProperty` returns `true` and that property is enumerable.

To check properties in JavaScript, we can use the `in` keyword. If an object property has its own value, it will return `true`.

Here is an example:

```
var girls = {
  name: 'Samantha',
  height: 'Tall',
  eyecolor: 'brown',
  address: null
};
'name' in girls; // true
'age' in girls; // false
```

Enumerating properties

In JavaScript, enumeration of an object's properties is done using the `for-in` loop.

Description

In JavaScript, enumerating properties are used in the `for-in` loop as this loop accesses all properties of an object. When we want to check the list of properties of an object, then we use the `for-in` loop to iterate properties. It assigns the name of the property to the loop variable.

Inherited objects are not enumerable, but properties that you add with these objects are enumerable.

Here is an example:

```
var student = {
  Name:"Ali",
  Age:"24",
  Edu:"Engineering"
}


Sudent.propertyIsEnumerable('Name');
// will return true since object's properties are enumerable

for(var property in student) {
  Console.log(property); //will log all properties
}
```

Property attributes

The information associated with every JavaScript property is called an **attribute**. Different types of property attributes are explained here.

Description

There are two types of JavaScript properties:

- Data property
- AccessorProperty (`getter` and `setter` properties)

There are four attributes that a property has:

- **Enumerable**: This checks whether the property is in a loop construct
- **Configurable**: This checks whether we can delete or modify a property
- **Writable**: This checks whether we can set the value of a property or not
- **Value**: This is a value of property and it can be of any data type in JavaScript

 The data property has all of the preceding attributes, while the accessor property does not have a value or writable attribute.

Object attributes

There are three types of object properties in JavaScript:

- **Named data properties**: These are normal object properties in which an object maps string name a to a value. Here is an example:

```
Var x={
prop:555
};

console.log(x.prop); //its get method
c.prop="xyz"; //its set method
```

- **Named accessor properties**: Functions that are used to get and set properties are known as **named accessor properties**. Here is an example:

```
Var x = {
  get name() {
    return getter;
  }
}
```

Here's another example:

```
var x = {
  set name(val) {
    console.log(val);
  }
}
```

- **Internal properties**: Some properties that are not accessible via language are called **internal properties** in JavaScript. These properties are purely for specification purposes. These properties have special names and are written inside square brackets. All objects have an internal property known as [[Prototype]]. The value of this property is either null or an object, which is used for implementing inheritance.

  It has two parts:

    ○ **Prototype**: This tells the prototype of an object
    ○ **Extensible**: This tells us whether we can or cannot add properties to an object

Serializing objects

Serializing an object means converting an object into bytes so that it can be stored in memory persistently, or it can be sent across the network. These bytes can then be deserialized into the original object.

Description

Serialization is used to store or preserve the internal state of an object. In serialization, an object can be transported or retrieved later. There are two methods of serialization in JavaScript:

- JSON.stringify
- JSON.parse

Here is an example:

```
Obj={a:1}
A=json.stringify(obj);
// creates a JSON String from an array or object

B=json.parse(A);
// parses a JSON Object 'A' in an object.
```

These methods can also retrieve and store objects, arrays, strings, true and false. Enumerable values are preserved or restored by the JSON.stringify() method.

Objects methods

Object methods are functions that are stored as object properties. These methods can be performed by calling them directly following a variable for which the function is to be called and a . (dot).

Description

Every object has methods, which are basically actions performed on it. A method is a property of an object.

The toLowerCase(), toUpperCase(), substr(), trim(), charAt(), and indexOf() methods are some of the examples of native (part of the core language) methods of a string object.

Here is an example using the toUpperCase() method:

```
var book = "JavaScript Reference!";
var result = book.toUpperCase();
```

The value of the result will be:

```
JAVASCRIPT REFERENCE!
```

Functions and methods

A function is a part of code that does a particular operation that is written by the user and called by name independently. A function may be passed some data and it may also return some data. On the other hand, you can think of methods as defined properties of objects that can be called with reference from the object of the class only. Objects that are associated with methods are basically window objects. The syntax of defining a method and a function is different in JavaScript. Methods are only used to define window objects. The way of defining a method is different than defining a function in JavaScript.

Invoking functions

The four different ways of invoking a function are as follows:

- Invoking a function as a function
- Invoking a function as a method
- Invoking a function as a constructor
- Invoking a function with a function method

All these methods were discussed in detail in the previous chapter. There is a different way of initializing the `this` keyword. When you call a function, it starts a function. However, when you invoke a function, it executes it.

Defining functions

When you define a function, your script will not execute, but when you invoke a function, the script will execute. A JavaScript function performs a particular task. When any object calls this function, it starts working. To define a function in JavaScript, we use the `function` keyword. A function can have multiple parameters depending on the task. You can find more detail for this in *Chapter 8, JavaScript Implementations, Syntax Basics, and Variable Types.*

Function arguments and parameters

In JavaScript, a function can have number of arguments. A function may be called with a number of arguments. If you do not provide any argument in a function, then it will become undefined. Arguments are optional in a JavaScript function. If you do not pass any argument in a function, then it will set it to default. Here is an example:

```
Function arg(x,y) {
  Console.log(x+y);
  Arg(2);
  Arg(2,1);
}
```

In this example, we passed two arguments in the function: arguments x and y. When the first function arg(2) is called, then a=2 and b will be undefined. When the second function is called, a=2 and b=1.

Parameters and return values

We know we can pass arguments in a function. A function returns a value to perform a different operation in your script. There are two ways to pass a value into a function:

- **Pass by value**: When we pass any variable (of primitive data types) as an argument in the function, we pass it by value. For example, first, the value is 2. After passing, it is 3:

```
var a=2;
console.log(a); // shows 2
functionpassVal(a);{
 a=3;
}
console.log(a); // shows 3
```

- **Pass by reference**: When you pass a value to an object, it is passed by reference:

```
functionpassingVariables(a, b, c) {
  a = a + 10;
  b.value = "changed";
  c = {value: "changed"};
}

varnum = 10;
varvar1 = {value: "unaffected"};
varvar2 = {value: "unaffected"};
```

```
passingVariables (num, var1, var2);

console.log(num);  // 20
console.log(var1.value);  // changed
console.log(var2.value);  // unaffected
```

Functions as namespace

Namespace is a set of logical identifiers grouped together. JavaScript does not provide a namespace facility by default. So, for creating namespaces in JavaScript, we declare a global object and make all functions and properties into that global object, for example:

```
var stud=student || {};
stud.student=function(name) {
  this.name ;
}
var s=new stud.student("Ali");
```

Closure

To write better code, we use closures in JavaScript. Better code means code that is creative and expressive. In JavaScript, you encounter closures repeatedly, whether you are a good JavaScript programmer or not. Depending on how you use closures in your code, it could be complex or easy.

Basically, closures are the inner functions of JavaScript used to access the outer function's scope. There are three scopes of a closure:

- Access of outer function variables
- Access to its own scope variables
- Access to its global variables

Inner functions also have access to outer function variables and parameters. In its own scope, variables are defined in curly brackets. Here is an example:

```
functionstudentName(name) {
  varstdName="Student Name";
  functionstdLastName(){
  returnstdName+name; }
  returnstdntLastName();
}
```

Function properties

To define a function in JavaScript, we use the `function` variable. This function can be called anywhere in your script. It could also be a function constructor. The attributes and their descriptions are as follows:

- `arguments`: This is an array passed to a function as an argument
- `argument.length`: This tells us the number of arguments in a function
- `constructor`: This is used to create an object
- `length`: This defines the number on an argument
- `prototype`: This allows a function to add object properties
- `arguments.callee`: This tells us which function is executing currently

Methods

Actions performed on objects are known as **methods** in JavaScript. They contain function definitions. They are stored as object properties in a script. For example, you can create a method like this in JavaScript:

```
Student.FullName = function() {
  // define your code here
}
```

Here `FullName` is both a property (`Student.FullName`) and a method (`Student.FullName()`). When you access object properties without brackets, this will return a function definition. Here is an example:

```
Name=Student.FullName;
```

Function constructor

A function constructor is used to define a function dynamically. A new operator is use to define a function with the constructor method. You can also pass as many arguments you want to use in your script to a constructor. The last argument will be the body of the function. It can also contain statements separated by commas. Here is an example:

```
varobj = new Function('a', 'b', 'return a*b;');
```

We cannot pass the same function name in a constructor as an argument, as it will create an error in the script. It can also create an unnamed function, known as an anonymous function.

Classes and modules

In JavaScript, we do not have any native approach to creating classes, but we can create a class using prototype inheritance and a constructor function.

Classes are containers for objects. We use classes to encapsulate a namespace and logic.

To instantiate a class, we can use the `new` keyword. Classes are similar to constructor functions. Here is an example:

```
function student(nameI) {
  This.name=name;
  this.age='18';
}
student.prototype.std=function() {
  //define some code
};
module.export=student;
```

 Modules are used to include and extend classes and properties easily. Modules attach properties to global objects to export module values.

Classes and their modules are extremely important and vital aspects of JavaScript. We will be covering the following topics in the subsequent sections:

- Classes and prototypes
- Constructors
- Java-style classes in JavaScript
- Augmented JavaScript
- Types of classes
- Subclasses
- Classes in ECMA5 script
- Modules

Classes and prototypes

In JavaScript, a class is an object with special types of properties and methods. It is used to create instances and define the behavior of instances. Instances' behavior changes dynamically and we have a special syntax to write it in JavaScript. Instances are created when special methods are invoked on a class.

Prototypes and functions are two different things in JavaScript. A constructor can be any function, but a prototype is a special kind of object. To define a behavior of any instance, we use a prototype. There are no special properties or methods a prototype has. When we modify a prototype, we have instances.

In simpler words, we can say that in JavaScript, a constructor can be any function that is responsible for creating an instance. On the other hand, a prototype can be any object that has no special methods or properties. Prototypes are responsible for an instance's behavior.

In JavaScript, the prototype and constructor functions act like a class, because a class has a constructor, and to define methods, you have a prototype:

Here is an example:

```javascript
//Constructor Function
var Cat = function(name) {
  this.Name = name;
  this.Meow = function() {
    console.log(this.Name + " meow");
  };
}

//Prototype object method
var Cat = function(name) {
  this.Name = name;
}

Cat.prototype.Meow = function() {
  console.log(this.Name + " meow");
};

//Both gives same results
var cat = new Cat("Capri");
cat.Meow();
```

There are no special properties or objects associated with a prototype. An object in your script can be an empty project or a prototype. When we say that any object can be a prototype, then this object will have functions and data types. Prototypes are not special kinds of objects, but classes are special kinds of objects in JavaScript.

Constructors

A class contains a set of objects, and for initialization of the objects, we use constructors. In a class, we can create objects using the new operator. We can define a class as a subclass to construct objects.

With a single property of prototype, a constructor is created. If we overwrite the prototype property, the reference to the constructor might be lost. In JavaScript, we use the `constructor` property to create a class from an object that is passed as an object. Here is an example:

```
var color = 'black';

function Cat() {
  // public property
  this.color = '';

  // private constructor
  var __construct = function(that) {
    console.log("I have a Cat!");
    that.color = 'brown';
  }(this)

  // getter
  this.getColor = function() {
    returnthis.color;
  }

  // setter
  this.setColor = function(color) {
    this.color = color;
  }

}

var b = new Cat();

console.log(b.getColor()); // should be brown

b.setColor('white');

console.log(b.getColor()); // should be white

console.log(color); // should be black
```

Defining a class

There are three ways of defining a class in JavaScript:

- Using a function
- Using object literals
- A singleton using a function

Using a function

You can create an object using the `new` keyword in a function. To access methods and properties, use the `this` keyword. There would be a conflict if you define a function with the same name in a class.

Using object literals

To define an object or array in JavaScript, we use literals. Here is an example:

```
Varobj= {};
Varobj=[];
```

Classes in the ECMA5 script

For specific objects' properties, the ECMA5 script added five methods. These methods are used to secure and restrict the extensibility of objects in the script. These methods are:

- Enumerable
- Writable
- Getter
- Setter
- Configurable

When we define a class in JavaScript, these methods are very useful. When you store an object, it sets an object ID for these methods. When we use a looping statement, it will return this object ID. All objects inherit the object ID, which is enumerable. To read a property, it will invoke the `getter` function, and there will be no `setter` function. So, it will be read-only. We cannot modify it, so it cannot be deleted.

Modules

The two very important aspects of modules are:

- **They have dependencies**: This means that when you write a module in your system, it is fully dependent on the function. We import dependencies from functions while creating our application.

- **They have exports**: If you leave some function and variable public in your system, anything can export these. For example, you have exported a function `$function`, module that depends on this function will also have access to this function.

A module can export a number of multiple variables and functions. To export these functions and variables, we use the `export` keyword. Here is an example:

```
Export function sub(a,b) {
   Return a+b;
}
```

We can also store a variable after exporting it. Here is an example:

```
Var string=function(a,b) {
   Return a+b;
}
```

Inheritance

JavaScript supports prototype inheritance. In other programming languages, objects and classes inherit from each other to use each other's properties and functions. However, in JavaScript, you have an object-based inheritance, which is called a prototype, in which objects use the properties of other objects. For example, if you have a `Person` object, then you can use the _proto_ attribute for that object to create another `Student` object:

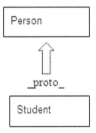

Prototype chaining

In JavaScript, you create new objects from existing objects. This process is called **prototype chaining**. It is similar to inheritance in object-oriented systems.

Description

Prototype is a property of the `constructor` function. When you add any object property to a prototype, it will add this property or method to the objects created by the constructor function. In prototype chaining, we create a function prototype using the properties of the `constructor` function. Using this, all methods or properties transfer to the `prototype` object from the `constructor` function. This method is very easy and useful for creating the `constructor` function to create objects. Here is an example:

```
function person(name) {
   this.name=name;
}
person.prototype= {
   sayHi:function() {
     console.log("something");
   }

   Function student(name) {
      This.name=name;
   }
}
Student.prototype=new Person();
Varstd=new student("Ali");
Std.sayHi();
```

In method resolution, first JavaScript checks objects for methods. When you use prototype chaining, it can override methods for prototypes of an object. So, the JavaScript construction function sets methods for objects.

Constructor stealing

In JavaScript, constructor stealing is also called **classical inheritance**. This method is use to inherit problems of prototype reference values.

Description

In constructor stealing, we call a super constructor in a subtype constructor. This idea is quite simple and easy. We use the `call()` and `apply()` methods for function calling. Here is an example:

```
function super() {
   this.name=["Ali"];
}
function sub() {
```

```
    super.call(this);
}

varstd=new sub();
std.name.push("Ali");
varstd1= new sub();
console.log(std1.name);
```

In this example, we used the `call()` method to call a super constructor for a newly created subclass instead of a subconstructor. This will initialize all objects in the `super()` function on `sub()`.

 When we use prototype chaining, the `constructor` function will allow us to pass arguments from a super constructor to within the subconstructor.

Combination inheritance

Combination inheritance is also called **pseudo-classical inheritance**. This is a combination of constructor stealing and prototype chaining.

Description

In combination inheritance, prototype chaining inherits properties and methods from a prototype, and constructor stealing inherits instances. In this way, we can reuse methods on prototypes by allowing methods to have their own properties. Here is an example:

```
functionSuperType(name) {
  this.name = name;
  this.colors = ['yellow', 'purple', 'indigo'];
}
SuperType.prototype.sayName = function() {
  //console.log(this.name);
};
functionSubType(name, age) {
  //inherit properties
  SuperType.call(this, name);
  this.age = age;
}
//inherit methods
SubType.prototype = new SuperType();
SubType.prototype.sayAge = function() {
  //console.log(this.age);
```

```
};
varinstance1 = new SubType('John Doe', 26);
instance1.colors.push('white');
//console.log(instance1.colors); //'yellow,purple,indigo,white'
instance1.sayName(); //'John Doe';
instance1.sayAge(); //26
varinstance2 = new SubType('Kate', 21);
//console.log(instance2.colors); //'yellow,purple,indigo'
instance2.sayName(); //'Kate';
instance2.sayAge(); //21
```

In this example, the SuperType constructor defines two properties: name and colors. The SuperType prototype has a single method called sayName(). The SubType constructor calls the SuperType constructor, passing in the name argument, and defines its own property called age. Additionally, the SubType prototype is assigned to be an instance of SuperType, and then, a new method called sayAge() is defined. With this code, it's then possible to create two separate instances of SubType that have their own properties, including the colors property, but all use the same methods. Addressing the downsides of both prototype chaining and constructor stealing, combination inheritance is the most frequently used inheritance pattern in JavaScript. It also preserves the behavior of instanceof and isPrototypeOf() to identify the composition of objects.

Prototypal inheritance

In prototypal inheritance, we use an object as a base for another object.

Description

In prototypal inheritance, there are no classes, only objects. To create an object, you can either create a totally new object or you can clone an existing object. New objects can be then extended with new properties.

Here is an example:

```
varobject=Object.create(null);
```

The preceding object has no prototype and is a clone of null:

```
var rectangle = {
  area: function () {
    returnthis.width * this.height;
  }
};

varrect = Object.create(rectangle);
```

In the preceding example, rect inherits the area function from rectangle. Here, rectangle is an object literal, an object literal is a way to create a clone of Object.prototype.

It can also be written as follows:

```
var rectangle = Object.create(Object.prototype);

rectangle.area = function () {
  returnthis.width * this.height;
};
```

We can extend the newly created object as follows:

```
rect.width=50;
rect.height=100;
console.log(rect.area());
```

We can create a constructor function that will clone rectangle for us and will extend it with the height and width properties:

```
var rectangle = {
  create: function (width, height) {
    var self = Object.create(this);
    self.height = height;
    self.width = width;
    return self;
  },
  area: function () {
    returnthis.width * this.height;
  }
};

varrect = rectangle.create(50, 100);

console.log(rect.area());
```

Parasitic inheritance

Parasitic inheritance is similar to prototypal inheritance.

Description

It simply works by creating a function that performs inheritance, object augmentation, and finally, it returns the object after completing each task:

```
Function abc(x) {
  Var clone=obj(abc);
```

```
    Clone.sayHi=function() {
    };
    return clone;
}

Var student= {
  Name="Ali";
};
Varstd=new abc(student);
Std.sayHi();
```

Here, in this example, we have the `abc()` function that has one argument, which is an object based on a new object. This object is passed to the `object` function and saves the resulting object into a `clone` variable. Now, the `clone` object will have a new object property, and at the end, we return the object.

Parasitic combination inheritance

A parasite is defined as an organism that lives inside another organism and relies on its resources. Similarly, in this inheritance, a child object relies on a parent object and extends its properties from it.

Description

The first constructor calls the subtype `prototype` and then it calls the subtype `constructor`. This is a very efficient way of creating new objects in JavaScript. At the end, the subtype will have all the properties of the super type. Here is an example:

```
function super(name) {
  this.name=["Ali"];
}
super.prototype.sayHi=function() {
  console.log("something");
}

function sub(age) {
  this.age=age;
  super.call(this,name);
}
sub.prototype=new super();
sub.prototype.sayHi();
```

The only difference between parasitic combination inheritance and combination inheritance is that, in the former one, the base constructor is called once, and in the latter one, the base constructor is called twice.

Subclasses

In every programming language, every subclass has a super class that inherits its properties and methods from. JavaScript is not a pure class-based programming language, but it follows some of the rules of OOP. We make classes in JavaScript using object notations.

In JavaScript, you can only perform inheritance using the `constructor` function or prototype. This inheritance is only done at run time, which means dynamically. Here is an example:

```
// super class
functionsuperClass() {
   this.bye = superBye;      //method 1
   this.hello = superHello;     //method 2
}

//sub class
functionsubClass() {
   this.inheritFrom = superClass;     //inherit-from method defines
                                      superclass
   this.inheritFrom();                //inherit from method called
   this.bye = subBye;                 method 1 overridden in subclass
}

functionsuperHello() {
   return "Hello from superClass";
}

functionsuperBye() {
   return "Bye from superClass";
}

functionsubBye() {
   return "Bye from subClass";
}
```

To run the preceding code execute following method:

```
functionprintSub() {
   varnewClass = new subClass();
   console.log(newClass.bye());
   console.log(newClass.hello());
}
```

Built-in objects

To add flexibility in language, JavaScript supports a number of built-in objects. The most commonly used objects are:

- Global
- Date
- Math
- RegExp (Regular Expression)
- Array

Implementations of these built-in objects are complex and different.

Global objects

Global objects are objects defined outside the function. Every function can access these variables because their scope is global for all.

When you do not declare a variable and assign a value to it, then it will automatically become global.

Description

When your code starts execution, functions and constants immediately become available. A global variable does not initialize with the new keyword. Basically, global objects are used to share same data to add properties. You can store methods within global objects in your script.

Objects that you cannot access directly for accessing those object we use global objects. We pass those object directly as arguments after declaring the global variable. You can create a number of instances and a number of global objects in your script.

A global object has a fixed number of properties. Multiple object instances can access this global object. Here is an example:

```
varstudentName="Ali"
functionmyStd(){    }

student=new Global("name");
student.age=18;
person=new Global("name");
post(person.age);
```

Date object

Date objects in JavaScript deal with date and time objects. For example, if we are writing a script and we need some functionality of date and time, then we can use this built-in object simply.

getTime()

This function is used to get the current time with respect to the number of milliseconds since January 1, 1970.

Parameters

There are no parameters passed.

Returns

The number of milliseconds since January 1, 1970.

Description

As the name states, this function is used to obtain the current time, in the form of milliseconds. We need to create a date object first.

```
var time = new Date();
time.getTime(); // This will output time as 1454905019871
```

getMilliseconds()

This function is used to get the current time with respect to the number of milliseconds.

Parameters

There are no parameters passed.

Returns

A number from 0-999.

Description

As the name states, this function is used to obtain the current time, in the form of milliseconds. We need to create a date object first.

```
var time = new Date();
time.getMilliseconds();
```

getMinutes()

This function is used to get the current time with respect to the number of minutes.

Parameters

There are no parameters passed.

Returns

A number from 0-59.

Description

This function is used to obtain the current time, in the form of minutes. We need to create a date object first.

```
var time = new Date();
time.getMinutes();
```

getHours()

This function is used to get the current time with respect to the number of hours.

Parameters

There are no parameters passed.

Returns

A number from 0-23 with 0 being midnight.

Description

This function is used to obtain the current time, in the form of hours. We need to create a date object first.

```
var time = new Date();
time.getHours();
```

getDate()

This function is used to get the current day.

Parameters

There are no parameters passed.

Returns

A number from 1-31.

Description

This function is used to obtain the current day. We need to create a date object first.

```
var time = new Date();
time.getDate();
```

getDay()

This function is used to get the current day in the week.

Parameters

There are no parameters passed.

Returns

A number from 0-6 with 0 being Sunday.

Description

This function is used to obtain the current day in the week. We need to create a date object first.

```
var time = new Date();
time.getDay();
```

getMonth()

This function is used to get the current month.

Parameters

There are no parameters passed.

Returns

A number from 0-11.

Description

This function is used to obtain the current month in the year. We need to create a date object first.

```
var time = new Date();
time.getMonth();
```

getFullYear()

This function is used to get the current year.

Parameters

There are no parameters passed.

Returns

The year in the YYYY format.

Description

This function is used to obtain the current year. We need to create a date object first.

```
var time = new Date();
time.getYear();
```

Set date methods

Methods are available in date objects to manipulate dates. We can also adjust the date dynamically. Here is an example:

```
var dob=new date();
dob.setDate(19.03.1990);
```

We can also set upcoming dates and the current date by using this function, for example:

```
var dob=new date();
dob.setDate(dob.getDate + 7);
```

The date set methods are:

- setTime()
- setMilliseconds()
- setMinutes()
- setMinutes()

- setHours()
- setDate()
- setDay()
- setMonth()
- setFullYear()

These methods are very similar to the date get methods described in the preceding term list.

We can also compare dates using the date object.

Math object

In JavaScript, the math object is used to perform mathematical operations.

This object has several mathematical functions. Here is an example:

- Math.E
- Math.PI
- Math.sqrt
- Math.Ln2
- Math.ln10

The math object has different methods. For example, we have the pow method that calculates the power of the first variable times the second.

```
Math.pow(base, exponent);
document.write(Math.pow(2,4));  // 16 here 2 is base and 4 is
exponent.
```

min()

This function is used to find out the the argument with the minimum value.

Parameters

The values to be evaluated are passed as parameters.

Returns

The argument with the minimum value.

Description

As the name suggests, this function is simply used to obtain the minimum value among all values in an argument

For example:

```
min(10, 56, 3, 26, -6, 4); //The value returned is -6
```

max()

This function is used to find the argument with the maximum value.

Parameters

The values to be evaluated are passed as parameters.

Returns

The argument with the maximum value.

Description

As the name suggests, this function is simply used to obtain the maximum value among all values in an argument.

For example:

```
max(10, 56, 3, 26, -6, 4); //The value returned is 56
```

random()

This function is used to generate a random number between 0 and 1.

Parameters

No parameters.

Returns

A random number between 0 and 1.

Description

The `random()` function is useful in generating random numbers. The value of the number will always lie between 0 and 1 (never exactly 1). For example:

```
Math.random();
```

round()

This function is used to round the number to its nearest integer value.

Parameters

The values to be evaluated are passed as parameters.

Returns

The rounded number.

Description

This method is used to create integer values after rounding them.

For example:

```
Math.round(4.3);// The value returned is 4
Math.round(4.8);// The value returned is 5
Math.round(4.5);// The value returned is 5
```

ceil()

This function is used to round a number up to the nearest and highest possible integer value.

Parameters

The values to be evaluated are passed as parameters.

Returns

The highest rounded number.

Description

This method is used to create integer values after rounding them to the higher integer.

For example:

```
Math.ceil(-6.2);// The value returned is -6
Math.ceil(6.2);// The value returned is 7
```

floor()

This function is used to round a number down to the nearest and lowest possible integer value.

Parameters

The values to be evaluated are passed as parameters.

Returns

The lowest rounded number.

Description

This method is used to create integer values after rounding them to the lower integer.

For example:

```
Math.floor(2.3);//The value returned is 2
Math.floor(-2.3);//The value returned is -3
```

The RegExp object

In JavaScript, for pattern matches in string, we use a regular expression. It is a very powerful and useful tool for expression pattern matching.

Parameters

The following are the parameters:

- **Pattern**: The text/pattern of the regular expression
- **Flags**: If specified, flags can have any combination of the following:
    - g: Global match
    - i: Ignore case
    - m: Multiline; treat beginning and end characters (^ and $) as working over multiple lines (that is, match the beginning or end of each line (delimited by \n or \r), not only the very beginning or end of the whole input string)

Returns

The return type of different regular expressions is different.

Description

Using a regular expression, you can make a complex task simple by writing few lines of codes. There are five methods in JavaScript:

- `RegExp.exec(pattern)`
- `RegExp.replace(pattern)`
- `RegExp.split(pattern)`
- `RegExp.match(pattern)`

Defining a regular expression

There are two ways of writing a regular expression in JavaScript. These are:

- RegExp constructor method
- Literal syntax

 There are differences between the `RegExp` object and global object. They look the same but act differently.

RegExp constructor

This method is used to dynamically construct a string search pattern. A regular expression in this method should be written in quotation marks. This method has three parameters. Here is an example:

```
var email=new RegExp("\d{2}","g");
```

In this example:

- E-mail is a required parameter to which regular expression values are assigned
- `\d` is a pattern parameter used to match regular expression
- `g` is global, which is a flag parameter. In this function, there are four types of parameters (`g`, `I`, `m` ,`u`).

Literal syntax

In literal notation, we write a regular expression without brackets. Here, i is a flag that shows to ignore case of the text whether it is uppercase, lowercase or any other. We have more flag objects such as the following ones:

- g: Global object
- i: Ignore case
- m: Multi search
- u: Unicode search

In regular expressions, we can have a global regular expression object, which will have information for each match case. A simple regular expression object has information about a particular regular expression:

```
var exp=\d{2}/i
```

String object

There are four string methods for pattern matching. In these objects, a pattern is sent with a parameter. These methods allow you to search, match, replace, and split patterns.

These methods are represented as follows.

Match(pattern)

This method is used to find a matching pattern within a string. Using the not (!) operator it can also be used to find non-matches.

The syntax is `string.Match(Expression)`.

Parameters

The string pattern that is to be matched.

Returns

It returns the result if a match is found or 0 or null if no match is found.

Description

This runs a search for matching strings in a regular expression. If the search is matched or successful then it will return an array of matching results, if not then it will return null or 0. It is also used to update properties in a regular expression.

Here is an example:

```
var str=("I have 10 dollars");
//The pattern below is used to find non-digits in a string
var parsestring= str.match(/\D/g);

// Outputs I, ,h,a,v,e, , ,D,o,l,l,a,r,s
```

Replace(pattern)

This method is used to replace a part of the string.

The syntax is `string.replace(stringSearched, stringReplacement)`.

Parameters

The string pattern that is to be replaced is passed as a parameter.

Returns

The string with the replaced value.

Description

This executes a search and is used for replacement of regular expression match resulted with alternative text. This is also used for replacement of regular expressions with specific and different `regExp` properties.

Here is an example:

```
var str1=("Apple Pie");
var parsestring1=str1.replace("Pie", "Cinnamon Roll");
```

Here the value of `parsestring1` is `Apple Cinnamon Roll`.

 Remember here that the search is case sensitive, so if you provide the value `parsestring1=str1.replace("piE", "Cinnamon Roll");` then no replacement is done.

Also, only the first occurrence of the pattern is replaced. Hence:

```
var str1=("Apple Pie , Banana Pie", "Strawberry PIE");
var parsestring1=str1.replace("Pie", "Cinnamon Roll");
```

Here the value of `parsestring1` is `Apple Cinnamon Roll`, `Banana Pie`, `Strawberry PIE`.

To perform a global search and replacement so that all occurrences are replaced we use the following code:

```
var str1=("Apple Pie , Banana Pie", "Strawberry PIE");
var parsestring1=str1.replace(/Pie/g, "Cinnamon Roll");
```

Here the value of `parsestring1` is `Apple Cinnamon Roll`, `Banana Cinnamon Roll`, `Strawberry PIE`.

For a global insensitive search, use the following code:

```
var str1=("Apple Pie , Banana Pie, "Strawberry PIE");
var parsestring1=str1.replace(/Pie/gi, "Cinnamon Roll");
```

Here the value of `parsestring1` is `Apple Cinnamon Roll`, `Banana Cinnamon Roll`, `Strawberry Cinnamon Roll`.

Split(pattern)

This is use to split a string in a regular expression.

The syntax is `string.split(separator,limit)`.

Parameters

A separator and limit are provided as optional parameters.

Returns

The split string is returned.

Description

With this method the string is split. Every word in the string is treated as a single element in an array. If a null string is passed as a parameter, the method causes each letter to be split into different characters. For example:

```
var str1 = "My Car is at the garage in Queens";
var parseString = str1.split("");
```

The value of `parseString` will be:

```
M,y, ,C,a,r, ,i,s, ,a,t, ,t,h,e, ,g,a,r,a,g,e, ,i,n, ,Q,u,e,e,n,s
```

Providing a limit will return a comma separated array of the words containing only the specified number of elements. For example:

```
var str1 = "My Car is at the garage in Queens";
var parseString = str1.split(" ", 3);
```

The value of `parseString` is `My,Car,is`.

Using a letter or letters as a separator will give the following results:

```
var str1 = "My Car is at the garage in Queens";
var parseString = str1.split("a");
```

The value of `parseString` will be:

```
My C,r is ,t the g,r,ge in Queens
```

Here is another example:

```
var str1 = "My Car is at the garage in Queens";
var parseString = str1.split("ar");
```

The value of `parseString` will be:

```
My C, is at the g,age in Queens
```

search(pattern)

This method is used to search for a particular string.

The syntax is `string.search(stringSearched)`.

Parameters

The string pattern that is to be searched is passed as a parameter.

Returns

It returns the position of the starting letter of the string if a match is found. If no match is found then it returns `-1`.

Description

It is used to find a match in a string. If a match is found it will send an index of that match otherwise, if a match is not found, it will return `-1`. Global flags are not supported by this method.

Here is an example:

```
var str1=("I have 10 dollars in my pocket");
var parsestring=str1.search("i");
```

The value of `parseString` here is 18.

 There are additional string methods available to perform other tasks on strings.
A detailed list of these methods can be found at `https://msdn.microsoft.com/en-us/library/ecczf11c(v=vs.94).aspx`.

Array objects

An array is a collection of objects.

To create an array in JavaScript, the elements of the collection are enclosed within square brackets and separated by commas, as seen here:

```
varcolors = ["red", "yellow", "blue"]
```

An array can also be initialized using the `new` keyword or by specifying their length between 0 and 232-1:

```
new array(first, second, third, … )
new array(7)     // creates an array of size 7
```

To access array elements, we can use an index notation:

```
varlastColor = colors[2];     // blue
```

Always remember that array elements always start with the zero index. Hence, the third element in the preceding array has the index of 2.

Array objects can hold all sorts of data, for example, strings, numbers, literals, dates, and even user-defined objects.

.Pop()

This method is used to *pop* an element out of an array.

Parameters

There are no parameters for this method.

Returns

It returns the *popped* element of the array.

Description

Here an array is considered as a stack and the elements that are last in the array are popped out first. This follows the LIFO principle.

Here is an example:

```
var sweets = ["Red Velvet", "Chocolate Mousse", "Strawberry
Delight", "Pineapple Sundae", "Black Forest"];
var element= sweets.Pop();
```

The value of the element here is `Black Forest`.

.Push()

This method is used to *push* an element into an array.

Parameters

There are no parameters for this method.

Returns

It returns the new length of the array.

Description

Here an array is considered as a stack and the elements that are pushed appear at the end of the array.

Here is an example:

```
var sweets = ["Red Velvet", "Chocolate Mousse", "Strawberry
Delight", "Pineapple Sundae", "Black Forest"];
var element= sweets.Push("Lemon Meringue");
```

The value of the element here is `6`.

.ToString()

This converts the elements in an array into a string. The elements appear as comma-separated strings.

Parameters

There are no parameters.

Returns

This returns a string containing the elements of the array.

Description

The `ToString()` function is used to convert an array into a string. The elements of the array appear in the string and are separated by a comma:

```
var sweets = ["Red Velvet", "Chocolate Mousse", "Strawberry
Delight", "Pineapple Sundae", "Black Forest"];
var StrSweets= sweets.ToString()
```

Here the value of `StrSweets` is:

```
Red Velvet,Chocolate Mousse,Strawberry Delight,Pineapple
Sundae,Black Forest
```

.ValueOf()

This method is also used to convert an array into a string.

Parameters

There are no parameters.

Returns

This returns a string containing the elements of the array.

Description

This is default behaviour of the array and works same as the `ToString()` function.

```
var sweets = ["Red Velvet", "Chocolate Mousse", "Strawberry
Delight", "Pineapple Sundae", "Black Forest"];
var StrSweets= sweets.ValueOf()
```

Here the value of `StrSweets` is:

```
Red Velvet,Chocolate Mousse,Strawberry Delight,Pineapple
Sundae,Black Forest
```

.Join()

This method is used to convert an array into a string. The elements are separated by the delimiter specified.

Parameters

A separator to separate the elements in the new string.

Returns

This returns a string containing the elements of the array separated by the delimiter specified.

Description

The `Join()` function is used to convert an array into a string. The elements of the array appear in the string and are separated by the delimiter:

```
var sweets = ["Red Velvet", "Chocolate Mousse", "Strawberry
Delight", "Pineapple Sundae", "Black Forest"];
var StrSweets= sweets.Join(*)
```

Here the value of `StrSweets` is:

```
Red Velvet * Chocolate Mousse * Strawberry Delight * Pineapple
Sundae * Black Forest
```

.Splice()

Splice, as the name suggests, is used to add new elements into the array. Unlike the `push()` method we can add elements in whichever position we want.

Parameters

The following are the parameters:

- Position
- Number of elements to be removed
- Elements to be added

Returns

The array as a string along with the new elements, if any.

Description

This method is used to remove and add elements in one step. We can specify where the new element is to be added and which elements are to be removed.

```
var sweets = ["Red Velvet", "Chocolate Mousse", "Strawberry
Delight", "Pineapple Sundae", "Black Forest"];
var StrSweets= sweets.splice(2, 0, "Lemon Meringue");
```

Here the value of `StrSweets` is:

```
Red Velvet,Chocolate Mousse,Lemon Meringue,Strawberry
Delight,Pineapple Sundae,Black Forest
```

.sort()

This method is used to sort an array into alphabetical order.

Parameters

No parameters.

Returns

The sorted array is returned.

Description

The sort method is used to sort an array, alphabetically.

Here is an example:

```
var sweets = ["Red Velvet", "Chocolate Mousse", "Strawberry
Delight", "Pineapple Sundae", "Black Forest"];
var StrSweets= sweets.Sort();
```

Here the value of `StrSweets` is:

```
Black Forest,Chocolate Mousse,Pineapple Sundae,Red
Velvet,Strawberry Delight
```

.reverse()

As the name suggests it reverses the order of the array.

Parameters

No parameters.

Returns

The reversed array is returned.

Description

The reverse method is used to sort an array, alphabetically, in reverse order.

Here is an example:

```
var sweets = ["Red Velvet", "Chocolate Mousse", "Strawberry
Delight", "Pineapple Sundae", "Black Forest"];
var StrSweets= sweets.reverse();
```

Here the value of StrSweets is:

```
Strawberry Delight,Red Velvet,Pineapple Sundae,Chocolate
Mousse,Black Forest.slice()
```

.slice()

As the name suggests, this method is used to slice up an array and create a new array using a part of the original array.

Parameters

The index at which we want the array sliced. The index of an array begins at 0. So the first element has index 0, the second element has index 1, and so on.

Returns

The sliced array containing the remaining elements is returned.

Description

The slice method is used to slice up an array and get the remainder of the array as a string.

Here is an example:

```
var sweets = ["Red Velvet", "Chocolate Mousse", "Strawberry
Delight", "Pineapple Sundae", "Black Forest"];
var StrSweets= sweets.slice(3);
```

Here the value of `StrSweets` is:

```
Pineapple Sundae,Black Forest
```

.concat()

This method is used to concatenate two or more arrays into a single array.

Parameters

The array to be concated is passed as the parameter.

Returns

This method returns the concated array.

Description

The `Concat()` method is used to create a single array by joining two or more arrays.

Here is an example:

```
var greenShades= ["Mint", "Basil", "Pine", "Emerald"];
var BlueShades=["Azure", "Cerulean", "Navy", "Aegan"];
var VioletShades= ["Lilac", "Orchid", "Mauve", "Wisteria"];
var CoolShades=greenShades.concat(BlueShades, VioletShades);
```

Here the value of `CoolShades` is:

```
Mint,Basil,Pine,Emerald,Azure,Cerulean,Navy,Aegan,Lilac,Orchid,
Mauve,Wisteria
```

11
Extending JavaScript and ECMAScript 6

ECMA 262 is a standard that defines the core features of the JavaScript language. The language that is defined by this standard is called **ECMAScript**. JavaScript is an implementation of ECMAScript. It runs in web browsers at the client end, while Node.js runs at the server end. ECMAScript 6 was released in June 2015. ES6 is a major update from ES5, which was released in 2009.

A complete language specifications draft of ES6 language specifications can be obtained from `https://people.mozilla.org/~jorendorff/es6-draft.html`.

Compatibility and goals

The ES6 compatibility chart shows which features of ES6 are supported in the current browsers. It also links all listed features to their specification guides.

It should be noted that some of the features might not be under compliance with their exact specifications. While working in Chrome, don't forget to enable the Experimental JavaScript flags.

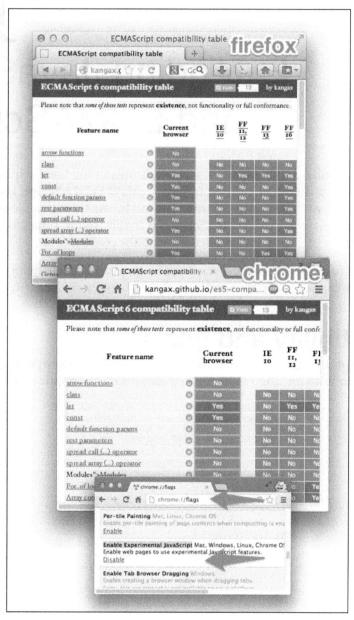

Reference: Use ECMAScript 6 Today

ECMA6 script has the following major goals:

- Default exports
- Static structure of modules
- Support for asynchronous and synchronous loading
- Used for dependencies between modules

JavaScript subset and extensions

Subsets are mostly defined for security purposes; scripts written using secure language subsets can be executed safely even if its source is untrusted, for instance, an ad server. Some of these subsets will be described later.

As JavaScript continued to evolve and allowed explicit extensions, newer versions were released. Many of the features were standardized. These extensions are compatible with modern browsers such as Firefox and Chrome. However, the implementation of non-standard extensions may require an external compiler because these features are being updated in major JavaScript engines now.

JavaScript subsets

As stated earlier, for execution security of untrusted code, we use subsets in JavaScript. For example, when we have a credit card checking script in which a credit card number is sent to a remote server, then for this type of information security, we use subset. By defining a subset, we check the behavior of a program that we have strictly not allowed. So, it means that we use subsets for a certain amount of code, and the other part of the code is omitted.

There are two goals of a JavaScript subset:

- The subset construct should be added to maximize coverage use of JavaScript constructs
- It is used to extend analysis to accommodate changes

These subset are defined for every reason.

The good parts: This is a subset that is part of the language used for the best and the worthy part of the script. The main goal of this subset is it purifies and simplifies code, and makes the script easier and more understandable. The good parts subset does not have an `eval()` function. It also eliminates the `continue` and `with` statements. It does not include function definition statements, and only defines function using the function definition expression. Using a function definition statement, it defines a function, and then, after defining the function, it does not use the function definition statement.

In subset curly brackets, we have a body of loops and conditional statements. If there is a single statement in the body, then it would not allow the brackets to be omitted.

Secure subsets

There are various implementations of secure subsets. Some of them are briefly described here.

ADsafe

ADsafe (`http://www.adsafe.org/`) was one of the first presented security subjects. It was proposed and created by Douglas Crockford. ADsafe uses tools such **asJSLint** (`http://www.jslint.com/`) to verify the unsafe code. It enforces good programming practices, so the likelihood of unsecure code executing correctly is much higher. It blocks the script from accessing the global variables or accessing the DOM directly. Instead, it allows the script to access the ADsafe object, which provides access to a secure API and indirect access to the DOM elements. ADsafe does not alter scripts and has no impact on its functionality. It enables us to determine quickly whether the script is safe to be placed on a page. It also works as a base that helps in the development of other secure subsets.

Dojox

The **dojox.secure** tool (`https://dojotoolkit.org/reference-guide/1.10/dojox/secure.html`) is a security subset inspired from ADsafe. It is an extension of the **Dojo** toolkit (`http://dojotoolkit.org`) and was developed by Kris Zyp. It is fully packed with components that ensure safe execution and loading of untrusted code, content, ads, and widgets from a different domain. It provides a sandbox environment and limited DOM elements for interaction:

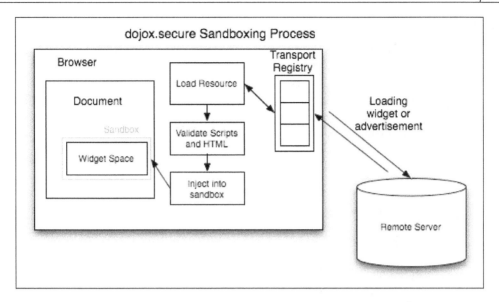

Caja

Caja (`https://developers.google.com/caja/`) is an open source secure subset powered by Google. Caja (which means "**box**" in Spanish) further defines two subsets:

- **Cajita** (which means "**small box**" in Spanish) is a narrow subset just like ADsafe and dojox.secure

- **Valija** (which means "**suitcase**" in Spanish) is a broader subset and is much more similar to ECMAScript in strict mode (with the `eval()` method removed)

Caja is a compiler tool that transforms third-party content such as HTML, CSS, and JS into secure code, which is then easy to embed in a website.

FBJS

FBJS (`https://github.com/facebook/fbjs`) is a JavaScript secure subset used by Facebook. It allows untrusted code to be executed in a secure environment. It transforms code to ensure security. During the transformation, all top-level identifiers are renamed by adding the module-specific prefix. Adding module specific prefix prevents querying any global identifiers. For example, you are developing an app having the `xyz123` ID, and there is a `foo()` function in the code. It will eventually become `xyz123_foo()`. Even function calls to `eval()` are redirected to a non-existent function.

Microsoft's web sandbox

Microsoft's **Web Sandbox** (`http://www.websandbox.org/`) defines a broad secure subset of JavaScript, HTML, and CSS. Sandbox implements host virtualization to provide security and extensibility. The untrusted code is executed in a virtual machine instead of running directly in a browser. A virtual machine quarantines the untrusted code, which prevents it from interacting with the elements outside the virtual machine. Let's take a look at the following block diagram:

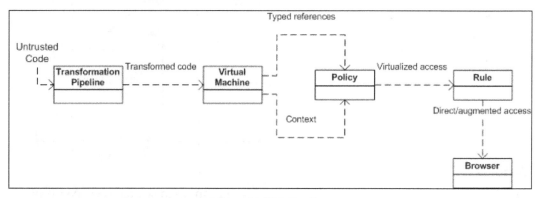

Microsoft's Web Sandbox

JavaScript extensions

Lots of new and useful features have been coded. They will be standardized with the release of ES6. ES6 was set to be officially released in June 2015. However, many of the features and extensions are already available on Firefox and Chrome (Experimental JavaScript flag has to be turned *on* in order to access some of the ES6 features). We will discuss the major features in the rest of the chapter.

Const

It works like variable keyword `var`. For declaring a constant, we use the word `const`. In order to use assignment we must declare constant.

> Values declared with the const can not be redeclared, redefined or reinitialized. JavaScript provide 8 constants through math object. One of them is PI. we can not reinitialize PI using const.

Let

The Let keyword is used for the block scoping of variables. The variables are declared at the start of the code instead of at the start of functions:

```
var name = "john";
console.log(name);
```

In the preceding example, the name john is the value of name logged in console. The declarations in JavaScript are moved to the top. The position of the variables declared or initialized in the scope of the function does not matter, and they will be hoisted to the top by default. JavaScript's default conduct is to move variable declarations to the top.

Hoisting is JavaScript's default behavior to move variable declarations to the top.

Variables in JavaScript are function scoped. This means, variables are available throughout the function, even if they are declared in a nested code block. Here is a short example in which we will log the output in the console of our client, that is, Chrome, Firefox, and so on:

```
var name = "john";
(function () {
  // var name = undefined;
  if (!name)
  { var name = "jane"; }
  console.log(name); // "jane"
}());
```

From the preceding example, the value of name used to log-in into the console is jane.

ES6 handles this issue with let. Let is very much like var. The only difference is that let is block scoped, and var is function scoped. We can rewrite the previous example using let, as shown here:

```
var name = "john";
(function () {
  // var name = undefined;
  if (!name) {
    let name = "jane";
  }
  console.log(name); // "john"
}());
```

Notice that although the value of name is `jane` inside the function, using the `let` keyword sets its scope to global and the value of name defaults to `john`. Hence, `john` is logged in the client's console.

 If we declare a variable as a constant, assign it some value, use the same constant somewhere else that changes its value, then its new value will be ignored. Like variables, we can add constants anywhere in our script without breaking our code.

Destructuring assignment

We can assign multiple values to the variables in a function using one command.

For each

The iteration of property value is done using this loop. The iteration of property name is done.

Iterator

The object for the next method is returned. The object that is returned has _ iterator_ property. The iterator is used for `iteratable` objects.

Generators

The generation of object is done here. A generated object is returned whenever a function invokes the `this` method. The `yield` keyword is used. The current execution of the function is specified by the generated object.

Array

The `iteratable` objects with the same values in the array are shorthanded by the use of array.

Generator expression

The functions are shorthanded for multiple `try-catch` expressions. The thing that is returned is the generated object wrapped in `{}` and not in `[]`. We use this for multiple values to variables in the function.

Scoped variables and constants

When we declare a variable, then it has a local scope and a global scope. We can define a variable anywhere in our script. When we declare a variable in JavaScript, we can assign a value to it at the time of declaration or later. Here is an example:

```
_xyz123; // variable declared without assigning a value to it
varabc = "Star"; //variable declared while assigning a value to it
```

In JavaScript, a variable is defined by a dollar sign the same as in query. In JavaScript, we create variables dynamically using the `var` keyword. Every variable has a name and a value associated with it. These values can be of any type, such as `number`, `array`, `string`, and so on. A variable name could be a combination of characters and numbers. Here is an example:

```
(a==undefined){
a=5}
```

A variable that is declared outside a function is a **global variable** having a global scope. This means that it can be accessed from anywhere within a script.

We can also declare a variable constant with the `const` keyword. A constant variable value is constant.

Constants can be defined using the `const` keyword as shown here:

```
Const a=5;
```

 The `const` and `let` keywords work in a similar way that they both are block scoped. However, in the case of `const`, values cannot be redeclared, redefined, or reinitialized. In short, const values are read-only.

Here is a working example:

```
const PI = 3.14159265359;

console.log("value of PI = " + PI); //value of PI = 3.14159265359

PI = 3.1415; //<------- Can not re-assign value to PI

console.log("value of PI = " + PI); //value of PI = 3.14159265359

const PI = 2.0312; //<------- Can not re-initialize value of PI
```

```
console.log("value of PI = " + PI); //Uncaught TypeError:
Identifier 'PI' has already been declared

var PI = 9.2144; //<------- Can not re-declare value of PI

console.log("value of PI = " + PI); //Uncaught TypeError:
Identifier 'PI' has already been declared.
```

The `class` variables are declared in the class but not within methods of any class, whereas the local variable exits within the methods of any class.

Shorthand functions

Shorthand function, also known as **expression closure**, is a technique to use simple functions in JavaScript. It is used to omit a function's curly brackets in the event; it returns a `true` or `false` statement. Similarly, if you omit the `return` keyword, it would also send you the exact same result.

The expression will be evaluated quickly after the argument list in your script by omitting the curly brackets and the `return` keyword.

Here is an example:

```
Let student=function(a)
A+1, yes
Function()
True,no
```

This behaves similarly like functions. They are defined with curly brackets and a `return` statement. This is very useful when we want to pass a function as an argument to a function.

Multiple catch clauses

In JavaScript, `try/catch` statements are use to handle exceptions present in the `try` code blocks.

The try clause

In the `try` block, the statements to be evaluated are executed.

If you want to deliberately throw an exception, we would use the `throw` statement. This will abort the execution of the remaining statements, and the control will move to the `catch` block.

The catch clause

After checking and encountering an error in the statements in the `try` block, the exception block is called. If the exception encountered is the same as the exception handled in the `catch` block, then the control immediately shifts to the `catch` block, and the statements within the `catch` block are executed.

The statements presented after the erroneous statement will *not* be executed, unless there is a `return` statement in the `finally` block.

A good practice is to use a conditional catch clause first if we anticipate that any exception will occur. An unconditional catch clause is placed last to handle all the remaining exceptions:

```
try {
  demotrycatchfunction(); // may throw any type of
  exceptions
}
catch (e) {
  if (e instanceofReferenceError) {
    // statements to handle ReferenceErrorexceptions
  } else if (e instanceofSyntaxError
) {
    // statements to handle SyntaxError exceptions
  }
  else if (e instanceofEvalError) {
    // statements to handle EvalError exceptions
  }
  else {
    // statements to handle any unspecified exceptions
    logMyError(e); // pass the exception object to the
    error handler
  }
}
```

The finally clause

This block will execute statements present within at end, whether an exception has occurred or not. The statements in a `finally` block execute irrespective of whether an error occurred. The `finally` block generally contains code that must be executed regardless of anything. Hence, we generally release resources and close connection inside a `finally` block. The syntax for writing a simple `try-catch-finally` block is as follows:

```
try {
   //try code - This is the Code block to try
}
catch(error) {
   //catch code - This is the Code block that handle errors
}
finally {
   //finally code - This is the Code block to be executed
   regardless of try catch results
}
```

We can also write this with a nested `catch` blocks like this:

```
try {
   //do something
}
catch (Exception e) {
   try {
     //do something with little likeliness of output
   }
   catch (Exception ex) {
     try {
       //do the minimum acceptable
     }
     catch (Exception e1) {
       //More try catches?
     }
   }
}
```

Here is an example showing the working of multiple catch clauses:

```
functionCheckEligibility(Age) {
  var result;
  try { //try block
    if (Age < 16 { //condition to be tested
    throw new Error("Children below the age of 16 are not allowed.
    Parent Supervision needed!"); //incase of false result, an
    error will be raised
    }
  result = age;
  }
  catch (e) { //catch block
    console.log(e.toString()); //error is converted to string and
    logged into the console
    throw e; //Uncaught Error
  }
  finally { // finally block - It will run in the end regardless
  of the try, catch results
    console.log("Age doesn't matter!");
  }

  return result;
};
```

Let's pass 14 as the argument to the function, as shown here:

```
CheckEligibility(14);
```

The output will be as follows:

```
Children below the age of 16 are not allowed. Parent Supervision
needed!
```

In try-catch statements, we must have at least one finally or
try-catch block. Try doesn't necessarily need a catch clause. If
a try statement does not contain at least one catch block, it must
contain a finally block. The possible exception handling clauses with
try-catch-finally are the try-catch, try-finally, or try-
catch-finally clauses.

E4X – ECMAScript for XML

It is an extension in JavaScript for support of XML extension with JavaScript. By using E4x, it provides easy access for XML document by the DOM interface. It is a server-side technology used in **Rhino** and **SpiderMonkey** because these are powerful extensions by all browsers.

Before E4X, it was very difficult and time consuming for reading and writing in XML. In JavaScript, E$X provides XML document as a XML object, which represents XML fragments as a `xmlList`. E4X supports special kinds of XML objects. This technique is used in client-side programming.

Here is an example:

```
varstudent=<student>
<studentInfo>
<name>Ali</name></studentInfo>
</student>
```

If we enter this XML into our JavaScript code, the E4X interpreter will handle it as an XML object in your script.

ECMAScript 6 features

ECMAScript 6, otherwise called **ECMAScript 2015**, is the most recent form of the ECMAScript standard. ES6 is an important upgrade to the language, and the first update to language since the release of ES5.1 in June 2011

A few of the new features of ES6 are:

- Arrow functions
- Classes
- Enhanced object literals
- Destructuring assignment
- Extended parameter handling
- Generator
- Modules
- Proxy

We will look at all these functions in the upcoming sections.

Arrow functions

Arrow functions are also known as **fat arrow functions**. It is a function and is similar to what we use in C#, Java, and Coffee Script. Statements and expression bodies are supported by arrows. The lexical of arrows is similar to its surrounding code. This is not the case in functions.

As the name suggests, arrow functions use a shorter syntax, an arrow (=>), for definition and in syntax.

For example, look at the following example:

```
// An empty arrow function returns undefined
let empty =()=>{};

(()=>"pine")()// returns "pine"

var simple = a => a >20?20: a;
simple(20);// 20
simple(10);// 10

let max =(a, b)=> a > b ?a : b;

// Easy array filtering, mapping, ...

varsampleArray=[7,4,1,0,3,5,11];
var sum =sampleArray.reduce((a, b)=> a + b);// The answer is 29
var even =sampleArray.filter(v => v %2==0);// The answer is [4, 0]
var odd =sampleArray.filter(v => v %2!=0);// The answer is [7, 1,
3, 5, 11]
var double =sampleArray.map(v => v *2);// The answer is[14, 8, 2,
0, 6, 10, 22]
```

An arrow function expression or a fat arrow function are shorter in syntax when compared with function expressions. Arrow function is used to bind the value of this. (It does not binds its own `arguments`, `super`, `this` or `new.target`). Arrow functions are anonymous.

The `yield` keyword is used to `pause` and `resume` a generator function (`function*` function keyword with an asterisk defines a `generator` function that returns a `Generator` object).

Classes

ES6 classes' syntax is simpler and easier than that of area syntactical sugar over the prototype-based object-oriented pattern. It is a syntactical sugar. One-time declaration makes class patterns easier to use and simplifies the use of class patterns. Classes support constructors, instance, prototype-based inheritance, static methods, and super calls.

Here is an example of writing a class in ES6 and ES5:

```
//ES5
functionsomeES5Class(fname, age) { // standard way to create an
object prototype i.e. constructor function
  this.fname = fname;
  this.age = age;
}


someES5Class.prototype.sayName = function() { //prototype property
enables us to add new functions to an existing prototype
  console.log(this.fname);
}


someES5Class.prototype.sayAge = function() { //prototype property
enables us to add new functions to an existing prototype
  console.log(this.age);
}


varmyInstance = new someES5Class('Talha', 25); //new keyword is
used with a constructor function to create new objects from the
same prototype
myInstance.sayName(); //the new method can then be called as a
regular member
myInstance.sayAge();


/*Output:
Talha
25*/


//ES6
classsomeES6Class { // ES6 class
  constructor(fname, age) { // a constructor is defined with
    default parameters
    this.fname = fname;
    this.age = age;
  }
```

```
  sayName() { //functions can be added to the class
    console.log(this.fname);
  }

  sayAge() { //functions can be added to the class
    console.log(this.age);
  }
}

varmyInstance = new someES6Class('Talha', 25); //new keyword is
used to create new objects from the class
myInstance.sayName(); //functions are the class members and can be
called directly
myInstance.sayAge();
/*Output:
Talha
25*/
```

Enhanced object literals

Object literals is one of the most popular patterns of JavaScript. JSON is based on object literals. The reason for its popularity is that it provides a very quick, short, and neat way to do key:value assignments, define methods, evaluate expressions, and make super calls. ES6 has extended the object literal syntax in various ways. This makes them more useful. Two types of extensions for object literals are explained here.

Property initializer shorthand

Earlier in ECMAScript 5, object literals were a comma-separated collection of name:value pairs. There was a likelihood of duplication while property values were being initialized.

Here is an example:

```
functioncreateStudent(StudentID, name, class) {
  return {
    StudentID: StudentID,
    name: name,
    class: class,
  };
}
```

In the preceding example, the `createStudent()` function creates a `student` object whose `name` and `class` properties are similar to the function parameters. This results in duplication of `name` and `class` properties, even though both behave differently.

To correct this, the initializer shorthand property was introduced in ECMAScript 6. This removed all the likelihood of duplication between property names and local variables.

For instance, `createStudent()` can be revised as follows:

```
functioncreateStudent(StudentID, name, class) {
  return {
    StudentID,
    name,
    class,
  };
}
```

In the event that property name will be the same as property estimation, you can simply incorporate property name without colon and value.

If the property of an object literal has no value, the JavaScript engine searches for a variable with a similar name in the surrounding. If the search procedure is successful, the value is assigned to the same party name in object literals.

Method initializer shorthand

With the advent of ECMAScript 6, many things improved, making the work of a web developer simpler. The syntax of writing methods in object literals improved to a great extent. Earlier, in ECMAScript 5, we needed to specify a name and write the complete function definition then and there.

Here is an example:

```
varcustomer = {
  name: "Samantha",
  logName: function() {
    console.log(this.name);
  }
};
```

With ECMAScript 6, the syntax became easier to code. Colon and function keywords have been removed. The same example can be rewritten as follows:

```
varcustomer = {
  name: "Samantha",
  logName() {
    console.log(this.name);
  }
};
person.logName();varobject = {
  // __prototype__
  __prototype__: theProtoTypeObj,
  // Shorthand for 'handler: handler'
  handler,
  // Methods
  toString() {
    // Super calls
    return "x " + super.toString();
  },
  // Dynamic property names
  [ 'property_' + (() => 20)() ]: 20
};
```

Template strings

Template strings amplify ECMAScript with syntactic sugar to build string. This component is like string introduction highlights in Perl, Python, and so on. You can likewise add a tag to permit redid string development, staying away from and counteracting infusion assaults or building complex information structures from string substance. They also enable us to create **domain-specific languages (DSLs)** to deal with content in a safe way.

Instead of adding more extending functionality to JavaScript strings, template strings provide a total new approach for string interpolation.

Basics

The simplest format of a template string is as follows:

```
literal${substitution_variable}literal
```

This is the most basic form of template strings which performs substitutions.

Template strings are enclosed within backticks (`) instead of single or double quotes. Here is an example:

```
letbasic_string = `Kung Fu Panda`;

console.log(basic_string);              // "Kung Fu Panda"
console.log(typeofbasic_string);        // "string"
console.log(basic_string.length);       // 13
```

In this example, a `basic_string` variable contains a simple JavaScript string. The template string syntax is only used to create the string value, which is then assigned to `basic_string`.

If there is a need to use a backtick in string, then you can escape it using a backslash (\\):

```
letbasic_string = `\`Kung Fu\` Panda.`;        // `Kung Fu' Panda
```

Multiline strings

In this type of string, we can add multiple lines in a single line of code. To insert a new line in a string, we have to include \n within the string manually, as follows:

```
letmultiline_string = "Kung Fu Panda, \n\
Releasing in 2016";

console.log(multiline_string);
```

The output of this is:

```
Kung Fu Panda
Releasing in 2016
```

We need to be careful regarding the whitespaces, as whitespaces within backticks are considered to be part of the string. All whitespaces before the second line are considered to be part of the string.

Destructuring assignment

In JavaScript, *destructuring* means pattern matching. In ES6, we can do efficient pattern matching in objects and arrays. Earlier, this was a long and complicated task. Here are some working examples written in a client console.

Fetching data from objects and arrays is very common in JavaScript. Object properties are usually stored in local variables for instant access. Let's take a look at the following code snippet:

```
var settings = {
  replay: true,
  save: false
};

// later

varlocalReplay = options.replay,
localSave = options.save;
```

ES6 made this easier by introducing destructuring assignments, which goes through an object or an array and stores specified values in the local variables. It allows binding using pattern matching for objects and arrays.

Array destructuring

All variables can be initialized and swapped at once instead of the conventional way of creating a temporary variable:

```
var [ first, last ] = ["one", "hundred"] // initialize
console.log(first + " to " + last); // one to hundred

[first, last] = [last, first] // variable swapping
console.log(first + " to " + last); // hundred to one
```

Multiple values from a function are returned with ease using array destructuring. We don't have to wrap around an object. To skip variables, you can leave the position of the array element blank:

```
function dob() {
  return [29, "November", 1990, "Thursday"];
}
var [date, month, year, day] = dob();
console.log("My date of birth is on " + date + " " + month); // My
date of birth is on 29 November
```

Object destructuring

Due to destructuring, variables can also be initialized from an object that is returned from a function even with deeply nested objects.

Destructuring enables variables to be initialized from an object that is returned by a function having deeply nested objects. Just like Array destructuring, we can skip the ones not needed. Here's the working snippet:

```
function dob() {
  return {
    date: 29,
    month: "November",
    year: 1990,
    time: {
      hour: 12, // nested
      minute: 35,
      meridian: "AM"
    }
  };
}

var { date: d, month: m, time : { hour: h, meridian: p } } =
dob();
// h is the nested property while year and minute is skipped

console.log("I was born on " + d + " " + m + " at " + h + " " +
p); // I was born on 29 November at 12 AM
```

Extended parameter handling

Functions are an important and fundamental part of any language. ES6 has introduced a number of incremental improvements in functions. This makes them less error prone and more powerful.

Functions allow any number of parameters to be passed irrespective of the number of parameters in the function definition. There are three types of these parameters that could be passed to functions:

- Default
- Rest
- Spread

Default parameter

ES6 lets us set default parameters. A parameter with a default value is considered optional. It binds trailing parameters to an array:

```
function multiply(x, y) {
  y = typeofy !== 'undefined' ?  y : 1;

  returnx*y;
}

multiply(10);
```

Rest parameter

Rest parameters replace the need for arguments and addresses common cases more directly. Rest parameters are indicated by three dots (...) preceding a parameter.

Here is an example showing the rest parameter:

```
//Rest Parameter
function sum(...nums) {
  var result = 0;
  nums.forEach(function(number) {
    result += number;
  });
  return result;
}
console.log(sum(1)); // 1
console.log(sum(1, 2, 3)); // 6
```

The named parameter becomes an array containing the rest of the parameters. Adding more than one named argument may cause syntax error.

Spread operator

Spread operator is very similar to the rest parameter, but it allows us to split the array to individual arguments, which are then passed to the function as separate arguments.

Here is an example showing the spread operator:

```
//Spread Operator
functionsum2(a, b, c) {
  return a + b + c;
}
varargs = [1, 2];
console.log(sum(...args, ...args, 3)); // 6
```

Here is an example showing the usage of default, rest, and spread parameters:

```
function sum() {
  return ;
}
console.log(sum(
(1, 2)
//Spread Operator

//Rest Parameter
//Default Parameter Values
//Default Parameter Values
functioninc(num, increment = 1) {
  returnnum + increment;
}
console.log(inc(2, 2)); // 4
console.log(inc(4)); // 5
```

Bindings

The `let` keyword is a new var. The declaration syntax for the `let` keyword is the same as for var. You can basically replace var with `let` to declare a variable but keep its scope to the current code:

```
functiongetCuisine(condition) {

  if (condition) {
    letcuisine = "Mediterranean";

    // other code

    returncuisine;
  }
  else {

    // cuisine does not exist here

    return null;
  }

  // cuisine does not exist here
}
```

Variables defined using `const` are considered to be constants, so the value cannot be changed once set. For this reason, every `const` variable has to be initialized:

```
// Valid constant
const ITEMS = 10;

// Syntax error: missing initialization
const ITEM;
```

Iterators and the for...of operator

We use iterators to allow customization of an object's iteration method/behavior, such as CLRIE numerable or Java Iterable. Generalize the `for..in` operator to custom iterator-based iteration with `for..of`. Iterators are an important feature of ECMAScript 6. When used in combination with new array methods and new types of collections (for example, sets and maps), iterators become even more important for the efficient processing of data.

Fibonacci numbers, or the Fibonacci arrangement, are the numbers in the accompanying whole number succession:

```
let fibonacci = {
  [Symbol.iterator]() {
    let x = 0, y = 1;
    return {
      next() {
        [x, y] = [y, x + y];
        return { done: false, value: y }
      }
    }
  }
}

for (vari of fibonacci) {
  // truncate the sequence at 3000
  if (i> 3000)
  break;
  console.log(i);
}
```

Generators

Custom iterators are a useful tool but it requires careful programming so that it can maintain its internal state explicitly. ES6 introduced generators which provide a powerful alternative. Generator allows us to create an iteration algorithm by writing a single function. This single function is able to maintain its own state.

A generator is a function that returns an iterator. The generator functions are denoted by embedding an asterisk (*) after the function keyword. A normal function becomes a generator if it contains a yield expression and uses function* syntax.

 It doesn't matter whether there is space between the function keyword and the asterisk.

The yield keyword is utilized within the generators function to indicate the qualities that the iterator must return when the next() method is called. So, in the event that you need to return unique values for each progressive call to next():

We can convert the previous iterator example to use a generator, as shown here:

```
let fibonacci = {
  *[Symbol.iterator]() {
    let prex = 0, cury = 1
    for (;;) {
      [ prex, cury ] = [ cury, prex+curv ] = [
        yield cury
    }
  }
}

for (let ni of fibonacci) {
  if (ni> 3000)
  break
  console.log(ni)
}
```

Better Unicode support

ES6 supports Unicode, including new Unicode literal form in strings, new RegExp u mode to handle code points, as well as new APIs to process strings at the 21-bit code points level. These updates enable us to create global apps in JavaScript. ECMAScript 6 enforces encoding of strings in UTF.

The supported Unicode examples are as follows:

```
// same as ECMAScript 5
"□".length == 2

// new RegExpbehaviour, opt-in 'u'
"□".match(/./u)[0].length == 2

// new form
"\u{1D306}"=="□"=="\uD834\uDF06"

// new String ops
"□".codePointAt(0) == 0x20BB7

// for-of iterates code points
for(var c of "□") {
  console.log(c);
}
```

Modules

ECMAScript 6 enables us to export and import symbols to and from modules without polluting the global namespace. It provides added support for modules for component definition. Runtime behavior is defined by a host-defined default loader. It is an implicitly asynchronous model; no code is executed until the necessary modules are available and processed:

```
export function sum(x, y, {
  return x + y
}

console.log("4π = " + math.sum(math.pi, math.pi, math.pi,
math.pi));

console.log("2π = " + sum(pi, pi));
```

Some additional features include export default and export *, as shown in the following code snippet:

```
exportvar e = 2.71828182846;

export default function(x) {
  returnMath.log(x);
}
console.log("2π = " + ln(e)*pi*2);
```

Module loaders

Module loaders are used primarily to resolve module specifiers, loading modules, and so on. They are responsible for downloading the required modules and binding them asynchronously. This brings to light the dependencies of a client script. The constructor is `Reflect.Loader`.

Module loaders support:

- Compilation hooks
- Nested virtualization
- Dynamic loading
- Global namespace isolation
- State isolation

Loader methods

- `System.module(source, options?)`: This is used to assess the JavaScript code in source to a module (which is delivered and returned non-concurrently by means of a guarantee)
- `System.set(name, module)`: This is used for the registration of the module created by System.module()
- `System.define(name, source, options?)`: This is used to assess the module code in source and registers the outcome

We can configure the default module loader, and new loaders can be constructed to evaluate and load code in isolated or constrained contexts:

```
System.import('libraries/math').then(function(mx) {
  console.log("π = " + (mx.pi));
});

// Create execution sandboxes - new Loaders
var loader = new Loader({
  global: fixup(window)
});
loader.eval("console.log('live to code!');");

// Directly manipulate module cache
System.get('jquery');
System.set('jquery', Module({$: $}));
```

Collections

Collections are used to create unique values collections of any type in JavaScript. In a collection of values, you can also add and remove values. There is no direct access to values in collection, and these are of array type.

In ECMAscript 6, collections are a new efficient way to store data. JavaScript arrays are similar to other programming language arrays with index. By use of these arrays, you can pull double and triple data and also stack data. There are many new types of collections in JavaScript. Here are some examples:

- Sets
- Maps
- WeakMap
- WeakSet

Sets

A `set` has a unique collection of values. The unique values of a set are also of object reference types. Values in sets cannot be duplicated. Before you access values from a `set`, you need to check whether the values are present or not.

We can add values in a `set` and also check the size of values in a set. Here is an example:

```
Var students=new set();
Students.add(10);
Students.add("Ali");
```

Maps

A `map` object is a `key/value` map. Any value in `map` may be used as a key or a value. Elements can iterate in a `map` in an insertion order, and it returns an array of a value or a key. There are two properties of `map`:

- `Map.length`: Returns the number of elements in a `map`
- `Map.prototype`: The `Map.prototype` property represents the prototype for the `map` constructor

Here are some of the methods of the `map` object.

Map.prototype.clear()

The `clear()` method removes all elements from a `map` object.

Returns

It returns nothing.

Parameter

There is no input parameter.

Description

After using this function, everything that we have initialized on map will be erased. The function has no parameter and returns nothing as it wipes out everything.

Here is an example of this method:

```
varmyMap=newMap();
myMap.set("pine","apple");
myMap.set(1,"apple");

myMap.size;// 2
myMap.has("cone");// will return false

myMap.has("pine")// will return true
```

Map.prototype.delete()

The `delete()` method removes the specified element from a `Map` object.

Returns

It returns `true` if a component in the map object existed and has been evacuated. It returns false if the component does not exist.

Parameter

A key is required. The key here is basically the element to be removed.

Description

This is different from `map.prototype.clear()` as it clearly removes a specific element instead of deleting every element on the map. We pass a key (the element to be deleted), and the function returns `true` or `false`, depending on the key.

Here is an example of this method:

```
varmyMap=newMap();
myMap.set("pine","apple");

myMap.delete("apple");// Returns true. Successfully removed.
myMap.has("apple");// Returns false. The "apple" element is no
longer present.
```

Map.prototype.entries()

This function is used to tell us about the key and value of elements on map.

Returns

It returns a new `iterator` object that contains a key and a value for every element on the map.

Parameter

There are no input parameters.

Description

This function is utilized for letting us know about the key and value of components on map.

Here is an example of this method:

```
varmyMap=newMap();
myMap.set("0","pine");
myMap.set(1,"apple");
myMap.set({},"cone");

varmapIter=myMap.entries();

console.log(mapIter.next().value);// ["0", "pine"]
console.log(mapIter.next().value);// [1, "apple"]
console.log(mapIter.next().value);// [Object, "cone"]
```

Map.prototype.forEach()

The `forEach` method executes the given callback once to every key/value pair in the map object.

Returns

It returns nothing.

Parameter

There are three parameters: the element `value`, element `key`, and the `map` object being traversed.

Description

The `forEach` strategy executes the given callback once to every key of the guide that really exists. It is not conjured for keys that have been erased. Nonetheless, it is executed for values that are available; however, they have the value defined.

Here is an example of this method:

```
functionlogMapElements(value, key, map) {
   console.log("m["+ key +"] = "+ value);
}
Map([["foo",3],["apple",{}],["cone",
undefined]]).forEach(logMapElements);
// logs:
// "m[pine] = 3"
// "m[apple] = [object Object]"
// "m[cone] = undefined"
```

Map.prototype.get()

A specific element from the map is returned using the `get()` method.

Returns

It returns the key that is used as a parameter (only if it is found in map); or else, it returns an error message.

Parameter

It requires a key that is to be returned from the map.

Description

We input a key that we want to find in the map, and the function returns it. It is used when we want to get the value of an element.

Here is an example of this method:

```
varmyMap=newMap();
myMap.set("apple","pine");

myMap.get("apple");// Returns "apple".
myMap.get("cone");// Returns undefined.
```

Map.prototype.has()

The function returns `true` (Boolean value) if the element exists and `false` if it does not.

Returns

It returns `true` if a component with the specified key exists in the `map` object. If not found, it returns `false`.

Parameter

A key is required.

Description

We pass a key in the function to check whether a certain element exists in the map or not. If the element exists, `true` is returned; otherwise, `false` is returned.

An example of this method is shown here:

```
varmyMap=newMap();
myMap.set("apple","pine");

myMap.has("apple");// returns true
myMap.has("cone");// returns false
```

Map.prototype.keys()

It returns keys for every element in the map.

Returns

It returns a new object that contains the keys of all elements on the map.

Parameter

There is no input parameter.

Description

The `keys()` strategy gives back another `iterator` object that contains the keys for every component in the `map` object in the insertion order.

An example of this method is shown here:

```
varmyMap=newMap();
myMap.set("0","pine");
myMap.set(1,"apple");
myMap.set({},"cone");

varmapIter=myMap.keys();

console.log(mapIter.next().value);// "0"
console.log(mapIter.next().value);// 1
console.log(mapIter.next().value);// Object
```

Map.prototype.set()

This is the procedure to add a new element on map.

Returns

It returns the map object.

Parameter

This is the key of the element to be added on map.

Description

The set() strategy includes another component with a predetermined key and value to a map object.

An example of this method is shown here:

```
varmyMap=newMap();

// Add new elements to the map
myMap.set("apple","pine");
myMap.set(1,"pineapple");

// Update an element in the map
myMap.set("apple","custard");
```

Map.prototype.values()

This is the method to get a new object containing values of each element.

Returns

It returns an object that has values of all components on map.

Parameter

There is no input parameter.

Description

The values() technique gives back another iterator object that contains the values for every component in the map object in the insertion manner.

Here is an example of this method:

```
varmyMap = new Map();

varkeyObj = {},
keyFunc = function () {},
keyString = "This is a sample string";

// setting the values
myMap.set(keyString, "value associated to 'This is a sample
string'");
myMap.set(keyObj, "value associated to a keyObj");
myMap.set(keyFunc, "value associated to a keyFunc");

myMap.size; // 3

// getting the values
myMap.get(keyString);    // "value associated to 'This is a sample
string'"
myMap.get(keyObj);       // "value associated to a keyObj"
myMap.get(keyFunc);      // "value associated to a keyFunc"

myMap.get("a string");   // "value associated to 'This is a sample
string'"
// because keyString === 'a string'
myMap.get({});           // undefined, because keyObj !== {}
myMap.get(function() {}) // undefined, because keyFunc !==
function () {}
```

WeakMap

It is the same as map, but there is some difference in it. It only accepts objects as keys. Primitive data types are not allowed in `WeakMap`. There is no garbage collection in a `WeakMap` because it doesn't reference to an object acting like a key. As a result of these differences, there is no method to access keys in `WeakMap`.

 Keys in `WeakMap` are not enumerable, which means that there is no method to give you a list of keys. There is size property available in `WeakMap`.

Here is an example:

```
varmyWeakMap1 = new WeakMap(),
myWeakMap2 = new WeakMap(),
varo1 = {},
o2 = function(){},
o3 = window;

myWeakMap1.set(o1, 37);
myWeakMap1.set(o2, "pineapple");
myWeakMap2.set(o1, o2);
myWeakMap2.set(o3, undefined);
myWeakMap2.set(myWeakMap1, myWeakMap2);

myWeakMap1.get(o2); // "pineapple"
myWeakMap2.get(o2); // undefined, because there is no value for o2
on myWeakMap2
myWeakMap2.get(o3); // undefined, because that is the set value

myWeakMap1.has(o2); // will return true
myWeakMap2.has(o2); // will return false
myWeakMap2.has(o3); // will return true

myWeakMap1.has(o1); // will return true
myWeakMap1.delete(o1);
myWeakMap1.has(o1); // will return false
```

WeakMap.prototype.clear()

This is used to remove all elements from the `WeakMap`. This is obsolete now, but is, however, still used in a few browsers.

Returns

It returns the key of the element to be removed from the `WeakMap` object.

Parameters

This is t key of the element to be removed from the `WeakMap` object.

Description

Here is an example:

```
varwm = new WeakMap();
varobject = {};

wm.set(object, "pine");
wm.set(window, "apple");

wm.has(object); // will return true
wm.has(window); // will return true

wm.clear();

wm.has(object)  // will return false
wm.has(window)  // will return false
```

WeakMap.prototype.delete()

This method is used to remove a specific object from `WeakMap`.

Returns

It returns `true` if an element in the `WeakMap` object has been removed successfully.

Parameters

This is the key of the element to remove from the `WeakMap` object.

Description

The `delete()` method removes the specified element from a `WeakMap` object.

Here is an example:

```
varwm = new WeakMap();
wm.set(window, "pineapple");

wm.delete(window); // Returns true. Successfully removed.

wm.has(window);    // Returns false. The window object is no
longer in the WeakMap.
```

WeakMap.prototype.get()

This method is used to retrieve a specific object from WeakMap.

Returns

It returns the element associated with the specified key or is undefined if the key can't be found in the WeakMap object.

Parameters

This is the key of the element to return from the WeakMap object.

Description

The key of the element to return from the WeakMap object.

Here is an example:

```
varwm = new WeakMap();
wm.set(window, "pine");

wm.get(window); // Returns "pine".
wm.get("apple");  // Returns undefined.
```

WeakMap.prototype.has()

This method is used to check whether the specified object exists in WeakMap.

Returns

It returns true if an element with the specified key exists in the WeakMap object; otherwise it returns false.

Parameters

It is the key of the element to test for presence in the WeakMap object.

Description

The has() method returns a Boolean indicating whether an element with the specified key exists in the WeakMap object or not.

Here is an example:

```
varwm = new WeakMap();
wm.set(window, "pine");

wm.has(window); // returns true
wm.has("apple");  // returns false
```

WeakMap.prototype.set()

This method is used to add an object to a specific location.

Returns

The WeakMap object.

Parameters

- Key: The key of the element to add to the WeakMap object
- Value: The value of the element to add to the WeakMap object

Description

The set() method adds a new element with a specified key and value to a WeakMap object.

Here is an example:

```
varwm = new WeakMap();
varobject = {};

// Add new elements to the WeakMap
wm.set(object, "pine").set(window, "apple"); // chainable

// Update an element in the WeakMap
wm.set(object, "cone");
```

Weakset

This is a collection of objects that don't stop its elements from being garbage collected. There is no looping, iteration, and learning in WeakSet. It has three methods.

WeakSet.prototype.add(someValue)

This method appends a new object at the end of the WeakSet.

Returns

The WeakSet.prototype.add(someValue) method returns Nothing

Parameter

The object to add to the WeakSet collection.

Description

The add() method appends a new object to the end of a WeakSet object.

An example of this method is as follows:

```
varmyWeakSet=newWeakSet();

myWeakSet.add(window);// add the window object to the WeakSet
created above

myWeakSet.has(window);// will return true
```

WeakSet.prototype.delete(someValue)

This method removes the specified object from WeakSet.

Returns

Returns true if the value is found in WeakSet and is deleted. Returns false if the value is not found.

Parameter

The value to be deleted is sent as a parameter.

Description

The delete() strategy expels the predefined element from a WeakSet object. It is used while we need to delete some element from WeakSet.

An example of this method is as follows:

```
varmyWeakSet=newWeakSet();
varmyObject={};

myWeakSet.add(window);

myWeakSet.delete(myObject);// Will return false
myWeakSet.delete(window);// Will return true.

myWeakSet.has(window);// Will return false.
```

WeakSet.prototype.has(someValue)

This method will return true if the object exists in WeakSet; otherwise, false is returned.

Returns

It returns `true` if a component with the predefined value exists in the `WeakSet` object; otherwise, it returns `false`.

Parameter

Requires a value that is to be searched.

Description

The `has()` technique gives back a Boolean demonstrating whether an item exists in `WeakSet` or not.

An example of this method is shown here:

```
varws=newWeakSet();
varobject={};
ws.add(window);

mySet.has(window);   // will return true
mySet.has(object);   // will return false
```

It has only arbitrary values. References of objects are held in a weak manner in a `WeakSet` object. They can also be garbage collectors. In `WeakSet`, there is no list of current objects because of the garbage collector. These objects are not enumerable.

Here is an example:

```
// Sets
varmySet = new Set();
mySet.add("apple").add("candy");
mySet.size === 2;
mySet.has("hello") === false;

// Maps
varmyMap = new Map();
myMap.set("boy", 27);
myMap.set(f, 25);
myMap.get(f) == 25;

// Weak Maps
varmyWeakMap = new WeakMap();
myWeakMap.set(s, { extra: 99 });
myWeakMap.size === undefined
```

```
// Weak Sets
varmyWeakSet = new WeakSet();
myWeakSet.add({ data: 99 });
```

Proxies

Proxies enable object creation with a wide range of behaviors available to host objects. They can be used for object virtualization, interception, logging/profiling, and so on. Proxies provide developers with an unprecedented control over objects and unlimited possibilities to define new interaction patterns.

Here is an example:

```
vartargetObject = {};
varhandlerObject = {
  get: function (receiver, book) {
    return `Title, ${name}!`;
  }
};

varproxyObject = new Proxy(target, handler);
proxyObject.world === 'Lahore!';

// Proxying a function object
vartargetObject = function () { return 'Target, I am'; };
varhandlerObject = {
  apply: function (receiver, ...args) {
    return 'Le proxy';
  }
};

var p = new Proxy(target, handler);
p() === 'Le proxy';
```

Symbols

A symbol is a unique type which can be used as an identifier for object properties. The symbol object is an implicit object wrapper for the symbol primitive data type.

Here is how you can create a new primitive symbol:

```
var symb = Symbol();
```

OR

```
var symb = Symbol('abc');
```

The preceding code creates two new symbols. `Symbol('abc')` does not force converts abc into an object but creates a new separate object.

```
Symbol('abc') === Symbol('abc'); //false
```

Using `Symbol()` with new keyword will throw a type error.

```
var symb = new Symbol(); // TypeError
```

This prevents creation of an explicit Symbol wrapper object instead of a new symbol value. Creating an explicit wrapper object around primitive data types were only supported until ES5. However, existing primitive wrapper objects like new Boolean, new `String` and new `Number` can still be created for legacy reasons.

And if it is necessary to create Symbol wrapper object, you can use the `Object()` function:

```
var symb = Symbol("abc");
typeof symb;        // "symbol"
var symbObj = Object(symb);
typeof symbObj;   // "object"
```

The `Object.getOwnPropertySymbols()` method returns an array of symbols and lets you find symbol properties on a given object.

Here is an example:

```
varSomeClass = (function() {

  var key = Symbol("key");

  functionSomeClass(privateData) {
    this[key] = privateData;
  }

  SomeClass.prototype = {
    doStuff: function() {
      ... this[key] ...
    }
  };

  returnSomeClass;
})();

var c = new SomeClass("bye")
c["key"] === undefined
```

The ECMAScript 6 standard uses a special notation to indicate symbols, prefixing the identifier with @@, such as @@create.

Subclassable built-ins

In ECMAScript 6, built-ins such as Date, Array, and DOM elements can be subclassed. Object construction for a function named Ctor now uses two phases:

- Call Ctor[@@create] to allocate the object and install any special behavior
- Invoke constructor on new instance to initialize it

The known @@create symbol is available via Symbol.create. Built-ins now expose their @@create syntax explicitly.

Here is an example:

```
// Pseudo-code of Array
classSomeArray {
  constructor(...args) { /* ... */ }
  static [Symbol.create]() {

  }
}

// User code of Array subclass
classSomeArray extends Array {
  constructor(...args) { super(...args); }
}

// Two-phase 'new':
// 1) Call @@create to allocate object
// 2) Invoke constructor on new instance
vararr = new SomeArray();
arr[1] = 123;
arr.length == 1
```

Promises

ECMAScript 6 introduced promises. It is a library used for asynchronous programming. It is a first-class representation of a value that may be made available in the future. Many existing JavaScript libraries already use promises.

Some of the methods for promises in ES6 are mentioned here.

Promise.All()

This method returns a promise that is resolved once all the promises in the iterable argument have been resolved. In the case of a rejection, it returns with the reason of the first-passed promise that was rejected.

Returns

The `Promise.All()` method returns nothing.

Parameter

An `iterable` object, such as an array.

Description

Promises returns result as an array of values. If any value in the array is not a promise, then it is converted using Promise.resolve. If any of the passed in promises rejects, then all promise are rejected and the reason of rejection of a promise is returned. It discards all other promise whether they have been resolved or not. If an empty array is passed, then this method resolves immediately.

An example of this method is shown here:

```
varprom1 = 6000;
varprom2 = new Promise(function(resolve, reject) {
  setTimeout(resolve, 100, "Here");
});

Promise.all([prom1, prom2]).then(function(values) {
  console.log(values); // [6000, "Here"]
});
```

Promise.prototype.catch()

This method is used only in cases where objects are rejected. It works the same as `promise.prototype.then()`.

Returns

The `promise.prototype.catch()` method returns nothing.

Parameter

- **One rejected**: A function called when the `promise` is rejected. This function has one argument, the rejection reason.

Description

The `catch()` technique gives back a `promise` and manages rejected cases. It behave similar as calling `Promise.prototype.then(undefined, onRejected)`.

An example of this method is as follows:

```
varprom1= new Promise(function(resolve, reject) {
  resolve('This was Successful!!');
});

prom1.then(function(value) {
  console.log(value); // "This was Successful!!"
  throw 'oh, no!';
}).catch(function(e) {
  console.log(e); // "Error found"
}).then(function() {
  console.log('Catch Done!');
}, function () {
  console.log('Not fired due to the catch');
});
```

Promise.resolve(value)

This method returns a `promise` object that is resolved by the specified value. If the value is associated to a then method, the returned promise will move to the then method, adopting its final state. Otherwise, the returned promise will be fulfilled with the specified value.

Returns

The `promise` object that is resolved with the given value.

Parameter

Let's take a look at the following parameters and their use:

- `onFulfilled`: A `function` called when the `Promise` is fulfilled
- `onRejected`: A `function` called when the `promise` is rejected

Description

The `Promise.resolve(value)` system gives back a `Promise` question that is determined with the given quality. On the off chance that the quality is a then able (that is, has a then technique), the returned promise will *follow* that then able, adopting its possible state.

The then() technique gives back a Promise. It takes two contentions: callback capacities for the achievement and disappointment instances of the Promise.

Using the then method

An example of this method is as follows:

```
varprom1=newPromise(function(resolve, reject) {
  resolve("This was a Success!");
  // or
  // reject ("Error Found Try Again!");
});

prom1.then(function(value) {
  console.log(value);//This was a Success!
},function(reason){
  console.log(reason);// Error Found Try Again!
});
```

Chaining

As the then() method returns a Promise, you can easily chain then calls:

```
varp2=newPromise(function(resolve, reject) {
  resolve(1);
});

p2.then(function(value) {
  console.log(value);// 1
  return value +1;
}).then(function(value) {
  console.log(value);// 2
});

p2.then(function(value) {
  console.log(value);// 1
});
```

You can also use chaining to implement one function with a Promise-based API on top of another such function:

```
functionfetch_current_data() {
  returnfetch("current-data.json").then((response)=> {
    if(response.headers.get("content-type")!="application/json") {
      thrownewTypeError();
    }
    var j =response.json();
```

```
   // maybe do something with j
   return j;// fulfillment value given to user of
   // fetch_current_data().then()
   });
}
```

Promise.reject(value)

This function returns a promise object that is rejected because of the passed value/reason.

Returns

The `Promise.reject()` method returns a simple output telling the reason for rejection.

Parameter

Reason why this promise is rejected.

Description

The static `Promise.reject()` function capacity gives back a `Promise` that is rejected. For troubleshooting purposes and specific mistake finding, it is helpful to make the reason an instance of error.

An example of this method is shown here:

```
Promise.reject("Testing Promise reject").then(function(reason) {
  // not called
},function(reason) {
  console.log(reason);// "Testing Promise reject"
});

Promise.reject(newError("fail")).then(function(error) {
  // not called
},function(error) {
  console.log(error);// Stacktrace
});
```

Promise.race(value)

This function returns a promise that is resolved or rejected the same way as the promises passed in iterable, with the value or reason from that promise.

Returns

The `Promise.race()` function returns a promise.

Parameter

An `iterable` object, such as an array.

Description

The `race` function gives back a `Promise` that is settled the same route as the initially passed `Promise` to settle. It determines or rejects, whichever happens first.

An example of this method is as follows:

```
varmyPromise1=newPromise(function(resolve, reject) {
  setTimeout(resolve,800,"first");
});
varmyPromise2=newPromise(function(resolve, reject) {
  setTimeout(resolve,300,"second");
});

Promise.race([myPromise1,myPromise2]).then(function(value) {
  console.log(value);// "second"
  // Both resolve, but myPromise2 is faster
});
```

Core math library APIs

ECMAScript 6 has made several new extensions to the prebuilt libraries, including core `Math` libraries, `arrays`, `string helpers`, and `Object.assign` for copying. These new methods help in speeding up the execution process, hence resulting in enhancing the performance of applications that may perform calculations and string manipulation. It also improves the speed of applications that must perform many calculations and string manipulations.

Numerous new library increases, including core Math libraries, array conversion helpers, string helpers, and `Object.assign` for copying. An example of using the Core Math Library APIs is as follows:

```
Number.EPSILON
Number.isInteger(Infinity) // will return false
Number.isNaN("NaN") // will return false

Math.acosh(3) // 1.762747174039086
Math.hypot(3, 4) // 5
```

```
Math.imul(Math.pow(2, 32) - 1, Math.pow(2, 32) - 2) // 2

"Neptune".includes("cd") // This will return false
"Mars".repeat(4) // This will be "MarsMarsMarsMars"

Array.from(document.querySelectorAll('*')) // Returns a real Array
Array.of(1, 2, 3) // Similar to new Array(...), but without
special one-arg behavior
[0, 0, 0].fill(2, 1) // [0,2,2]
[24, 14, 23, 57, 89, 75, 33].find(x => x == 33) // 33
[24, 14, 23, 57, 89, 75, 33].findIndex(x => x == 14) // 1
[1, 2, 3, 4, 5].copyWithin(3, 0) // [1, 2, 3, 1, 2]
["x", "y", "z"].entries() // iterator [0, "x"], [1,"y"], [2,"z"]
["x", "y", "z"].keys() // iterator 0, 1, 2
```

Binary and octal literals

ECMAScript 6 introduced binary and octal literal notations, for binary (b) and octal (o). Both these notations are a little similar to hexadecimal literal notation for prepending 0x or 0X to a value.

The new octal literal format begins with 0o or 0O, while the new binary literal format begins with 0b or 0B. Each literal type must be followed by one or more digits; 0-7 for octal and 0-1 for binary. Here's an example:

```
// ECMAScript 6
varvalue11 = 0o65;      // 53 in decimal
varvalue22 = 0b100;     // 4 in decimal

0b111110111 === 503 // will return true
0o767 === 503 // will return true
```

Reflect API

The `reflect` object is a single object that contains functions related to the reflection API. As the name suggests, it is merely a reflection of the objects so that one can observe them closely, regardless of who the object was created by. The `reflect` object is not a `function` object. It does not have a `constructor` method. It cannot be invoked as a function, because it does not have a `call` method.

Reflect API is known to be the inverse of Proxy API.

Here is a list of methods a `reflect` object has.

Reflect.get(target, prop, [receiver])

This method allows you to get the property of an object. This method is similar to property accessors syntax (`object[propertyKey]`).

Returns

The `reflect` object returns the value of property.

Parameter

The parameters are target objects on which to get property, the name of property, and the value.

Description

The static `Reflect.get()` method works like getting a property from an object (`target[propertyKey]`) as a function.

An example of the get method is as follows:

```
// Object
varobject={a:4,b:5};
Reflect.get(object,"b");// 5

// Array
Reflect.get(["first","second"],1);// "second", since array starts
with 0 index

// Proxy with a get handler
var x ={p:9};
varobject=newProxy(x, {
  get(a,b,c){returnb +"meow";}
});
Reflect.get(object,"woof");// "woofbar"
```

Reflect.set(target, prop, value, [receiver])

This method allows you to set a property of an object. This method is also similar to property accessor syntax.

Returns

The `Reflect.set(target, prop, value, [receiver]` returns a Boolean value indicating whether property was successful or not.

Parameter

Parameters are target objects, name of the property, the value to set, and the receiver.

Description

The static `Reflect.set()` strategy works like setting a property on an item.

An example of this method is shown here:

```
// Object
varobject={};
Reflect.set(object,"property","value");// will return true
object.property;// "value"

// Array
vararr=["cow","cow","cow"];
Reflect.set(arr,1,"goat");// will return true
arr[1];// "goat"

// It can truncate an array.
Reflect.set(arr,"length",1);// will return true
arr;// ["goat"];

// With just one argument, propertyKey and value are "undefined".
varobject={};
Reflect.set(object);// will return true
Reflect.getOwnPropertyDescriptor(object,"undefined");
// { value: undefined, writable: true, enumerable: true,
configurable: true }
```

Reflect.has(target, prop)

This method allows you to check whether an object holds a specific property. This method is similar to the in operator.

Returns

The `Reflect.has(target, prop)` returns a Boolean value indicating whether the target has a property or not.

Parameter

The target object and the property key (name of property to check) is passed.

Description

The static `Reflect.has()` technique works like the in operator as a function.

An example of this method is shown here:

```
Reflect.has({a:0},"a");// will return true
Reflect.has({a:0},"b");// will return false

// returns true for properties in the prototype chain
Reflect.has({a:0},"toString");

// Proxy with .has() handler method
object=newProxy({}, {
  has(s,d){returns.startsWith("cat");}
});
Reflect.has(object,"catastrophe");// will return true
Reflect.has(object,"camel");// will return false
```

Reflect.apply(target, receiver, args)

This method is used to call a target function with a specified set of arguments.

Returns

The `Reflect.apply(target, receiver, args)` method returns nothing.

Parameter

Target function to call. `thisArgument` and `ArgumentList` is passed as parameters.

Description

The static `Reflect.apply()` technique calls an objective function with specified arguments.

An example of this method is shown here:

```
Reflect.apply(Math.floor, undefined,[3.999]);
// 3;

Reflect.apply(String.fromCharCode, undefined,[80, 97, 107, 105,
115, 116, 97, 110]);
// "Pakistan"

Reflect.apply("".charAt,"stars",[2]);
// "a"
```

Reflect.construct(target, args)

This method allows you to call a `constructor` function with multiple arguments. It is just like calling new function (…args).

Returns

The `Reflect.construct(target, args)` returns nothing.

Parameter

The target function to be called, an argument list, and the new target (constructor to be used) are parameters.

Description

The `Reflect.construct` method permits you to conjure a constructor with a variable number of contentions (which would likewise be conceivable utilizing the spread operator consolidated with the new operator).

An example of this method is shown here:

Using `Reflect.construct()`:

```
var d =Reflect.construct(Date,[2015,1,5]);
dinstanceofDate;// will return true
d.getFullYear();// 2015
```

Using `newTarget`:

```
functionmyConstructor(){}
var result =Reflect.construct(Array,[],myConstructor);

Reflect.getPrototypeOf(result);// myConstructor.prototype
Array.isArray(result);// will return true
```

Reflect.getOwnPropertyDescriptor(target, prop)

This method is just like `Object.getOwnPropertyDescriptor()`. This method returns a property descriptor of a specific property if it exists on an object; otherwise, undefined is returned. The only difference between these two is the way non-object targets are handled.

Returns

The `Reflect.getOwnPropertyDescriptor(target, prop)` method returns a property descriptor object.

Parameter

The target object in which to look for property, and property key (name of the property to be applied) are the parameters.

Description

The `Reflect.getOwnPropertyDescriptor` system gives back a property descriptor of the given property in the event that it exists on the object, indistinct something else undefined is returned if property does not exists. The main contrast to `Object.getOwnPropertyDescriptor()` is the manner by which non-object targets are taken care of.

An example of this method is shown here:

Using `Reflect.getOwnPropertyDescriptor()`:

```
Reflect.getOwnPropertyDescriptor({a:"bye"},"a");
// {value: "bye", writable: true, enumerable: true, configurable:
true}

Reflect.getOwnPropertyDescriptor({x:"bye"},"y");
// undefined

Reflect.getOwnPropertyDescriptor([],"length");
// {value: 0, writable: true, enumerable: false, configurable:
false}
```

Difference to `Object.getOwnPropertyDescriptor()`:

If the first argument to this method is not an object (a primitive), then it will cause a `TypeError`. With `Object.getOwnPropertyDescriptor`, a non-object first argument will be coerced to an object at first:

```
Reflect.getOwnPropertyDescriptor("woof",0);
// TypeError: "woof" is not non-null object

Object.getOwnPropertyDescriptor("dummy",0);
// { value: "d", writable: false, enumerable: true, configurable:
false }
```

Reflect.defineProperty(target, prop, desc)

This method is similar to `Object.defineProperty()`. This method allows us to modify the property of an object. The `Object.defineProperty()` method returns an object or returns a type error if the property is not defined successfully. The `Reflect.defineProperty()` method returns `true` if the property was defined successfully. Otherwise, it returns `false`.

Returns

The `Reflect.defineProperty(target, prop, desc)` method returns a Boolean demonstrating regardless of whether the property was effectively characterized.

Parameter

Target object, property key, and attributes are the parameters.

Description

The `Reflect.defineProperty` technique permits the exact expansion to or change of a property on an object. For more subtle elements, see the `Object.defineProperty`, which is comparative. `Object.defineProperty` gives back the objects or tosses `TypeError` if the property has not been effectively characterized. `Reflect.defineProperty`, then again, essentially gives back a Boolean demonstrating regardless of whether the property was effectively characterized.

An example of this method is shown here:

Using `Reflect.defineProperty()`:

```
http://haseeb.deeurl.com/client-demos/everydayadvice/v3/={};
Reflect.defineProperty(object,"x",{value:7});// will return true
object.x;// 7
```

Checking if property definition has been successful:

With `Object.defineProperty`, which returns an object if successful or throws a `TypeError` otherwise, you would use a `try...catch` block to catch any error that occurred while defining a property. As `Reflect.defineProperty` returns a Boolean success status, you can just use an `if...else` block here:

```
if(Reflect.defineProperty(target, property, attributes)) {
  // will return success
}
else{
  // will return failure
}
```

Reflect.getPrototypeOf(target)

This method returns a prototype of the specified object. It is similar to the `Object.getPrototypeOf()` method.

Returns

The `Reflect.getPrototypeOf(target)` method returns the prototype of object or null.

Parameter

The target object for which we need the prototype is passed as a parameter.

Description

The static `Reflect.getPrototypeOf()` method is the same technique as `Object.getPrototypeOf()`. It gives back the model (that is, the estimation of the inside `[[Prototype]]` property) of the predetermined item.

An example of this method is shown here:

```
Reflect.getPrototypeOf({});// Object.prototype
Reflect.getPrototypeOf(Object.prototype);// will return null
Reflect.getPrototypeOf(Object.create(null));// will return null
```

Reflect.setPrototypeOf(target, newProto)

This method sets the prototype of object to another object or to null. This method is the same as the `Object.setPrototypeOf()` method.

Returns

The `Reflect.setPrototypeOf(target, newProto)` method returns a Boolean showing regardless of whether the model was effectively set.

Parameter

The target object and prototype are parameters.

Description

The `Reflect.setPrototypeOf` method changes the prototype (that is, the value of the internal `[[Prototype]]` property) of the specified object.

An example of this method is shown here:

```
Reflect.setPrototypeOf({},Object.prototype);// will return true
Reflect.setPrototypeOf({},null);// will return true

Reflect.setPrototypeOf(Object.freeze({}),null);// will return false

var target ={};
varprototype=Object.create(target);
Reflect.setPrototypeOf(target,prototype);// will return false
```

Reflect.deleteProperty(target, prop)

This method is used to delete properties from an object. This method is similar to the delete operator as a function.

Returns

The `Reflect.deleteProperty(target, prop)` method returns a Boolean value telling us whether the property is deleted or not.

Parameter

The target object and the name of the property to be deleted are parameters.

Description

The `Reflect.deleteProperty` method permits you to erase a property on an object. It returns boolean value indicating if the property was successfully removed or not, regardless of whether the property was effectively characterized. It is almost similar to the non-strict delete operator.

An example of this method is shown here:

```
varobject={a:11,b:12};
Reflect.deleteProperty(object,"a");// will return true
object;// { y: 12 }

vararr=[11,12,13,14,15];
Reflect.deleteProperty(arr,"3");// will return true
arr;// [11, 12, 13, , 15]

// Returns true if no such property exists
Reflect.deleteProperty({},"bar");// will return true

// Returns false if a property is unconfigurable
Reflect.deleteProperty(Object.freeze({bar:1}),"bar");// will
return false
```

Reflect.enumerate(target)

This method returns an iterator with enumerable own and inherited properties of the target object.

Returns

Returns an iterator with the enumerable own and acquired properties of the objective object.

Parameter

Target object on which to get property is passed in the function.

Description

The `Reflect.enumerate()` method returns an iterator with the enumerable own and inherited properties of the target object.

An example of this method is shown here:

```
varobject={a:98,b:99};

for(var name ofReflect.enumerate(object)) {
  console.log(name);
}
// logs "a" and "b"
```

Reflect.preventExtensions(target)

This is the same method as `Object.preventExtensions()`. It prevents us from adding more properties (extensions) to an object.

Returns

Returns a Boolean demonstrating regardless of whether the objective was effectively set to forestall expansions.

Parameter

Target object on which we have to prevent extensions.

Description

The static `Reflect.preventExtensions()` method keeps new properties from always being added to an object (that is, counteracts future augmentations to the item). It is like `Object.preventExtensions()`, yet with a few contrasts.

An example of this method is as follows:

```
varblank={};
Reflect.isExtensible(blank);// === will return true

Reflect.preventExtensions(blank);
Reflect.isExtensible(blank);// === will return false
```

Reflect.isExtensible(target)

This method allows us to check whether new properties can be added to an object or whether the object is extensible or not. This method is similar to the `Object.isExtensible()` method.

Returns

A Boolean value indicating whether the target is extensible or not.

Parameter

The target object that has to be checked for its extensibility.

Description

The static `Reflect.isExtensible()` technique figures out whether an item is extensible (whether it can have new properties added to it). It is like `Object.isExtensible()`, yet with a few contrasts.

An example of this method is shown here:

```
var blank ={};
Reflect.isExtensible(blank);
```

The preceding function will return `true`.

Reflect.ownKeys(target)

This method returns the object's own property keys.

Returns

The `Reflect.ownKeys(target)` method returns an array of target objects.

Parameter

Target object from where to get keys.

Description

The static `Reflect.set()` strategy works like setting a property on an object.

Here is an example of this method:

```
Reflect.ownKeys({a:5,b:6,c:7});
Reflect.ownKeys([]);

varsymbol=Symbol.for("dirt");
varsymbolb=Symbol.for("sky");
varobject={[symbol]:0,"string":0,"99":0,"4":0,
[symbolb]:0,"100":0,"-7":0,"second string":0};
Reflect.ownKeys(object);
```

Tail calls

Calls in tail position won't be able to grow the stack without any limits. It helps in making recursive algorithms safe and secure in the safe of unbounded inputs.

Example

The following function produces a factorial of any number passed to it. There is a tail call in the end of the function which recalls the function. Previously, we used to get a stackoverflow error, but ES6 is safe for handling arbitrary inputs.

If the output is out of range, it will simply display infinity:

```
function factorial(n, acc) {
 'use strict';
 if (n <= 1) return acc;
 return factorial(n - 1, n * acc);
}
console.log(factorial(5, 1)); //120
console.log(factorial(200, 1)); //Infinity

// Stack overflow in most implementations today,
// but safe on arbitrary inputs in ES6
console.log(factorial(10000000, 1));
```

12
Server-side
JavaScript – NodeJS

Node.js is a relatively new server platform that is built on JavaScript. One of the main features of Node is that it is a non-blocking server. This means that resource-intensive tasks will not tie up the server. Node.js can then handle many concurrent connections. It can also handle real-time communications more easily than a blocking server.

One of the main uses of Node.js is as a web server. This is a perfect task as serving web pages usually involves reading files and connecting to a database. It is able to serve more clients while either of these two actions are executing. This is very different compared to a blocking server. A blocking server would have to wait for all the resources to return before it could respond to more requests.

 Note that this reference will only be Node.js specific; we will not cover any frameworks or libraries in this chapter.

The most popular frameworks are useful and should be utilized whenever possible, but our focus will only be on functions and modules that are included with Node.js. There will be no coverage of **Express** (arguably, the most used Node.js framework). Most importantly, we will cover the building blocks of Node.js that Express and its dependencies are built on.

A great book that covers frameworks and more is *Building Scalable Apps with Redis and Node.js* by Packt Publishing.

In this chapter, the following groups of references will be described, accompanied with examples:

- File and process management:
    - Modules
    - OS (operating system)
    - Process
    - File
    - Path
    - REPL (Read Eval Print Loop)
    - Errors

- Utilities:
    - Events
    - Crypto
    - Buffer
    - Console
    - Npm (Node Package Manager)
    - Stream

- Net modules:
    - createServer
    - net.Server

- HTTP:
    - Server
    - IncomingMessage
    - ServerResponse
    - clientRequest

File and process management

We will start our overview of Node.js with the basics. This will include loading modules, managing processes, handling files and paths, and **REPL (Read Eval Print Loop)**. These are things that virtually any Node.js project will need.

Modules

Node.js is a modular system. Much of the functionality of Node.js is contained in modules that must be loaded at runtime. This makes the knowledge of loading and building modules a core requirement to using Node. Here are the references you can use for your Node modules:

- `require()`
- `modules.export`

require()

This loads the module at the given path:

```
require(path)
```

Return value

The return value will be an object. The properties of this object will vary, depending on what is loaded. We will cover `module.exports` next, which is what module designers and even you can use to set the value of this return value.

Description

The `require()` function is used to load the module at a path, where the path can be a core module (a module packaged with Node.js), directory, file, or module (a project that you or someone else has built). As a result, it is very versatile. The `require()` function will try to resolve the passed-in path in this order: the core module, the directory or file if the path begins with "./", "/", "../", and then the module, take a look at the following description for more information. You then need to check the require function in different locations for all of this to work:

- You will first look for a core module. The core modules can be viewed in the source of Node.js under the lib directory. We will cover the most prolifically used modules in this chapter.

- Next, require would load the path as a file if the string begins with "./","/", or "../". These are current directory, root directory, and parent directory, respectively.

- If the filename is not found, require will then try appending `.js`, `.json`, or `.node`. This means that the `require (./data/models)` function and `require (./data/models,js)` will load the same file. If require does not find a file, then it will try to load the path as a directory. This means it will look for either an `index.js` file or the main property inside `package.json`. Require will then either use `index.js` or `package.json` to load as a file.

- Finally, if the path does not start with "./", "/", or "../" and it is not a core module, require will search for a `node_modules` folder. The first directory will be the `current` directory. After that, each directory will be a parent directory, all the way up to the `root` directory. In addition to this, require will also search the paths in the `NODE_PATH` environment variable.

As a quick summary, here is the order that require will use:

- Core module (no relative path)
- File module (relative path)
- Folder module (relative path)
- The `node_modules` module (no relative path)

Here are some examples of how the require function is used to load core modules, files, or modules:

```
var http = require('http'); //loads a core module
```

As you can see from the comment, this example will load the HTTP core module:

```
var data = require('./data'); //loads a directory
```

This example shows you how to load a directory:

```
var dataModels = require('./data/models'); //loads the file
models.js
```

This one will load a file:

```
var redis = require('redis'); //loads a module
```

Finally, this one will load a module.

Every Node.js project will use require many times, so knowing how and where it will load is important.

Here is a simple example that demonstrates require and how it works with `module.exports`.

Here is the file that will be loaded with require, `requireTest.js`, and it will be loaded from a relative path:

```
module.exports = 'This value is from requireTest';
```

Here is how to load this value in a Node.js script:

```
var requireTest = require('./requireTest');
console.log(requireTest);
```

module.exports

The `module.exports` property is a convenience property used in a module to expose the functionality of the module outside the scope of the current file.

Return value

The `module.exports` property is the return value from the module. This can seem misleading though. We will not return `module.exports`. It is the object or properties set at `module.exports` that are available from this module.

Description

The `module.exports` property is the link from the current file into the scope of the calling file. Any variables defined in the current file will not be in the scope of file that calls it. To make the variables available, you must either set them as the value of `module.exports` or as properties of `module.exports`. This functionality is the mechanism that Node.js uses with require. Exports can be set to any type: string, integer, function, object, and many others. Functions allow us to either pass in values or create a `constructor()` function. Objects can be created and then used to overwrite the exports object or can be added to the exports object as properties. We have all of JavaScript's function- and object-creation tricks at our disposal.

 A quick note is that require will cache output. This means consecutive calls to the same module will return the same instance of an object.

Examples of the `constructor()` function being used are shown here:

- This allows an object to be passed in:

```
module.exports = function Foo(bar) {do something with
bar};
```

- This allows the export function to be executed:

```
module.exports = function FooConstructor() {};
```

- The `foo` property will be used in the following two examples:

```
module.exports = {foo: foo()};
module.exports.foo = foo();
```

The OS module

Here are the most important functions and properties of the `os` module. The `os` module allows you to get information from the operating system. This is important as we may need to know the hostname or how many CPUs are currently available.

All the functions that we will look at now assume that `var os = require('os')` is already in the file.

hostname()

This will return the hostname of the device:

```
.hostname()
```

Description

An example of how the `os.hostname()` function is used is shown here. In this case, it will return the hostname of the current computer used. It will not return the domain suffix of the computer:

```
os.hostname();
```

cpus()

This will return the number of CPUs of the current device:

```
.cpus()
```

Description

We will get an array of objects that map to each CPU. The objects will have the model, speed, and times:

- Model and speed are the processor model and speed of the CPU, respectively. Note that, most of the time, model and speed will not be relevant to our code.

- Times has the breakdown of how many milliseconds the CPU has spent in `user`, `nice`, `sys`, `idle`, and `irq`.

This information can be used, most of the time, to find out how many CPUs the machine has. It is good to know this information, as Node.js is single threaded and we can launch multiple processes in a cluster for each CPU.

Here is an example of getting the number of CPUs on a computer:

```
var cpus = os.cpus().length;
```

networkInterfaces()

This gets a list of network interfaces:

```
.networkInterfaces()
```

Description

This will be an object that contains all the network interfaces. Each property maps to an interface and it will have an array of all the IP addresses (IPv4 and IPv6).

As an example, this is how you can get the object that has all the interfaces for a computer:

```
var network = os.networkInterfaces();
```

The process module

Process is an object that allows us to get access to events on the process. We can also get access to `stdin`, `stdout`, and `stderr`. These are global objects that will be available in any file or context.

stdout

The `stdout` object is a writable stream.

```
stdout
```

Description

This is the stream that will connect to `stdout`. Note that streams will be covered later in this chapter under Utilites. If we are running Node.js as a console application, this is where we could write to `stdout` if needed. Most streams in Node are non-blocking, but writes to stdout and stderr are blocking.

We also can use `stdout` to find out whether Node.js is running in TTY. We can access `process.stdout.isTTY`. This is a Boolean value.

The example here will show us how to write a message to the `stdout` stream. By default, this will be sent to the `process.stdout.write` console. This will write to `stdout`.

stderr

The `stderr` object is a writable stream.

```
stderr
```

Description

This is similar to `stdout`, with the key difference being it writes to `stderr`. This is very useful for console applications as we can write to the console what is happening.

As an example, this writes to the `stderr` stream. By default this will write to the console.

```
process.stderr.write("Something seems to have gone wrong.");
```

stdin

This is a readable stream that maps to `stdin`.

```
stdin
```

Description

This maps to the standard stream, stdin, in the same way stdout and stderr map to the stderr streams. The difference is that the stdin object is readable, while the others are writable. Anything that is piped into this process can be read out using process.stdin. To read from a readable stream, we will have to listen for two possible events that let us know how we can retrieve data. The first is readable, and the other is data. We will cover this more in depth when we get to the stream section.

For instance, this example takes the data that is sent in through stdin and sends it to stdout using the readable event:

```
process.stdin.on('readable', function() {
  var data = process.stdin.read();
  if(data !== null) process.stdout.write(data);
});
```

argv

This is all the command-line arguments passed in:

argv

Description

The argv commands will be an array of all the arguments passed into this script. Arguments are split by spaces. This means that debug=true (which has no spaces) will be one argument, and debug = true (a space between each word) will be three. This is an important distinction to keep in mind if you want to pass values in arguments. Arguments 0 and 1 will always be the node and the path and filename of the current script.

Here is an example:

```
process.argv.forEach(function(val){ if(val === 'debug'){ debug();
} });
```

Signal events

Signal events allow you to listen for the standard POSIX signals:

```
process.on({signal, callback});
```

Description

All of the POSIX signals, except SIGKILL and SIGSTOP, can be listened for. In addition to these signals, you can also listen for some Windows signals. Here is the list of signals:

- SIGUSR1: This is a user-defined signal. In Node.js, it is usually used to start the debugger.

- SIGTERM: This is the signal to terminate.

- SIGINT: This is the signal to interrupt. It is usually sent by pressing *Ctrl + C.*

- SIGPIPE: This lets a process know when it is trying to pipe to a nonexistent process.

- SIGHUP: This is the signal that tells a process that the terminal it was running in has hung up.

- SIGBREAK: This is non-POSIX and is used by Windows. It should be used in a manner similar to SIGINT.

- SIGWINCH: This is the signal to tell the process that the window has changed size.

Here is an example of listening for SIGINT, which recognizes that *Ctrl + C* was pressed:

```
process.on('SIGINT', function(){
  //ctrl+c was pressed
});
```

process.env

This object contains the environment variables:

```
process.env
```

Description

The process.env object is a simple JavaScript object that contains all the environment variables. Each property will be a string.

A great place to put configuration settings is in the environment when building an extensible application. The process.env object can then be used to check whether the current environment is in production or even to just store the configuration settings.

Here is an example of checking for environment and setting a value from the environment:

```
if(process.env.NODE_ENV !== 'production')
  //do test stuff
var redisHost = process.env.REDIS_HOST;
```

kill

This will send a signal event to a process:

```
process.kill(pid, [signal])
```

Description

This will send any of the signal events that are defined in the signal events section, which that we covered earlier. This is essentially running the POSIX kill command.

We can use this kill command to send the current process a signal, using `process.pid`, or to send another process that we have a reference to the kill signal.

Here is an example of killing the specific process ID 4634:

```
process.kill(4634, 'SIGTERM');
```

pid

This gets the current `pid`:

```
process.pid
```

Description

It is the `pid` (process ID) of the process.

This is an example of `process.kill` and `process.pid` used together:

```
process.kill(process.pid, 'SIGTERM');
```

cwd

This gets the current working directory:

```
process.cwd()
```

Here is an example that set the `cwd` variable to the current working directory of the process:

```
var cwd = process.cwd();
```

File functions

This section is not a true module, like the previous section on process. This section will focus on any of the functions or modules that allow us to read, write, or find files and directories.

__filename

This returns a string of the current filename:

```
__filename
```

Description

The `__filename` command returns the current filename. This can be different, depending on which file is being executed. A module that is being executed will return its filename instead of the main entry point.

Here is an example of logging the current filename to the console:

```
console.log(__filename);
```

__dirname

This is a string of the current directory:

```
__dirname
```

Description

Much like `__filename`, this will return the currently executing file's directory. The `__dirname` command is used many times when a relative path needs to be created.

> Both the `__filename` and `__dirname` variables are available in any file being executed by Node.js. They are determined per file, so they are correct for each file that gets executed.

This example assumes Express has been loaded as express:

```
//express is loaded
app.use(express.static(__dirname + '/static'));
```

The file module

We will now look at a list of key functions in the file module. All of these functions just run the underlying POSIX commands.

Each of the commands we cover will have an asynchronous and synchronous version of each function. The synchronous function will be the same name, with Sync appended, for example, open and openSync. In a way, the asynchronous versions are more like Node.js, in that, they let the event loop process without holding up execution.

Each asynchronous function will need a callback function defined as the last parameter. This function will be in the form of function(err, result). We will cover this when we get to handling errors. The quick takeaway is that the first parameter, err, will be null if no error occurred, or it will have the error.

In the current versions of Node.js, you need not use a callback function, but this will become an exception in v0.12.

The synchronous functions will not process anything in the event loop until the function returns. While this seems against the Node.js non-blocking paradigm, it makes sense in certain cases, for example, when a specific file must be opened before anything else can process. This means that the classic try/catch is needed to handle any exceptions or errors.

In almost every circumstance, the asynchronous version is the one that should be used.

Each example is under the assumption that the fs variable already exists. Here is the code that sets the fs variable to the fs module:

```
var fs = require('fs');
```

stat

This returns fs.Stats, which is an object with information about the queried file or directory:

```
fs.statstat(path, callback)
fs.statSync(path)
```

Description

The `stat` variable gets the the data that would be returned after running `stat()` on the operating system. The `stat` object is an instance of `fs.Stats`. This object gives us useful functions such as `isFile()` and `isDirectory()`. In addition to this, `fs.Stats` has many properties. We can see the modified time, access time, and file size.

There are more functions and properties, but these are the most likely used.

The `fs.lstat()` and `fs.fstat()` functions will both return an `fs.Stats` object when pointed to a file. The difference is that `lstat` will run against a link instead of following the link to the file or directory. The `fstat` runs against a file descriptor instead of a path.

Here is an example that loads a file named `test.txt` in the same directory as the code file and logs the `fs.Stats` object:

```
fs.stat(__dirname + '\test.txt', function(err, stats){
  console.log(stats);
});
```

open

This returns a file descriptor of the path passed in:

```
fs.open(path, flags, [mode], callback)
fs.openSync(path, flags, [mode])
```

Description

This will open a file in the path passed in. There are many flags that can be passed. They are described here:

- `r`: Read only, errors when file does not exist
- `r+`: Read and write, errors when file does not exist
- `rs`: Read synchronous, here, "synchronous" only refers to the filesystem caching data and not synchronous such as `openSync`
- `rs+`: Read and write synchronous
- `w`: Write
- `wx`: Write, errors when file exists
- `w+`: Read and write, file is created or truncated
- `a`: Append, file is created
- `ax`: Append, errors when file exists

- a+: Read and append, file is created
- ax+: Read and append, errors when file exists

The flags allow you to open, read, and write a file, whether it exists or not. This means that most of the time, a call to `fs.exists` is not required as one of the flags will give you the answer you need.

The mode parameter is the permissions that are used if a file is created. It defaults to `0666`.

Finally, the callback returns a file descriptor. With this, data can be read or written using `fs.read` or `fs.write`.

This is an example of opening the file `test.txt`:

```
fs.open(__dirname + '\file.txt', 'r', function(err, fd){
  //fd is available to be read from
});
```

read

This reads from a file descriptor:

```
fs.read(fd, buffer, offset, length, position, callback)
fs.readSync(fd, buffer, offset, length, position)
```

Description

The `read()` function takes a lot of parameters to run. We need a file descriptor, which we get from open, a buffer, and the size of the file. In the example, we used `fs.stat` to get the file size.

Here is a full example of opening a file and reading from it:

```
fs.stat(__dirname + '/test.txt', function(error, stats) {
  fs.open(__dirname + '/test.txt', 'r', function(err, fd){
    var buffer = new Buffer(stats.size);
    fs.read(fd, buffer, 0, stats.size, null, function(err,
    bytesRead, buffer){
      console.log(buffer.toString('utf8'));
    });
  });
});
```

readFile

This is a simplified version for reading a file:

```
fs.readFile(filename, [options], callback)
fs.readFileSync(filename, [options])
```

Description

The `readFile()` function greatly simplifies the process of reading a file in Node.js. In the previous function, `fs.read`, we needed to set everything up before we tried to read the file. The `readFile()` function allows us to just pass a filename and get a buffer back of what is in the file.

The `optional options` object takes a flag and an encoding property. The flag property is the same as the flag from `fs.open`, so any of them can be used. The encoding is used for the buffer that is returned in the callback.

Here is an example that demonstrates how much easier it is to load a file with `readFile`. The example is also using the `optional options` parameter:

```
var filename = __dirname + '/test.txt';

fs.readFile(filename, {flag: 'r', encoding: 'utf8'}, function(err,
data){
  console.log(data.toString('utf8'));
});
```

close

This will close a file descriptor:

```
fs.close(fd, callback)
fs.closeSync(fd)
```

Description

It is important to close any files that we open in our scripts. If we get a file descriptor from `fs.open`, we will need to call `fs.close` on that file descriptor at some point.

This is an example of closing a file descriptor:

```
fs.close(fd, function(err){
  //handle err here
});
```

write

This writes to a file descriptor:

```
fs.write(fd, buffer, offset, length, position, callback)
fs.writeSync(fd, buffer, offset, length, position)
```

Description

The `write()` function takes a file descriptor and buffer to write to a file. Much like read, we have to pass in quite a few parameters to make this work.

In the following example, we are reading a file into a buffer and then writing that buffer back out to another file. The offset and length are both integers that we need to pass in. The position can be an integer, but it can also be `null`. `Null` will start writing at the current position in the file.

Just like read, write can be complex. Here is a full example of reading from one file and writing to another:

```
var fs = require('fs');
var filename = __dirname + '/test.txt';
var writeFile = __dirname + '/test2.txt';

fs.stat(filename, function(error, stats) {
  fs.open(filename, 'r', function(err, fd) {
    var buffer = new Buffer(stats.size);
    fs.read(fd, buffer, 0, stats.size, null, function(err,
    bytesRead, buffer) {
      fs.open(writeFile, 'w', function(err, writeFD) {
        //will create a file named test2.txt with the contents
        from test.txt
        fs.write(writeFD, buffer, 0, buffer.length, null,
        function(err, bytesWritten, writeBuffer) {
          console.log(writeBuffer.toString('utf8'));
        });
      });
    });
  });
});
```

writeFile

This is a simplified function to write to a file:

```
fs.writeFile(filename, data, [options], callback)
fs.writeFileSync(filename, data, [options])
```

Description

Exactly like the difference between read and `readFile`, `writeFile` is a simplified version of write. We just pass in a filename and a string or buffer, and it will write the file.

The callback only returns an error when it occurs.

`readFile` and `writeFile` seem like the best choices in most cases, and in fact, this is most likely true. The main thing that you give up using these functions is control. You can only read an entire file or write an entire file.

 With read or write, you can read any portion and write any portion of a file. This is an important difference to keep in mind.

Here is an example of `writeFile`:

```
var filename = __dirname + '/write.txt';
var buffer = new Buffer('Write this to a file.', 'utf8');
fs.writeFile(filename, buffer, {encoding: 'utf8', flag: 'w'},
function(err){
  if(null !== null){
    //do something
  }
});
```

appendFile

This function allows us to append a file:

```
fs.appendFile(filename, data, [options], callback)
fs.appendFileSync(filename, data, [options])
```

Description

appendFile exists because writeFile will only write an entire file. So, we need another function to add to a file. This is where giving up some control for ease comes in. If we were using a file descriptor and write, then we could choose to start writing at the end of the file. This is effectively appending the file:

Here is an example of appendFile:

```
var filename = __dirname + '/write.txt';
var buffer = new Buffer('Append this to a file.', 'utf8');
fs.appendFile(filename, buffer, {encoding: 'utf8', flag: 'w'},
function(err){
  if(null !== null){
    //do something
  }
});
```

The path module

The path module is separate from the file module. Path is concerned with fixing paths, whereas file is concerned with working with files and directories. Many times, these modules will be used together.

The functions covered are the most used and most useful. You will most likely need to locate paths relative to your current project, and this is what the path module is for:

 Note that the path module does not check for the existence of path modifications. It essentially only makes changes to the string value of a path.

Just like the other modules, the example assumes that the path module has been loaded:

```
var path = require('path');
```

normalize

This returns a string of the path with any oddities fixed:

```
path.normalize(pathString)
```

Description

Normalize will fix many problems associated with reading paths. A great example of this is the difference between Windows and Unix paths. Unix uses forward slashes, and Windows uses backslashes. Normalize will return the correct slashes based on the system it is executed on.

In addition to this, normalize will also remove the current directory and parent directory shortcuts, (. and .. respectively). It will also remove double slashes from a directory. It normalizes any paths passed in.

Here is an example of using Unix slashes on a Windows system. This example will change all the slashes to backslashes:

```
var pathString = "/unix/style/path/separators";
console.log(path.normalize(pathString));
```

join

This returns a string of all the paths joined together:

```
path.join([pathString1], [...])
```

Description

Join makes it easy to create a path from partial paths. This seems like something that can be done with concatenation, but it is easy to forget about path separators. Join will make sure that the path separators will all be in the correct spots.

Here is an example of `join`. The example will take all the parameters and join them together with the correct slash for your system:

```
console.log(path.join('path', 'separators', 'added'));
```

resolve

This returns the string of the path based on the parameters:

```
path.resolve([pathString], [...])
```

Description

This can be viewed as the cd command executed for each parameter. The paths passed in can be relative or full paths. A relative path will add to the returned path, and a full path will be used whole.

Here are two examples:

- Relative paths, will return `/home/josh/test`:

  ```
  console.log(path.resolve('/home/josh/node', '..', 'test'));
  ```

- A full path will return `/home/brian/node`:

  ```
  console.log(path.resolve('/home/josh/node', '/home/brian/node'));
  ```

relative

This returns the difference between the `to` and `from` paths:

```
path.relative(from, to)
```

Description

The path returned can be used with `cd` to change to the new directory.

Here is an example that will return `../../brian/node`, because you must go up two parent folders and over to `brian/node` to get from one to the other:

```
var from = '/home/josh/node';
var to = '/home/brian/node';
console.log(path.relative(from, to));
```

dirname

This returns a string of the directory name:

```
path.dirname(pathString)
```

This example will return the directory that the current file is in. If the file was in the directory `/home/users/jjohanan/node`, then the example will return `/home/users/jjohanan/node`:

```
console.log(path.dirname(__filename));
```

basename

This returns a string of the final part of a path:

```
path.basename(pathString, [ext])
```

Description

This will either return the filename or directory depending on what path is passed in. The optional `ext` parameter will remove that portion from the return value if it exists.

Here are two examples, one involving a file and the other a directory:

- This will return `test`:
  ```
  console.log(path.basename('/home/josh/test.js', '.js'));
  ```

- This will return `josh`:
  ```
  console.log(path.basename('/home/josh'));
  ```

extname

This returns a string of the extension of the path. If there is no extension, a blank string is returned:

```
path.extname(pathString)
```

Here are two examples:

- This example will return `.js`:
  ```
  console.log(path.extname('/home/josh/test.js'));
  ```

- This example will return a blank string:
  ```
  console.log(path.extname('/home/josh'));
  ```

REPL

REPL stands for **Read Eval Print Loop**. What this means is that it is an interactive console. We can enter in a command (**Read**). The command will be executed (**Eval**). The output of the command will will be printed to the console (**Print**). Finally, we can do this as many times as we want (**Loop**). REPL is great to run a few lines of code to see what they will do.

node

This starts Node.js in the REPL mode:

```
node
```

Description

The main way REPL will be used is by calling it directly. This can be done by executing Node.js without a file to serve, by running just `node`. Once `node` has returned with a prompt, we can add commands and see what happens when we run them. This is perfect to test a few lines of code.

Here is a quick example of logging in to the console; first run `node` to get a prompt and then run the command:

```
node
//wait for >
console.log('hey this REPL!');
```

Handling errors

Errors are a part of any development project. We must be able to handle errors in a graceful way. If we do not, then we are creating bad experiences for our users. Even worse, we could be opening up a vector for attack. A stack trace that gets sent to an end user can give out many details.

This will be a special section that deals more with design patterns than with actual code reference. Node.js is an asynchronous event-driven platform. For the major part, most people have not worked on a platform like this and can make mistakes when handling errors. We feel that handling errors is very important.

The core of this information comes from Joyent, one the major forces behind `Node.js` today. You can find more information on Joyent at `https://www.joyent.com/developers/node/design/errors`.

Types of errors

Errors can be split into two types: **operational** and **programmer** errors. Operational errors are errors that occur during the operation of an application. A database server not being accessible is an example. These errors can be planned for and handled gracefully.

Next is programmer errors, which are errors in the literal sense. For example, a piece of code is malformed or an unexpected condition has come up. These are very hard to plan for (if we had planned for them, then they wouldn't be errors!). These will almost always break the server, so we can come back through the logs to find what went wrong.

Error design patterns

Now that we know the two different types of errors, let's look at the three ways of alerting an application that has an error. The three ways are throwing the error, asynchronous callback, and emitting an error event:

- The first pattern of throwing the error is built into JavaScript. This pattern is great for any synchronous code. If we are doing any synchronous operations and an error occurs, we should throw it. When handling a synchronous call, we should wrap the function call in a `try`/`catch` block. Here is an example with `JSON.parse`, which runs synchronously and throws an error when a non-JSON string is passed to it:

```
try{
    JSON.parse(jsonObject);
} catch (ex) {
    //do something with this error
}
```

- The next pattern is using an asynchronous callback. Many built-in Node functions do this already. The pattern is to use a callback that has the signature `function(error, result)`. The first parameter will either have an error or be null or undefined. We can implement this ourselves whenever we write an asynchronous function. If there is an error, return it in the callback as the first parameter.

> When handling errors like these, we must put an error check in every callback function. This is important, as not doing this can silently swallow errors.

A good example of this is asynchronous and synchronous `filesystem` module calls. For example, read takes a callback, and `readSync` should be wrapped in a `try`/`catch` block.

Here is an example callback and check for error:

```
fs.read(path, function (err, data) {
    if(err !== null)
        //handle error
})
```

Finally, we can emit an error event. This is used for asynchronous functions as well. Whether we implement a callback or event is a personal choice, but it should be clear which one is being used. It is also a best practice to just implement one. Many times, an event is used when there is a long running asynchronous process. Reading data from a network socket is an example. A socket does not always give the data in one simple pass, so events are set up. One of those events is an error event. To handle this, we just need to listen for that event. Here is an example of listening for the error event of a socket:

```
socket.on('error', function(error){
    //handle error here
})
```

Utilities

In the next group of modules, we will look at utilities. The functions chosen here are used across many different types of applications. We will cover everything from events and cryptology to buffers and npm.

Events

Events are used in many built-in Node objects. This is because emitting and listening for events is the perfect way to let another function know when to start executing. This is especially true in the asynchronous world of Node.js. Anytime we use the on function of an object, it means that it has inherited from EventEmitter. All of the examples will assume that the events variable is already created as follows:

```
var events = require('events');
```

EventEmitter

This is the parent class that can be inherited from to create a new EventEmitter:

```
events.EventEmitter
```

Description

Node.js has a fully featured event system that we can easily inherit from and implement. We do not need any extra frameworks or custom code. EventEmitter is the class to inherit from, and we will get every function in the rest of this section available.

Here is an example of setting up a custom the `EventEmitter` parameter:

```
var util = require('util');
var events = require('events');

function MyEventEmitter(){
    events.EventEmitter.call(this);
    this.test = function (emitThis) {
        this.emit('testEvent', emitThis);
    }
}

util.inherits(MyEventEmitter, events.EventEmitter);

var myEE = new MyEventEmitter();

myEE.on('testEvent', function (data) { console.log(data) });

myEE.test('test');
```

on

This function adds a listener for a specific event:

```
emitter.on(event, listenerFunction)
emitter.addListener(event, listenerFunction)
```

Description

The `on` function has become the preferred naming convention to add listeners to events. As an example, jQuery uses the exact same function name for their event listeners. The `event` handler is a string name of the event that will be emitted. The `listenerFunction` parameter is what will be executed when the event is emitted.

The `listenerFunction` parameter can be an anonymous function or a reference to a function. The preferred way of adding a listener is with a reference to a function. This will allow us to remove this specific listener at a later time.

Here is an example based on our new `MyEventEmitter` class:

```
var quickLog = function (data) {
    console.log('quickLog: ' + data);
}
myEE.on('testEvent', quickLog);
```

once

This works just like `on`, except it only executes once and then removes itself as a listener:

```
emitter.once(event, listenerFunction)
```

removeListener

This is the function that is used to remove a listener from an event:

```
emitter.removeListener(event, function)
```

Description

When we are done listening for this event, we will want to remove our listener. This will help prevent memory leaks. If we added an anonymous function as the listener, then we cannot remove it as we do not have a reference to it. Using our previous example from `on`, we will remove the listener:

```
myEE.removeListener('testEvent', quickLog);
```

removeAllListeners

This function will remove every listener for all events or a specific event:

```
emitter.removeAllListeners([event])
```

Description

This is essentially the nuclear option to remove listeners. This is indiscriminate with listeners. The `removeAllListeners` parameter will even remove listeners we did not add. Use this as a last resort.

An example that removes all the listeners from this event is shown here. If the event was left blank, it would remove all listeners for all events:

```
myEE.removeAllListeners('testEvent');
```

setMaxListeners

This function sets the number of listeners before Node.js and warns about a possible memory leak:

```
emitter.setMaxListeners(numberOfListeners)
```

Node.js has a helpful warning when the number of listeners exceeds a threshold. The default value is 10, so when you add the eleventh listener, Node.js will warn:

```
(node) warning: possible EventEmitter memory leak detected. 11
listeners added. Use emitter.setMaxListeners() to increase limit.
```

As a general rule, this is true. If we keep adding listeners to an event, there is a great chance for a memory leak. However, there will be times when we will need more than 10 listeners on an event. This is where we use setMaxListeners. If we set the max listeners to zero, then we can add as many as we want.

Here is an example of setting the max listeners to 50:

```
myEE.setMaxListeners(50);
```

emit

This is how we fire off an event:

```
emitter.emit(eventName, [argument], [...])
```

If we have extended an object to be an event emitter, then we will want to emit some events! This is the function to do that. It will execute all the event listeners that have attached themselves to this event based on eventName.

Here is an example that shows a listener being added and then emitting an event:

```
myEE.on('testEvent', function (data) { console.log(data) });
myEE.emit('testEvent', 'Emit This!', 'Another Argument!');
```

Crypto

Every modern application needs cryptography. A great example of Node.js using cryptography is with HTTPS. We will not explore the inner workings of HTTPS as there is a module (the https module) that does this for us. We will look at the cryptographic functions used to hash, store, and check passwords.

In the same way as the other modules, we will require the crypto module and have it available for use in our examples. Here is what we will need:

```
var crypto = require('crypto');
```

createHash

This function will return a crypto.Hash object:

```
crypto.createHash(algorithm)
```

Description

The algorithms that can be used will be different for each system as it relies on OpenSSL. We can find out the algorithms that crypto can use by calling `crypto.getHashes()`. This will return an array of strings that can then be passed into `createHash` as the algorithm.

The return object from this function is a `crypto.Hash` object, which is covered in the next section.

Here is an example that creates an MD5 hash:

```
var md5 = crypto.createHash('md5');
```

The hash object

This is the object that is returned from `crypto.createHash`:

```
hash.update(data, [encoding])
hash.digest([encoding])
```

Description

Once we get a reference to the Hash object that has been returned, you will see that it has two functions. The first is update, which allows us to add to the data that will be hashed. This can be called multiple times. This is important if we want to hash a stream input.

The next function is digest. This will return digest based on the algorithm the hash object was created with. The string encoding for this function can be hex, binary, or BASE64.

Here is a full example of reading data from a file and then calculating the MD5 hash of the file.

```
var f = file.readFileSync(__dirname + '/test.txt');

var md5 = crypto.createHash('md5');
md5.update(f);
console.log(md5.digest('base64'));
```

> Do not use hashing for passwords. The next function we will cover is much more secure than a simple hash. A digest hash is great for checking if some data has changed, as the hashes will be different if even one bit is different. In addition to this, it can be used as a key or identifier. A great example is using it for a memory cache and using the hash as the key. If the data is the same, the key will be the same.

pbkdf2

This function will use HMAC-SHA1 multiple times to create a derived key:

```
crypto.pbkdf2(password, salt, iterations, keyLength, callback)
crypto.pbkdf2Sync(password, salt, iterations, keyLength)
```

Return Type

Both `pbkdf2` and `pbkdf2Sync` will return a derived key as a buffer.

Description

Pbkdf2 (password-based key derivation function 2) is designed for password storage. It is better than hashing because it is difficult. Hashing is designed to be a quick calculation. This is bad because modern CPUs can calculate thousands upon thousands of hashes a second. This makes cracking a hashed password easy.

Pbkdf2 fixes this using a work factor in iterations. The higher the iterations, the longer the calculation will take. Now, instead of calculating thousands a second, we can slow a CPU down to just a few a second. This is a significant decrease.

These are the parameters used:

- `password`: This is the string we want to create a derived key for.
- `salt`: This is a string that is combined with the password. Doing this ensures that the same password will not have the same hash if `salt` is different.
- `iterations`: This is the work factor that instructs the function how many times to repeat. This can be increased as CPUs become faster. Currently, at least 10,000 should create a reasonably secure derived key.
- `keyLength`: This is the desired length of the returned derived key.

Here is an example of creating a derived key for the string `password` and `salt`:

```
crypto.pbkdf2('password', 'salt', 10000, 32, function (err, key) {
    console.log(key.toString('base64'));
});
```

randomBytes

This returns cryptographically strong pseudo-random data:

```
crypto.randomBytes(length, [callback])
```

Return type

A buffer is returned.

Description

Random data is needed for various functions. While no data can truly be random, there are varying levels of randomness. The randomBytes parameter is random enough to use for cryptographic functions. A perfect use of randomBytes is for a salt to be used in pbkdf2. The salt variable is combined with the password to create a different hash even if the passwords are the same.

This function can be executed asynchronously or synchronously. It depends on whether there is a callback, which it would then execute asynchronously.

Here is a function to create a random salt for pbkdf2. If you compare this example to the previous one, you will see that this example outputs a unique string each time, while the previous one does not:

```
var random = crypto.randomBytes(256);

crypto.pbkdf2('password', random.toString('base64'), 10000, 32,
function (err, key) {
    console.log(key.toString('base64'));
});
```

pseudoRandomBytes

This returns pseudo-random data:

```
crypto.pseudoRandomBytes(length, [calback])
crypto.pseudoRandomBytes(length)
```

Return Type

A buffer is returned.

Description

This functions exactly like randomBytes, except it is not cryptographically strong. This means that we should not use it with any cryptographic functions such as pbkdf2.

We can use it for anything else that requires randomness, a filename, or a cache key for example.

Here is a simple example of executing this function asynchronously:

```
crypto.pseudoRandomBytes(256, function (err, randomData) {
    console.log(randomData.toString('base64'));
});
```

Buffer

Node.js uses buffers internally for many things. We have seen this as we have had buffers returned for many functions. This is because anytime raw data or binary data needs to be stored, it will be stored in a buffer.

Buffers have a few quirks about them that we must keep in mind. First, buffers store data, but to utilize the data held inside them, we must encode it. We will cover the encodings and how to do this in this section. Second, buffers cannot be resized. When they are created, we must give a length, and that will always be the length of that buffer. We can, of course, create a new buffer that is larger and then copy over the data. Finally, a buffer is a global. We do not need to have `var buffer = require('buffer')`. Also, it can be utilized in any file at any time.

Buffer creation

The initialization function of a buffer is as shown in the following code snippet:

```
new Buffer(size)
new Buffer(array)
new Buffer(str, [encoding])
```

Return value

This returns a buffer object.

Description

There are three different ways to initialize a buffer. The first function uses an integer of the given size, the next one uses an array, and the final method can use just a string. The encoding is optional, as it defaults to UFT8.

This example demonstrates initializing using an array with the `hello` string in ASCII:

```
var hello = [72, 101, 108, 108, 111];
var buffer = new Buffer(hello);
console.log(buffer.toString('ascii'));
```

index

This gets the value at the specific index in the buffer:

```
buffer[index]
```

Return Value

This returns the value at the index.

Description

This works much like an array. Here is an example of getting the first index in the buffer:

```
var buffer = new Buffer('Hello!');
console.log(buffer[0]);
```

toString

This returns the buffer as a string based on the encoding:

```
buffer.toString([encoding], [start], [end])
```

Return Value

This returns a string.

Description

This is most likely the function that you will use to get the data out of a buffer. The first parameter is encoding, which is one of the following:

- ASCII
- UTF8
- UTF16LE
- BASE64
- Binary
- Hex

All the parameters are optional, so this means that they all have default values. Encoding is defaulted to UTF8, start is 0, and end is the end of the buffer.

Here is an example of creating a buffer and retrieving the data out of it. It explicitly defines each of the parameters:

```
var buffer = new Buffer('Hello this is a buffer');
console.log(buffer.toString('utf8', 0, buffer.length));
```

toJSON

This returns the contents of the buffer as a JavaScript object:

```
buffer.toJSON()
```

Return Value

This returns an array with the contents of the buffer.

Description

This will return contents of the buffer mapped to an array. This example is similar to the previous example, but with `toJSON`:

```
var buffer = new Buffer('Hello this is a buffer');
console.log(buffer.toJSON());
```

isBuffer

This is a class method that will determine whether an object is a buffer:

```
Buffer.isBuffer(objectToTest)
```

Return Value

This returns a Boolean value.

Description

Remember that this is a class method, so it can be executed without a new instance of buffer. Here is an example of using the function:

```
var buffer = new Buffer('Hello this is a buffer');
console.log(Buffer.isBuffer(buffer));
```

write

The following code writes to the buffer.

```
buffer.write(stringToWrite, [offset], [length], [encoding])
```

Return value

This returns an integer of the number of bytes written.

Description

This function will write the string passed into the buffer. Much like the other buffer functions, there are many optional parameters that have defaults. The default offset is 0, the length is `buffer.length - offset`, and the encoding is UTF8.

This example writes to a buffer twice using the return value from the first write to append the second string:

```
var buffer = new Buffer(12);
var written = buffer.write('Buffer ', 0, 7, 'utf8');
console.log(written);
buffer.write('time.', written);
console.log(buffer.toString());
```

byteLength

This function will get the length of a string in bytes based on the encoding:

```
buffer.byteLength(string, [encoding])
```

Return value

This returns an integer of the number of bytes needed.

Description

Buffers cannot be resized after initializing, so we may need to know how big a string is beforehand. This is where `byteLength` comes in.

Here is an example that determines the size of a string and then writes it to the buffer:

```
var byteLength = Buffer.byteLength('Buffer time.', 'utf8');
var buffer = new Buffer(byteLength);
var written = buffer.write('Buffer time.', 0, buffer.length, 'utf8');
console.log(buffer.toString());
```

readUInt

This will get an unsigned integer at a certain spot in the buffer:

```
buffer.readUInt8(offset, [noAssert])
buffer.readUInt16LE(offset, [noAssert])
buffer.readUInt16BE(offset, [noAssert])
buffer.readUInt32LE(offset, [noAssert])
buffer.readUInt32BE(offset, [noAssert])
```

Return Value

This returns an unsigned integer of the size used, 8 for `readUInt8`.

Description

Not all data stored in a buffer is exactly a byte. Sometimes, data will need to be read in 16-bit or 32-bit chunks. In addition to this, you can also specify whether the data is little endian or big endian, denoted by `LE` or `BE` in the function name, respectively.

The offset is which spot in the buffer to start at. The `noAssert` parameter will run validation if the offset size is in the buffer. By default, it is `false`.

Here is an example of setting data and then reading the data out with `readUInt16`:

```
var buffer = new Buffer(2);
buffer[0] = 0x1;
buffer[1] = 0x2;
console.log(buffer.readUInt16LE(0));
console.log(buffer.readUInt16BE(0));
```

writeUInt

This writes an unsigned integer to a buffer:

```
buffer.writeUInt8(value, offset, [noAssert])
buffer.writeUInt16LE(value, offset, [noAssert])
buffer.writeUInt16BE(value, offset, [noAssert])
buffer.writeUInt32LE(value, offset, [noAssert])
buffer.writeUInt32BE(value, offset, [noAssert])
```

Description

This is the exact opposite of the `readUInt` function. Sometimes, we need to write data that is larger than one byte in length. These functions make it simple.

The `noAssert` parameter is optional, and it defaults to `false`. This will not run any validation on the value or offset.

Here is an example of writing `UInt16` to the buffer:

```
var buffer = new Buffer(4);
buffer.writeUInt16LE(0x0001, 0);
buffer.writeUInt16LE(0x0002, 2);
console.log(buffer);
```

 Note that there are more read and write functions of this type for the buffer class. Instead of creating a very redundant section, I will list them. Remember that they work in the same fashion as the functions we have covered: `readInt8`, `readInt16LE`, `readInt16BE`, `readInt32LE`, `readInt32BE`, `readDoubleLE`, `readDoubleBE`, `readFloatLE`, and `readFloatBE`. There is a `write()` function that maps to each one of these as well.

Console

This is much like the console that is present in most modern browsers. The console essentially maps to `stdout` and `stderr`. This isn't a module, and each function is not very complex, so let's jump right in.

log

This writes to `stdout`:

```
console.log(message, [...])
```

Description

This is probably the most used console function. It is great for debugging, and the output can be combined with piping to write to a file for a history. The multiple parameters create a string-like function.

Here is an example of using multiple parameters:

```
console.log('Multiple parameters in %s', 'console.log');
```

dir

This is an alias for `util.inspect`:

```
console.dir(object)
```

Description

Many times, the output of `console.log` and `console.dir` will be similar. However, when trying to look at an object, `console.dir` should be preferred.

time and timeEnd

These two functions are used together to mark the start and end of a timer:

```
console.time(label)
console.timeEnd(label)
```

Description

These two functions will always be used together. The `console.time` parameter will start a timer that can be stopped with `console.timeEnd` by passing the same label. When `timeEnd` is called, it will log the elapsed time between start and end in milliseconds.

Here is an example that uses `setTimeout`:

```
console.time('simple-timer');
setTimeout(function () {
    console.timeEnd('simple-timer');
}, 500);
```

trace

This logs to the console and includes a stack trace:

```
console.trace(message, [...])
```

Description

This works much like `console.log`. The first parameter can be treated like a formatted string, with the other parameters supplying the additional input. The main difference is that `console.trace` will include a stack trace when it logs to the console.

Here is a simple example:

```
console.trace('This should be the first line.');
```

npm (Node Package Manager)

npm is not a Node.js module like. We will look at some of npm's features and uses, as almost every Node.js project will use npm.

Most modern platforms have a way of grouping together code that serves a function or purpose called packages. Node.js uses npm to track, update, pin, and install these packages.

init

This initializes a node module by creating `package.json` in the current directory:

```
npm init
```

Description

An interactive console session will ask you quite a few questions and use the answers to build a `package.json` file for you. This is a great way to kick off a new module. This will not delete your current the `package.json` file or any of the current properties if the `package.json` file exists.

package.json

This is the file that has all the information about your project.

Description

This is not a function or command, but it is the most important file in your project. It is what determines all the information about your project. Although technically, the only properties needed are name and version, there are many properties that can be set. If this file was created using npm in it, you will have quite a few already filled out. It would be tedious to list out all the possibilities. Here are just a few of the most useful: name, version, scripts, dependencies, devDependencies, authors, and license.

The npm docs at `https://www.npmjs.org/doc/files/package.json.html` go through all the settings their uses.

install

This is the command to install a package:

```
npm install
npm install [package] [@version] [--save | --save-dev]
```

Description

This is the main way to install new packages and their dependencies. If `npm install` is called without any parameters, it will use `package.json` and install all the dependencies.

This command also allows you to install packages by executing it with the name of the package. This can be augmented by adding a version. If the version is omitted, it will install the newest version. In addition to this, you can use save flags that create a property in dependencies or devDependcies.

This is not the entire list of what `npm install` can do, but it is the most used list.

update

This will update a package to the newest version:

```
npm update [package]
```

Description

This command will update all the packages or a specific package to the newest version.

shrinkwrap

This will explicitly define all the dependencies for a project:

```
npm shrinkwrap
```

Description

This is different from the basic list of dependencies in `package.json`. Most packages have requirements of their own. When a package is installed, npm will go out and find the newest version that matches the dependency's specified version. This can lead to different versions of packages installed when run at different times. This is something that most developers want to avoid.

One way to combat this is to run `npm shrinkwrap`. It will create `npm-shrinkwrap.json`. This file will explicitly define the versions currently installed recursively for every package installed. This ensures that when you run `npm install` again, you will know what package versions will get installed.

run

This will run an arbitrary command:

```
npm run [script]
```

Description

The `package.json` file has a property named scripts. This is an object that can have a list of commands that can be run by npm. These scripts can be anything that runs from the command line.

There are three commands on npm that use these scripts objects. These are `npm test`, `npm start`, and `npm stop`. These commands map to test, start, and stop the scripts object, respectively.

Here is an example for a scripts object from `package.json` and the way to call it from npm:

```
package.json:
  "scripts": {
    "hey":  "echo hey"
}
npm run hey
```

Stream

Stream is an interface that is used by many internal objects. Any time data needs to be read or written, it is most likely done through a stream. This fits with the Node.js asynchronous paradigm. If we are reading a large file from the filesystem, we would create a listener to tell us when each chunk of data is ready to be read. This does not change if that file is coming from the network, an HTTP request, or `stdin`.

We are only going to cover using a stream, in this book. The stream interface can be implemented with your own objects as well.

Streams can be readable, writable, or duplex (both). We will cover readable and writable streams separately.

Readable

This is, of course, a stream that we can get data out of. A readable stream can be in one of the two different modes, flowing, or non-flowing. Which mode it is in depends on which events are listened for.

To put a stream in the flowing mode, you will just have to listen for the data event. Conversely, to put a stream in the non-flowing mode, you will have to listen for the readable event and then call the `stream.read()` function to retrieve data. The easiest way to understand the modes is to think about the data as a lot of chunks. In the flowing mode, every time a chunk is ready, the data event will fire, and you can read that chunk in the callback of the data event. In the non-flowing mode, the chunk will fire a readable event, and then, you will have to call read to get the chunk.

Here is a list of events:

- readable
- data
- end
- close
- error

Here are two examples, one that uses flowing and one that uses non-flowing:

```
var fs = require('fs');
var readable = fs.createReadStream('test.txt');

readable.on('data', function (chunk) {
    console.log(chunk.toString());
});
var fs = require('fs');
readable.on('readable', function () {
    var chunk;
    while (chunk = readable.read()) {
        console.log(chunk.toString());
    }
});
```

read

Use with a non-flowing readable stream:

```
readable.read([size])
```

Return value

This returns either a string, buffer, or null. A string is returned if the encoding is set. A buffer is returned if the encoding is not set. Finally, null is returned when there is no data in the stream.

Description

This reads from a stream. Most of the time, the optional parameter size is not needed and should be avoided. Only use this with a non-flowing stream.

Here is a simple example that reads a file:

```
readable.on('readable', function () {
    var chunk;
    while (chunk = readable.read()) {
        console.log(chunk.toString());
    }
});
```

setEncoding

This sets the encoding of the stream:

```
stream.setEncoding(encoding)
```

Description

By default, a readable stream will output a buffer. This will set the encoding of the buffer, so a string is returned.

Here is the opening example with setEncoding used:

```
readable.setEncoding('utf8');
readable.on('readable', function () {
    var chunk;
    while (chunk = readable.read()) {
        console.log(chunk);
    }
});
```

resume and pause

These functions pause and resume a stream:

```
stream.pause()
stream.resume()
```

Description

Pause will stop a stream from emitting data events. If this is called on a non-flowing stream, it will be changed into a flowing stream and be paused. Resume will cause the stream to start emitting data events again.

Here is an example that pauses the stream for a few seconds before reading it:

```
readable.pause();
readable.on('data', function (chunk) {
    console.log(chunk.toString());
});
setTimeout(function () { readable.resume();}, 3000);
```

pipe

This allows you to take the output of a readable stream and send it to the input of a writable stream:

```
readable.pipe(writable, [options])
```

Return Value

This returns the writable stream so that piping can be chained.

Description

This is exactly the same as piping output in a shell.

A great design paradigm is to pipe from a stream to another stream that transforms the stream and then pipe that to the output. For example, you want to send a file over the network. You would open the file as a readable stream, pass it to a duplex stream that would compress it, and pipe the output of the compression to a socket.

Here is a simple example of piping output to stdout:

```
var readable = fs.createReadStream('test.txt');
readable.pipe(process.stdout);
```

writable

This is the stream the data goes to. This is a little simpler as there are really only two functions that matter: write and end.

Here are the events and details of when they fire:

- drain: This fires when the internal buffer has written all the data
- finish: This fires when the stream has been ended and all the data has been written
- error: This fires when an error occurs

It is important to note that a stream can be given more data than it can write in a timely fashion. This is especially true when writing to a network stream. Because of this, the events `finish` and `drain` to let your program know that the data has been sent.

write

This function writes to the stream:

```
writable.write(chunk, [encoding], [callback])
```

Return value

This returns a Boolean value if the stream has written completely.

Description

This is the main function of a writable stream. Data can be a buffer or string, encoding defaults to UTF8, and the callback is called when the current chunk of data has been written.

Here is a simple example:

```
var fs = require('fs');
var writable = fs.createWriteStream('WriteStream.txt');

var hasWritten = writable.write('Write this!', 'utf8', function () {
    console.log('The buffer has written');
});
end
```

This will close the stream, and no more data can be written:

```
writable.end([chunk], [encoding], [callback])
```

Description

When you are done writing to a stream, the end function should be called on it. All the parameters are optional, a chunk is data that you can write before the stream ends, encoding will default to UTF8, and the callback will be attached to the finish event.

Here is an example to end a writable stream:

```
var fs = require('fs');
var writable = fs.createWriteStream('WriteStream.txt');

writable.end('Last data written.', 'utf8', function () {
    //this runs when everything has been written.
});
```

The net module

The net module in Node.js allows us to create network connections. The connections that are created will be streams that we can write to and read from. This section will focus on just network connections and not HTTP. Node.js has a full HTTP module, and we will cover that in the next section.

All the functions assume that the net module has been loaded like this:

```
var net = require('net');
```

createServer

This function will create a TCP server:

```
net.createServer([options], [listener])
```

Return value

This returns a net.Server object.

Description

This function allows us to listen for connections. The returned object will be a net.Server object, and the connection listener will be passed to a net.Socket object. We will cover both of these objects shortly.

Here is a simple example that shows us how to listen and write to a socket. Each connection will have to be manually closed:

```
var net = require('net');
var server = net.createServer(function (connection) {
    connection.write('You connected!');
});
server.listen(5000, function () {
    console.log('Listening on port 5000');
});
```

net.Server

We will now look at the net.Server object. All of the functions in the next section will need to a have a Server object created through createServer.

The net.Server parameter is an EventEmitter that will emit events. Here is a list of the events with the event argument if there is one:

- Connection: net.Socket
- close
- Error: Error
- listening

Here is an example that uses all of the events:

```
var net = require('net');
var server = net.createServer();
server.on('listening', function () {
    console.log('I am listening');
});
server.on('connection', function (socket) {
    console.log(socket);
    socket.end();
    server.close();
});
server.on('error', function (err) {
    console.log(err);
});
server.on('close', function () {
    console.log('The server has stopped listening');
});
server.listen(5000);
```

listen

This starts accepting connections:

```
server.listen(port, [host], [backlog], [callback])
```

Description

Creating a server does not get it to start listening to requests. We will have to give the listen function at least a port. The host is optional, as it will listen on all IPv4 addresses, and the backlog will be the queue of connections. Finally, the callback will be called when the server starts listening.

You may get EADDRINUSE. This just means that the port is already being used by another process.

Here is an example that defines all the parameters:

```
server.listen(5000, '127.0.0.1', 500, function () {
    console.log('Listening on port 5000');
});
```

close

This closes the current server:

```
server.close([callback])
```

Description

This will stop the server from creating new connections. This is important to remember because it will not close the current connections.

The callback is called when there are no more connections.

address

This gets the port and address:

```
server.address()
```

Description

This will give you the port and IP address where this server is listening.

getConnections

This gets the number of connections:

```
server.getConnections(callback)
```

Return Value

This returns an integer.

Description

This does not give any information on each connection. It only returns the number. This is a great way to see whether there are any connections. The callback function will need to be in the form of *function(err, connections)*.

connect

This easily creates a connection to the specified address:

```
net.connect(port, [host], [connectListener])
net.createConnection(port, [host], [connectListener])
```

Return value

This returns a `net.Socket` object.

Description

This function does not do anything that you cannot do with a socket. It is a convenient function that returns a `net.Socket` object.

For the parameters, a port is required, the host will default to localhost, and `connectListener` will be added to the connect event of the newly formed `net.Socket` object.

Here is an example that will connect to a server we just created and send data every second:

```
var net = require('net');
var server = net.createServer();
server.on('listening', function () {
    console.log('I am listening');
});
server.on('connection', function (socket) {
    socket.on('data', function (d) {
        console.log('from client: ' + d);
    });
});

server.listen(5000);

var client = net.connect({ port: 5000, host: 'localhost' }, function
() {
    setInterval(function () {
        client.write('hey!');
    }, 1000);
});
```

net.Socket

This section will be similar to the net.Server section. The net.Socket parameter is the object that is returned anytime a connection is made. It can also be used to create a new connection.

It is a readable and writable stream. This is the only way to send and receive data from a net.Socket.

Here is the list of events along with details of when they fire:

- connect: On connection.
- data: When data is received.
- end: When the socket has ended.
- timeout: When the socket has timed out from inactivity. The socket is still open at this point.
- drain: When all the data in the write buffer has been sent.
- Error: On error.
- close: When the socket closes.

As net.Socket is a readable stream, there is no read function. You will have to listen for the data event to the get the data.

Here is an example of using a socket to connect to a local server:

```
var server = net.createServer();
server.on('listening', function () {
    console.log('I am listening');
});
server.on('connection', function (socket) {
    socket.on('data', function (d) {
        console.log('from client: ' + d);
    });
});

server.listen(5000);

var client = new net.Socket();
client.on('connect', function () {
    setInterval(function () {
        client.write('Hey!');
    }, 1000);
});

client.connect(5000, 'localhost');
```

connect

This creates a connection:

```
socket.connect(port, [host], [listener])
```

Description

This is the function that actually creates a connection. Much like net.connection, the port is required, the host will default to localhost, and the listener just maps the function to the connection event.

Here is an example that connects locally and writes to the connection:

```
var client = new net.Socket();
client.on('connect', function () {
    setInterval(function () {
        client.write('Hey!');
    }, 1000);
});

client.connect(5000, 'localhost');
```

write

This sends data out on the socket:

```
socket.write(data, [encoding], [callback])
```

Description

The socket is buffered because it is very easy to queue up more data than can be sent over the network. This is done automatically by Node.js, but you should be aware of this, as buffering will use up memory as it is holding the data to be sent.

The encoding parameter will default to UTF8, but any of the encodings we have discussed can be used. The callback will be called once the data has been written over the socket.

Here is an example with all of the parameters defined:

```
var client = new net.Socket();
client.on('connect', function () {
    client.write('This is the data', 'utf8', function(){
        console.log('Data has been sent');
    });
});

client.connect(5000, 'localhost');
```

end

This starts the closing process of the socket:

```
socket.end([data], [encoding])
```

Description

This is effectively closing the socket. We cannot say for sure, but the reason could be that the server could send some data back, although the socket will close shortly.

You can send some data before the socket closes, and this is what the optional parameters are for:

```
Here is an example that closes a socket.
var client = new net.Socket();
client.on('connect', function () {
    client.end('I am closing', 'utf8');
});

client.connect(5000, 'localhost');
```

The HTTP module

We will cover the HTTP server module. Technically, you could write your HTTP server using the net module, but you do not have to.

Some of these functions are very similar to the net module functions. This should make sense as HTTP, at its core, is a network server.

All of these functions and objects are also used with the HTTPS module. The only difference is that for the options of createServer and https.request, you can pass certificates.

All of the following examples assume that the module has been loaded:

```
var http = require('http');
```

createServer

This creates an HTTP server:

```
http.createServer([requestListener])
```

Return Value

This returns an `http.Server` object.

Description

Much like `net.createServer`, this is required to serve anything. The `requestListener` parameter is attached to the request event.

Here is a simple example that just logs to the console any time a request is made:

```
var server = http.createServer(function (req, res) {
    console.log('Someone made a request!');
    res.end();
});
server.listen(8080);
```

http.Server

This is the server object that is returned from `http.createServer`. This is the object that will respond to all requests.

We will start with the functions and look at each event separately as the events are important to handling requests.

listen

This tells the server to listen on the supplied port, path, or file descriptor:

```
server.listen(port, [host], [callback])
server.listen(path, [callback])
server.listen(fd, [callback])
```

Description

Although this function has three different ways to execute, you will most likely only use the network listener. In fact, the other two listeners are difficult, if not impossible, to even execute on Windows. Let's cover the last two quickly.

The path listener will use a local socket server, and the file descriptor will need a handle. If this sounds foreign, it means you will use the other method.

The network listener requires that the port be used. The host will default to localhost if nothing is passed in. In all the functions, a callback will be attached to the listening event.

Here is an example of listening on a network port with all the parameters defined:

```
var server = http.createServer();
server.listen(8080, 'localhost', function(){
    console.log('The server is listening');
});
```

close

This closes the server:

```
server.close([callback])
```

Description

This will stop the server from listening. The callback will be attached to the close event.

Here is a simple example:

```
var server = http.createServer();
server.listen(8080, 'localhost', function () {
    server.close(function () {
        console.log('Server has closed');
    });
});
```

Events

The `http.Server` parameter is an `EventEmitter` object. The events are also where the majority of work will be done.

request

This event fires when a request comes in:

```
server.on('request', function (req, res) { });
```

Description

If you only listen to one event, this is the event to listen for. It has the `request` and the server's response. The `req` attribute will be `http.IncomingMessage`, and the `res` attribute will be `http.ServerResponse`. We will look at both of these objects in this section. In addition to this, `req` implements a readable stream interface, and `res` implements a writable stream interface.

Here is an example of listening for a request:

```
server.on('request', function (req, res) {
    res.end();
    console.log('A request was received');
});
```

close

This event fires when the server closes:

```
server.on('close', function () { });
```

upgrade

This event fires when the client sends an HTTP upgrade:

```
server.on('upgrade', function (req, socket, buffer) { });
```

Description

An upgrade request asks the web server to change protocols. If you are implementing another protocol other than HTTP you should listen and deal with this event. A great example of this is a WebSocket upgrade.

The req attribute is the request, the socket will be a net.Socket, and buffer is a Buffer.

IncomingMessage

This is the request object when listening for the request event or from http.clientRequest. This is a readable stream.

headers

The HTTP headers from the request:

```
message.headers
```

Description

Sometimes, you will want to make decisions based on the information in the headers. Here is an example using headers to check for basic authentication:

```
server.on('request', function (req, res) {
    if (req.headers.authorization !== undefined)
        //do a check here
    res.end();
});
```

method

This gets the HTTP method of the request:

```
message.method
```

Description

This returns the method as a string in uppercase. Here is an example for GET:

```
server.on('request', function (req, res) {
    if (req.method === 'GET')
        res.write(req.method);
    res.end();
});
```

url

This is the URL that was requested:

```
message.url
```

Description

This will be a string of the URL, including any query parameters. You can parse the string yourself or use Node's query string module and use the `parse` function.

Here is a simple example that will serve any files in the current directory. Remember that this is only an example and does no error checking:

```
server.on('request', function (req, res) {
        var file = fs.createReadStream('.' + req.url);
        file.pipe(res);
});
```

data

This is the data event from the readable stream interface.

Description

If you have an incoming message, most likely, you would want to know what is in the message. As it is a readable stream, we will need to listen for the data event to get all the data out. When the data is exhausted, the end event will fire.

Here is an example that creates listeners for the data and end event:

```
var data = '';
response.on('data', function (chunk) {
    console.log(chunk);
    data += chunk;
});

response.on('end', function () {
    console.log(data);
});
```

ServerResponse

This is the response that the HTTP server creates for the event request. Each request needs a response, and this is it. This implements a writable interface.

writeHead

This will write the HTTP response header:

```
response.WriteHead(statusCode, [headers])
```

Description

This writes the header for the response. This needs to be called before `response.write`. If it is not, then the server will send it for you with the headers you have set.

`statusCode` is the HTTP status code of the response. A `header` is an object with the name of the header as a property and the value as the value.

Here is an example that writes the header:

```
server.on('request', function (req, res) {
    res.writeHead(200, { 'Content-Type': 'text/html' });
    res.end();
});
```

statusCode

This sets the status code of the response:

```
response.statusCode
```

Description

This is used instead of `response.writeHead`. If this is called after `writeHead` has been executed, then it will not change the response header. It must be called instead of it.

Here is an example that uses `statusCode`:

```
server.on('request', function (req, res) {
    res.statusCode = 404;
    res.end();
});
```

setHeader

This writes a specific header:

```
response.setHeader(name, value)
```

Description

In the same way that `statusCode` must be called instead of `writeHead`, `setHeader` must be called instead of `writeHead`. This can be called multiple times to set multiple headers.

Here is an example of using `statusCode` and `setHeader` together:

```
server.on('request', function (req, res) {
    res.statusCode = 200;
    res.setHeader('Content-Type', 'text/html');
    res.setHeader('Custom-Header', 'Custom-Value');
    res.end();
});
```

write

This is the function that writes the response body:

```
response.write(chunk, [encoding])
```

Description

The `response.write` parameter is a writable stream, so this interface can be used. A chunk can be a buffer or string. The encoding is optional as it will default to UTF8. Here is an example that writes a simple HTML page as the response:

```
server.on('request', function (req, res) {
    res.statusCode = 200;
    res.setHeader('Content-Type', 'text/html');
    res.write('<html><body><h1>Hello!</h1></body></html>');
    res.end();
});
```

end

This ends the response:

```
response.end([data], [encoding])
```

Description

The `response` parameter is a writable stream, so we must end the stream when we are done writing. Data is any optional data that needs to be written, and encoding will default to UTF8. All of the examples for response have used `res.end`. If you do not end the response, the browser will wait for a response from the server.

http.request

This makes a request using HTTP:

```
http.request(options, [callback])
```

Return value

This returns an `http.ClientRequest` object.

Description

Node.js allows you to consume HTTP as well as serve it. The options object has many properties that can be set. Here is a list of them:

- host
- hostname
- port
- localAddress

- socketPath
- method
- path
- headers
- auth
- agent

Every option is not required for each request. Most of the time, only hostname, port, path, and method are needed to make a request. The options parameter can also be a URL as a string.

The callback will be attached to the response event. The request object is a writable stream so that data can be sent to the server. Here is an example that makes a request to Packt Publishing:

```
var request = http.request({
    host: 'www.packtpub.com',
    port: 80,
    path: '/',
    method: 'GET'
}, function (res) {
    console.log(res);
});

request.end();
```

http.get

This is the convenience method for a GET request:

```
http.get(options, [callback])
```

Return value

This returns a http.ClientRequest object.

Description

This works in a manner similar to http.request, except it automatically sends an empty request and calls the end function. If you are only making a GET request, this can save some boilerplate code.

Here is an example that requests Packt Publishing:

```
http.get('http://www.packtpub.com', function (res) {
    console.log(res);
});
```

http.clientRequest

This is the object that is returned from `http.request`.

write

This writes to the server in the request:

```
request.write(data, [encoding])
```

Description

The `http.clientRequest` attribute is a writable stream. It is writable as you may need to send data to the remote server, for example, when making a POST request.

This works like all the other writable streams, so data can be a buffer or string, and encoding will default to UTF8.

end

This ends the request:

```
request.end([data], [encoding])
```

Description

When you are writing to a stream, you must end the stream with this function. Without doing this, the connection will stay and/or timeout. Data is optional and can be a buffer or string, while encoding will default to UTF8.

response

This is the response event. It lets you know that the remote server has responded:

```
request.on('response', function(response){})
```

Description

This event fires when the remote server responds. The response object in the callback will be `http.incomingMessage`.

If no response handler is added, the server response will be discarded. If there is a response handler, then Node.js will start to buffer the response to memory. If you do not read it back out, you can cause the server to crash.

Here is an example listener that reads the data from the response:

```
var request = http.request({host: 'www.google.com', path: '/', port:
80, method: 'GET'});

request.on('response', function (response) {
    var data = '';
    response.on('data', function (chunk) {
        console.log(chunk);
        data += chunk;
    });

    response.on('end', function () {
        console.log(data);
    });
});
```

Bootstrap – The Stylish CSS Frontend Framework

13

Bootstrap is a frontend framework and open source tool for developing websites and applications using HTML and CSS.

Twitter Blueprint was the initial name given to Bootstrap. Mark Otto and Jacob Thornton developed Bootstrap and used Twitter as the framework for consistency. According to Twitter developer Mark Otto:

> *"A super small group of developers and I got together to design and build a new internal tool and saw an opportunity to do something more. Through that process, we saw ourselves build something much more substantial than another internal tool. Months later, we ended up with an early version of Bootstrap as a way to document and share common design patterns and assets within the company."*

The first official release of Bootstrap was August 19, 2011. There are currently three versions of Bootstrap. However, Bootstrap 4 has been announced but its final version is yet to be released.

Introduction to Bootstrap foundations

Bootstrap is compatible with the most recent versions of many web browsers including Firefox, Opera, Internet Explorer, Google Chrome, and Safari browsers.

The HTML5 doctype

To get started with Bootstrap, the following piece of code for HTML5 doctype must be included in every bootstrap project:

```
<!DOCTYPE html>
<html lang="en">
  ...
</html>
```

Mobile first

Bootstrap is very mobile friendly. Mobile First styles are all included in a library and not scattered among various files. For accurate rendering and touch zooming, add the viewport meta tag to `<head>`:

```
<meta name="viewport" content="width=device-width, initial-scale=1.0">
```

Zooming can be disabled by setting the property user-scalable to no in the viewport meta tag, as shown here:

```
<meta name="viewport" content="width=device-width, initial-scale=1.0, maximum-scale=1.0, user-scalable=no">
```

Responsive images

Images can be made to respond to various screen sizes using a simple class, as follows:

```
<img src="..." class="img-responsive" alt="Responsive image">
```

Containers

In bootstrap, all the web page content and the grid system is wrapped inside a main container. These containers are not nestable.

There are two types of containers, they are as follows:

- Responsive fixed width container, for example:
  ```
  <div class="container"></div>
  ```

- Responsive full width container, for example:
  ```
  <div class="container-fluid"></div>
  ```

Getting started

It's now time to get started with your first Bootstrap project or website. You can get Bootstrap from various sources. For a kick start, here are a few sources for you to get your hands on Bootstrap.

The Github project

Bootstrap is an open source project from the creators of Twitter. You can download it from their GitHub repository or any other command-line interface you prefer.

Downloading Bootstrap

You can easily download Bootstrap from the following link: `https://github.com/twbs/bootstrap/releases/download/v3.3.5/bootstrap-3.3.5-dist.zip`

Installing with bower

You can install Bootstrap with `bower` using the following command:

```
$ bower install bootstrap
```

Installing with npm

You can install Bootstrap with `npm` using the following command:

```
$ npm install bootstrap
```

Installing with composer

You can install Bootstrap with `composer` using the following command:

```
$ composer require twbs/bootstrap
```

Layouts

Layouts help you to define a standard structure or the skeleton for your websites. There are three types of layouts:

- Fixed layouts
- Fluid layouts
- Responsive layouts

Fixed layouts do not change with screen size and all styles are static. Fluid layouts make the `div` elements flow to the bottom if they cannot be accommodated across the width of the viewing screen. Responsive layouts keep a very close eye on and respond to the adjusting screen sizes. These options can be used as described in the following sections.

Fixed layouts

A fixed layout of a website has a wrapper (which wraps or contains all columns) of a constant width, that is, which cannot be changed no matter how small or how big the screen resolution is. The wrapper or the container cannot be moved and is set to a fixed position. The reason why many web designers prefer fixed layouts is due to ease in usage and customization.

Description

In fixed layout, column widths are fixed and cannot be changed. The syntax for declaring fixed layouts for your website is as follows:

```
<body>
  <div class="container"> <!--This line is for declaring fixed
  layouts-->
  </div>
</body>
```

Everything inside the `container` class in the preceding code will be fixed for every device in which this code is executed.

Fluid layouts

A fluid layout acts just like a liquid and adjusts itself according to the screen resolution of the user at runtime. The components of such layouts mainly contain percentage widths and thus adjust to the user's screen effectively. Such layouts are more user friendly and make the website look better. It also improves accessibility and interface.

Description

Fluid layouts adjust themselves according to the screen resolution they receive using predefined percentage widths. The syntax for declaring fluid layouts for your website is shown here:

```
<div class="container-fluid"> <!--declaration of a fluid
container-->
  <div class="row-fluid">
    <div class="span3"> <!--spans 3 columns -->
      <!--Sidebar content-->
    </div>
```

```
    <div class="span5"> <!--spans 5 columns -->
      <!--Body content-->
    </div>
  </div>
</div>
```

Bootstrap's grid system allows up to 12 columns across the page.

In the preceding example, span3 combines three columns and span5 combines five columns, and together they complete the whole page adjusting the layout according to the screen resolution.

Responsive layouts

Responsive layouts provide a design for a website depending on the number of conditions, which include ratios, widths, display types, and so on. Such layouts automatically adjust and adapt to any screen size, thus providing better accessibility and optimal viewing experience to the user.

Description

Responsive layouts are a growing trend among web designers as they offer less hassles in customization and implementation.

The following example code shows how you can include responsive features using meta tags along with a Bootstrap stylesheet:

```
<meta name="viewport" content="width=device-width, initial-scale=1.0">
<link href="assets/css/bootstrap-responsive.css" rel="stylesheet">
```

Supported devices

To provide effective layouts on a number of different devices, Bootstrap can support many media queries in one file. The following table shows the range of devices that are supported:

Label	Layout width	Column width	Gutter width
Large display	1200px and up	70px	30px
Default	980px and up	60px	20px
Portrait tablets	768px and up	42px	20px
Phones to tablets	767px and lower	Fluid columns, no fixed width available	
Phones	480px and lower	Fluid columns, no fixed width available	

Referenced from: http://getbootstrap.com/css/#grid-options

The grid system

Use rows and columns to create a grid of a specific size and add data to it. Here are a few guidelines to keep in mind:

- Place rows in a `.container(fixed-width)` or `.container-fluid(full-width)` methods for accurate alignment.

- Horizontal groups of columns can be created using rows. Insert data in columns, and only columns may be immediate children of rows.

Padding is used by columns for creating gutters. That cushioning is counterbalanced in lines for the first and the last section by means of negative edge on `.lines`. Initiate columns by specifying the number columns. Not more than 12 columns can be initiated in a row, all extra columns will jump on a new line. Grid classes apply to devices with screen widths greater than or equal to the breakpoint sizes, and overrides grid classes targeted at smaller devices.

The grid options cheat sheet

The following table shows some effective ways in which the Bootstrap grid system can be used to work for multiple devices:

	Large Device (>=1200 px)s	Medium Devices (>=992 px)	Small Devices such as Tablets (>=768px)	Extra small devices such as Phones (<768px)
Grid behavior	Collapsed to start, horizontal above breakpoints			Horizontal at all times
Max container width	1170px	970px	750px	None (auto)
Class prefix	`.col-lg-`	`.col-md-`	`.col-sm-`	`.col-xs-`
# of columns	12			
Max column width	95px	78px	60px	Auto
Gutter width	350px (15px on each side of a column)			
Nestable	Yes			
Offsets	Yes			
Column ordering	Yes			

source: `www.getbootstrap.com/css/`

Media queries

Media queries help the website to adjust the styles according to the screen size. We can use the media queries in our LESS files in order to create the key breakpoints in our grid system. Observing the cheat sheet, we can write media queries. Let's take a look at the following code snippet:

```
/* Large Device (>=1200 px) */
 @media (min-width: @screen-lg-min) { ... }

/*Medium Devices (>=992 px)*/
@media (min-width: @screen-md-min) { ... }

/* Small Devices such as Tablets (>=768px) */
@media (min-width: @screen-sm-min) { ... }

/* Extra small devices such as Phones (<768px)*/
/* No media query as this is the default*/
```

We occasionally expand on these media queries to include a max width to limit CSS to a narrower set of devices:

```
/* Large Device (>=1200 px) */
@media (min-width: @screen-lg-min) { ... }

/*Medium Devices (>=992 px)*/
@media (min-width: @screen-md-min) and (max-width: @screen-md-max)
{ ... }

/* Small Devices such as Tablets (>=768px) */
@media (min-width: @screen-sm-min) and (max-width: @screen-sm-max)
{ ... }

/* Extra small devices such as Phones (<768px)*/
@media (max-width: @screen-xs-max) { ... }
```

Responsive column resets

We need these types of columns because sometimes in a grid, not all the columns end with the same alignment due to a varying amount of data in it. However, responsive columns will ensure that everything is perfectly aligned. Let's take a look at the following code snippet:

```
<div class="row">
<div class="col-xs-6 col-sm-3" style="background-color:pink">.
col-xs-6 .col-sm-3</div>
```

```
    <div class="col-xs-6 col-sm-3" style="background-
    color:brown;">.col-xs-6 .col-sm-3</div></div>
    <!-- Add the extra clearfix for only the required viewport -->

    <div class="clearfix visible-xs-block"></div>

    <div class="col-xs-6 col-sm-3" style="background-
    color:orange;>.col-xs-6 .col-sm-3</div>
    <div class="col-xs-6 col-sm-3" style="background-
    color:black;>.col-xs-6 .col-sm-3</div>
</div>
```

Offsetting columns

Sometimes, we need to place a column or start a column with some free space offset. So, we set an offset from where the column needs to begin:

```
<div class="row">
  <div class="col-md-4">.col-md-4</div>
  <div class="col-md-4 col-md-offset-4">.col-md-4 .col-md-offset-
  4</div>
</div>

<div class="row">
  <div class="col-md-3 col-md-offset-3">.col-md-3 .col-md-offset-
  3</div>
  <div class="col-md-3 col-md-offset-3">.col-md-3 .col-md-offset-
  3</div>
</div>
<div class="row">
  <div class="col-md-6 col-md-offset-3">.col-md-6 .col-md-offset-
  3</div>
</div>
```

Nesting columns

As the name suggests, nesting columns are an embedment of a column within a column. Let's take a look at the following code snippet:

```
<div class="row">
  <div class="col-md-9">
    Level 1: .col-md-9
    <div class="row">
      <div class="col-md-6">
        Level 2: .col-md-6
```

```
        </div>
        <div class="col-md-6">
          Level 2: .col-md-6
        </div>
      </div>
    </div>
</div>
```

Column ordering

Column ordering can also be changed by moving columns to right or left. The following code shows how columns can be moved:

```
<div class="row">
  <div class="col-md-9 col-md-push-3">.col-md-9 .col-md-push-
  3</div>
  <div class="col-md-3 col-md-pull-9">.col-md-3 .col-md-pull-
  9</div>
</div>
```

LESS variables and mixins

LESS mixins and variables are used to quickly instantiate a layout using specific values given through variables and mixins.

Mixins

Mixins are mainly used together with grid variables to provide CSS styles for individual elements.

Description

Mixins, as the name suggests, are a way of including or mixing a group of properties from one rule set into another rule set. The following example shows the make-row() mixin:

```
make-row (@gutter: grid-gutter-width) {
  margin-left : (@gutter / -2);
  margin-right : (@gutter/ -2);
  &: extend( .clearfix all);
}
```

The make-row() mixin generates styles for the wrapper element, which contains all the columns. It uses the value from the @gutter parameter to calculate the left and right margins for a row.

Variables

The media query point from where columns start floating, total number of columns and gutter width are determined by variables. This information is provided by variables in order to generate predefined grid classes and for custom mixins as well.

Description

Variables are used along with mixins to generate styles for individual elements.

The following piece of code predefines some variables that are used in mixins as default values:

```
//Number of columns in the grid.
@grid-columns: 12;

//padding between columns. Divided in half for left and right.
@grid-gutter-width: 30px;
//point at which the navbar collapses.
@grid-float-breakpoint: 768px;
```

Typography

Typography is the art and technique of arranging type elements to make written language legible, readable, and appealing when displayed with the use of headings, bold fonts, italic fonts, strong fonts, lists, and so on.

Headings

In Bootstrap, all headings from `h1` to `h6` are available from HTML. Headings are mainly used to highlight the main topics under discussion. The heading text should be included between proper HTML heading tags, for example, `<h1>` Here is the heading text `</h1>`. The heading size decreases as the heading number increases, providing the facility to highlight the main topics and subtopics. This technique helps in managing a proper design for the website.

Here are a few examples of how headings can be used:

```
<h1> This is a Bootstrap heading H1</h1>
<h2> This is a Bootstrap heading H2</h2>
<h3> This is a Bootstrap heading H3</h3>
<h4> This is a Bootstrap heading H4</h4>
<h5> This is a Bootstrap heading H5</h5>
<h6> This is a Bootstrap heading H6</h6>
```

Body

All the HTML tags related to typography and design must be included within the body tags, for example, text, hyperlinks, images, tables, lists, and so on. The following code shows a paragraph tag, which shows the text in a paragraph:

```
<p>...</p>
```

Lead body

The lead class helps make the text inside the tags stand out. The method of its declaration is as stated here:

```
<p class="lead">...</p>
```

Emphasis

Emphasis basically affiliates the size and font of the text to its importance in a document. For example, larger text would have more importance than smaller text or text in italics might contain a reference from another resource.

Small text

The text within the `small` tags is mainly reduced to 85% of the original size. This technique is mainly used to lessen the importance of the text:

```
<small>...</small>
```

Bold text

The text within the `strong` tags is made more visible by making it larger and bolder. This helps in increasing the emphasis of the text in the document:

```
<strong>...</strong>
```

Italics text

The text within the `em` tags is italicized. This technique is mainly used to denote references, among many other uses:

```
<em>...</em>
```

Alignment

Alignment is a basic technique used to align a paragraph to the left, right, or center of the screen, regardless of the screen resolution:

```
<p class="text-left">Text here will be left-aligned</p>
<p class="text-center"> Text here will be center-aligned </p>
<p class="text-right"> Text here will be right-aligned </p>
```

Abbreviations

The customized `<abbr>` element of HTML can be used with the following syntax as shown in the following code snippet.

Basic

The `<abbr>` tag shows a smaller version of text and is expanded when the mouse is hovered over it:

```
<abbr title="attribute">Here is an example of an attribute
tag</abbr>
```

The output of this code will show the attr abbreviation.

Initialism

Initialism has the same functionality as the basic abbreviation but with smaller text:

```
<abbr title="HyperText Markup Language" class="initialism">HTML
using Initialism</abbr>
```

Addresses

Address tags are used to accommodate all text related to an address. The following example shows the format:

```
<address> …
  <strong>Packt PublishingPublishing.</strong><br>
  Berwick House, <br>
  35 Livery St, <br>
  Birmingham B3 2PB,<br>
  United Kingdom <br>
  <abbr title="Phone">P:</abbr> +44 121 265 6484
</address>
```

Blockquotes

Blockquotes are mainly used for quoting text from another source. They are used with paragraph tags for quoting a paragraph:

```
<blockquotes> … </blockquotes>
```

Tables

Tables are used to clearly display the contents in an organized form so that data is easily accessible and readable.

#	Category	Item	ItemID
1	Apparel	Blue Shirt	App_BlueShirt
2	Apparel	White Coat	App_WhiteCoat
3	Accessories	Leather Belt	Acc_LeatherBelt

Basic

In the preceding table, is the basic version of a Bootstrap table with light padding and horizontal dividers only. The syntax is as follows:

```
<table class="table"> ... </table>
```

Striped rows

The structure of striped rows is the same as that of the basic table, its style is similar to the strips of zebra crossing, that is, lighter and darker alternative rows:

```
<table class="table table-striped"> ... </table>
```

Bordered table

This class converts a table into equal divisions with visible boundaries. Each division contains a single value:

```
<table class="table table-bordered"> ... </table>
```

Hover rows

This class adds the feature that highlights the row on which the mouse hovers:

```
<table class="table table-hover"> ... </table>
```

Condensed rows

A more squeezed and smaller version of a table can be achieved by decreasing the padding between rows:

```
<table class="table table-condensed"> ... </table>
```

Contextual classes

Contextual classes when applied to table rows or cells, give them predefined colors. Here are a few available classes:

- `.active`: This class applies a hover color to the table row
- `.success`: This class applies green color to the table row
- `.info`: This class applies blue color to the table row
- `.warning`: This class applies yellow color to the table row
- `.danger`: This class applies red color to the table row

We can set entire rows or individual cells to display a certain color to denote a particular message. Here is an example of how this can be achieved:

```
<!-- Contextual classes when applied on rows -->
<tr class="active">...</tr>
<tr class="success">...</tr>
<tr class="warning">...</tr>
<tr class="danger">...</tr>

<!-- Contextual classes when applied on cells (`td` or `th`) -->
<tr> <td class="active">...</td>
<td class="success">...</td>
<td class="warning">...</td>
<td class="danger">...</td> </tr>
```

Responsive tables

Responsive tables adjust themselves to scroll horizontally on small devices. The difference is only visible on small devices:

```
<div class="table-responsive">
  <table class="table"> ... </table>
</div>
```

Lists

Lists are used to group data in a certain order, or it can be ungrouped to display data in a sequential form.

Lists can be of the following types:

- Unordered
- Ordered
- Unstyled
- Inline
- Description

Unordered lists

An unordered list is a collection of items in which the order does not matter. Here is the syntax of an unordered list:

```
<ul>
   <li>...</li>
   <li>...</li>
</ul>
```

Ordered lists

An ordered list is a collection of items where the order does matter. Here is the syntax of an ordered list:

```
<ol>
   <li>...</li>
   <li>...</li>
</ol>
```

Unstyled lists

Unstyled lists can be ordered or unordered with the removal of the left margin and the default list style. Here is the syntax of an unstyled list:

```
<ul class="list-unstyled">
   <li>...</li>
   <li>...</li>
</ul>
```

Inline lists

Inline lists arrange all items of a list into a single line or row. Here is the syntax of an inline list:

```
<ul class="list-inline">
  <li>...</li>
  <li>...</li>
</ul>
```

Description lists

A description list contains the list items along with their descriptions. Here is the syntax of a description list:

```
<dl>
  <dt>...</dt>
  <dd>...</dd>
</dl>
```

Horizontal description

The horizontal description class does the same thing as the description list class with the only difference being the placement of the corresponding description of the list item in the same line. Here is the syntax of an horizontal description list:

```
<dl class="dl-horizontal">
  <dt>...</dt>
  <dd>...</dd>
</dl>
```

Forms in Bootstrap

Form elements are various elements used in Bootstrap to make navigation and GUI more appealing and satisfying. Use of various text boxes, buttons, and so on enable better output.

There are three types of layout for forms:

- Vertical forms
- Inline forms
- Horizontal forms

Vertical forms

Vertical forms are the default layout of bootstrap forms. The attribute used here is role and the value of it is set to form to provide better accessibility and automatic and default styling for the form. The syntax for this is as follows:

```
<form role="form"> … </form>
```

Inline forms

Many a time, we also come across forms in which the elements of the forms are present inline and in a single line and left aligned. Inline forms are required to have the form-inline class for the <form> element. The syntax for this as follows:

```
<form class="form-inline" role="form"> … </form>
```

Horizontal forms

A horizontal form is the most nifty of this set and is broadly used on web pages to collect data from website users. The appearance and performance of this form is something that sets it apart from the other two types of forms. This form aligns labels and groups of form controls in a horizontal layout.

Horizontal forms are required to have the form-horizontal class for the <form> element. Additionally, labels are to have the control-label class for the <label> element. The syntax is as follows:

```
<form class="form-horizontal" role="form"> … </form>
```

Inputs for forms in Bootstrap

All different input types supported by HTML are available to use even in Bootstrap, making it simple for someone from an HTML background to grasp the concepts. Inputs such as textarea, password, radio button, checkbox and many more are supported in Bootstrap.

The syntax for a simple text box as a means of input is as follows:

```
<input type="text" class="form-control" placeholder="Text input"
id ="txtName">
```

If we want the text altered to not show the actual letters being typed in, then we can use the input type as password. The syntax for using the input type as password is as follows:

```
<input type="password" class="form-control" placeholder="Text
input" id="txtPassword">
```

Textarea

The textarea is an area that holds text entered by the user; it can hold small words to large paragraphs. The syntax for textarea is as follows:

```
<textarea class="form-control" rows="44"></textarea>
```

The preceding line tells the control that the textarea must span four rows.

Help text

The help block provides block-level help text for form controls:

```
<span class="help-block">  </span>
```

Checkbox

The checkbox control allocates a box to a certain group of related options that can be selected by clicking on the box. This feature is used when the user is required to select only from the given options. The syntax for adding a checkbox is as follows:

```
<div class="checkbox">    </div>
```

Here is the syntax to add a checkbox that is disabled:

```
<div class="checkbox disabled">     </div>
```

Select list

The select class control triggers a dropdown menu that contains a group of options from which only one can be selected at a time. Its syntax is as follows:

```
<select class="form-control"> … </form>
```

Radio button

The radio class control does the same as the checkbox except that the user can choose only one option at a time. Its syntax is as follows:

```
<div class="radio"> … </div>
```

Here is the syntax to add a radio class that is disabled:

```
<div class="radio disabled">    </div>
```

Static control

The static class control allows the user to insert text in a horizontal form next to its corresponding label. Text can be added next to a form label in a horizontal form using the "form-control-static" class within paragraph tags. The form-static-control class must be used.

The following example inserts the static text—Web Developer's Reference Guide:

```
<p class="form-control-static">Web Developer's Reference Guide<p>
```

Input focus

The input class lets an input field automatically focus when the page loads. Its syntax is as follows:

```
<input class="form-control" id="focusedInput" type="text" value="...">
```

Disabled input

The disabled attribute disables input in a particular text box, it cannot be clicked on or used. To use this, the disabled attribute can be added to a <fieldset> tag to disable all of its controls.

Validation states

These classes give meaning to input controls when returning a message from the server such as fields that were left empty or when an incorrect combination is entered.

Validation states can be used by adding .has-success, .has-warning, or .has-error in a class. This is shown in the following code:

```
<div class="form-group has-success"> … </div>
<div class="form-group has-warning"> … </div>
<div class="form-group has-error"> … </div>
```

Control sizing

Users can easily set the height of various columns as per their requirement.

We can easily set heights and widths using classes such as `.input-lg` and `.col-lg-*`:

```
<input class="form-control input-lg" type="text"
placeholder=".input-lg">
<div class="col-xs-2"> … </div>
```

Images

We can add classes to an `<img>` element for image manipulation using built-in CSS styles:

```
<img src="..." alt="..." class="img-rounded">
<img src="..." alt="..." class="img-circle">
<img src="..." alt="..." class="img-thumbnail">
```

The preceding code will create the following images:

 Note that Internet Explorer 8 lacks support for rounded corners in images.

Icons (Glyphicons)

Glyphicons are small icons used to help the user understand the meaning of a function. For example, an e-mail will have an envelope icon, search would have a magnifying glass icon, and so on. Some Glyphicons are shown in the following diagram:

More than 250 Glyphicons in font format are present in the **Glyphicon Halflings** set. Here is how to add Glyphicons in Bootstrap:

```
<span class="glyphicon glyphicon-search"></span>
```

All the available Glyphicons can be found at `http://getbootstrap.com/components/`.

Navigation elements

Bootstrap supports multiple types of navigation element and can be used as described in the following code:

Tabs

The `tab` class creates small tabs on the navigation bar, and each tab provides a link to different pages:

```
<ul class="nav nav-tabs"> … </ul>
```

The tabs basically are links to other pages or websites; thus, the `tab` class should be declared within the link tags, as shown in the preceding code.

Pills

The `pill` class has the same functionality as the `tab` class, with the only difference being the styling. The tabs now appear like pills:

```
<ul class="nav nav-pills"> … </ul>
```

Justified

Adding an additional class of `nav-justified` would allow tabs or pills to automatically adjust themselves according to the screen resolution. The tabs or pills are given equal widths:

```
<ul class="nav nav-tabs nav-justified"> … </ul>
```

Disabled links

Adding a `disabled` class to a tab or pill in a navigation bar would remove the hover state, disabling the access to the link:

```
<ul class="nav nav-pills">
  ...
    <li class="disabled"><a href="#">Disabled link</a></li>
  ...
</ul>
```

Remember to place the actual link in place of #.

The navigation bar

Navigation in Bootstrap helps in navigating through the website. It allows quick access to the links a user visits often.

Default

The `navbar` class is used to create a simple navigation bar by including `.navbar` and `.navbar-default` in the navigation tab:

```
<nav class="navbar navbar-default" role="navigation">
```

To make a scalable, responsive menu bar that collapses to a dropdown when displaying on mobile devices, use the following class to wrap the bar:

```
<div class="navbar-header">
```

Forms

You can also put forms within a navigation bar by adding the `.navbar-form` class:

```
<form class="navbar-form navbar-left" role="search">
```

Buttons

Similar to the `navbar` class, `.navbar-btn` adds a button to the bar that can perform many useful functions:

```
<button type="button" class="btn btn-default navbar-btn"> …
</button>
```

Text

By adding the `.navbar-text` class, we can also add text to the navigation bar:

```
<p class="navbar-text"> … </p>
```

Non-nav links

The `navbar-link` class allows us to add standard links that are not in the `navbar` navigation component:

```
<p class="navbar-text navbar-right">
  <a href="#" class="navbar-link"></a>
</p>
```

Fixed to top

Adding the `navbar-fixed-top` class within the `<nav>` tabs allows `navbar` to dynamically position itself at the top of the page. Here is its syntax:

```
<nav class="navbar navbar-default navbar-fixed-top"
role="navigation">
```

Fixed to bottom

The `navbar-fixed-bottom` class allows the navigation bar to sit right at the bottom of the page. Here is its syntax:

```
<nav class="navbar navbar-default navbar-fixed-bottom"
role="navigation">
```

Static top

The `navbar-static-top` class adds a new feature to the navigation bar that allows the element to scroll along with the page. Here is its syntax:

```
<nav class="navbar navbar-default navbar-static-top"
role="navigation">
```

Inverted navbar

The `navbar-inverse` class only changes the color of the navigation bar and turns it into the opposite color. For example, `navbar` gets a black background with white text:

```
<nav class="navbar navbar-inverse" role="navigation">
```

Panels

Panels are simple boxes that contain plain text. Panels are mostly used in order to present important information in a visually favorable way.

Basic

A basic panel consists of a single box containing some text. The method of its declaration is shown here:

```
<div class="panel panel-default"> … </div>
```

Heading

The `panel-heading` class adds an additional box above the basic panel, which contains its heading or title. Both boxes are of different colors by default. Here is the syntax:

```
<div class="panel-heading">This is a Panel Heading</div>
```

Footer

The `panel-footer` class adds a box beneath a basic panel which also contains text of some sort. Here is the syntax:

```
<div class="panel-footer">This is a Panel Footer</div>
```

Group

Panels under the `panel-group` class are grouped together. Here is the syntax:

```
<div class="panel-group">
```

Breadcrumbs

Breadcrumbs serve as a helping tool that keeps track of the path you take to visit different pages. Using breadcrumbs, you can know the current location of a page on a website.

Breadcrumbs are used to find out the current page's path in a navigation hierarchy.

Here is a sample code:

```
<ol class="breadcrumb">
  <li><a href="#">Home</a></li>
  <li><a href="#">Library</a></li>
  <li class="active">Data</li>
</ol>
```

Labels and badges

Labels and badges offer help tools that keep track of the progressive factors, such as numerical indicators, counts, percentages, and so on, by keeping counts or by showing the status of a website being loaded and so on.

Labels

Labels are associated with different headings or titles which help in keeping records of counts or give tips among other things. Labels can be declared as follows:

```
<h3>This is an example Heading<span class="label label-
default">This is an example label</span></h3>
```

Badges

Badges are the same as labels with the only difference being the shape. Badges have more curved shapes than labels. They are mainly used to notify the user of the new changes, unseen e-mails, and so on. Let's take a look at the following code snippet:

```
<a href="#">Check EMailsEMails <span class="badge">4545</span></a>
```

Pagination

Pagination is the grouping of data on various pages like a textbook where data of same importance is usually posted on the same page for better accessibility. Pagination is highly scalable and provides larger click areas which are hard to miss. Pagination can be used along with tables and is useful for paginating search results.

Default

Following is a basic example of bootstrap pagination:

```
<ul class="pagination">
    <li>
      <a href="#" aria-label="Previous">
        <span aria-hidden="true">&laquo;</span>
      </a>
    </li>
    <li><a href="#">1</a></li>
    <li><a href="#">2</a></li>
    <li><a href="#">3</a></li>
    <li><a href="#">4</a></li>
    <li><a href="#">5</a></li>
```

```
<li>
  <a href="#" aria-label="Next">
    <span aria-hidden="true">&raquo;</span>
  </a>
</li>
</ul>
```

Adding .active to <li> will highlight the current page link:

```
<li class='active'><a href="#">3</a></li>
```

Adding .disabled to <li> will disable the page link and make it unclickable:

```
<li class='disabled'><a href="#">3</a></li>
```

Pager

The next and previous links are used in pagination for quick access. Pagers are mainly used by simple sites such as magazines, newspapers, or blogs, and so on. Here is the syntax:

```
<ul class="pager"> ... </ul>
```

Progress bars

A basic progress bar is a rectangular bar that fills according to the level of progress achieved. These bars are mainly used for the purpose of showing current progress regarding an action.

Here is the code to create progress bars:

```
<div class="progress">
  <div class="progress-bar" role="progressbar" aria-
  valuenow="505"
      aria-valuemin="0" aria-valuemax="100" style="width:505%">
  </div>
</div>
```

For more types visit: http://www.w3schools.com/bootstrap/
bootstrap_progressbars.asp.

Advanced Bootstrap/JavaScript plugins

Bootstrap can benefit from powerful JavaScript libraries to display various kinds of dynamic content on web pages. Bootstrap plugins require jQuery as a dependency. These include buttons, dropdowns, tooltips, alerts, tabs, and more. We will now cover how to use them.

Buttons

Buttons in Bootstrap can be used under various combinations.

Basic

The `btn-group` class generates a default grey button with curved edges that can trigger any function when clicked on by the user:

```
<div class="btn-group"> … </div>
```

Button toolbar

The `btn-toolbar` class groups together all buttons that are included in the `btn-toolbar` class:

```
<div class="btn-toolbar" role="toolbar"> … </div>
```

Sizing

The `sizing` class is used to size groups of buttons at once by just adding `btn-group-*`.

The declaration is shown here:

```
<div class="btn-group btn-group-lg">...</div>      //large
<div class="btn-group">...</div>      //normal
<div class="btn-group btn-group-sm">...</div>      //small
<div class="btn-group btn-group-xs">...</div>      //extra small
```

Nesting

Creating drop-down menus with a series of buttons can be done by placing a `btn-group` within a `btn-group` as shown here:

```
<div class="btn-group" role="group" aria-label="...">
  <button type="button" class="btn btn-default">Alpha</button>
  <button type="button" class="btn btn-default">Beta</button>
```

```
<button type="button" class="btn btn-default">Gamma</button>

<div class="btn-group" role="group">
  <button type="button" class="btn btn-default dropdown-toggle"
  data-toggle ="dropdown"> List of Top Publishers</button>
  <ul class="Top Publishers">
  <li><a href="https://www.packtpub.com/"> Packt
  Publishing</a></li>
  <li><a href="http://www.oreilly.com/"> O'Reilly</a></li>
  </ul>
</div>
</div>
```

Vertical variation

The btn-group-vertical class arranges a group of buttons in a vertical fashion. Here is the syntax:

```
<div class="btn-group-vertical"> ... </div>
```

Justified link variation

The btn-group-justified class allows the button groups to adjust themselves according to any screen resolution and provides equal widths to the buttons. Here is the syntax:

```
<div class="btn-group btn-group-justified"> ... </div>
```

Dropdowns

Dropdown menus are triggered when a button is clicked on the dropdown by the user. Dropdowns are mainly used to access additional related links.

Single button

The btn btn-default dropdown-toggle class changes a button into a simple dropdown menu. Its declaration is shown in the following code:

```
<button type="button" class="btn btn-default dropdown-toggle"
data-toggle="dropdown">
  <span class="caret"></span>
</button>
```

Split button

The `btn btn-danger` class does not change the button entirely into a dropdown, rather it splits a button into two parts where one performs a simple button function and the other becomes a dropdown menu:

```
<div class="btn-group">
  <button type="button" class="btn btn-danger">Action</button>

<button type="button" class="btn btn-danger dropdown-toggle" data-
toggle="dropdown">
  <span class="caret"></span>
  <span class="sr-only">Toggle for Dropdown</span>
  </button>
</div>
```

Tooltips

Tooltips are small boxes that pop up when the pointer is hovered over an element.

To create a tooltip, add the `data-toggle="tooltip"` attribute to an element. Add the `data-toggle="tooltip"` attribute to an element to create a tooltip. To specify the text that is displayed inside a tooltip, use the `title` attribute:

```
<a href="#" data-toggle="tooltip" title="Tooltip">…</a>
```

Positioning

The positioning tool is used to position a popup box of tooltips, for example, when a box may pop up on the top or bottom or to the left or right of an element:

Here is the syntax for positioning it at the top:

```
<a href="#" data-toggle="tooltip" data-
placement="top" title="Tooltip">Tooltip at the top</a>
```

Here is the syntax for positioning it at the bottom:

```
<a href="#" data-toggle="tooltip" data-
placement="bottom" title="Tooltip"> Tooltip at the bottom</a>
```

Here is the syntax for positioning it on the left of the element:

```
<a href="#" data-toggle="tooltip" data-
placement="left" title="Tooltip">Tooltip at the left</a>
```

Here is the syntax for positioning it on the right of the element:

```
<a href="#" data-toggle="tooltip" data-
placement="right" title="Tooltip"> Tooltip at the right</a>
```

 Remember to place the actual link in place of #.

Popovers

Popovers and tooltips have the same functionalities with the only difference that for popovers to appear, the element needs to be clicked on by the user. They are used to present additional information regarding the element.

Basic creation

Popovers can be generated using the following piece of code:

```
<a href="#" data-toggle="popover" title="Popover Header" data-
content="Some content inside the popover">Toggle popover</a>
```

Positioning

Popovers can be positioned on the top or bottom or to the left or right of the element using the following code.

Here is the syntax for positioning the popovers at the top:

```
<a href="#" title="Header" data-toggle="popover" data-
placement="top" data-Content="Content"> Popover at the top </a>
```

Here is the syntax for positioning it at the bottom:

```
<a href="#" title="Header" data-toggle="popover" data-
placement="bottom" data-content="Content"> Popover at the bottom
</a>
```

Here is the syntax for positioning it on the left:

```
<a href="#" title="Header" data-toggle="popover" data-
placement="left" data-content="Content"> Popover at the
leftleft</a>
```

Here is the syntax for positioning it on the right:

```
<a href="#" title="Header" data-toggle="popover" data-
placement="right" data-content="Content">PopoverPopover at the
right </a>
```

Remember to place the actual link in place of #.

Closing

The `popover` class allows the popover to close when you click elsewhere:

```
<a href="#" title="Dismissible popover" data-toggle="popover"
data-trigger="focus" data-content="Click anywhere in the document
to close the popover">Click here to close popover</a>
```

Alerts

Bootstrap provides the utility of displaying alert messages. The code for its declaration is shown here. Bootstrap also allows you to assign different colors to alert messages to signify different situations. Bootstrap requires jQuery, and $ in this syntax means we are invoking jQuery. Let's take a look at the following code:

```
<button type="button" class="close" data-dismiss="alert" aria
label="Close"> <span aria-hidden="true">&times;</span> </button>
```

The syntax of an alert is as follows:

```
$().alert():
```

This listens for click events on its elements having data-dismiss-alert. The syntax is as follows:

```
$().alert('close'):
```

This removes an alert from the DOM. The element will fade out if it includes the `.fade` and `.in` classes.

Tabs

Tabs are used in navigation bars to provide quick access to different links or pages. Tabs need to be individually activated, as follows:

```
<div class="container">
  <h1>Alpha Zoo</h1>
  <ul class="nav nav-tabs">
    <li class="active">
    <li><a href="#">Exhibit A to Exhibit H</a></li>
    <li><a href="#">Exhibit I to Exhibit M</a></li>
    <li><a href="#">Exhibit N to Exhibit Y</a></li>
    <li><a href="#">Mini Aquarium</a></li>
```

```
   <li><a href="#">Alpha Aviary</a></li>
   <li><a href="#">Adopt an animal for just $4</a></li>
 </ul>
 <br>
 <p>Welcome to our Zoo! We take pride in the happy animals we
 house.</p>
</div>
```

We can use the `fade` class to fade the content of tabs after viewing them:

```
<div class="tab-content">
  <div role="tabpanel" class="tab-pane fade in active"
  id="homepage">...</div>
  <div role="tabpanel" class="tab-pane fade"
  id="profile">...</div>
  <div role="tabpanel" class="tab-pane fade" id="posts">...</div>
  <div role="tabpanel" class="tab-pane fade"
  id="settings">...</div>
</div>
```

Accordions

Many a time, we come across scenarios wherein we need to manage large amounts of information within a single page. Placing all this content on a single page may lead to the creation of a very long page, and scrolling up or down may be frustrating for the person using the website. Accordion widgets are used to solve this problem, as they are used on websites to manage the large amount of content and navigation lists. They are basically collapsible panels inside which information is placed. With the Bootstrap collapse plugin, its very simple to create accordions.

This code creates an accordion with panel components:

```
<div class="panel-group" id="accordion">
  <H1> Welcome to Alpha Zoo </H1>
  <p>Welcome to our Zoo! We take pride in the happy animals we
  house.</p>
  <div class="panel panel-default">
    <div class="panel-heading">
      <h4 class="panel-title">
        <a data-toggle="collapse" data-parent="#accordion"
        href="#collapse1">
        Exhibit A to Exhibit H</a>
      </h4>
    </div>
    <!--Data for Panel 1-->
    <div id="collapse1" class="panel-collapse collapse in">
      <div class="panel-body">
```

```
          These exhibits are for animals from the tropical regions
          of the planet. Take a guided tour through Exhibit A, our
          largest exhibit housing our bengal tigers Uri and Kayla
          with their cubs at exhibit A or simply feed our talking
          toucan Charlie in Exhibit D.
          <a href='#'> See more</a>
        </div>
      </div>
    </div>
    <!--Data for Panel 2-->
    <div class="panel panel-default">
      <div class="panel-heading">
        <h4 class="panel-title">
          <a data-toggle="collapse" data-parent="#accordion"
          href="#collapse2">
          Exhibit I to Exhibit M</a>
        </h4>
      </div>
      <div id="collapse2" class="panel-collapse collapse">
        <div class="panel-body">
          This is the second panel. The content for the second panel
          will go in here.
        </div>
      </div>
    </div>
  </div>
</div>
```

Modals

Modal plugins are popup windows or boxes that are displayed at the top of the page. A modal looks like this:

Modal size

The modal dialog boxes come in two sizes. Small modals can be used for dealing with small functions, whereas large modals can be used to prompt large datasets.

Small

The modal-dialog modal-sm class creates a small modal. Here is the syntax:

```
<div class="modal-dialog modal-sm">
```

Large

The modal-dialog modal-lg class creates a large modal. Here is the syntax:

```
<div class="modal-dialog modal-lg">
```

Media objects

Media objects are abstract object styles that can be used for making blog comments or other descriptive thumbnails:

- `.media`: This class floats a `media` object to the right or left of a content block
- `.media-list`: This class forms an unordered list of items:

```
<div class="media">
  <a class="pull-left" href="#">
    <img class="media-object" data-src="holder.js/64x64">
  </a>
  <div class="media-body">
    <h4 class="media-heading">This is the Main Media
    heading </h4>
  </div>
<div>

<ul class="media-list">
  <li class="media">
    <a class="pull-left" href="#">
      <img class="media-object" data-src="holder.js/64x64">
    </a>
    <div class="media-body">
      <h4 class="media-heading">This is a Media heading
      </h4>
      <!-- Nested media object -->
    </div>
  </li>
</ul>
```

Carousels

The carousel plugin allows you to make elements move in a circle while viewing each element one by one.

Carousels show components by cycling through them. This can be done using the following code, which creates a carousel of animal photographs:

```
<div id="myCarousel" class="carousel slide" data-ride="carousel">
<!-- Indicators -->

<ol class="carousel-indicators">
  <li data-target="#myCarousel" data-slide-to=
  "0" class="active"></li>
  <li data-target="#myCarousel" data-slide-to="1"></li>
  <li data-target="#myCarousel" data-slide-to="2"></li>
  <li data-target="#myCarousel" data-slide-to="3"></li>
</ol>
```

```
<!-- Wrapper for slides -->

  <div class="carousel-inner" role="listbox">
    <div class="item active">
      <img src="Emperor_Penguin.jpg" alt="Emperor Penguin">
    </div>
    <div class="item">
      <img src="bengal_tiger.jpg" alt="Tiger">
    </div>
    <div class="item">
      <img src="african_elephant.jpg" alt="Elephant">
    </div>
    <div class="item">
      <img src="australian_kiwi.jpg" alt="Kiwi">
    </div>
  </div>

  <!-- Left and right controls -->

  <a class="left carousel-
control" href="#myCarousel" role="button" data-slide="prev">
    <span class="glyphicon glyphicon-chevron-left" aria-
    hidden="true"></span>
    <span class="sr-only">Previous</span>
  </a>
  <a class="right carousel-
control" href="#myCarousel" role="button" data-slide="next">
    <span class="glyphicon glyphicon-chevron-right" aria-
    hidden="true"></span>
    <span class="sr-only">Next</span>
  </a>
</div>
```

Typehead

A Typehead is just another form of textbox that provides text predictions as the user types into the text box and may look something like this if programmed to type ahead the states of the US:

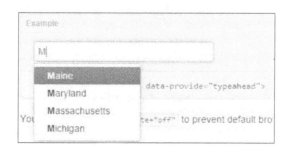

How to create typehead

The following code shows how you can create a simple typehead textbox:

```
<input type="text" data-provide="typeahead">
```

Usage of typehead via JavaScript

We can call the typehead using the following code:

```
$('.typeahead').typeahead()
```

For a complete implementation, visit `https://twitter.github.io/typeahead.js/examples/`.

Scrollspy

The **Scrollspy** plugin allows the navigation targets to automatically update themselves when the user scrolls up or down.

Scrollspy can help in identifying the section of the page you have reached while scrolling randomly and makes finding required data much easier. The Scrollspy plugin can normally be activated in two ways, which we will see now.

Activating Scrollspy via a data attribute

The data attribute allows spying on a particular element by adding `<data-spy="scroll"` to the element:

```
<body data-spy="scroll" data-target=".navbar">...</body>
```

Activating Scrollspy via JavaScript

Scrollspy can also be triggered by JavaScript by selecting the element and executing the `scrollspy()` function:

```
$('#navbar').scrollspy()
```

Affix

The **affix** plugin is used to lock an element to an area on a page.

The affix plugin can be activated using data attributes or JavaScript. Affix plugins are used to place social icons on websites, where they are locked in one place so that they can be accessed by the user any time.

Activating the affix plugin via a data attribute

Use the following method to activate the `affix` tool:

```
<div data-spy="affix" data-offset-top="200">...</div>
```

Activating the affix plugin via JavaScript

We can also activate the `affix` tool via JavaScript manually using the following code:

```
$('#navbar').affix()
```

Customizing Bootstrap

Since Bootstrap is a very heavy project, including all its repositories is not actually required, and even if you do, this could put enormous load on your website, making it sluggish and affecting user experience. To get the Bootstrap engine suited to your specific needs, go to `http://getbootstrap.com/customize/` and import a style file with the settings you need. You can also import your existing settings file on the preceding link, add or remove options within the GUI, and get an updated version without writing a single line of code.

Websites built with Bootstrap

WordPress is out there, and a lot of big websites and companies are using it. Twitter's website itself is made with Bootstrap. Take a look at some famous websites built with the Bootstrap framework:

* `https://www.engineyard.com/`

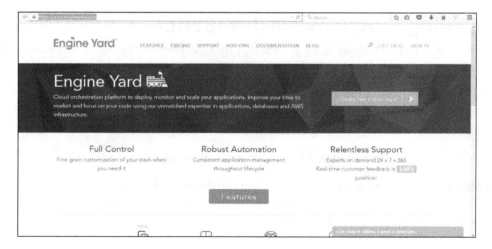

- `http://www.hublot.com/en/`

- `https://www.fliplingo.com`

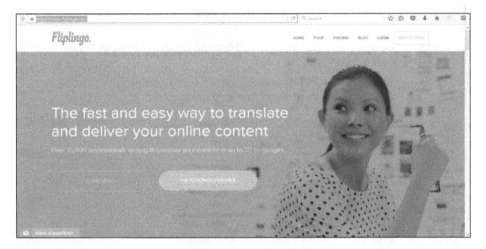

Bootstrap resources

The Internet is full of Bootstrap resources; here are a few:

- `www.wrapbootstrap.com`: You can buy or sell at **WrapBootstrap**. It is a huge marketplace for premium templates and themes.

- `www.bootswatch.com`: *Bootstrap themes* are released under the MIT license and maintained by the community on GitHub. Themes are built for the latest version of Bootstrap.

- `www.startbootstrap.com`: **Startbootstrap** is an easy way to learn and develop Bootstrap, as it contains thousands of starter themes and templates, even for Bootstrap 3.

- `www.themes.getbootstrap.com`: These are the official *Bootstrap themes* and templates from the creators of Bootstrap and include dashboards, admins, and marketing sites.

Here are a few more resources for Bootstrap, but there are many more. You can surf through these sites and gain some more knowledge about the working and intricacies of Bootstrap:

- `http://expo.getbootstrap.com/`
- `https://bootstrapbay.com/blog/built-with-bootstrap/`
- `http://builtwithbootstrap.com/`
- `http://getbootstrap.com/getting-started/#examples`

As of now, Bootstrap version 4 alpha has been launched. All the JavaScript plugins have been rewritten in ECMAScript6, Completely shifted from LESS to SASS and IE8 support has been dropped.

Here is official blog post: `http://blog.getbootstrap.com/2015/08/19/bootstrap-4-alpha/`

jQuery – The Popular JavaScript Library

jQuery is an open source JavaScript library. jQuery makes JavaScript programming much simpler.

The following are the notable corporate members of the jQuery foundation:

- **WordPress**: (http://wordpress.org/)
- **IBM**: (http://ibm.com/)
- **NeoBux**: (http://www.neobux.com/)
- **Mozilla**: (http://www.mozilla.org/)
- **Intel's Open Source Technology Center**: (http://software.intel.com/en-us/oss)
- **Adobe**: (http://adobe.com/)

You can find all about jQuery at their official website (www.jQuery.com).

The evolution of JQuery

jQuery has been evolving since day one. There are two major releases available for download. The versions 1.x and 2.x differ in a way; 1.x is more stable and supports older browsers as well; whereas, 2.x has the same API as 1.x but without the support for legacy browsers.

 A legacy browser is an older version of a browser that has not been updated to the latest available version.

If you are using jQuery for a project, you can get another version that takes fewer resources and is faster to load.

Getting started

To get started with developing jQuery, you can download jQuery software by visiting `https://jquery.com/`. In the following sections, we will cover a few download links.

Installing JQuery

We can download jQuery from `http://jquery.com/download/`.

There are two versions of jQuery available for download: compressed and uncompressed.

To choose your option, go to the preceding link and right-click on **Save as** and select **My Computer** and download it.

jQuery 1.x

We can download the minified version from `http://code.jquery.com/jquery-1.11.3.min.js`.

For development, we can download the version 1.x from `http://code.jquery.com/jquery-1.11.3.js`.

jQuery 2.x

We can download the minified version from `http://code.jquery.com/jquery-2.1.4.min.js`.

For development, we can download the version 2.x from `http://code.jquery.com/jquery-2.1.4.js`.

Using jQuery

jQuery is an extremely powerful JavaScript library. Here are a few sample pieces of code to give you a head start on your next project.

If you have downloaded the jQuery library to your hard disk and plan to use it from there, then you can include the following code in your HTML `<head>` tag:

```
<script src="js/jquery.min.js"></script>
```

Here, `js` is a folder in the root directory of your project.

 To avoid longer loading time and performance issues, scripts should be added to the end of the `<body>` tag because when the browser loads the web page (let's say, `sample1.html`) and the scripts are at the end of the body tag, the browser can render the content of the page (the body) and only start loading scripts afterward.

Another preferred approach is to use the Google hosted libraries; these provide faster rendering to your pages and jQuery code than using your own hosted jQuery libraries. You can use the Google developer hosted libraries with the following piece of code:

```
<script src="https://ajax.googleapis.com/ajax/libs/
jquery/2.1.3/jquery.min.js">
</script>
```

The jQuery syntax is used to perform any specific action on elements of HTML.

The basic syntax is as follows:

```
$(selector).action()
```

Here is the description:

- `$`: `$` is used to access the jQuery object.
- `(selector)`: The `query (or find)` HTML elements using familiar CSS-style selector syntax. For example, you can select by element name, type, class or id.
- jQuery `action()`: For example, it can be events like click, keypress, focus and so on.

Selectors

As the name suggests, `selector` attributes are used to select various elements of HTML. The `selector` attributes basically support the CSS selectors.

Selectors begin with a `$` sign followed by parentheses: `$()`

Element selectors

Element selectors select elements using their name. For example, if a paragraph is written in the tags <p>, you can select this paragraph using its name, that is, p:

```
$("p")
```

Parameters

The name of the element to be chosen is passed as a parameter.

Returns

The element selectors returns the element.

Description

The element selectors select elements using their name. For example, if a paragraph is written in the tags <p>, you can select this paragraph using its name.

ID selectors

ID selectors select elements using their ID. Each element of the HTML can have its own identifying ID and it can be accessed using #. For example, to access the element with the ID text, we can use the following syntax:

```
$("#text")
```

Parameters

The pound sign (or number sign) or a hash sign followed by the ID name is passed as a parameter.

Returns

This returns the element using the ID passed as a parameter.

Description

This selects elements using their ID. IDs are usually used to uniquely identify DOM elements that are accessed through the pound symbol in Javascript or the hash sign.

Class selectors

Class selectors select the elements using the class name. For example, a class named sample can be accessed by the following syntax:

```
$(".sample")
```

Parameters

A dot/period followed by the name of the class is passed as a parameter.

Returns

This returns the elements using the Class name passed as parameter.

Description

This selects the elements using the class name.

Events

JQuery makes it easier to response when user interacts with the web page. For example, we can perform several tasks when they click somewhere, scroll the document, hover on field or anything like that. Whenever user interacts with the web page, an event is occurred. We can use event handling to execute our code.

Mouse events

These are the events that are instantiated as soon as the user activates any of the functions related to the mouse. In the following sections, we will cover the description of each mouse event.

.click()

The click event takes a DOM object and calls the function if or when it is clicked by the user.

Parameters

The click event receives a callback function.

Returns

This returns the response generated by the function called on click.

Description

The click event uses the ID to get what the user has clicked on and accordingly calls its respective function defined inside the body.

Here is an example of its usage.

HTML Code:

```
<div id="clicked">
   //function to be called after clicked
</div>
```

jQuery Code:

```
$( "#clicked" ).click(function() {
  alert( "Function for .click() called." );
});
```

.dblclick()

We can attach a handler to the double-click event of an HTML element using the .dblclick() jQuery method.

Parameters

The dbclick event receives a callback function.

Returns

This returns the response generated by the function called on **double click**.

Description

The dblclick event uses the ID to get what the user had double clicked on and accordingly calls its respective function.

Here is an example of its usage.

HTML Code:

```
<div id="clicked">
   // function to be called after clicked
</div>
```

jQuery Code:

```
$( "#clicked" ).dblclick(function() {
  alert( "Function for .dblclick() called." );
});
```

.hover()

The `hover` event uses the ID to get what the user had his mouse on and accordingly calls its respective function.

Parameters

The `hover` event receives a callback function.

Returns

This returns the response generated by the function called **on hover**.

Description

The `hover` event uses the ID to get what the user had his mouse on and accordingly calls its respective function.

Here is an example of its usage.

HTML Code:

```
<ul>
  <li>Lahore</li>
  <li>Karachi</li>
  <li>Peshawar</li>
  <li>Sialkot</li>
</ul>
```

jQuery Code:

```
$( "li" ).hover(
  function() {
    $( this ).append( $( "<span> (*)</span>" ) ); // "this" is
    used to access the current object itself
  }, function() {
    $( this ).find( "span:first" ).remove();
  }
);
```

.mousedown()

The `.mousedown` event is activated when the user left-clicks on the mouse and highlights a specific text.

Parameters

The `.mousedown()` function which gets executed when the element is clicked.

Returns

This returns the response generated by the function called **on click**.

Description

The event is activated when the user left-clicks and highlights some specific text.

Here is an example of its usage.

HTML Code:

```
<div id="myTarget">
  Click here
</div>
```

jQuery Code:

```
$( "#myTarget" ).mousedown(function() {
  alert( "Function for .mousedown() called." );
});
```

.mouseenter()

The event is activated when the mouse is hovered over the selected text and a function is called accordingly.

Parameters

The `mouseenter` event receives a callback function.

Returns

This returns the response generated by the function called **on mouse enter**.

Description

This event is activated when the mouse is hovered over the selected text and a function is called accordingly. The event related to the `mouseenter()` is fired only once, so it does not matter if you hold the cursor over an element, the function assigned through this function is executed only once.

Here is an example of its usage.

HTML Code:

```
<div id="external">
   External
   <div id="internal">
     Internal
   </div>
</div>
<div id="myLog"></div>
```

jQuery Code:

```
$( "#external" ).mouseenter(function() {
   $( "#myLog" ).append( "<p>Function for .mouseenter()
   called.</p>" );
});
```

.mouseleave()

The `.mouseleave` event is activated when the cursor is moved away from the HTML element.

Parameters

The `mouseleave` event receives a callback function.

Returns

This returns the response generated by the function called **on clicked**.

Description

The event is activated when the mouse is left. The function is called accordingly.

Here is an example of its usage.

HTML Code:

```
<div id="external">
  External
  <div id="internal">
    Internal
  </div>
</div>
<div id="myLog"></div>
```

jQuery Code:

```
$( "#external" ).mouseleave(function() {
  $( "#myLog" ).append( "<p> Function for .mouseleave()
  called.</p>" );
});
```

.mousemove()

The .mousemove event is triggered when the mouse is being moved within an element.

Parameters

The mousemove event receives a callback function.

Returns

This returns the response generated by the function called on mouse move.

Description

This event is triggered when the mouse is being moved within an element.

Here is an example of its usage.

HTML Code:

```
<div id="myTarget">
  Move here
</div>
<div id="other">
  Trigger the Function
</div>
<div id="myLog"></div>
```

jQuery Code:

```
$( "#myTarget" ).mousemove(function( event ) {
   // the event keyword identifies the mousemove event in the case
   of this example
   var msg = "Function for .mousemove() called at ";
   msg += event.pageX + ", " + event.pageY;
   $( "#myLog" ).append( "<div>" + msg + "</div>" );
});
```

.mouseout()

The `.mouseout` event is triggered when the mouse pointer leaves the boundaries of the element. Any HTML element can be bound to this event.

Parameters

The `mouseout` event receives a callback function.

Returns

This returns the response generated by the function called when the mouse moves out of the targeted element.

Description

The `mouseout` event is triggered when the mouse pointer leaves the element.

Here is an example of its usage.

Required HTML Code:

```
<div id="external">
   External
   <div id="internal">
     Internal
   </div>
</div>
<div id="other">
   Trigger the Function
</div>
<div id="myLog"></div>
```

Required jQuery Code:

```
$( "#external" ).mouseout(function() {
  $( "#myLog" ).append( "<p>Function for .mouseout() called.</p>"
  );
});
```

.toggle()

This .toggle() function is used to bind multiple handlers to matching elements that are executed on alternate clicks.

Parameters

The parameters of the toggle() function are duration, easing, and callback.

The duration parameter is optional and is used to specify the speed of the hide and show effect. The possible values are fast, slow, and milliseconds. The default is 400 ms.

The easing parameter is optional and is used to specify the easing() function that is to be used for animation. The default value is string.

The callback parameter too is optional and is used to specify the function that is to be called once the animation is complete.

Returns

This returns the output of the function that is called.

Description

This function is used to check the visibility of an element and then alternate between the hide() and show() methods. The callback is always fired once the animation is complete and only once for the element that finds a match.

Here is an example of its usage.

Required HTML Code:

```
<ul>
  <li>Mercury</li>
  <li>Venus</li>
  <li>Earth</li>
  <li>Mars</li>
</ul>
```

Required jQuery Code:

```
$(document).ready(function() {
  $("ul").click(function() {
    $("li").toggle("slow", function() {
    });
  });
});
```

Keyboard events

The keyboard events are triggered on Keyboard functions, for example, when a button/key is pressed or released, and so on. Keyboard events can be controlled with the following built-in jQuery functions. The available functions are KeyDown, KeyPress, and KeyUp.

The only practical difference between KeyDown and KeyPress is that KeyPress relays the character resulting from a KeyPress event and is only called if there is one.

For example, if you press *A* on your keyboard, you'll get this sequence of events:

- KeyDown: KeyCode=Keys.A, KeyData=Keys.A, Modifiers=Keys.None
- KeyPress: KeyChar='a'
- KeyUp: KeyCode=Keys.A

.keydown()

The keydown event is instantiated when a key is pressed by the user.

Parameters

The keydown event sends the key pressed as a parameter.

Returns

This returns the output of the function that is called when a key is pushed down.

Description

The keydown event is instantiated when the user presses a key, which calls the function to be executed.

Here is an example of its usage.

Required HTML Code:

```
<form>
  <input id="myTarget" type="text" value="KeyPress">
</form>
```

Required jQuery Code:

```
$( "#myTarget" ).keydown(function() {
  alert( "Function for .keydown() called." );
});
```

The preceding sample code selects the div element with the myTarget ID and triggers the alert function when a key is pressed down.

.keypress()

The keypress event is instantiated when a key is pressed by the user.

Parameters

This sends the key pressed as parameter.

Returns

This returns the output of the function called by the key press.

Description

The keypress event is instantiated when the user presses a key, which calls the function to be executed.

Here is an example of its usage.

Required HTML Code:

```
<form>
  <fieldset>
    <input id="myTarget" type="text" value="Tomato">
  </fieldset>
</form>
```

Required jQuery Code:

```
$( "#myTarget" ).keypress(function() {
  console.myLog( "Function for .keypress() called." );
});
```

The preceding sample code selects the `div` element with the `myTarget` ID and triggers the alert function when a key is pressed.

.keyup()

The `keyup` event occurs when the key that is pressed is released by the user.

Parameters

This sends the key pressed as a parameter.

Returns

This returns the output of the function that is called when key is released.

Description

The event occurs when the key pressed is released by the user.

Here is an example of its usage.

Required HTML Code:

```
<form>
  <input id="myTarget" type="text" value="Hello there">
</form>
```

Required jQuery Code:

```
$( "#myTarget" ).keyup(function() {
  alert( "Function for .keyup() called." );
});
```

The preceding sample code selects the `div` with the `myTarget` ID and triggers the alert function when a key is released.

Form events

Form events are when elements inside a form are bound to jQuery. These events are helpful when it comes to processing data entered via forms. These events can be used on elements inside the `<form>` tags. We will now cover the description of each form event.

submit()

The submit event, as the name suggests, is fired when a form is submitted.

Its syntax is $(selector).submit(function).

Parameters

The parameter taken is the function that is to be run once the form is submitted.

Returns

This event does not return anything.

Description

The submit() function is a form event. It is used to bind form elements with a function that needs to be called whenever a form is submitted.

Required HTML Code:

```
<form action="">
  User ID: <input type="text" name="UsrID" value="KA112"><br>
  Password: <input type="password" name="password"
  value="Password"><br>
  <input type="submit" value="Submit">
</form>
```

Required JQuery Code:

```
$(document).ready(function() {
  $("form").submit(function() {
    alert("Form Submitted!");
  });
});
```

change()

The change event is fired whenever the value of an element in a form changes.

Its syntax is $(selector).change(function).

Parameters

The parameter taken is the function that is to be run once the value of the selected element changes.

Returns

This event does not return anything.

Description

This event is used to bind the event to a function that needs to be called whenever a value inside a form element changes. This function works only on the `<input>`, `<textarea>`, and `<select>` elements.

Required HTML Code:

```
<select name="ShadesOfGreen">
  <option value="Jade">Jade</option>
  <option value="Mint">Mint</option>
  <option value="Emerald">Emerald</option>
  <option value="Moss">Moss</option>
</select>
```

Required JQuery Code:

```
$(document).ready(function() {
  $("select").change(function() {
    alert("Option Changed");
  });
});
```

blur()

The `blur` event is fired whenever an element in a form loses its focus and the user moves to the next element in the form.

Its syntax is `$(selector).blur(function)`.

Parameters

The parameter taken is the function that is to be run once the element loses focus.

Returns

This event does not return anything.

Description

The `blur` event is used to call a function whenever an element loses its focus.

Required HTML Code:

```
User ID: <input type="text">
Gender: <select name="Gender">
  <option value="Male">Male</option>
  <option value="Female">Female</option>
</select>
```

Required JQuery Code:

```
$(document).ready(function() {
  $("input").blur(function() {
    alert("User ID lost foucs");
  });
});
```

focus()

The `focus` event is fired whenever an element in a form gets its focus.

Its syntax is `$(selector).focus(function)`.

Parameters

The parameter taken is the function that is to be run once the element is in focus.

Returns

This event does not return anything.

Description

The `focus` event is used to call a function whenever an element is in focus. An element is generally *in focus* when we select it with the mouse or use the *Tab* key to navigate to it. This event is triggered only when the specified element is in focus and not the element's children.

The focus event is generally used with the `blur` event.

Required HTML Code:

```
User ID: <input type="text" name="UsrID"><br>
Email ID: <input type="text" name="emailID">
```

Required JQuery Code:

```
$(document).ready(function() {
  $("input").focus(function() {
    $(this).css("background-color", "#cccccc");
  });
  $("input").blur(function() {
    $(this).css("background-color", "#ffffff");
  });
});
```

focusin()

This event is fired whenever an element or its child is in focus.

Its syntax is `$(selector).focusin(function)`.

Parameters

The parameter taken is the function that is to be run once the element is in focus.

Returns

This event does not return anything.

Description

The `focusin` event is used to call a function whenever an element is in focus. This event is also called whenever a child element is in focus.

Required HTML Code:

```
<div>
  Name: <input type="text" name="fullname"><br>
  Email: <input type="text" name="email">
</div>
```

Required JQuery Code:

```
$(document).ready(function() {
  $("div").focusin(function() {
    $(this).css("background-color", "#cccccc");
  });
});
```

focusout()

The `focusout` event is fired whenever an element or its child is out of focus.

Its syntax is $(selector).focusout(function).

Parameters

The parameter taken is the function that is to be run once the element is in focus.

Returns

This event does not return anything.

Description

This event is fired whenever an element or its child loses its focus. This event is generally used along with the `focusin` event.

Required HTML Code:

```
<div>
  Name: <input type="text" name="fullname"><br>
  Email: <input type="text" name="email">
</div>
```

Required JQuery Code:

```
$(document).ready(function() {
  $("div").focusin(function() {
    $(this).css("background-color", "#cccccc");
  });
  $("div").focusout(function() {
    $(this).css("background-color", "#ffffff");
  });
});
```

Document events

Document events are generally fired whenever a document is loaded. In the following sections, we will cover the description of each document event.

resize()

The `resize` event is fired whenever the user resizes the window. Its syntax is as follows:

```
$(selector).resize(function)
```

Parameters

The parameter taken is the function that is to be run once the window is resized.

Returns

This event does not return anything.

Description

The `resize` event is used to call a function when the user resizes the window.

Required HTML Code:

```
<p></p>
```

Required JQuery Code:

```
$(document).ready(function() {
  $(window).resize(function() {
    $("p").text("Window resized!!");
  });
});
```

scroll()

The `scroll` event is fired whenever the user scrolls in the (scrollable) element. We can use this event to bind it to a function. Its syntax is as follows:

```
$(selector).scroll(function)
```

Parameters

The parameter taken is the function that is to be run once the user scrolls on the element.

Returns

This event does not return anything.

Description

The `scroll` event is fired whenever the user scrolls in an element.

Required HTML Code:

```
<div style="border:1px solid
   black;width:200px;height:100px;overflow:scroll;">Lorem ipsum
   dolor sit amet, consectetur adipiscing elit. Curabitur vehicula
   ultrices nulla vel facilisis. Curabitur elementum lorem non
   massa porttitor accumsan. Cras eu leo tincidunt, pulvinar neque
   et, tempus dolor. Nam condimentum nisl vel quam posuere, vitae
   malesuada nunc molestie. Aliquam pulvinar diam eu magna sagittis
   efficitur. Vestibulum tempor, leo accumsan maximus hendrerit, ex
   nisi rutrum sapien, nec ultricies tellus nisl ac lacus.
   Phasellus sed ligula augue.
</div>

<p></p>
```

Required JQuery Code:

```
$(document).ready(function() {
   $("div").scroll(function() {
      $("p").text( "Text Scrolled!");
   });
});
```

Effects and animations

Custom animations and effects can be added to various elements to enhance your interface using varying designs and colors.

animate()

The `animate()` function uses some built-in animations to animate objects in and off the view.

Its syntax is as follows:

```
(selector).animate({styles},speed,easing,callback)
```

Parameters

The animate function accepts the parameters `duration`, `easing`, and `callback`.

The `duration` parameter is optional and is used to specify the speed of the hide and show effect. Its possible values are fast, slow, and milliseconds. The default is 400ms.

The `easing` parameter is optional and is used to specify the easing function that is to be used for the animation. The default is `string`.

The `callback` parameter too is optional and is used to specify the function that is to be called once the animation is complete.

Returns

Animations return the modified object containing all the modifications.

Description

Custom animations and effects can be added to various elements to enhance your interface using varying designs and colors.

stop()

The `stop()` method stops the animation of the selected element.

Its syntax is `$(selector).stop(stopAll,goToEnd);`

Parameters

This takes two Booleans, which are both set to false by default, as parameters.

Returns

This does not return anything.

Description

This function stops running the animation as soon as it is called. If the first parameter is set to `true`, this removes all the other animations for the element. If the second parameter is set to `true`, it quickly finishes the current animation.

Here is an example of its usage.

Required HTML Code:

```
<div id="sample">
  <img id="sample" src="myImage.png" alt="" width="1" height="2">
</div>
```

Required jQuery Code:

```
$( "#sample" ).hover(function() {
  $( this ).find( "img" ).stop( true, true ).fadeOut();
}, function() {
  $( this ).find( "img" ).stop( true, true ).fadeIn();
});
```

The preceding sample code creates a nice fade effect without the common problem of multiple queued animations.

Hide, show, and toggle

Elements can be set to hide and show, where hide makes the elements disappear from the eye of the user and show does the opposite.

hide()

The `hide()` function, if applied on an HTML element, hides it from view. This can be used in generating dynamic content based on user activity. The following is its syntax:

```
$(selector).hide(speed,callback);
```

Parameters

This takes speed in milliseconds and the callback function as parameters. The values taken as parameters are as follows:

- `Fast`
- `Slow`
- `Time` in milliseconds

Returns

This does not return anything.

Description

This function is equivalent to setting the CSS property `display: none` for the selected element. It also saves the original display property for future use.

Here is an example of its usage.

Required HTML Code:

```
<div id="sample">
</div>
<img id="myImage" src="myImage.jpeg" alt="" width="1" height="2">
```

Required jQuery Code:

```
$( "#sample" ).click(function() {
  $( "#myImage" ).hide( "slow", function() {
    alert( "Animation complete." );
  });
});
```

show()

The `show()` function, if applied on an HTML element, makes the hidden element visible. This can be used to control and manipulate dynamic content based on user activity, for example, making certain form options visible after a certain checkbox is selected. The following is its syntax:

```
$(selector).show(speed,callback);
```

Parameters

This takes speed in milliseconds and the callback function as parameters. The values taken as parameters are as follows:

- `Fast`
- `Slow`
- `Time` in milliseconds

Returns

This does not return anything.

Description

This function removes the `display:none` property from the element and reverts it to the original. For example, if an element has a property `display:inline-block` and was hidden using the hide function, it will set the display back to inline-block.

Here is an example of its usage.

Required HTML Code:

```
<div id="sample">
</div>
<img id="myImage" src="myImage.jpeg" alt="" width="1" height="2">
```

Required jQuery Code:

```
$( "#sample" ).click(function() {
  $( "#myImage" ).Show( "slow", function() {
    alert( "Animation complete." );
  });
});
```

toggle()

The `toggle()` function, if applied on an HTML element, toggles with the visibility of that element:

```
$(selector).toggle(speed,callback);
```

Parameters

This takes the speed in milliseconds and the callback function as parameters. The values taken are as follows:

- `Fast`
- `Slow`
- `Time` in milliseconds

Returns

This does not return anything.

Description

This function is used to toggle with the visibility of the elements.

This function should not be confused with the mouse event function `toggle()`, which was explained previously. To ensure which `toggle()` function is being used. Check the parameters passed to the function.

Here is an example of its usage.

Required HTML Code:

```
<div id="sample">
</div>
<img id="myImage" src="myImage.jpeg" alt="" width="1" height="2">
```

Required jQuery Code:

```
$( "#sample" ).click(function() {
  $( "#myImage" ).Show( "slow", function() {
    alert( "Animation complete." );
  });
});
```

Fade

Fade can be used to set the visibility of elements.

fadeIn()

The `fadeIn()` function is similar to the `show()` function in functionality, but `fadeIn()` comes with a nice fading transition effect.

Its syntax is `$(selector).fadeIn(speed,callback);`.

Parameters

This takes speed in milliseconds and the callback function as parameters. The values taken as parameters are as follows:

* `Fast`
* `Slow`
* `Time` in milliseconds

Returns

This does not return anything.

Description

This works in a similar way to the show() function but with a fade transition.

Here is an example of its usage.

Required HTML Code:

```
<div id="sample">
  Click here
</div>
<img id="myImage" src="myImage.png" alt="" width="1" height="2">
```

Required jQuery Code:

```
$( "#sample" ).click(function() {
  $( "#myImage" ).fadeIn( "slow", function() {
    // Animation complete
  });
});
```

The preceding sample code selects the div element with the sample ID and fades in the image with the myImage ID with slow animation.

fadeOut()

The fadeOut() function is similar to the hide() function in functionality, but it comes with a nice fading transition effect.

Its syntax is as follows: $(selector).fadeOut(speed,callback);

Parameters

This takes speed in milliseconds and the callback function as parameters. The values taken as parameters are as follows:

- Fast
- Slow
- Time in milliseconds

Returns

This does not return anything.

Description

The `fadeOut()` function works in a similar way to the `hide()` function but with a fade transition.

Here is an example of its usage.

Required HTML Code:

```
<div id="sample">
  Click here
</div>
<img id="myImage" src="myImage.png" alt="" width="1" height="2">
```

Required jQuery Code:

```
$( "#sample" ).click(function() {
  $( "#myImage" ).fadeOut( "fast", function() {
    // Animation complete
  });
});
```

fadeToggle()

The `fadeToggle()` function automatically toggles an element's display property from `none` to `block`, `inline`, and so on.

Here is an example of its syntax:

```
$(selector).fadeToggle(speed,callback);
```

Parameters

This takes speed in milliseconds and the callback function as parameters. The values taken as parameters are as follows:

- `Fast`
- `Slow`
- `Time` in milliseconds

Returns

This does not return anything.

Description

If an element is already hidden, `fadeToggle()` will make it visible and vice versa.

Here is an example of its usage.

Required HTML Code:

```
<div id="sample">
  Click here
</div>
<img id="myImage" src="myImage.png" alt="" width="1" height="2">
```

Required jQuery Code:

```
$( "#sample" ).click(function() {
  $( "#myImage" ).fadeToggle( 2000, function() {
    // Animation complete
  });
});
```

fadeTo()

The `fadeTo()` function adjusts the opacity of the target element to the given value.

Its syntax is as follows:

```
$(selector).fadeTo( duration, opacity [, complete ] )
$(selector).fadeTo( duration, opacity [, easing ] [, complete ] )
```

Parameters

This takes duration in milliseconds as parameters. The values taken as parameters are as follows:

- `Fast`
- `Slow`
- `Time` in milliseconds

The other parameter is opacity for the target element. The value lies between `0` and `1` and the final parameter is the callback function.

Returns

This does not return anything.

Description

The `fadeTo()` function is similar to the `fadeIn()` method. But the user can specify the target opacity here. For example, set an element to 50% opacity by pacing 0.5 as the opacity.

Required HTML Code:

```
<div id="sample">
  Click here
</div>
<img id="myImage" src="myImage.png" alt="" width="1" height="2">
```

Required jQuery Code:

```
$( "#sample" ).click(function() {
  $( "#myImage" ).fadeTo( "Fast", 0.5, function() {
    // Animation complete
  });
});
```

Sliding

Sliding methods are used to slide the elements in up or down directions. The `slideDown()` function will make element visible, while the `slideUp()` function will hide the contents of the element.

slideDown()

The `slideDown()` function slides down the selected element with the specified speed.

Here is an example of its syntax:

```
$(selector).slideDown(speed,callback);
```

Parameters

This this takes speed in milliseconds and the callback function as parameters. The values taken as parameters are as follows:

- `Fast`
- `Slow`
- `Time` in milliseconds

Returns

This does not return anything.

Description

The `slideDown()` function makes a hidden element visible with a nice sliding effect.

Here is an example of its usage.

Required HTML Code:

```
<div id="sample">
  Click here
</div>
<img id="myImage" src="myImage.png" alt="" width="1" height="2">
```

Required jQuery Code:

```
$( "#sample" ).click(function() {
  $( "#myImage" ).slideDown( "slow", function() {
    // Animation complete.
  });
});
```

slideUp()

The `slideUp()` function slides up (hides) the selected element with the specified speed.

Here is an example of its syntax:

```
$(selector).slideUp(speed,callback);
```

Parameters

Takes speed in milliseconds and the callback function as parameters. The values taken as parameters are as follows:

- `Fast`
- `Slow`
- `Time` in milliseconds

Returns

This does not return anything.

Description

This function hides the selected element with a nice sliding effect in the upward direction.

Here is an example of its usage.

Required HTML Code:

```
<div id="sample">
  Click here
</div>
<img id="myImage" src="myImage.png" alt="" width="1" height="2">
```

Required jQuery Code:

```
$( "#sample" ).click(function() {
  $( "#myImage" ).slideUp( "fast", function() {
    // Animation complete.
  });
});
```

slideToggle()

The `slideToggle()` function toggles between `slideUp()` and `slideDown()` for the selected element with the specified speed.

Here is an example of its syntax:

```
$(selector).slideToggle(speed,callback);
```

Parameters

This takes speed in milliseconds and the callback function as parameters. The values taken as parameters are as follows:

- `Fast`
- `Slow`
- `Time` in milliseconds

Returns

This does not return anything.

Description

Just as `fadeToggle()` switches transitions between two states, `slideToggle()` can slide an element up or down.

Here is an example of its usage.

Required HTML Code:

```
<div id="sample">
  Click here
</div>
<img id="myImage" src="myImage.png" alt="" width="1" height="2">
```

Required jQuery Code:

```
$( "#sample" ).click(function() {
  $( "#myImage" ).slideToggle( "fast", function() {
    // Animation complete.
  });
});
```

Callback

Multiple lines of statements are queued rather than being executed simultaneously. A callback function queues the statements and executes them one by one.

Its syntax is as follows:

```
var callbacks = $.Callbacks();
```

The object created can be used to add, remove, instantiate, and disable callbacks. The supported functions are `callbacks.add()`, `callbacks.remove()`, `callbacks.fire()`, and `callbacks.disable()`.

callbacks.add()

This function is used to add all the functions in an array that are to be called later.

Parameters

This takes flags as strings as its parameters.

Returns

This method returns the callback's object to which it is associated with, (this).

Description

The `callbacks.add()` function adds the function to the callback array.

Here is an example of its usage.

Required jQuery Code:

```
function myFunc1( value ) {
  console.myLog( value );
}

function myFunc2( value ) {
  console.myLog( "myFunc2 says: " + value );
  return false;
}

var callbacks = $.Callbacks();
callbacks.add( myFunc1 );

// Outputs: meow!
callbacks.fire( "meow!" );

callbacks.add( myFunc2 );

// Outputs: woof!, myFunc2 says: woof!
callbacks.fire( "woof!" );
```

callbacks.fire()

The `callbacks.fire()` function invokes the callbacks in a list with any arguments that have been passed.

Parameters

This takes a list of arguments to pass back to the callback list.

Returns

This returns the callback objects onto which it is attached.

Description

The `callbacks.fire()` function is used to invoke the callbacks in a list with the arguments. The preceding example could be referenced.

callbacks.remove()

The `callbacks.remove()` function is used to remove a function from the array.

Parameters

This takes flags as strings as its parameters.

Returns

This returns the callbacks object onto which it is attached.

Description

This removes the function from the callback array. The preceding example could be referenced.

callbacks.disable()

The `callbacks.disable()` function disables the call of the next function in the array.

Parameters

This does not take any parameter.

Returns

This returns the callbacks object to which the object is attached.

Description

The execution of the next function in the array is prevented using the `callbacks.` `disable()` function:

```
var sound = function( value ) {
  console.log( value );
};

var callbacks = $.Callbacks();

// Add the above function to the list
callbacks.add( sound );

// Fire the items on the list
callbacks.fire( "Woof!" );

// Disable further calls being possible
callbacks.disable();

callbacks.fire( "Meow" );
```

Chaining

A varying amount of statements can be executed by chaining them on the same element. Each statement will be executed one after the other.

The value returned from each chained action is a new jQuery object. Chaining can be done by appending one action to the previous action; for example:

```
$("#p1").css("color", "blue").slideDown(100).slideUp(35);
```

Here, the actions `slideUp()` and `slideDown()` are performed one after the other.

jQuery and the document object model

The DOM defines a standard for accessing HTML and XML documents:

> *"The W3C Document Object Model (DOM) is a platform and language-neutral interface that allows programs and scripts to dynamically access and update the content, structure, and style of a document."*

The following are some ways of DOM manipulation in jQuery:

- `text()`: This sets or returns the text content of the selected elements
- `html()`: This sets or returns the content of the selected elements
- `val()`: This sets or returns the values of form fields

jQuery traversing

You can traverse through the elements in the order they are combined. All the elements are mostly combined in the form of a tree, and we can traverse them starting from the root.

 Elements are not *combined* per se, but they are rather structured or modeled within the document object.

Let's take a look at the following image:

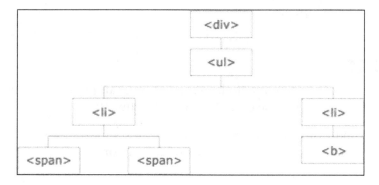

Let's take a look at the following description:

- The `<div>` element is the parent of `<ul>` and an ancestor of everything inside it
- The `<ul>` element is the parent of both the `<li>` elements and a child of `<div>`
- The left `<li>` element is the parent of `<span>`, child of `<ul>`, and a descendant of `<div>`
- The `<span>` element is a child of the left `<li>` and a descendant of `<ul>` and `<div>`
- The two `<li>` elements are siblings (they share the same parent)
- The right `<li>` element is the parent of `<b>`, child of `<ul>`, and a descendant of `<div>`
- The `<b>` element is a child of the right `<li>` and a descendant of `<ul>` and `<div>`

Ancestors

An ancestor is a parent!

We will cover three useful jQuery methods for traversing up the DOM tree in the following sections.

parent()

The `parent()` function returns the parent of selected element.

Parameters

This takes no parameter, but it is called as a function of the jQuery object.

Returns

This returns the parent of the element.

Description

This function returns the parent of the selected element:

```
$(document).ready(function() {
  $("span").parent();
});
```

parents():

The `parents():` function returns an array of parents of the selected element till root.

Parameters

This takes no parameter but is called as a function of the jQuery object.

Returns

This function returns all the parents of an element.

Description

The `parents():` function returns an array of parents of the selected element till root:

```
$(document).ready(function() {
  $("span").parents();
});
```

parentsUntil():

```
$(selector).parentsUntil(stop,filter);
```

The `parentsUntil()` method returns all ancestors between the `selector` and `stop` element.

An ancestor element is a parent, grandparent, great-grandparent, and so on.

Parameters

Stop an optional parameter that indicates where to stop the search for matching ancestor elements. Filter an optional parameter usually an expression to narrow down the search between selector and stop.

Returns

This returns all parents between the two selected elements.

Description

This function returns the parents between two selected elements:

```
$(document).ready(function() {
  $("span").parentsUntil("div");
});
```

Descendants

A child of the parent is called its descendant.

In the following sections, we will cover two useful jQuery methods for traversing down the DOM tree.

children()

The `children()` function returns the children of the selected element.

Parameters

This takes no parameters but it is called as a function of the jQuery object.

Returns

This returns an array of HTML elements that are children of the target element.

Description

This function returns the children of the selected element:

```
$(document).ready(function(){
  $("div").children();
});
```

find()

The `find()` function returns an array of children up to the child that has no children of its own, which is also called a **leaf**.

Parameters

The `find()` function takes the HTML element as parameters.

Returns

This returns all the children of the target element.

Description

This function returns an array of children up to the leaf of the tree:

```
$(document).ready(function() {
  $("div").find("span");
});
```

Siblings

Siblings are elements that share a same parent.

There are many useful jQuery methods for traversing sideways in the DOM tree, which we cover here.

siblings()

```
$(selector).siblings(filter);
```

The `siblings()` function returns all the siblings of the selected element.

Parameters

Filter is an optional parameter usually an expression to narrow down the search among all siblings.

Returns

This returns all the siblings of the element.

Description

This function returns all the siblings of the selected element using the `filter` parameter:

```
$(document).ready(function() {
  $("span").siblings("div");
});
```

next()

```
$(selector).next(filter);
```

Filter is an optional parameter usually an expression to narrow down the search for next sibling.

Parameters

This takes no parameters, but is called as a function of the jQuery object.

Returns

This returns the next siblings of the element.

Description

This function returns the next siblings of the selected element using the `filter` parameter:

```
$(document).ready(function(){
  $("span").next();
});
```

nextAll()

```
$(selector).nextAll(filter);
```

The `nextAll()` function returns an array of the next siblings of the selected element.

Parameters

Filter is an optional parameter usually an expression to narrow down the search for all next sibling.

Returns

This returns an array of all the next siblings of the target element.

Description

This function returns an array of the next siblings of the selected element using the parameter:

```
$(document).ready(function() {
  $("span").nextAll();
});
```

nextUntil()

```
$(selector).nextUntil(stop, filter);
```

The nextUntil() function returns an array of next siblings of the selected element between two specified elements.

Parameters

Stop an optional parameter that indicates where to stop the search for next matching sibling elements.

Filter an optional parameter usually an expression to narrow down the search for sibling elements between selector and stop.

Returns

This returns all the next siblings of the element.

Description

This function returns an array of next siblings of the selected element between two elements:

```
$(document).ready(function() {
  $("span").nextUntil('H4');
});
```

prev()

```
$(selector).prev(filter);
```

The prev() function returns the previous siblings of the selected element.

Parameters

Filter is an optional parameter usually an expression to narrow down the search for previous sibling.

Returns

The prev() function returns the previous siblings of the element.

Description

This function returns the previous siblings of the selected element using the filter parameter:

```
$(document).ready(function() {
  $("span").prev();
});
```

prevAll()

```
$(selector).prevAll(filter);
```

The prevAll() function returns an array of the previous siblings of the selected element.

Parameters

Filter is an optional parameter usually an expression to narrow down the search for all previous siblings.

Returns

The prevAll() function returns the array of all the previous siblings of the element.

Description

This function returns an array of the previous siblings of the selected element using the parameter:

```
$(document).ready(function() {
  $("span").prevAll();
});
```

prevUntil()

The prevUntil() function returns an array of the previous siblings of the selected element between two elements.

Parameters

This takes the element up to which the search of siblings is limited.

Returns

This returns an array of all the previous siblings of the element.

Description

This function returns an array of the previous siblings of the selected element and the parameter:

```
$(document).ready(function() {
  $("span").prevUntil("Div");
});
```

Filtering

The filtering method is used to locate a specific element based on its location.

first()

The first() function outputs the first element of the selected elements.

Parameters

The first() function takes the selected element as parameter.

Returns

This returns a jQuery object that stores a reference to the first item from an array of items matching the provided selector string.

Description

This function outputs the first element of the selected elements. The following example outputs the first H1 heading inside the <div> tag:

```
$(document).ready(function() {
  $("div H1").first();
});
```

last()

This function returns the last element of the selected elements.

Parameters

The `last()` function takes the selected element as parameter.

Returns

This returns a jQuery object that stores a reference to the last item from an array of items matching the provided selector string.

Description

This function outputs the last element of the selected elements. The following example outputs the last `H1` heading inside the `<div>` tag:

```
$(document).ready(function() {
  $("div H1").last();
});
```

eq()

The `eq()` function returns the element specified at the corresponding index number, provided that we begin the numbering from 0. Hence, the first element will have its index number as 0, the second element will have the index number 1, and so on.

Parameters

The `eq()` function takes the selected element and the index number as parameters.

Returns

This returns the element at the specified index number.

Description

This function returns the element specified at the corresponding index number. The following example returns the fifth `div` element:

```
$(document).ready(function() {
  $("div").eq(4);
});
```

filter()

The `filter()` function is used to obtain a list of elements that satisfy a particular condition. All the elements that satisfy the specified condition will be returned.

Parameters

The element to be searched and the condition that the element must satisfy are taken as parameters here.

Returns

This returns a list of elements that satisfy a specified condition.

Description

The `filter()` function is useful for searching and obtaining a list of elements that satisfy a specified condition. In the following example, we will search and obtain a list of all the `<div>` elements that have their class named as `Feedback`:

```
$(document).ready(function() {
   $("div").filter(".Feedback");
});
```

 The `not()` method is the reverse of the `filter()` method. If you want to find elements that do not satisfy the mentioned condition, `not()` can be used.

Using AJAX in jQuery

Asynchronous JavaScript and XML (AJAX) was the base building block of **Single Page Applications (SPAs)**. This method is used to update the content of a web page without reloading the whole page. This method helps save precious resources and decreases the time taken for loading a page considerably, since only parts of the page are reloaded and not the entire page.

More than often, you have visited the Google search page for searching answers to your questions. Have you noticed how the page displays results as you type into the search box and provides useful suggestions of related searches? Or the product filters on Amazon and Ebay websites. These effects are achieved with AJAX.

The jQuery Ajax load

The `load()` method loads data from a server and puts the returned data into the selected element.

Its syntax is as follows:

```
$(selector).load(URL,data,callback);
```

Parameters

The `load()` method take the URL, `data`, and `callback` as parameters.

The `callback` parameter can have the following parameters:

- `responseTxt`: This parameter contains the resulting content when successful
- `statusTxt`: This parameter contains the status of the request, that is, `success`, `notmodified`, `error`, `timeout`, `parsererror`
- `xhr`: This parameter contains the `XMLHttpRequest` object

Returns

The data from the URL is placed in the selected element.

Description

The `load()` method loads data from a server and puts the returned data into the selected element. The following example loads the `Sample.txt` file into the specified `<div>` tag:

```
$("#div1").load("Sample.txt" , function(responseTxt, statusTxt, xhr);
```

jQuery Ajax Get

The `Get` request gets the data from the server with an HTTP `GET` request:

- `GET`: This requests data from a specified resource

Its syntax is as follows:

```
$.get(URL,callback);
```

Parameters

This takes the URL and callback as parameters. Here the `callback` parameter is optional.

Returns

The `Get` request returns the data fetched from the URL.

Description

The Get request gets the data from the server with an HTTP GET request:

```
$.get("Sample.html", myfunction(data)
```

The required HTML file is as follows:

```
<p> This is the data from the Sample.html file</p>
```

The preceding code will fetch the data from the html file and the line **This is the data from the Sample.html** will be displayed in an alert box on triggering.

jQuery Ajax Post

The Post request gets data from the server with an HTTP POST request:

- POST: This requests data from a specified resource

Its syntax is as follows:

```
$.post(URL, data, callback);
```

Parameters

This takes URL, data, and callback as parameters. Here, the data and callback parameters are optional.

Returns

This returns the data fetched from the URL.

Description

This gets data from the server with an HTTP POST request:

```
$.post("Sample.html", myfunction(data)
```

The required HTML file is as follows:

```
<p> This is the data from the Sample.html file</p>
```

The preceding code will fetch the data from the HTML file and **This is the data from the Sample.html** will be displayed in an alert box when triggered.

Miscellaneous jQuery functions

Here are a few more jQuery functions.

noConflict()

Different scripts cannot work at the same time. Hence, in order to remove the conflicts, we use the `noConflict()` function.

Its syntax is as follows:

```
$.noConflict()
```

Parameters

An optional parameter for this method is `removeAll`. This parameter is used to release the control over all jQuery variables. It's a Boolean value. If present, it indicates that the control over all values must be released.

Returns

This method does not return anything.

Description

The $ symbol is used by various JavaScript libraries, which if used alongside jQuery may cause issues. The `noConflict()` function returns the control of the $ symbol to the other library.

The following code shows how one event has to wait when the other event is in process:

```
$.noConflict();
jQuery(document).ready(function() {
  jQuery("button").click(function() {
    jQuery("p").text("jQuery is still working!");
  });
});
```

param()

The `param()` method is used to create a serialized representation of an object.

Its syntax is as follows:

```
$.param(object)
```

Parameters

Object and trad are the parameters used in this function. Trad is an optional parameter and is used when a traditional param serialization is needed. This parameter is optional.

Returns

This returns a serialized representation of the object.

Description

The param() method is used to generate a serialized representation of an object or an array. This is mostly used where a query string is to be generated. The following example creates a query string for the student object:

```
$(document).ready(function() {
   StudentObj = new Object();
   StudentObj.name = "Kate";
   StudentObj.age = 21;
   StudentObj.class = "Micro-Processors";
   $("button").click(function() {
     $("div").text($.param(StudentObj));
   });
});
```

index()

The index() method is used to find out the position of an element.

Its syntax is as follows:

```
$(selector).index()
```

Parameters

The element whose position is to be found is taken as a parameter.

Returns

This method returns the index position of the first occurrence of the specified element, which is relative to the selector or specified element.

Description

The `index()` method is used to get the position of the element that is passed as a parameter. The first occurrence of that element is searched for and its position is returned. If the particular element is not found, then `-1` is returned. The position numbering begins at `0`.

The following example finds the position of the `div` element and returns its index in an alert box:

```
$(document).ready(myfunction() {
  $("div").click(myfunction() {
    alert($(this).index());
  });
});
```

each()

The `each()` function is used to run a specific function for every element that matches the criteria.

Its syntax is as follows:

```
$(selector).each(function(index,element))
```

Parameters

The only parameter this takes is the `function(index, element)`. Here the position of the selector can be specified at `index` and the element can be specified in `element`.

Returns

This method does not return anything.

Description

The `each()` function runs the specified function for each and every element that matches the criteria. In the following example, an alert is created every time the `<div>` tag is encountered:

```
$(document).ready(function() {
  $("button").click(function() {
    $("div").each(function() {
      alert($(this).text())
    });
  });
});
```

data()

The `data()` method is used to obtain data from the selected element. It is also used to submit data to the selected element.

Its syntax is as follows: `$(selector).data(name)`

Parameters

```
$(selector).data(name,value);
```

To attach data to element, parameters passed are name and value. that name is then used to retrieve the data value.

Returns

This returns data from the selected element.

Description

The `data()` function is used to attach data to or from an element. In the following example, we first attach the data to the `<div>` element:

```
$(document).ready(function() {
  $("#btnAttach").click(function() {
    $("div").data("greetingmsg", "Welcome To Alpha Zoo");
  });
  $("#btnGetAttached").click(function() {
    alert($("div").data("greetingmsg"));
  });
});
```

removeData()

The `removeData()` method is used to remove data that was previously attached to the element with the `data()` method.

Its syntax is `$(selector).removeData(name)`.

Parameters

The name of the data that is to be removed is taken as a parameter.

Returns

This does not return anything.

Description

As the name suggests, the `removeData()` method is used to remove data that was already set. The following example removes data that was set on the `<div>` tag:

```
$("#btnRemoveData").click(function() {
  $("div").removeData("greetingmsg");
  alert("Message from the site" + $("div").data("greetingmsg"));
});
```

jQuery plugins

Plugins are used to create a modular part of an application using various elements that can be used in multiple projects. Here is a simple demonstration:

```
(function( $ ) {
  $.myFunc.showLinkLocation = function() {
    this.filter( "a" ).append(function() {
      return " (" + this.href + ")";
    });
    return this;
  };
}( jQuery ));
```

 For more support on creating custom plugins, you can visit `https://learn.jquery.com/plugins/basic-plugin-creation/`.

The jQuery community is huge. Developers have made some really great jQuery plugins and extensions that you can use in your projects. All these projects are available free of cost; however, there are some paid options too. The following are some great jQuery plugins:

- **NIVO Slider**: This is one of the oldest and most popular image gallery plugins by **Dev7Studios**. It has a built-in image cropping system and comes with many themes and visual transitions.

- **nanoGALLERY**: This is another great image gallery plugin that comes with navigation, lightbox, lazy load, thumbnails, and many more goodies. It is also compatible with Bootstrap.

- **MixItUp**: This plugin will help you make AJAX filters for your portfolio and galleries with smooth animations.

- **jQuery Knob**: This is an extremely innovative jQuery plugin that makes touchable and clickable dials. Even if you are not using it in your projects, you should definitely take a look at its implementation.

- **Tubular**: This plugin lets you set a YouTube video as your web page's background.

- **Arc Text**: This plugin converts your text into arc shapes. You can use your mouse to push and pull the text to shape them in arcs.

jQuery resources

If you are hungry for more jQuery goodies, head over to this great website called **jQuery Rain** at www.jqueryrain.com. They have over 3500 jQuery plugins and tutorials with working demonstrations and sample codes.

15
AngularJS – Google's In-Demand Framework

Angular is an application framework that helps you create web applications. It builds off of HTML and JavaScript to make the creation of dynamic applications easier. Angular extends and is a superset of JavaScript at the same time. You can use plain old JavaScript and Angular to build your application.

This creates a double-edged sword. On the positive side, it is much easier to build dynamic user interfaces and keep your code maintainable and testable. On the other side, you must learn the overall concept of how an Angular application is built, which Angular piece goes where. This is very different to any other JavaScript application you may have built.

If all you have ever built is user interfaces with **jQuery**, **BackBone**, or plain old JavaScript, then much of Angular will seem new and different.

We will try to cover Angular in a hierarchical way. We will start at the top with containers that hold other parts and objects and end functions that can be used across many objects. We will also touch upon testing, as it is a core part of how Angular is built.

Let's not waste any more time and jump right to it.

All of the examples assume that you have loaded Angular so that the `angular` object is available.

 If you are unsure on how to load Angular, visit the official Angular page at `https://angularjs.org/`.

Modules (ngApp)

This is the high-level container for all the other parts of your application. There are more functions than those listed here, but they will be described in the section they relate to. For example, you can use `module.controller` to create a controller, but this function will be under the controller section.

module

Modules are the first basic building block of an Angular application:

```
angular.module(moduleName, [dependencies], [configFunction])
angular.module(moduleName)
```

Parameters

- `moduleName`: This is a string that will identify the module. It should be unique.

- `dependencies (optional)`: This is an array of module names that this module is dependent on.

- `configFunction (optional)`: This is a function that will configure the module. See *config* section.

Return value

This is an Angular module object.

Description

This function will either create a new module or retrieve a module. This depends on whether we pass in an array of dependencies. If dependencies are omitted, then a module is retrieved. Conversely, if we include an array of modules to load (the array can also be empty), then a module will be created.

When you have a group of objects that work together, it is a good idea to put them into a module. Do not worry about creating too many modules. A module should have one and only one clear function. Then, all the objects that it needs to accomplish that function would be packaged with it.

Here are a few examples of creating modules:

- This creates a new module: var firstModule = angular. module('firstModule', []);

- This retrieves a module named firstModule: var firstModule = angular.module('firstModule');

- This creates a module that relies on firstModule: var secondModule = angular.module('secondModule', ['firstModule']);

config

This allows you to configure providers:

```
module.config(configFunction)
```

Parameters

- The configFunction function is the function that will be executed.

Return value

This is an Angular module object.

Description

This is the function that should be used to configure providers. We will cover providers later in this chapter, but there are a few examples in this section. This allows for providers to be created before the module actually executes.

The providers will be injected into this function when called. For example, you can use $provide or $routeProvider and they will be available. If you want to use a custom provider, it would have to be created before config. The custom object will need provider appended to the name for it to be available in config.

Here are a couple of examples using providers:

- This example uses $provide. The provider will be available later as firstProvider:

```
firstModule.config(function ($provide) {
  $provide.provider('firstProvider', function () {
    this.$get = function () {
      return function () { alert('First!'); }
    }
  });
});
```

- This example creates a provider first. It is injected as `firstProvider` in `config` and used later:

```
firstModule.provider('first', function () {
  this.$get = function () {
    return function () { alert('First!'); }
  }
});
firstModule.config(function (firstProvider) {
  console.log(firstProvider);
});
```

run

This function is executed after config:

```
module.run(runFunction)
```

Parameters

- The `runFunction` function is the function that will be executed.

Return value

This is an Angular module object.

Description

The `run()` function gets executed after `config`. At this point, all modules will be loaded. It is the first function called after the module is initialized after `config`. What you do in this function will depend on the module.

Here is an example that sets a scope variable. The variable will be available in the module in later functions:

```
firstModule.run(function ($rootScope) {
  $rootScope.test = 'test';
});
```

Routing (ngRoute)

The `ngRoute` module is a module that will allow you to configure routing in your application. Routing is listening for changes to the location and then automatically responding to those changes with a new controller and template. It uses `ngView`, `$routeProvider`, and `$route`.

 Your module will need to depend on `ngRoute` to use these directives and services. We will also need to include the Angular route JavaScript in our HTML.

ngView

This works with the `$route` service as a spot for content:

```
<ng-view [onload=''] [autoscroll='']/>
<element ng-view [onload=''] [autoscroll='']/>
```

Parameters

- `onload(Angular expression)`: This evaluates on load.

- `autoscroll(Angular expression)`: Whether or not `$anchorScroll` is used with this `ngView`. By default, it is disabled. Otherwise, it will evaluate whether the expression is true or not.

Return value

This is a directive.

Description

When routing, you will need to mark a part of your application where dynamic content can be loaded. This is what `ngView` does. When a route is matched, it will load the new content where `ngView` is. An example will be provided for all of `ngRoute` at the end of the section.

$routeProvider

This is a provider that lets you configure routes:

```
$routeProvider.when(path, route)
$routeProvider.otherwise(route)
```

Parameters

- path(string): This is what the location will be matched against. It can contain named groups by using a colon (:group), can include a star to match multiple parts (:group*), and can be optional (:group?).

- route(object): This object tells Angular what to do when the route matches. The object can have these properties (not an inclusive list):

  - controller
  - template
  - templateUrl
  - resolve

Return value

This returns $routeProvider, so it is chainable.

Description

This is the provider that can be used to configure all of the routes. It can be injected into module.config.

$route

This is the actual service that provides which route definition has been matched. This is an object that can be injected directly into a controller.

Properties

- current(object): This object has the current variables based on the route that was matched. This will include $route, loadedTemplateUrl, locals, params, and scope.

- routes(object): This has all the routes configured.

Events

These events can be listened for the $route object:

- $routeChangeStart: This event is fired before the actual route change

- $routeChangeSuccess: This event is fired after a route has been resolved

- $routeChangeError: This event is fired if any of the route promises are rejected

Description

This is a service that can be injected into each controller. The controller can then look at the properties to get information about the route that was matched. The routing matching will happen without your intervention and then you can update your controller's scope when the route is loaded.

$routeParams

This is a service that will return the parameters of the loaded route. This will only give you parameters after a route has resolved, so you may need to use `$route.current.params`. This can be injected into a controller.

Here is an example using all of the directives and services in ngRoute. First, we have an HTML body tag. This will also include an inline template named `main.html`. This template will echo out the `$route` and `$routeParams` objects:

```
<body ng-app="firstModule">
  <div ng-view></div>
  <a href="#/main/1">Main</a>

  <script type="text/ng-template" id="main.html">
    <pre>$routeParams = {{$routeParams}}</pre>
    <pre>$route = {{$route}}</pre>
  </script>

</body>
```

Here is the script that will execute this. First is the creation of the module, then the configuration of `$routeProvider` and, finally, the definition of a controller for the provider to use:

```
var firstModule = angular.module('firstModule', ['ngRoute']);

firstModule.config(function ($routeProvider) {
  $routeProvider.when('/main/:id', {
    controller: 'MainController',
    templateUrl: 'main.html'
  });
});

firstModule.controller('MainController', function ($scope, $route,
$routeParams) {
  $scope.$route = $route;
  $scope.$routeParams = $routeParams;
});
```

Dependency injection

Angular makes use of dependency injection everywhere. Dependency injection is when a function does not initialize the dependencies it needs. Instead, they are injected into the function as parameters. For example, when a module needs a route provider, it asks for one. The module does not care how or when the route provider was created; it just wants a reference.

You actually use the injector in everything you do in Angular. Angular just does it for you. We will look at $injector and understand how it works but, most likely, you will not need to use these functions.

Dependency injection in Angular

We will quickly cover the common ways that objects are injected into functions in Angular. Using a controller as an example, we will cover the two most common methods. Both of these are using Angular's injection behind the scenes:

- **Defining the variables in a function**: You just have to pass the name of the object you need injected. Here is an example that uses $scope and a service:

```
firstModule.controller('DIController', function ($scope,
customService) {
  //$scope and customService are available here
  console.log($scope);
  console.log(customService);
});
```

- **Using an array to list the dependencies**: You can get the exact same result using an array. The elements of the array will be the objects you need as strings. Finally, you will just need to have a function as the last element in the array. The function can even rename the variable if needed. Here is the same example in the array format:

```
firstModule.controller('DIController', ['$scope',
'customService', function (newScope, custom) {
  // newScope and custom are available here
  console.log(newScope);
  console.log(custom);
}]);
```

 Only the array format is minification safe. The first function will not work once the source has been minified.

injector

Use this to get an Angular injector that you can invoke:

```
angular.injector(modules)
```

Parameters

- The `modules(array)` array is a list of the modules you want to load. You must include `ng`.

Return value

This returns an injector object. See `$injector` section.

Description

You can create this object to use Angular's injector object. List out the references you want and then invoke your function.

Here is an example that gets a reference to the `$http` service:

```
var injector = angular.injector(['ng']);
var injectTest = function ($http) { console.log($http); };
injector.invoke(injectTest);
```

$injector

You will very rarely ever need to create an injector in Angular. It will be provided for you. You can get a reference to the injector by injecting it or retrieving it from a current module. Here are examples for both:

- You can get a reference from any element inside of the module:

  ```
  var injector = angular.element(document.body).injector();
  ```

- You can have it injected into a function. Here is an example using `config`:

  ```
  firstModule.config(function ($routeProvider, $injector) {
    console.log($injector);
  });
  ```

Methods

- `annotation`: This returns an array of the objects that will be injected
- `get(name)`: This returns the service with its name
- `invoke(function)`: This will execute the function injecting the dependencies
- `has(name)`: This allows you to determine whether a service exists

Description

Angular will do this automatically for you, but it is always good to have an idea of what is happening. This is especially true with something that works just like `$injector`. Each time a function executes with dependencies, Angular will invoke the function from the injector, sending the correct parameters if they have been created and registered.

Controllers

Controllers are one of the core units of any Angular application. Controllers are used to create a small part of a module that requires its own scope. Each module can have many controllers. Controllers should be small and focused on one task.

Each controller should really only worry about the data and any events that modify that data. This means a controller should not modify the DOM, change output or input, or share state with another controller. Each of these should use the Angular solution, directives or filters, and services, respectively.

Controllers are created from a module reference, so they are tied to modules. Here is an example of creating a simple controller:

```
firstModule.controller('SimpleController', ['$scope', function
($scope) {
  $scope.hey = "HEY!";
  console.log($scope);
}]);
```

This module can then be attached to a DOM element with `ngController`:

```
<div ng-controller="SimpleController">
  {{ hey }}
</div>
```

ngController

This is a core part of how Angular maps to the model-view-controller pattern.

```
<element ng-controller />
```

Parameters

- The ng-controller(expression) attribute is a string that will tell Angular which controller is tied to this element.

Description

A controller needs a part of the document to attach. This directive will bind the controller, with its scope, to this element.

If a controller has been defined in a route, then you should not add this directive to the page. The router will take care of binding to the correct element.

Here is an example of using ngcontroller to create an alias for the controller:

```
<div ng-controller="SimpleController as simple">
  {{ simple.hey }}
</div>
```

$scope

This is the most important part of a controller. This is the where you should place everything you are tracking for this controller. This includes any functions that modify the scope.

The $scope controller is injected into the controller by declaring a dependency to it (see dependency injection). There are built-in functions and properties (see Scopes), but because it is just a JavaScript object, you can add your own functions and properties. These will map directly to the template in the controller.

Here is an example of a controller that defines one property, hey, and a function, changeHey. It is important to note that there are no references to DOM references at all in this function:

```
firstModule.controller('SimpleController', ['$scope', function
($scope) {
  $scope.hey = "HEY!";
  $scope.changeHey = function () {
    $scope.hey = $scope.hey === 'HEY!' ? 'OK!' : 'HEY!';
  };
}]);
```

Here is the template with all the data binding in the HTML document:

```
<div ng-controller="SimpleController">
  {{ hey }}
  <input type="text" ng-model="hey"/>
  <button ng-click="changeHey()">{{hey}}</button>
</div>
```

Angular will know what `hey` is in this element because it is scoped to just `SimpleController`.

Data binding and templates

A controller uses HTML as its templating language. You can bind a value from the controller's scope just by surrounding it in double brackets (`{{ }}`). That is really all there is to it!

For some elements such as `input`, `select`, and `textarea`, you cannot just add the value of a `scope` object to bind them. You will have to use the `ngModel` directive.

The `$scope` section has a great example of binding scope values to the template.

Event binding

Angular uses directives to bind events. In the `$scope` section, the example uses `ngClick` to listen for the click event on a button.

See the *Directives*, *Event Binding* section for a list of the most used event directives.

Scope

The `$scope` object that gets injected into controllers has some functionality. In addition to this, we will look at the hierarchies and digest cycle of scopes.

Digest cycle

This is an important concept to understand with scopes. The digest cycle, from a high level, is a cycle that checks to see whether any scope variables have been changed. If they have, it then executes a function. Take binding a scope variable to the template with `{{variable}}`. The digest cycle will now watch this variable and, anytime it changes, it will update the template. If the variable is bound anywhere else, it will be updated as well. This is how Angular "magically" makes values auto update.

A few things to keep in mind is that not everything in the scope is watched. The easiest way to have it watched is to bind it. You can also manually watch values. Also, remember that performance issues can arise when you are watching many variables. The digest cycle goes through all the watchers.

$digest

This is how you can start the digest cycle:

```
scope.$digest()
```

Description

This will manually kick off the digest cycle for the scope. In most cases, this does not need to be called. For example, `$digest` does not need to be called after updating a value from a click event when handled through Angular. Angular will start the digest cycle for you. A good rule of thumb is that if you are changing or updating a value from an Angular event or directive in a controller, you would not need to call `$digest`.

One case where you may need to call it is when dealing with an asynchronous call in a custom directive.

$watch

This allows you to watch a value or computed value in the digest cycle:

```
scope.$watch(watch, listener)
```

Parameters

- `watch(string or function)`: This is what you want to watch. A string will be evaluated as an expression. The function will have access to the scope through the first parameter. Using a function allows you to watch not only for values, but also calculated values of variables in the scope.

- `listener(function)`: This function will have the `function(newVal, oldVal, scope)` signature. This is the function that will execute when the value changes.

Return value

This is a function to deregister the watch.

Description

This is how to manually add a watch to the digest cycle. There are two main reasons to do this. The first is that you will need to run a custom function when a value changes. The other is that you will need to watch a combination or calculation of a value in $scope.

Here is an example that has a watch for a string and a function. The basis of the example is from *Controllers, $scope* sections. The first watch listens for the hey variable in the scope. The other one watches to see whether the value of hey has three or more characters. It will only fire when this threshold has been crossed and not fire again until it is crossed in the opposite direction:

```
$scope.$watch('hey', function (newVal, oldVal, scope) {
  alert('Hey was changed from ' + oldVal + ' to ' + newVal);
});

$scope.$watch(function (scope) {
  return scope.hey.length >= 3;
}, function (newVal, oldVal, scope) {
  console.log('Hey listener');
});
```

$apply

This is a way to manually start the digest cycle:

```
scope.$apply(func)
```

Parameters

* The func(function or string) attribute is a string, it would be evaluated as an expression. If it is a function, the function would be executed.

Return value

This is the return value of the function or expression.

Description

This will manually kick off the digest cycle. Much like $digest, this should not be called for the most part, except for specific situations. The most common situation is when a scope value has been changed outside of Angular, for example, an asynchronous AJAX call that has a reference to a scope value. The update happens outside of the digest loop and Angular does not know as it did not use any Angular methods.

This leads to a best practice to always use Angular's services and functions. If you do so, you should never have to run $apply.

Another best practice is to run your function inside $apply. Angular will catch any errors that are thrown and you can deal with them the Angular way.

Here is an example that updates the scope inside setTimeout after 2 seconds. As the digest loop has finished, it will not see this change unless $apply is called:

```
setTimeout(function () {
  $scope.$apply(function () { $scope.hey = 'Updated from
  setTimeout'; });
}, 2000);
```

Hierarchies

Angular applications only have one root scope but many child scopes. When a variable is referenced, it will check the current scope it is in and then check the parent. This will happen all the way up to the root scope. This is very similar to how JavaScript objects work with the prototype property. You can find more about this in *Chapter 8, JavaScript Object-orientated Programming*.

Services

The role services play in an Angular application is clear, but there can be confusion around the creation of services. This is because there are three very similar ways to create a service in Angular. We will look at each of these and why they should be used.

A service in Angular is an object that can be an authority on data (meaning it is the only source of some data). A great example is the route provider as it is the only object that provides route information. It is a singleton that all modules utilize, a way to keep data in sync between controllers, or all of these! A great example of a service that you will most likely need is $http. It makes AJAX requests for you. You can build a service that returns data from your API and you do not have to worry about creating AJAX calls in each and every controller.

Another example is the `$route` and `$routeParams` services. When you have a reference to the `$route` service, you can always find out what route has been matched. The `$routeParams` service will let you know the parameters.

Services should be used anytime you have the need to write the same code more than once. You can pull it out and put it into a service. In addition to this, services should be created for any data that will be used by more than one controller. The controller can then ask the service for the data. This will keep this data the same across multiple controllers.

All of the functions listed can be called from the module or off the `$provide` injectable object.

Factory, service, and provider will all rely on an HTML template of this:

```
<div ng-controller="SimpleController">
  {{ service }}
</div>
```

Factory

This is the method to create factories:

```
module.factory(name, getFunction)
```

Parameters

- `name(string)`: This is the name that the service will be known by. This can be used for dependency injection.
- `getFunction(function or array)`: This is the function that will return the service. This can also be an array that lists the dependencies.

Return value

This is an Angular module object.

Description

The service factory is great when you need a singleton. No configuration other than what is done in the `factory()` function is done. The object will be the same each time it is injected.

Here is a simple example that will return the name of the service. The example also creates a dependency on $http:

```
firstModule.factory('firstFactory', ['$http', function ($http) {
  var serviceName = 'firstFactory';
  return {
    getName: function(){return serviceName;}
  };
}]);
```

Service

Services can be initialized with new keyword:

```
module.service(name, constructor)
```

Parameters

- name(string): This is the name of the service
- constructor(function or array): This will be the function that is called as the constructor

Return value

This is an Angular module object.

Description

The key distinction between a service and a factory is that it can be initialized with new. Here is an example that depends on $http:

```
firstModule.service('firstService', ['$http', function ($http) {
  return function (name) {
    var serviceName = name;

    this.getName = function () {
      return serviceName;
    };
  };
}]);
```

Here is the controller that will initialize the service:

```
firstModule.controller('SimpleController', ['$scope',
'firstService', function ($scope, firstService) {
  var first = new firstService('First Service Name');
  var second = new firstService('Second Service Name');
  $scope.service = second.getName();
}]);
```

Provider

The function that provides the most control of the setup of a provider:

```
module.provider(name, provider)
```

Parameters

- name(string): This is the name of the provider
- provider(function or array)

Return value

This is an Angular module object.

Description

This is the final and most complex way to build a service. It must return an object with a $get method. You should use this when you must have this object ready for configuration. This is the only provider that can be injected during the configuration phase of application startup. The word "provider" will be appended to the name of this. For example, if you named your provider my, it will be injected using myProvider. Here is an example provider that has its name injected during configuration. First up is the provider definition:

```
firstModule.provider('first', function () {
  var serviceName;

  return {
    configSet: function (name) {
      serviceName = name;
    },
    $get: function () {
      return {
```

```
        getName: function () { return serviceName; }
      };
    }
  }
});
```

Next is the configuration. Notice how it is injected using `firstProvider`:

```
firstModule.config(['firstProvider', function (firstProvider) {
  firstProvider.configSet('firstProvider123');
}]);
```

Finally, here is the controller:

```
firstModule.controller('SimpleController', ['$scope', 'first',
function ($scope, firstProvider) {
  $scope.test = firstProvider.getName();
}]);
```

Value

This sets a value in the module:

```
module.value(name, value)
```

Parameters

- `name(string)`: This is the name of the value
- `value(object)`: This can be anything

Return value

This is an Angular module object.

Description

A value is something that is set and then can be injected later. Values can only be injected into a controller or service, not during configuration.

Here is a simple example of value:

```
firstModule.value('appTitle', 'First App');
```

Constant

This creates a constant variable in a module:

```
module.constant(name, value)
```

Parameters

*   `name(string)`: This is the name of the value
*   `value(object)`: This can be anything

Return value

This is an Angular module object.

Description

This is very similar to value, except that this can be used in the `config` function and that the value cannot be decorated.

Here is a simple example of constant:

```
firstModule.constant('appTitle', 'First App');
```

$http

This is the service used to make HTTP calls:

```
$http(config)
```

Parameters

*   `config(object)`: This object has the following properties:
    *   `method(string)`: This is the HTTP method.
    *   `url(string)`: This is the URL.
    *   `params(string or object)`: This is the params for the request. An object will be mapped key to value for this.
    *   `data(string or object)`: This is the data to be sent in the request.
    *   `headers(object)`: This sets the headers for the request.
    *   `xsrfHeadername(string)`: This is the name of the header for XSRF.
    *   `xsrfCookieName(string)`: This is the name of the cookie for XSRF.

    °   `cache(Boolean)`: This is used to decide whether to cache data or not.

    °   `responseType(string)`: This is used to decide what the request type will be.

Return value

A promise will be returned.

Description

If you are familiar with jQuery's AJAX function, then you are familiar with this. This is Angular's way of making any `XMLHttpRequests`. For most things, you will use one of the convenience methods that make using `$http` easier.

Convenience methods

You can use all of the HTTP methods as functions: `GET`, `POST`, `HEAD`, `PUT`, `DELETE`, and `PATCH`. We will just look at `GET`, `POST`, and `JSONP` closely.

 `GET`, `POST`, and `JSONP` will cover most, if not all, of many people's needs for `$http`. If this does not, view the `$http` documentation at `https://docs.angularjs.org/api/ng/service/$http`.

Each function will take the URL as the first parameter and a `config` object, which is the same `config` object that `$http()` gets.

GET

This is a `GET` request:

```
$http.get(url, config)
```

Description

This executes a simple `GET` request. Here is an example of a factory that uses `$http.get`:

Here is the factory:

```
firstModule.factory('httpService', ['$http', function ($http) {
  return {
    test: function () { return $http.get('test', {params:
    'test'}); }
  }
}]);
```

This returns a promise that the controller can then use:

```
firstModule.controller('SimpleController', ['$scope',
'httpService', function ($scope, httpService) {
  httpService.test().success(function (data, status) {
    console.log(data);
  })
  .error(function (data, status) { console.log('An error
  occured');}); });
}]);
```

POST

This is a POST request:

```
$http.post(url, config)
```

Description

This will make a POST request. Here is a factory that makes a POST and an example that uses localhost. Remember that you must be running a server that responds to POST requests for this to work:

```
firstModule.factory('httpService', ['$http', function ($http) {
  return {
    test: function () { return $http.post('http://localhost/post',
    { data: 'HEY' }); }
  }
}]);
```

jsonp

When you have to make a cross origin request, you should use JSONP. This will allow you to use the data instead of the request being blocked based on security.

Notable services

I will list out some useful services that can be injected, with a short blurb about each:

- `$anchorScroll`: This parameter allows you to scroll to the element in the hash
- `$animate`: This parameter allows DOM manipulations
- `$cacheFactory`: This allows caching
- `$http`: See `$http`
- `$interval`: This uses Angular's way to call `setInterval`
- `$location`: This gets the information about `window.location`
- `$rootScope`: This returns the root scope for the application
- `$route`: See `Routing`
- `$q`: This allows promises to be added in our project
- `$timeout`: This uses Angular's way to call `setTimout`

This is not a comprehensive list as Angular has many services and can create and include more. These are the ones that you will most likely use in your applications.

Promises

In JavaScript, many actions are asynchronous. A great example of this is an AJAX request. When the request is sent, you do not know when or even if a request will be returned. This is where promises come in.

A promise is an object that will promise to run a function once an asynchronous event has happened. In our example, the event will be the request returning. This could be in a few milliseconds or longer, depending on the timeout setting.

In addition to tracking successful events, promises can be rejected. This allows the object that was waiting for the response to do something different.

 Visit `https://promisesaplus.com/` for the complete specification for using promises in JavaScript. Promises or promise-like objects are applicable in almost any JavaScript that you may write.

$q

This is the service that implements promises:

```
$q.defer()
```

Return value

This returns a deferred object.

Description

This is the core of building and using promises. The first thing is to get a deferred object, which will have to resolve and reject functions. When the action is successful, call the `resolve` function; when it fails, call `reject`. Finally, return the promise with `defer.promise`.

With the promise, you can call `then`, which takes two functions. The first will be called when `resolve` is called, and the second will be called when `reject` is called. The promise can be passed around and have `then` called multiple times.

Anytime you are doing anything asynchronous, you should use promises. With Angular, you should use $q as it is tied in with rootscope.

Here is an example where a function will succeed when the number is even and fail when the number is odd. Then, it is executed twice, logging to the console, whether it succeeded or failed. Note that the function is created in the controller, but a utility function like this should be put a service into production:

```
firstModule.controller('SimpleController', ['$scope', '$q',
function ($scope, $q) {
  function qTest(number) {
    console.log($q);
    var defer = $q.defer();

    if (number % 2 === 0) {
      defer.resolve(number);
    } else {
      defer.reject(number);
    }
    return defer.promise;
  };
```

```
qTest(2)
  .then(function (n) { console.log('succeeded!'); }, function
  (n) { console.log('failed!'); });

qTest(3)
  .then(function (n) { console.log('succeeded!'); }, function
  (n) { console.log('failed!'); });

}]);
```

Expressions

Expressions are a feature of Angular. They are a subset of JavaScript commands in addition to some Angular function. Expressions are used in many places in Angular. For example, anytime you bind data, you can use an expression. This makes understanding expressions important.

An expression will be evaluated to a value, to a true statement, to a function in scope, or to a variable in scope. This makes them powerful, but they do have some limitations.

Expressions in JavaScript

You can use some JavaScript, but not all JavaScript in an expression. Here are some of the things that you can and cannot do in JavaScript using expressions:

- You can use a string, number, Boolean, array literal, or object literal
- You can use any operators, for example, `a + b`, `a && b`, or `a || b`
- You can access properties on an object or look up values in an array
- You can make function calls
- You cannot use flow control statements in an expression, for example, an `if` statement

Context

When an expression is evaluated in Angular, it will use the scope that it is in. This means that you can use any object or function that is accessible in the scope. One difference is that you will not get access to the global `window`. For example, you will not be able to use `window.alert` in an expression.

Directives

Directives are what Angular uses to connect to the **Document Object Model (DOM)**. This allows Angular to separate the concerns of what each part of the application should do. This means that a controller should never touch the DOM. A controller should only work through directives to change the DOM.

Normalization

When using directives, Angular must parse the DOM and figure out what directives apply to it. This is done by normalizing all the elements and tags. Normalization will remove any ";" "," "-", or" _". It will also remove x- and `data-` from the beginning of any attributes. For example, when looking for `ngModel`, all of the following will match:

- `x-ng:model`
- `data-ng_model`
- `ng-model`
- `ng:model`

 If you are concerned with HTML 5 validation, then you should use the `data-` normalization.

Scope

Scopes inside directives can become very confusing. We will look at a few examples of the different ways to use scope.

First up is just inheriting the scope. This means that the directive will use whatever value the variable has in the controller's scope. In this example, `test` will have to be set in the controller's scope:

```
firstModule.directive('firstTest', function () {
  return {
    template: 'This is the test directive. Test: {{test}}'
  };
});
```

@ binding

The next scope modification will be to isolate the scope. You can set the scope property of the returned Directive Definition Object (see the next section). What you use here will change how the scope is built. An @ symbol will read in the value as a one-way bind into the scope. An = symbol will create a two-way bind. Each of these can have the name of the attribute used after them.

For example, to bind one way to the attribute scope-test, use: `@scopeTest`. Here is an example that does that:

```
firstModule.directive('firstTest', function () {
  return {
    restrict: 'AE',
    scope: {
      test: '@scopeTest'
    },
    template: 'This is the test directive. Test: {{test}}'
  };
});
```

This can be used like this:

```
<div first-test scope-test="Scope Test Value"></div>
```

= binding

Here is the example using =. The controller will need to have a variable in scope to pass to the directive. Here is the directive:

```
firstModule.directive('firstTest', function () {
  return {
    restrict: 'AE',
    scope: {
      test: '='
    },
    template: 'This is the test directive. Test: {{test}}'
  };
});
```

The directive is then used like this:

```
<div first-test test="fromControllerScope"></div>
```

Notice that the attribute used to connect the scope was called `test`. This is because we only used =, instead of =nameOfVariable.

& binding

This is the final way is to pass a function in. This is done with &. When creating a directive with isolated scope, you run into a problem with letting the controller know when to take an action. For example, when a button is clicked, the & binding allows the controller to pass in the reference to a function and have the directive execute it.

Here is an example directive:

```
firstModule.directive('firstTest', function () {
  return {
    restrict: 'AE',
    scope: {
      testAction: '&'
    },
    template: '<button ng-click="testAction()">Action!</button>'
  };
});
```

The template now has a button that will call testAction when clicked. The testAction parameter that will execute is passed in from the controller and lives in the directive's scope.

Here is the DOM of this directive:

```
<div first-test test-action="functionFromController()"></div>
```

Another situation comes up where you will need to pass information from the directive to the controller, for example, the event object or a variable from the scope. Here is an example that shows how Angular makes the $event object available in functions.

Here is the directive:

```
firstModule.directive('firstTest', function () {
  return {
    restrict: 'AE',
    scope: {
      testAction: '&'
    },
    template: '<button>Action!</button>',
    link: function ($scope, element) {
      element.on('click', function (e) {
        $scope.$apply(function () {
```

```
        $scope.testAction({ $e: e, $fromDirective: 'From
        Directive' });
      });
    });
  }
};
});
```

The key is the `link` property. This runs after compilation of the directive and is bound to the instance of the directive. This is important if you have a repeating directive. Next you listen for click using a jQuery-like API called JQLite. From here, we must call `$apply` because we are outside of Angular and it will not pick up any changes made here. Finally, we executed the expression that was passed in creating two variables, `$e` and `$fromDirective`, that will be available in the function in the controller.

Here is what the directive will look like in the DOM:

```
<div first-test test-action="functionFromController($e,
$fromDirective)"></div>
```

The two variables, `$e` and `$fromDirective`, need to be called the same thing as you defined in the directive.

Modifying DOM

Angular makes very clear separation of concerns. This helps prevent hard-to-trace bugs from appearing. One of the separations is that controllers should not modify the DOM. Where does one modify the DOM then? In directives.

Directives are the only piece of your Angular application that should have any knowledge of what elements are in the DOM. When a DOM modification needs to be made, it should be the directive that does it.

Angular includes a jQuery-like library called jQLite. It has many of jQuery's DOM manipulation functions. If you know jQuery, you already know jQLite.

Here is a simple example of a directive that adds a `div` element when a button is clicked. The example uses jQLite's `append` function:

```
firstModule.directive('firstTest', function () {
  return {
    restrict: 'AE',
    scope: {
      testAction: '&'
    },
```

```
      template: '<button>Add a DIV!</button>',
      link: function ($scope, element) {
        element.on('click', function (e) {
          element.append('<div>I was added!</div>');
        });
      }
    };
  });
```

Event binding

In an Angular application, only directives should be listening for DOM events, for example, the click event. This makes it very clear where the handlers reside.

Here is an example that binds to the click event of the element and logs to the console:

```
firstModule.directive('firstTest', function () {
  return {
    restrict: 'AE',
    scope: {
      testAction: '&'
    },
    template: '<button>Add a DIV!</button>',
    link: function ($scope, element) {
      element.on('click', function (e) {
        console.log(e);
      });
    }
  };
});
```

Additionally, directives can let a controller pass in a function and execute it when an event happens (see = binding). Finally, the directive can even pass parameters into the controller from the directive. A great example is the event object that is returned from the event (see & binding).

Directive definition object

The directive definition object is the object that tells Angular how to build a directive.

Here are the most used properties and a quick overview of what they do:

- `priority`: A directive with a higher priority will be compiled first. This defaults to `0`.

- `scope`: See *Directives, Scope* section for a much more in depth overview.

- `controller`: This can be confusing, but controller is used to share logic between directives. Another directive can share the code in the controller by using require and listing the name of the required directive. That directive's controller will be injected into the `link` function. The function will have the following definition: `function($scope, $element, $attrs, $transclude)`.

- `require`: A string of the directive that is required. Prepending `?` will make this optional, `^` will search the element and parents throwing an error if not found, and `?^` will search the element and parents, but is optional. The function instance will be shared across directives.

- `restrict`: This will restrict the ways you can define the directive in the DOM. Here are the options, with `E` and `A` being the most commonly used ones:
    - E: This stands for element
    - A: This stands for attribute and default
    - C: This stands for class
    - M: This stands for comment

- `template`: HTML as a string or a function that returns a string that has the definition of `function(element, attrs)`.

- `templateUrl`: Loads the template from this URL.

- `link`: This is where any DOM manipulations or listeners are put. This function will have this definition: `function(scope, element, attrs, requiredController, transcludeFunction)`. If another directive is required, then its `controller` property would be the `requiredController` parameter.

Controller vs link

When to use the `controller` or `link` function can be very confusing when building directives. You should view the `controller` function as the interface that another directive can use. When a directive is required by another directive, the controller return value is injected into the `link` function. This will be the fourth parameter. The object is then accessible from `link`. The `link` function is used for any DOM manipulations or listeners.

Key directives

Here are some of the most often used directives.

ngApp

This is the root of your Angular application:

```
<element ng-app></element>
```

Parameters

- The `ng-app (string)` attribute is the name of the default module.

Description

This will set the root element of the application. This can be put on any element, including the root HTML element.

This will automatically bootstrap Angular loading the module that is defined in `ng-app`.

ngModel

This binds data from the scope to elements:

```
<input ng-model [ng-required ng-minlength ng-maxlength ng-pattern
ng-change ng-trim]></input>
```

Parameters

- `ng-model (string)`: This will be a variable in the scope
- `ng-required (boolean)`: This sets this input as required
- `ng-minlength (int)`: This sets the minimum length
- `ng-maxlength (int)`: This sets the maximum length

- `ng-pattern(string)`: This is the regular expression that the value must match

- `ng-change(expression)`: This is the Angular expression that will execute on value change

- `ng-trim(boolean)`: This decides whether or not to trim the value

Description

This is used to bind variables in the controller's scope to input elements (text, select, or textarea). This will be a two-way binding, so any changes in the variable will update all occurrences of it.

Here is a simple example with text input:

```
<input ng-model="test" type="text"/>
  {{test}}
```

ngDisabled

This can disable an element:

```
<input ng-disabled></input>
```

Parameters

- If the `ng-disabled(expression)` attribute evaluates to true, the input will be disabled.

Description

This allows you to disable an input easily through code. The expression can bind to a scope variable or just evaluate what is in the expression.

Here is a simple example that disables a text input:

```
<input ng-disabled="true" type="text"/>
```

ngChecked

This can make an element checked:

```
<input ng-checked></input>
```

Parameters

- The ng-checked(expression) attribute is the Angular expression that should evaluate to a JavaScript Boolean value.

Description

This is the Angular way to check or uncheck a checkbox based on something in the controller.

Here is an example:

```
<input ng-checked="true" type="checkbox"/>
```

ngClass

This sets the class of an element:

```
<element ng-class></element>
```

Parameters

- The ng-class(expression) attribute can be a string, array, or an object map.

Description

When the expression is a string or array, then the value of the string or the values of the array will be applied as classes to the element. These can be tied to variables in the scope, of course.

Here is an example of using a string to set the class. Here is the style that will be applied:

```
.double { font-size: 2em; }
```

Here is the code to apply it:

```
<div ng-class="classString">Text</div>
<input type="text" ng-model="classString" />
```

The class is tied to the value of the classString variable. The input is bound so that any change will update the class on div. Once you type in double, it will apply the style.

Here is an example using an object map. The object's property name is the class that will be applied and the value must be `true`. Here is a similar example utilizing the same class:

```
<div ng-class="{double: classString}">Text</div>
<input type="text" ng-model="classString" />
```

You will notice that once you type anything into the input, the class will be applied. This is because a non-blank string will be `true`. You can use this to apply as many classes as needed using more properties.

ngClassOdd and ngClassEvent

These set the class of an odd or even element, respectively:

```
<element ng-class-odd></element>
<element ng-class-even></element>
```

Parameters

- The `ng-class-odd` or `ng-class-even (expression)` attributes must evaluate to a string or an array of strings that will become the class(es) for the element.

Description

These two directives are related and can even be applied to the same element. If a repeated element is odd, then `ng-class-odd` will evaluate and the same is true for `ng-class-even`.

Here is an example that will make every odd element twice the size and every even element half the size. Here are the styles:

```
.odd { font-size: 2em; }
.even { font-size: .5em; }
```

Here are the elements. The `ul` attribute creates the data to be repeated, and each `span` parameter statically sets the class to either odd or even. You can use variables in scope as well:

```
<ul ng-init="numbers=[1,2,3,4]">
  <li ng-repeat="number in numbers">
  <span ng-class-even="'even'" ng-class-
  odd="'odd'">{{number}}</span>
  </li>
</ul>
```

ngRepeat

This is a template that can be repeated:

```
<element ng-repeat></element>
```

Parameters

- The ng-repeat(repeat_expression) attribute is similar to an expression, but it has a few syntax differences. Go to the description for the full explanation.

Description

Many times you will have data that has a similar template, but changes for each row of data. This is where ng-repeat comes in. The ng-repeat function will repeat the HTML that you have for each item in the repeat expression.

The repeat expression is an expression that tells ng-repeat what items are going to be looped over. Here is a rundown of some expressions:

- item in collection: This is the classic foreach statement. It will loop over each item in a collection (an array, for example). The item parameter will be available inside the template.

- (key, value) in collection: If your data is in an object and you want to be able to associate the name of the property to the value, then you will need to do use this.

- item in collection track by grouping: This allows for grouping. The grouping will only give you one item for each unique value of grouping.

- repeat expression | filter: You can filter any of these expressions to give you a subset of the data.

Here is an example using an unordered list. Here is the controller:

```
firstModule.controller('SimpleController', ['$scope', function
($scope) {
  $scope.items = [{id: 1, name: 'First' }, {id: 2, name:
  'Second'}];
}]);
```

Here is the HTML for the controller:

```
<div ng-controller="SimpleController">
  <ul>
    <li ng-repeat="item in items track by item.id">
      ID: {{item.id}}
      Name: {{item.name}}
    </li>
  </ul>
</div>
```

ngShow and ngHide

These can show or hide elements, respectively:

```
<element ng-show></element>
<element ng-hide></element>
```

Parameters

- The ng-show or ng-hide(expression) attributes will be evaluated to true or false, and the element will either by shown or hidden.

Description

These directives allow you to show or hide content based on the data in the scope.

Here is an example that uses a counter to show or hide elements. You can use ng-hide and use the opposite logic. Here is the controller:

```
firstModule.controller('SimpleController', ['$scope', function
($scope) {
  $scope.count = 0;
  $scope.increase = function () { $scope.count++; };
}]);
```

Next is the HTML:

```
<div ng-controller="SimpleController">
  <div ng-show="count == 0">Count is zero: {{count}}</div>
  <div ng-show="count > 0">Count is greater than zero:
  {{count}}</div>
  <button ng-click="increase()">Increase Count</button>
</div>
```

ngSwitch

This creates a switch statement:

```
<element ng-switch>
<element ng-switch-when></element>
<element ng-switch-default></element>
</element>
```

Parameters

- `ng-switch(expression)`: This is an expression that returns a value. This value will be used when evaluating `ng-switch-when`.

- `ng-switch-when(expression)`: When the value matches this expression, then this element will be visible.

- `ng-switch-default`: This element will show when `ng-switch-when` does not match.

Description

This directive works much like the JavaScript `switch` statement. Different cases are tested against, and the one that matches is used. If none of the cases match, then a default element is used.

Here is an example that jumps between even and odd. Here is the controller:

```
firstModule.controller('SimpleController', ['$scope', function
($scope) {
  $scope.count = 0;
  $scope.increase = function () { $scope.count++; };
}]);
```

Then comes the HTML:

```
<div ng-controller="SimpleController">
  <div ng-switch="count % 2">
    <div ng-switch-when="0">Count is Even: {{count}}</div>
    <div ng-switch-when="1">Count is Odd: {{count}}</div>
  </div>
  <button ng-click="increase()">Increase Count</button>
</div>
```

ngClick

This is used to define the click handler:

```
<element ng-click></element>
```

Parameters

- The ng-click(expression) attribute is what will be evaluated when the element is clicked. A function can be used, and the event object is available using the function($event) function definition. Any other variables in scope can be passed as well, for example, $indexin a repeater.

Description

This directive allows you to run JavaScript on the click of an element. Usually, this is used with a function that is in the scope.

Here is an example that will increment a scope variable. First, here are the controller's scope variables:

```
$scope.counter = 0;
$scope.functionFromController = function (e) { $scope.counter++;
};
```

Next, this is the element with the ng-click directive. In this example, you do not use the event object, but it demonstrates how to get it to the controller function:

```
<button ng-click="functionFromController($event)">Click
Me!</button>
{{counter}}
```

ngDblclick

This is used to define the double-click handler:

```
<element ng-dblclick></element>
```

Parameters

- The ng-dblclick(expression) function, a function can be used and the event object is available using the function($event) function definition. Any other variables in scope can be passed as well, for example, $index in a repeater.

Description

This directive is very similar to `ngClick`. When the element is double-clicked, the expression will be evaluated.

This is an example of a div that will increment a counter when double-clicked. Here are the controller's variables:

```
$scope.counter = 0;
$scope.functionFromController = function (e) { $scope.counter++;
};
```

Here is the element and directive:

```
<div ng-dblclick="functionFromController($event)">Double Click
Me!</div>
{{counter}}
```

ngMousedown, ngMouseup, ngMouseover, ngMouseenter, and ngMouseleave

These are used to define the mouse event handlers:

```
<element ng-mousedown></element>
<element ng-mouseup></element>
<element ng-mouseover></element>
<element ng-mouseenter></element>
<element ng-mouseleave></element>
```

Parameters

- In the `ng-mouse*(expression)` function, a statement or function can be used, and the event object is available using the `function($event)` function definition. Any other variables in the scope can be passed as well, for example, `$index` in a repeater.

Description

These are grouped together as they are all related. When the mouse takes the action (down, up, over, enter, or leave), the expression will be evaluated.

This example is a little crazy, but it demonstrates how to use these events. Here is the relevant portion of the controller:

```
$scope.counter = 0;
$scope.functionFromController = function (e) { $scope.counter++;
};
```

Here are the directives:

```
<div ng-mousedown="functionFromController($event)" ng-
mouseup="functionFromController($event)"
  ng-mouseenter="functionFromController($event)" ng-
  mouseleave="functionFromController($event)"
  ng-mouseover="functionFromController($event)">Mouse Over
  Me!</div>
{{counter}}
```

ngMousemove

This is used to define the mouse move handler:

```
<element ng-mousemove</element>
```

Parameters

- In the ng-mousemove(expression) function, a statement or function can be used, and the event object is available using the function($event) function definition. Any other variables in the scope can be passed as well, for example, $index in a repeater.

Description

This fires when the mouse moves. Unless the directive is on the entire page, the event will be limited to only the element it is applied to.

Here is an example that will display the mouse's *x* and *y* coordinates. Here are the relevant scope variables:

```
$scope.x = 0;
$scope.y = 0;
$scope.functionFromController = function (e) {
  $scope.x = e.pageX;
  $scope.y = e.pageY;
};
```

Then comes the directive:

```
<div ng-mousemove="functionFromController($event)">Move the mouse
to see the x and y coordinates!</div>
{{x}}
{{y}}
```

ngKeydown, ngKeyup, and ngKeypress

These are used to define the key press handlers:

```
<element ng-keydown></element>
<element ng-keyup></element>
<element ng-keypress></element>
```

Parameters

- In the ng-key* (expression) function, a statement or function can be used, and the event object is available using the function ($event) function definition. Any other variables in the scope can be passed as well, for example, $index in a repeater.

Description

These will fire when the key is pressed or released.

Here is an example that will retrieve the key code from the key that was pressed down. Here are the relevant scope variables:

```
$scope.keyCode = 0;
$scope.functionFromController = function (e) {
  $scope.keyCode = e.keyCode;
};
```

Next comes the directive:

```
<input type="text" ng-keydown="functionFromController($event)"/>
Which key: {{keyCode}}
```

ngSubmit

These are used to define the submit handler:

```
<form ng-submit></form>
```

Parameters

- In the ng-submit (expression) function, a statement or function can be used, and the event object is available using the function ($event) function definition. Any other variables in the scope can be passed as well, for example, $index in a repeater.

Description

This directive is used to capture the `submit` event of a form. If the form does not have an action attribute, then this will prevent the form from reloading the current page.

Here is a simple example that logs the event object to console on `submit`. Here is the directive:

```
<form ng-submit="functionFromController($event)"><input
type="submit" id="submit" value="Submit" /></form>
```

Next comes the controller code:

```
$scope.functionFromController = function (e) {
  console.log(e);
};
```

ngFocus and ngBlur

These are used to define the focus and blur handlers, respectively:

```
<input, select, textarea, a, window ng-focus></input>
<input, select, textarea, a, window ng-blurs></input>
```

Parameters

- In the `ng-focus(expression)` function, a statement or function can be used, and the event object is available using the `function($event)` function definition. Any other variables in the scope can be passed as well, for example, `$index` in a repeater.

Description

The `ngFocus` handler will fire when the element gains focus, and `ngBlur` will fire when it loses focus. Here is an example with a text input that logs the event to console:

```
<input type="text" ng-focus="functionFromController($event)"/>
```

Here is the controller code:

```
$scope.functionFromController = function (e) {
  console.log(e);
};
```

ngCopy, ngCut, and ngPaste

```
<element ng-copy></element>
<element ng-cut></element>
<element ng-paste></element>
```

Parameters

- ng-copy, ng-cut, or ng-paste(expression): A statement or function can be used, and the event object is available using the function($event) function definition. Any other variables in the scope can be passed as well, for example, $index in a repeater.

Description

These are the events that will be fired when text is either cut, copied, or pasted. Here is an example that uses all three:

```
<input type="text" ng-cut="functionFromController($event)" ng-copy="functionFromController($event)" ng-paste="functionFromController($event)" />
```

Here is the controller code:

```
$scope.functionFromController = function (e) {
  console.log(e);
};
```

Globals

This next group of functions can be executed from anywhere in Angular without having to inject them. They are mainly utility functions that allow you to do things easier or do things the Angular way.

Extend

This provides a way to combine two objects:

```
angular.extend(srcObject, destObject)
```

Parameters

- srcObject(object): The object that extends will copy the properties from
- Destobject(object): The object that extends will copy the properties to

Return value

This returns a reference of destObject.

Description

In JavaScript, there is no in-built way to extend an object using another object. This function does just that.

Here is a simple example that will extend one object with the other's property:

```
var first = { first: '1' };
var second = { second: '2' };
var extended = angular.extend(first, second);
//extended will be {first:'1', second:'2'}
```

noop

This is the no operation function:

```
angular.noop()
```

Parameters

- The any or none functions are used as these functions does nothing, you can pass in no parameters or as many as you want.

Return value

This will return undefined.

Description

It is useful to have a function do no operation (noop). A great example of this is when you have a function as a parameter that is optional. If it is not passed in, you can run noop instead.

This is a simple example that demonstrates the scenario explained earlier:

```
function test(doSomething) {
  var callback = cb || angular.noop;
  callback('output');
}
```

isUndefined

This checks to see whether something is undefined:

```
angular.isUndefined(object)
```

Parameters

- The `object (any type)` function can be any variable.

Return value

This returns a Boolean value.

Description

This states whether or not the variable is defined.

Copy

This makes a copy of an object:

```
angular.copy(srcObject, [destObject])
```

Parameters

- `srcObject (any type)`: This is the source object to be copied.
- `destObject (same type as srcObject)`: This is optional. If it is supplied, it would be the destination of the copy operation.

Return value

This function returns the copy of `srcObject`. If `destObject` is supplied, it would be returned.

Description

When you need to make a copy of an object instead of modifying the original object, use this function.

Bind

This binds a function to an object:

```
angular.bind(self, function, [args..])
```

Parameters

- `self(object)`: This will set `this` (the inner self-reference) in the function
- `Function(function)`: This is the function that is being bound
- `Args(any type)`: These are the arguments that will be bound to the function

Return value

This is the new bound function.

Description

This creates a new bound function that will execute in the context of self. This allows you to define a function and then execute it many times in different contexts. This is further extended by binding arguments as well.

This is a contrived example, but demonstrates the principles. First is a function that depends on the context to execute. It will add the first parameter to `this` and multiply that result:

```
function addAndMultiply(toAdd, toMultiply) {
  return (this + toAdd) * toMultiply;
}
```

Next, you will use `angular.bind` to create a new function:

```
var newFunc = angular.bind(4, addAndMultiply, 1);
```

This can be executed, and the return value will be 5 times the multiplier. In `newFunc`, `this` is 4, and `toAdd` is 1, so the inner parens will always be 5. For example this will return 10:

```
newFunc(2);
```

Forms

Forms are a core part of sending data to a server in HTML. As a result of this, Angular has some extra features that work with forms.

ngModel

Each form input will need `ngModel` defined to store the value in the scope. See *Directives, ngModel* for more information.

Here is a simple form that binds two text inputs:

```
<form name="form">
  First Name: <input type="text" name="firstname" ng-
  model="data.firstName" />
  Last Name: <input type="text" name="lastName" ng-
  model="data.lastName" />
</form>
{{data.firstName}} {{data.lastName}}
```

CSS classes

Angular will automatically add CSS classes to the form and elements that you can then target with CSS. Here is the list of CSS classes and when they are applied:

- `ng-valid`: This denotes that the form or element is valid
- `ng-invalid`: This denotes that the form or element is invalid
- `ng-pristine`: This denotes that the control has not been changed
- `ng-dirty`: This denotes that the control has been changed

Validation

Angular has features that make validation very easy. First, Angular will use any of the HTML 5 input types. These allow the browser to do some validation, but Angular will still track any errors.

Next, you can use any of the built-in validation directives of `ngModel`. The list is `required`, `pattern`, `minLength`, `maxLength`, `min`, and `max`. See *Directives, ngModel* for more info about each. When an input fails validation, the value will not be passed into the bound scope variable.

Here is an example that sets a minimum length on `firstName`:

```
<form name="form">
  First Name: <input type="text" name="firstname" ng-
  minlength="10" ng-model="data.firstName" />
  Last Name: <input type="text" name="lastName" ng-
  model="data.lastName" />
</form>
{{data.firstName}} {{data.lastName}}
```

When a form is given a `name` attribute, it is bound to the scope as that name. When inputs are given names in a form, they are bound to that form. This allows you to use other directives with these values.

Here is an example that will show an error message when the text input does not meet the minimum length of 10:

```
<form name="form">
  First Name: <input type="text" name="firstname" ng-
  minlength="10" ng-model="data.firstName" />
  <div ng-show="form.firstname.$invalid">First name must be 10
  characters!</div>
  Last Name: <input type="text" name="lastName" ng-
  model="data.lastName" />
</form>
{{data.firstName}} {{data.lastName}}
```

The validation message will only show when the field is invalid.

The form will have `$dirty`, `$invalid`, `$pristine`, and `$valid` as properties that can be used in directives or in scope. The inputs will have the same properties and additionally an `$error` object that will have each of the failed validations as a property. In the preceding example, this means that `form.firstname.$error.minLength` will return `true` when the input has failed that validation and `false` when it is valid.

Custom validators

When you need to create your own logic, you can build a custom validator. You will need to create a new directive, require `ngModel`, and pass the value through the `$parsers` object of the `ngModel` controller when it is passed into the `link` function. Then, use `$setValidity` based on whether or not the value passed validation.

Here is an example of a custom validator where you cannot have the value of the input set to `josh`:

```
firstModule.directive('notJosh', function () {
  return {
    require: 'ngModel',
    link: function (scope, element, attrs, ctrl) {
      ctrl.$parsers.unshift(function (viewValue) {
        if (viewValue.toUpperCase() === 'JOSH') {
          ctrl.$setValidity('notJosh', false);
          return undefined
        }
        else {
          ctrl.$setValidity('notJosh', true);
          return viewValue;
        }
      });
    }
  }
});
```

Testing

Testing should always be a major part of any development project. Angular has been built from the beginning to be testable. It has clear separation of concerns; for example, you do not need to build a full DOM to test a controller. Angular also uses dependency injection everywhere, which makes mocking up objects very easy.

Unit testing with Jasmine and Karma

Jasmine and **Karma** are two tools that allow you to quickly and easily test your Angular code.

Jasmine

This is the actual unit testing library that we will use. Jasmine is a behavior-driven testing framework and is really easy to write.

Karma

Karma is the test runner that will watch your files and automatically kick off your tests. It runs on Node.js, so you must have it installed. You can then install Karma with npm:

```
install karma-jasmine
```

Karma can watch your test files and rerun them whenever any of the files change. You can also debug tests in the browser if there are any issues. It is a great complement to Jasmine, and Google recommends both for testing.

ngMock

The ngMock handler is used to help mock up your application when testing. When testing, you will not want to create an entire DOM to load just one module. This is where ngMock can create a controller instance for use, and we can then test it.

Module

This allows you to load a module:

```
module(moduleName)
```

Parameters

- The moduleName(string) function take

Description

You do not have a root element to put ng-app on, so module allows us to load a module to get access to its controllers, services, and directives. You should only use this function in tests after loading ngMock.

Inject

This gets the Angular inject services:

```
inject(toBeInjected)
```

Parameters

- The toBeInjected(function) function works much like other injected functions. List out the objects to be injected, and they will be available in the function body.

Description

Use inject to get access to built-in Angular services, such as $controller and $compile, or use it to get access to a loading module's services.

Inject can load dependencies if they are wrapped with underscores. For example, inject would load $compile if it is used as _$compile_. This is done because in a test, we will need to create a reference to the $compile service, and most likely, we would want to use $compile as the variable name. The underscores allow you to inject it and use the $compile variable.

$httpBackend

This can create a mock response:

```
$httpBackend.when(requestType, url, [requestParameters],
[headers])
$httpBackend.expect(requestType, url, [requestParameters],
[headers])
$httpBackend.respond(response)
```

Parameters

- requestType (string): This is the HTTP method of the request
- url (string): This is the URL of the request
- requestParameters (object): These are the parameters of the request
- headers (object): These are the headers for the request
- response (string, object): This is the response of the request

Return value

This returns a handler that can call respond.

Description

Making AJAX calls is a perfect example of something that should not be done in a unit test. There are too many things out of your control for unit testing. The $httpBackend handler is provided by ngMock so that you can create a mock response.

The handler must match the expected method and URL at the very least. You can also match the optional parameters and headers if you plan on making specific requests with them.

When the request is matched, you can send back a string or object as the response. This allows you to create a test that uses $httpBackend, as you know what the response is going to be.

The difference between expect and when is that expect has to be called in the test, whereas when does not have that requirement.

Unit testing controllers

Here is an example of a simple unit test for a controller. First, you must create a controller and then load it in our test:

```
var firstModule = angular.module('firstModule', ['ngMock']);
firstModule.controller('SimpleController', ['$scope', function
($scope) {
  $scope.test = 'HEY!';
}]);
```

You can now create the test. In the test, you must load the firstModule module, inject $controller, and create an instance of SimpleController. Here is the test:

```
describe('SimpleController', function () {
  var scope = {};
  var simpleCtrl;
  beforeEach(module('firstModule'));

  it("should have a scope variable of test", inject(function
($controller) {
    expect(scope.test).toBe(undefined);
    simpleCtrl = $controller('SimpleController', { $scope: scope
    });
    expect(scope.test).toBe('HEY!');
  }));
});
```

Unit testing directives

This example will show you how to test a directive. First, create the directive:

```
firstModule.directive('simpleDirective', function () {
  return {
    restrict: 'E',
    scope:{
      test: '@'
    },
```

```
      replace: true,
      template: '<div>This is an example {{test}}.</div>'
    };
  });
```

Next, you will need to load the module, inject $compiler and $rootscope, compile the directive, and finally, start the digest loop at least once to bind any values:

```
describe('simpleDirective', function () {
  var $compile, $rootScope;
  beforeEach(module('firstModule'));
  beforeEach(inject(function (_$compile_, _$rootScope_) {
    $compile = _$compile_;
    $rootScope = _$rootScope_;
  }));

  it('should have our compiled text', function () {
    var element = $compile('<simple-directive
    test="directive"></simple-directive>')($rootScope);
    $rootScope.$digest();
    expect(element.html()).toContain('This is an example
    directive.');
  });

});
```

Unit testing services

The final testing example will test a service. First, create a service:

```
firstModule.factory('firstFactory', ['$http', function ($http) {
  return {
    addOne: function () {
      return $http.get('/test', {})
      .then(function (res) {
        return res.data.value + 1;
      });
    }
  }
}]);
```

Next, you will have to load the module, inject $httpBackend and the service factory, create a response, and load the response. Notice the use of $httpBackend.flush(). This will send the response to any open requests:

```
describe('firstFactory', function () {
  var $httpBackend, testingFactory, handler;

  beforeEach(module('firstModule'));
  beforeEach(inject(function (_$httpBackend_, firstFactory) {
    $httpBackend = _$httpBackend_;
    handler = $httpBackend.expect('GET', '/test')
    .respond({ value: 1 });
    testingFactory = firstFactory;
  }));

  it('should run the GET request and add one', function () {
    testingFactory.addOne()
    .then(function (data) {
      expect(data).toBe(2);
    });
    $httpBackend.flush();

  });
});
```

Index

objects, creating
  about 435
  new keyword 435
  object.create() method 436
  object literal 435
object type 369
observer pattern 442
observers/subscribers 442
ol element
  attributes 16
  description 16
once function 579
on click 662
on clicked 663
on function 578
on hover 661
on mouse enter 662
opacity() CSS function 313
opacity CSS property 247
open 566, 567
OpenType Font (OTF) 318
operators
  about 384
  arithmetic operator 385
  assignment operators 393
  binary operator 384
  logical operator 390, 391
  relational operators 396
  ternary operator 385
  unary operator 385
optgroup element
  about 51
  attributes 51
  description 51
option element
  attributes 52
  description 52
order CSS property 181
ordered lists 629
OR operator 392
orphans CSS property 224
OS module
  about 558
  cpus() function 558
  hostname() function 558
  networkInterfaces() function 559

outline CSS property
  auto 277
overflow CSS property 252
overflow-x CSS property 253
overflow-y CSS property 253

P

package.json 591
Pac-Man shape mask 259
padding CSS property 145, 146
page box
  about 233
  bleed CSS property 233
  marks CSS property 234
page-break-after CSS property 230
page-break-before CSS property 230, 231
page-break-inside CSS property 231
pagination
  about 640
  default 640
  pager 641
paging
  about 229
  page-break-after CSS property 230
  page-break-before CSS property 230
  page-break-inside CSS property 231
panels
  about 638
  basic 639
  footer 639
  group 639
  heading 639
param element
  about 35
  attributes 35
  description 35
parameter handling
  about 512
  default parameter 513
  rest parameter 513
  spread operator 513
param() method 705
parasitic combination inheritance 468
parasitic inheritance 467
parent() function 693

www.ingramcontent.com/pod-product-compliance
Lightning Source LLC
Chambersburg PA
CBHW081447050326
40690CB00015B/2704

* 9 7 8 1 7 8 3 5 5 2 1 3 9 *